The life of John Fisher, Bp. of Rochester in the reign of King Henry VIII, with an appendix of illustrative documents and papers;

John Lewis

F.

THE
LIFE

OF

DR. JOHN FISHER,

BISHOP OF ROCHESTER IN THE REIGN OF KING HENRY VIII

WITH AN

APPENDIX OF ILLUSTRATIVE DOCUMENTS AND PAPERS.

BY THE REV. JOHN LEWIS, A.M.

AUTHOR OF THE LIFE OF JOHN WICKLIFFE, D.D., BISHOP PECOCKE,
ETC

NOW FIRST PRINTED FROM THE ORIGINAL MANUSCRIPT
PREPARED BY THE AUTHOR FOR THE PRESS

WITH AN INTRODUCTION,

BY

T HUDSON TURNER, ESQ

VOL. I.

LONDON:
JOSEPH LILLY, 19, KING STREET, COVENT GARDEN.
1855.

CONTENTS OF VOL. I.

INTRODUCTION.

The life of Bishop Fisher now presented to the
public supplies an important deficiency in English
Biography for with the single exception of the short
and partial memoir published by Dr. Bailey in 1655
and subsequently reprinted in 1739 and 1740, the
career of this prelate who occupies so prominent a
place in a remarkable era of English History, has
received but little attention from the successive writers who with very different aims have treated of the
stormy times in which he flourished. It may, indeed,
be justly remarked that the circumstance of his
suffering nearly at the same time, and for the same
offence as Sir Thomas More has greatly contributed
to obscure the merits of his unfortunate case—writer
after writer has lavished his entire stock of historical
compassion and reflection upon the fate of the Chancellor who, owing to his public position, undoubted
learning, ingenious works and the interesting record
of his son-in-law has obtained a greater share of
commiseration from his contemporaries and posterity,
than the aged Bishop whose sphere of action was
more retired, and whose character and acquirements
as they were less dazzling than those of the witty

B

lawyer and politician have been less generally understood and appreciated.   However notwithstanding
the unfavourable relation in which he stands in the
page of history to Sir Thomas More, there is some
reason to believe that the balance of opinion among
some of the contemporaries of these eminent persons
was materially in favour of the Bishop.   Sir Richard
Morysine in a treatise* dedicated to Cromwell and
published hardly two years after they had suffered,
thus considers the merits of their respective cases.

" It is quite possible that the Bishop of Rochester
who had spent by far the greatest part of his life in
the study of those authors whose sole object was to
establish the authority of the Roman Pontiff, it is
quite possible, I say, that *he* may have believed the
Pope to be the Vicar of Christ.   But there are many
reasons why I cannot persuade myself that More always entertained this opinion.   He discusses this text
in his great dialogues which he wrote in English,
' Tu es Petrus, et super hanc petram, ædificabo
Ecclesiam meam, &c.' and this also, ' Ego rogavi ne
deficiat fides tua, &c.' and says that the faith of Peter
had failed him, that of the Church never.   Therefore
' rogavi ne deficiat fides tua ' was spoken not to
Peter but to the Church, whence it follows that Christ
and not Peter is the foundation of the Church, &c."

The entire passage is worth perusal; the above

* Apomaxis calumniarum convitiorumque, &c.   Joannis Cochlæi.
Lond. 1537, 4to. p. 76.

quotation, however, is sufficient to prove that if Morysine a creature of the government could venture to think well of the Bishop's motives he merely echoed the general sentiments of the time. It is true that Cochlæus replied and is considered to have worsted Morysine in this part of his argument, but it is only so far as regards his attempt to palliate the enormity of inflicting the punishment of death for a theoretical point of belief.

The progressive steps in the fall of Bishop Fisher have been either confused or overlooked by the generality of historical writers, and the merit of being the first to investigate and narrate them belongs to the author* of this work.

It was entirely lost sight of that Henry's first motive to disgrace the Bishop was the opposition he had made to the King's divorce from Catharine of Arragon. It appears probable that, but for the ill will he incurred by his resolute conduct during the course of that business, he would not have been so hardly dealt with for his communications with Elizabeth Barton, and his concealment of her absurd prophecies—offences utterly disproportioned to the sentence passed upon him by the Act 25. Hen. VIII. viz. forfeiture and im-

---

* The reader may be also referred to an acute and ingenious paper in the Archæologia, v. xxv. by John Bruce, Esq. F. S. A. who, being unaware of the existence of this work in a printed form, consulted the same original materials for the illustration of the same point, viz. the legal pretext for Fisher's execution. This essay has been used with advantage by Dr. Lingard in the last edition of his History of England

prisonment for life—but it had been determined to ruin him and this punishment, for which he was permitted to compound, was merely a preparatory infliction. The next snare laid for him was his being required to swear to the preamble of the Act of Succession, which, as was perhaps expected, he refused to do, excepting so far as related to the Succession only; this was followed by a second attainder and deprival of his Bishoprick, and finally he appears to have been insidiously entrapped into a denial of the King's Supremacy, but whether he actually denied it or not, it is certain he was tried and executed for that offence. Passing over the whole of these intermediate persecutions, for such they undoubtedly were, most authors have confined themselves to his denial of the Supremacy and left their readers to infer that Fisher like More suffered no trouble but on this account.

A late author* has endeavoured to shew that Fisher was executed for other treasons than the mere denial of the King's Supremacy—it is not worth while to enter into any detailed examination of his arguments since they are effectually disproved by a copy of the Bishop's Indictment which will be found in the Appendix†—with such evidence all doubt respecting the fact must be dispelled. Henry, however, appears, to have been fully conscious of the atrocity of the whole of the proceedings against Fisher and More, and with a meanness worthy of the ferocity which

* Turner's History of Hen. VIII. vol. ii. p. 387.
† No. XXXV.

sent them to the scaffold when he was reproached for his severity insinuated that they had been guilty of far more heinous crimes, and dictated the following letter which Cromwell wrote to the English ambassador at the Court of France.

" Sir, after my most hertie recommendacions these shalbe to advertise you the xvijth day of this moneth I receyved from you by your servaunte a paket of lettres which indelayedlie I delyvered to the Kinges highnes, and conferred with his grace theffects both of your lettres and all others within the saide packet, being dyrected as well to his highnes as to me.   And after his highnes had with me perused the hole contentes thoroughe of your saide lettres, perceyvyng not onelie the likelyhod of the not repayre thither into Fraunce of Philip Melancton, but also your communicacions had with the Frensh King uppon your demaunde made of the Kinges highnes pencions, with also your discrete answers and replicacions made in that behalf, for the which his Majestie gyveth unto you his hertie and condigne thankes, ye shalle understonde that his highnes comaunded me to make you answer in this wise folowing.   First as touching the Kinges money his highnes doubteth not but seeng both the Frensh kyng and also the grèt maister hathe promysed you it shalbe dispeched, ye wille as the case shall requyre not ceasse to call uppon them till it be despeched.   And ferther considering that the saide Frensh King uppon your saide demaund of the saide pencions so sodaynelie fell into comunicacyone with you aswell of his ffrendeship and huma-

nyte shewed to the Kinges highnes, alledging that he
at all tymes hathe answered for the Kinges highnes
and specyally when he was last at Marcelles with Pope
Clement, with other thinges as in your saide lettres
appereth, as also concerning thexecucyons lately don
here within this realme, the Kynges highnes somwhat mervaileth thereat and thinketh it good that,
as of yourself, ye take som occasion at convenyent
tyme and oportunyte to renovate the saide comuni-
cacion both with the Frensh Kyng or at the lest with
the grete maister, sayeng unto them that where the
saide Frensh King alledgeth that he hathe at all
tymes answered for the Kynges highnes in his cause,
and specyally with the saide Pope Clement at Marcelles, affirmyng his procedinges to be just and upright concerning the matrymony, as ye do wryte,
Albeit the Kynges highnes procedinges in all his
affaires within this realme being of suche equyte and
justnes of themself as they bee, nedeth not the defence or assistence ageynst Pope Clement or any
other foreyn power, having Goddes worde and lawes
onely sufficient to defende hym, [with thopynyons of
the moste famous clerkes of Christendome],* yet in
that that the saide Frensh Kyng hathe as he sayeth
answered at all tymes on the Kinges parte, he hathe
done nothing but the parte of a brother in justefieng
and verefieng the trewth, and so contynuying shall
do as aperteyneth to a prynce of honour, which the

---

* This sentence is erased in the original draft from which this copy
is taken

Kinges highnes doubtith not he hathe and will do, onelie in respecte to the veryte and trewth besides the amyte betwixt both them justlie requyring the same.

And concerning thexecucyons don within this realme ye shall say to the saide Frensh King, that *the same were not so mervelous extreme as he alledgeth for touching Mr. More and the Bisshop of Rochester with such others as were executed here, their treasons conspiracies and practises secretely practised aswell within the realme as without to move and styrre discension and to sowe sedycyone within the realme, intending therbye not onlye the distrucsyon of the Kynge but also the hole subversion of the same, being explaned and declared, and oppynlye detect and so manifestly proved afore them that they coulde not avoyde nor denye it, and they thereof lawfully convycted and condempned of high treasoun by the due order of the lawes of this realme, so that it shall and maye well appere to all the worlde that they havyng such malice roted in their hertes ayenst their prynce and sovereigne and the totall distructione of the commen weale of this realme were well worthie if they had had a thousande lyves to have suffered ten tymes a more terrible deth and execucyon then any of them did suffer.*

And where as the saide Frensh King sayeth that as touching such lawes as the Kinges highnes hathe made he will not medle withall alledging it not to be mete that one prynce should desyre another to chaunge his lawes, sayeng that his be to olde to be chaunged, to that ye shall sey that such lawes as the

Kinges highnes hath made here be not made without substaunceyall groundes by grete and mature advise, counsaile and deliberacion of the hole polycie of this realme, and are in deade no new lawes but of grete antiquyte and many yeres passed were made and executed within this realme, as now they be renovate and renewed onelie in respecte of the common weale of the same. And it is not a litle to his highnes mervaile that the saide Frensh King ever wolde counsaile or advise him if in case hereafter any such like offenders should happen to be in this realme that he should rather banish them then in such wise execute them. And speciallie considering that the saide Frensh King himself in comoning with you at that time not onelie confessed thextreme execucions and grete bruyllie of late don in his realme, but also that he now intendeth to withdraw the same and to revoke and call home agayne such as be out of his realme; the Kinges highnes therefore taketh his saide advise and counsaile straungely supposing it neyther thoffice of a frende nor of a brother that he wolde determyne himself to call home into his realme agayne his subjectes being out of the same for spekkyng ageynst the Bisshop of Romes usurpyd auctoryte, and counsaile the Kinges highnes to banysshe his traytours into straunge partes where they might have good occasyon, tyme place and oportunyte to worke their feates of treason and conspiracie the better ayenst the Kinges highnes and this his realme. In which parte ye shall somwhat engreve the matier after suche sorte as it may well appere to the saide

Frensh King that not onelie the Kynges highnes myght take those his consailes and communycacions with you both straungelie and unkindely, thinking the same not to procede of mere amyte and frendeship, but also using such polycie and austeryte in proponyng the same with the saide Frensh King and the grete M^r., taking such tyme and oportunyte as may best serve for the same, as they may well perceyve the Kinges highnes procedinges here within his realme both concerning the saide execucions and all other thinges to be onelie grounded uppon justice and the equyte of his lawes which be no new lawes but auncyent lawes made and established of many yeres passed within this realme and now renovate and renewed as is aforsaid for the better order weale and suretie of the same. And ye may fferther saye that yf the Frenche Kyng and his counsayll well consyder as the owt to do that it were moche better to advaunce the ponyshment off trayters and rebelles ffor theyr offences thenne to punyshe suche as do speke ageynst the usurpid auctoryte. And touching suche wordes as the saide Frensh King spake unto you concerning how Mr. More dyed and what he saide to his doughter going to his judgement, and also what exhortacions he should gyve unto the kinges subjectes to be trew and obedient to his grace I assure you that there was no suche thing, whereof the gret M^r., promysed you a double at length. In that the kinges pleasure is that ye shull not onelie procure the saide double and sende it hither, but also sey unto the saide Frensh King that the Kinges high-

nes can not otherwise take it but veray unkyndely
that the saide Frensh King or any of his counsaile at
whose handes he hathe so moche meryted and to
whom he hath mynistred so many grete benefites
pleasures and comodytees, shoulde so lightlie gyve
eare faith and credence to any suche vayne brutes
and fleeng tales, not having first knowlege or adver-
tisement from the Kynges highnes here and his counsaile of the veryte and trewth, affirming it to be the
office of a frende if he harde any such tales of so
noble a prynce, rather to have put the tellers to sylens
or at the lest not to have dyvulget the saide untyll
suche tyme as the Kinges Majestie being soo dere a
freend hadde bene advertysyd therof and the trewthe
known; before he should so lightlie beleve or alledge
any suche reporte; which argueth playnelie not to
remayne in the saide Frensh Kynges brest such inte-
gryte of herte and syncere amyte towardes the Kynges
highnes and his procedinges as his highnes alwayes
hertoffore trustyd too, which thing ye may propone
and alledge unto the saide Frensh King and the grete
M^r. or to oon of them with such modestie and so-
brenes as ye thinke they may perceyve that the
Kinges highnes hathe good and just cause sumwhat
in this parte to take theyr lyght credytt unkyndelye "*

*   *   *   *   *   *   *   *   *

(at Thornebery, the 23rd day of August.)

* This letter is copied from the original draft in Cromwell's
handwriting preserved in MS Harl 288, fol. 39-46, it appears to
have been corrected and interlined according to the King's dictation
The concluding portion of it may be seen in Strype's Memorials

It is to this letter that Mr. Lewis refers (vol. ii. p. 210.) upon the authority of Strype, and it is singular he should not have thought it worthy of a place in the Appendix, as it throws so much light upon the character and policy of Henry at this time. That the whole of the assertions respecting Fisher, are false is shewn by the indictment already mentioned, that they are equally false in the case of Sir Thomas More may be seen by referring to Roper's Life where the words and letters to which, probably, the French King alluded and of which he seems to have had copies are printed.* The unblushing impudence with which Henry asserts that his " new" laws were but revivals of ancient ones, is surprising—as in making this declaration he could not have calculated upon the French King's ignorance of their character and effects, which were already notorious throughout Europe.

There is one point in the life of Fisher upon which

Ecclesiastical, v. 1. part, 2. p. 251-2, Oxford: 1812, 8vo. Strype has indeed printed it entire, but his version differs in some points from the present, and was certainly taken from another copy; according to him the address ran thus, " To my right loving friend Sir John Wallop, Knyght, the Kinges Ambassadour resident in the Corte of Fraunce "—whereas the copy here given is indorsed in a later hand, " Mr. Secretary Cromwelle his letter by the Kynges directyones to the Lydger Ambassador in Fraunce touchinge speches used to him by the Frenche Kyng concernynge the Executyons of Sir Thomas More and Fysher bushope of Rochestere in H. 8. his tyme." Lydger for Leaguer would make it appear that it was written to one of Henry's envoys to the Leaguers of Smalcald, which could not have been the case, Wallop was the person addressed.

* See Lewis's Edition, 8vo. 1731. p. 98-102.

Mr. Lewis has but slightly touched, viz. how far his elevation to the dignity of Cardinal, hastened the King's determination to put him to death. He gives the sayings recorded in Bailey without advancing any opinion upon them or testing their probability. The following extract from Mr. Bruce's valuable paper shews the little credit to which they are entitled.

"A reason for the harsh proceedings against Fisher, which has been very commonly insisted upon, is that his injudicious appointment by the Pope to the dignity of the purple, 'alarmed the government' and awakened the sleeping vengeance of the King, who instantly determined to put him upon his trial. . Fisher's appointment as Cardinal took place on the 21st of May, and the commission to try him was dated on the 2nd of June, before the news of the appointment at Rome could have been received in London. This seems to prove that the determination to bring him to trial must have preceded his appointment. Indeed, no one who considers the manner in which he was first tempted by the council, and afterwards betrayed by Rich, into the declaration which was fatal to him, can think that it had not for some time been determined to put him upon his trial. Whether the appointment did not hasten his execution is another question upon which some persons may doubt. In Fisher's instance I can find nothing but what seems to mark a leisurely proceeding in a settled and determined course. His appointment to the purple was on the 21st of May, the commission to try him was on the 2nd of June, the news of his appointment reached London several days before the 12th of June, but he was not tried until the 17th, and then, to the general surprise, five days elapsed before the order arrived for his execution. I cannot here trace the hurry of alarm which some writers have imagined. Such transactions were often dispatched in the reign of Henry VIII. in a far shorter time, and would have been got through more quickly in Fisher's instance, if the arrival of the Cardinal's hat in England in time to be placed upon its owner's living head, had been a subject of alarm. Indeed, if it can be considered settled that the determination to put him upon his trial, or in other words, if the desire to get rid of him, existed before the English Court were aware he had been appointed a Cardinal, the other question is of minor importance, since it would have been a solecism in the unrelenting character of Henry VIII. if he had paused between the wish to destroy and its accomplishment.

" There are various statements of the feelings with which Fisher himself viewed his appointment; but there can be no reason to doubt his own account upon oath, which will be found in the Appendix,* that when the news was told him he declared that if the Cardinal's hat were layed at his feet he would not stoop to take it up, he did set so little by it."†

The proceedings of Pope Paul III. upon the news of the judicial murder of his newly made Cardinal

---

* Coll. no. XLI. † Archæologia, vol. xxv. p. 85-6.

will be found in Chaco's Lives of the Roman Pontiffs and Cardinals, whence the spirited letter announcing it to Ferdinand King of the Romans, which had been seen and abridged by Hall, is now extracted entire, and may be added to the number of opinions concerning the death of Fisher quoted by Mr. Lewis in the second volume of this Work. It is worthy of remark that the Pope acknowledges he had conferred the dignity upon him with a view to his preservation.

Paulus Papa III. Dilecto Filio Ferdinando Regi Romanorum Illustri.*

Charissime Fili salutem, et Apostolicam benedictionem. Non dubitamus jam tuæ serenitati auditum esse de inexorabili nece bonæ memoriæ Joannis Episcopi Roffensis, et Cardinalis nostri, tuamque Majestatem, ut est omni pietate conspicuam, tum dignitate, et sanctitate hominis, tum gratiâ ipsâ, et causâ mortis vehementer fuisse commotam. Nam sive Episcopalem, et Cardinalitiam dignitatem, in quâ Sancti Apostoli referuntur, sive genus mortis per carnificem, sive causam veritatis et justitiæ, pro quâ vir ille sanctus occubuit, consideramus, omnia hujusmodi sunt, ut sicut ab impiissimo profecta sunt, ita potentissimi Regis animum et aures gravissimè offendere debeant. Cum enim Henricus Angliæ Rex separatâ à se impiè, et injustè charissimâ in Christo filiâ nostrâ Catharinâ Angliæ Reginâ, materterâ tuâ,

* Vitæ et Res Gestæ Pontificum Romanorum et S. R. E Cardinalium, &c Alphonsi Ciaconi Ordinis Prædicatorum, &c. operâ descriptæ, ab A. Oldomo S. I. recognitæ, 4 tom. fol. Rom. 1677. tom. 3, p. 574-5.

cum quâ matrimonium mediante Sedis Apostolicæ
dispensatione contraxerat, prolemque ex eâ susceperat,
vivente ipsâ Catharinâ Annam adulteram propriâ
auctoritate uxorem duxisset, et ad velandum facinus
suum, matrimonii cum ipsâ Catharinâ validitatem, et
Apostolicæ Sedis potestatem negasset, Ecclesiamque
Anglicanam, et Regnum illud Sedis Apostolicæ tribu-
tarium ab ejusdem Sedis obedientiâ subtraxisset, seque
in hæreticorum numerum multipliciter retulisset,
multaque alia indigna, et impia commisisset; cumque
hæc bonis omnibus desplicerent, ut debent, quotquot
improbarent ductionem adulteræ, capi, necari, car-
cerarique et ultimo supplicio affici fecit; atque hanc
ejus impietatem toto triennio patienter tulit universa
Christianitas, et hæc Sedes Apostolica, quæ licet illum
Regem feudatarium habebat, pastorali tamen clemen-
tiâ toleravit hæc tamen indigna, et resipiscentiam in
dies ipsius Henrici sperando patienter expectavit,
quòque in irritum cesserint, hæc novissima declarant.
Cum enim Nos in eâ Cardinalium creatione, quam
proximè habuimus, ipsum Roffensem, ad ornan-
dam ejus virtutem et sanctitatem, in numerum
Cardinalium retulissemus, sperantes eam dignitatem,
quæ ubique solita est haberi sacrosancta, non solùm
ad amoliendam perniciem, sed, et ad salutem, et li-
berationem esse valituram; in hâc re Henricum se
similem esse voluit, tum sui qui multos alios simili
ex causâ necavit, tum Henrici II., progenitoris sui,
cujus odio, et persecutione B. Thomas martyr Episc.
Cantuariensis occubuit. Nec tamen hic Henricus illius
impietatem retulit, verùm et longè superavit. Ille

enim unum, hic multò plures, ille unius particularis,
hic universalis Ecclesiæ jura tuentem, ille Archiepiscopum, hic R. E. Cardinalem neci tradidit.   Ille de-
nique qui se puigare Alexandro III. coactus est, cul-
pam in alios rejecit, pœnitentiam sibi à Romano
Pontifice impositam humiliter suscepit, hic obstina-
tissimo animo sceleratissimum factum tuetur, non
solùm non ductus pœnitentiâ, verùm pertinax, et
rebellis, hostisque factus.   Non quia læsus à Romanâ
Ecclesiâ, à quâ est titulo Defensoris decoratus, quem
ipse titulum ingratissimè ad offensionem fidei retorsit,
sed quia etiam multipliciter læsit.   Cum igitur fili
charissime Sancta Romana, et universalis Ecclesia
magno vulnere dedecore ignominiâque violata sit,
patientia ejus semper novas Henrici injurias provo-
caverit, necessariumque sit cauterio uti, una cum
Venerabilibus fratribus nostris S. R. E. Cardd. ad
tuam Majestatem, quæ cum suis progenitoribus semper justitiam, probitatem, religionem coluit, et hanc
Sedem semper filiali observantiâ reverita est, confugi-
mus, tuam opem, auxilium, et favorem in tantis Ecclesiæ injuriis implorantes, teque per viscera miseri-
cordiæ D. N. Jesu Christi enixè obsecrantes, ut cum
viâ juris et justitiæ demum Henricum censuræ con-
temptorem, atque in eâ ultra biennium insordescen-
tem, hæreticum, schismaticum, adulteium notorium,
publicum homicidam, et *in* sacrilegum rebellem, et
criminis læsæ majestatis multipliciter reum, piop-
terea dicto Regno à jure ipsum privatum declarare
intendimus, Tu cum serenissimo Cæsare fratre tuo, et
cæteris Principibus, quorum opem pariter advocamus,

executioni justitiæ faveas, sicuti speramus, et te pro optimi principis officio, esse facturum, sicut autem plenius ex nuntii ad te missi verbis intelliges. Datum Romæ apud Sanctum Marcum, die 22 Julii, Anno 1535.

The Bishop's wretched condition and straitened means, during his severe imprisonment in the Tower, are described by himself in a letter to Cromwell which will be found in the Appendix,* and to one of those fortunate accidents which have handed down to us so many of the ephemeral papers and memoranda of by gone days, which would seem from their very nature to have been most liable to destruction, we are indebted for the preservation of an account of the weekly sums allowed for his support and that of his fellow sufferer Sir Thomas More, while in confinement ; it occurs in a paper entitled "The Charges of certayne persons in the towre."†

"The Bysshope of Rochester for xiiijth monthys after **xx.** s. le weke   Sm^a } lvj. li

Sir Thomas More for iijth monthis unpayd after x. s. le weke and his servainct v. s. weke. } ix. li.

Twenty shillings a week ought certainly to have supplied the Bishop with more necessaries than he appears to have enjoyed, but doubtless Master Lieutenant had his profit upon the sum charged: after all however Fisher was better treated than More, who was allowed five shillings less and had a servant to share the pittance with him.

* Coll. No. XXVIII.

† MS. Cotton. Titus B. I. fol. 155.

figure was designed to be laid upon it: the figure
however, if there was one, is not yet discovered.
The monument is now removed to a small vacant bit
of a Court on the north side of the chapel, to the
east, &c.

" Nov. 1st 1773, All Saints, Mr. Ashby calling upon
me informed me that the Chapel, in which this monument was found, was built by Bishop Fisher, on
whose execution the Tomb was taken to pieces and
thrown aside: for in some of the old accounts, a
trifling sum is charged for defacing Bishop Fisher's
Tomb. As there is no resisting this testimony, the
monument wants no other explication.

" I was told by Mr. Essex 1774, that this tomb, by
being exposed under the drippings of the north side
of the Chapel all the winter, is entirely spoiled and
shivered by the wet and frost.

" Peter Torregiano, a Florentine, made the Tomb in
Westminster Abbey for King Henry VII. and his
mother, the Countess of Richmond: it is probable
therefore that he gave the design for this of Bishop
Fisher, in the same shape and taste as the latter, v.
Mr. Walpole's Anecdotes on Painting, vol. 1, p. 102,
104, Edit. 2nd. Little conception of it is to be
drawn from my draft on the other side* but from the
Countess' tomb."

Mr. Baker was at some pains to obtain an au-
thentic portrait of Fisher; and in the third volume
of his collections,† there is an almost obliterated

* There is a rough pen and ink sketch opposite this description.

† MS. Harl. 7030

drawing of him, apparently after Holbein; it bears no resemblance however to the genuine drawing by that Master in the Royal Collection; the features are entirely different, nor can we reconcile the two by supposing that the former was painted when the Bishop was in the prime of life; the latter was taken only ten years before his death, as it bears the date of 1525; it agrees in every respect with the description which Hall gives of his personal appearance. It is presumed that Baker's drawing was made from the copy he obtained of a picture at Longleat, the seat of the Marquis of Bath, concerning which the following correspondence is found in Cole's Collections.*

" *To the very Rev. Mr. Baker, B. D. and Fellow of St. John's College in Cambridge.*

Longleat, July, 25th.

Dear Sir,

We are here of opinion that the vol. of Hollingshead wch you mention, contains things omitted in most copies, tho' perhaps not all, which are found in some. But that cannot be exactly known, 'till it be compared with some other Copie, which contains the omissions. My L^d will take it very kindly, if you will be pleased, as you propose, to send that volume to Mr. Bedford: and his L^dship will send B^p Fisher's Picture to London to have a copy taken for you there by a good hand. Mr. Bouchier lately called here in his way from the Bath, and in

* Vol. 30, fol. 119 et seq.

with the face, and with the description. I have likewise in the same case sent some papers of Mr. Harbin's, who gives his service. Mr. Wanley came to town with us, and I have not seen him since: when I do see him, I will put him in mind of his promise, if he have not yet written to you. I am, dear Sir, your humble Servt,

R. Jenkin.

My humble service to Mr. Billers, Mr. Browne, and all our Friends. I shall write to my tutor by this night's post."

*   *   *   *   *   " The Picture here " mentioned is that, I suppose, now hanging in the " Gallery of the master's Lodge in St. John's College " in Cambridge, and is not like that published among " Houbraken's Collection of Heads, painted by Hol- " ben: this in St. John's being a very mortified and " meagre personage with a crucifix by him, as I re- " collect it. All these letters were directed to Mr. " Baker as Fellow of St. John's College." [*Cole.*]

There is a portrait of Fisher among Houbraken's Heads, after a picture by Holbein which at the publication of that work was in the possession of a Mr. Richardson:* it resembles the drawing in the Royal Collection, but differs from it in the costume.†

---

* The Novelist ?

† " I saw in Nov. 1766 an indifferent Picture of Bishop Fisher, with one of Sir Tho. More, Abp. Plunket &c, on a Staircase near the Prior's apartment, of the English Benedictines at Paris but a most

It is immaterial to enquire whether the Latin version of Fisher's life preserved in one of the volumes of Baker's Collections * be an original work or merely an amplified version of the English one, the writer of this notice inclines to the latter opinion, admitting however that he has had no opportunity of examining any other MS. of the Latin than the one already alluded to, which was transcribed by Baker from a MS. then in the possession of Roger Gale.

The author of the English life was probably Dr. Richard Hall, but Pits not always an infallible guide, is the only authority for this supposition. He tells us† that Hall studied at Christ's College Cambridge, that he was subsequently compelled to fly into Belgium, " to avoid the persecution of the heretics," and that after one or two changes of residence he died at St. Omer, 26th Feb. 1604. He mentions also that he saw and conversed with him at Douay, about the year 1580, and enumerates in a list of his works, " The Life of John Fisher Bishop of Rochester, in English,"‡ which he had himself seen in the Library

admirable one of Sir Tho. More, by Holbein, in the fine Collection of the Duke of Orleans at the Palais Royal at Paris." Cole's MSS. vol. 7, p. 126^b.

* MS. Harl. 7030.

† De Script. Angl. pp. 802-3 Ed. 1619, 4to.

‡ Mr. Baker was inclined to attribute the Latin version to Hall but his argument in the following note is of no great weight, besides being opposed to the evidence of Pits who had known the man and seen his work, " This life is cited by J. C. student in Divinitie, (iste J. C. erat ni fallor, Josephus Creswellus) in a Book written anno. 1620, with permission, entitled *The Theatre of Catholique*

timony to the contrary owing to the erasure of the Bishop's insignia from all conspicuous places which took place after his execution, there is every reason to believe that he never bore any such arms, the Coat attributed to him by Cole and figured in vol. 45 of his Collections, p. 165 is Azure, a dolphin embowed en fesse between three ears of corn, or, within a bordure engrailed of the same.*

Dr. Fiddes the biographer of Wolsey issued proposals for a life of Fisher, which was to have been published in 1725; in the compilation of it he had the use of Baker's MSS the work however did not appear, owing it is said to his having lost his manuscript: the subject was afterwards taken up by Alban Butler to whom Cole communicated the notes which he had made respecting the Bishop :† whatever collections he left behind him were subsequently destroyed by Mr. Charles Butler who communicated the fact in a letter to Mr. Bruce by whom this information was obligingly furnished to the writer of these remarks. It is probable that Butler and Lewis were engaged on the same work at the same time.

Of the various writings of Bishop Fisher nothing need be said in this place, as they are correctly enumerated by the Author, who has also carefully analised his controversial works, now remembered only in connection with the history of the Reformation;

* See also p. 21 ante note, and MS. Harl. 7047 fol 206.

† They may be seen in the seventh volume of his Collections, pp 1, 126, 127, 128,—his curious letters to Butler are in vol. 25, pp 17^b, et seq

of his minor productions the sermon preached at the funeral of Henry VII. is, perhaps, the most valuable, since it contains many curious details of the superstition or hypocrisy of that prudent and parsimonious prince.*

The learning of the bishop was probably, as respectable as that of the generality of his more remarkable contemporaries of the English Church and laity, but his natural abilities if we may judge of them by his writings appear to have been of an inferior order; in his polemical tracts he skilfully employed the defensive weapons of argument supplied by the Scholastic Theologians whom he had long and carefully studied, but he did not, or could not, aid them by his own original views or expositions; his style was unusually prolix even for the age in which he wrote; and the highest praise that can be awarded to his Latinity is that it occupies a middle station between the barbarity of the monkish writers and the pseudo-classicality of the sixteenth century.

The few remains of his epistolary correspondence both in English and Latin are collected in the Appendix† with the exception of one letter which was accidentally omitted although Mr. Lewis had used

---

* See vol. 1. cap. iii. pp. 30-33.

† Mr. Lewis copied some of these letters from printed works, the originals however are still extant in the following MSS.

Appendix No. XXVIII. MS. Cotton. Cleop. E. vi. fol. 172,

Appendix No. XXX.   ib.   fol. 162.

Appendix No. XXXIII. (Cranmer to Cromwell) MS. Harl. 283, fol. 120.

it. It will be found annexed to these remarks together with another paper relating to his examination in the Tower.

These letters are so few in number, and were written under such peculiar circumstances, that they can hardly be admitted as evidence, in an estimate of his character, of any other merit than his meekness and humility.

Exalted by the Roman Catholics to the dignity of a martyr and almost to that of a saint, Fisher's merits were long and gratefully remembered by the church whose tenets he had so strenuously defended, while the intolerance and horrible persecutions of a succeeding reign, led the Protestants to regard him, though both intolerant and an abettor of persecution, with some favour and more compassion, but by neither party hitherto has justice been rendered to his memory. Without attending to the indiscriminate eulogists of his own sect who did not hesitate to compare him with St. John the Baptist, or to the vituperations of those writers of the reformed faith who suppressed or were ignorant of his positive merits, we may truly say of him that with great opportunities to advance his own interest at court, he remained invariably contented with the preferment he had first obtained, that his life was devoted to the encouragement of learning in others and the acquisition of it himself, that he was modest and affable, ever ready to extend his aid and protection to the needy and deserving, and that the sincerity of his conduct and piety is placed beyond doubt by the stedfastness with which he encountered death in defence of the religious principles in which he had been educated, which he had vindicated with his pen, and which he conscientiously believed to be true.*

T. H. TURNER.

May 10th, 1839.

---

* Strictly speaking he suffered for denying the King's supremacy only, but as that point involved a mighty train of consequences which the Bishop could not but have foreseen, to have admitted it would have been to deny all those articles of belief with respect to which he had asserted the Pope's authority.

[No. I.*]

MS. Cott. Vespasian. F. xiij. fol. 154 b.

Master Cromwel, after my right humble comendations I beseiche you to have some pytye of me, considryng the case and condition that I ame in ; and I dowt not but yf ye myght see in what plyte that I ame ye woulde have some pyte uppon me, for in goodfaythe now almoste this six weekys I have badde a grevous cowighe with a fever in the bigynnynge thereof, as dyvers other heare in this countre bathe hadde, and dyvers have dyed thereof. And now the mattyer is fallen downe in to my leggis and feit, with suche swellinge and aiche that I maye nother ryde nor goo, for the which I beseiche you eftsonys to have some pyte uppon me and to spare me for a season, to thende the swellinge and aiche of my leggis and feit maye swaige and abait, and then by the grace of our Lorde I shall with all speide obeye your commaundement, Thus fare ye weall, at Rochestre the xxviij. daye of January.

By your fathefull Beadman,

JO. ROFFS.

[No. II.†]

Interrogatories, ministered, on the Kinges behalf, [*unto*] John Fissher, Doctour of Divinitie, late Busshop [*of Rochester*], the 14th daie of June, in the 27 yere of [*the reign of*] King Henrie thEight, within the Towre [*of London, by the*] right worshipfull Mr. Thomas Bedyll, [*Mr. Doctour Abridge*] Mr. Richard Layton, and Mr. Richard [*Curwen being of the*] Kinges Counsaill, in the presence of Harrie [*Pelstede and John*] Whalley, witnesses, and me, John ap Rice, notary [*Publick*], with thansweres of the said Mr. Doctour Fissher to the [*same*].

* Referred to in Vol. II. Chap. XXXII. p. 118, and there stated to be No. 17 in the collection &c. but it was omitted.

† See vol. II. chap. XXXV. p. 160 et seq.

in defence of the religious principles in which he had
been educated, which he had vindicated with his pen,
and which he conscientiously believed to be true.*

T. H. TURNER.

* Strictly speaking he suffered for denying the King's supremacy
only, but as that point involved a mighty train of consequences
which the Bishop could not but have foreseen, to have admitted it
would have been to deny all those articles of belief with respect to
which he had asserted the Pope's authority.

[No. I.*]

MS. Cott. Vespasian. F xiij. fol. 154 b.

Master Cromwel, after my right humble comendations I beseiche
you to have some pytye of me, considryng the case and condition
that I ame in; and I dowt not but yf ye myght see in what plyte
that I ame ye woulde have some pyte uppon me, for in goodfaythe
now almoste this six weekys I have hadde a grevous cowighe with
a fever in the bigynnynge thereof, as dyvers other heare in this
countre hathe hadde, and dyvers have dyed thereof.   And now the
mattyer is fallen downe in to my leggis and feit, with suche swellinge
and aiche that I maye nother ryde nor goo, for the which I beseiche
you eftsonys to have some pyte uppon me and to spare me for a
season, to thende the swellinge and aiche of my leggis and feit maye
swaige and abait, and then by the grace of our Lorde I shall with
all speide obeye your commaundement,   Thus fare ye weall, at
Rochestre the xxviij. daye of January.

By your fathefull Beadman,

JO. ROFFS.

[No. II.†]

Interrogatories, ministered, on the Kinges behalf, [*unto*] John
Fissher, Doctour of Divinitie, late Busshop [*of Rochester*],
the 14th daie of June, in the 27 yere of [*the reign of*] King
Henrie thEight, within the Towre [*of London, by the*] right
worshipfull Mr. Thomas Bedyll, [*Mr. Doctovr Alridge*] Mr.
Richard Layton, and Mr. Richard [*Curwen being of the*]
Kinges Counsaill, in the presence of Harrie [*Pelstede and
John*] Whalley, witnesses, and me, John ap Rice, notary
[*Publick*], with thanswrres of the said Mr. Doctour Fissher
to the [*same*].

* Referred to in Vol. II. Chap. XXXII. p. 118, and there stated to be No. 17
in the collection, &c but it was omitted
† See Vol. II. Chap. XXXV p 160, et seq.

THE

LIFE

OF

DR. JOHN FISHER,

BISHOP OF ROCHESTER.

CHAP. I.

1. JOHN FISHER was born, according to Dr. Hall, and George Lily, in the year 1459, though others reckon the year of his birth about 1461, not much before St. Alban's field. By the Latin writer of his Life he is said to have been seventy-seven years old when he was beheaded, and consequently was born A. D. 1458. The Bishop

Life of Bp. Fisher, MS. at the Royal Society. Moreri reckons the time of his birth about 1455.

B

himself observed to the King, in his speech to him at the public commencement at Cambridge, that when he was made a Bishop, 1504, he was very [a] young; and yet if he was born 1459, he was then forty-five years old. According to the same reckoning, he must have been twenty-four years old when admitted in the University. For all which reasons, it seems as if the time of his birth was fixed too early at 1459, and, that he was not born till about six years after, *viz.* 1465.

2. However this be, it is agreed by all, that the place of Mr. Fisher's birth was the town of Beverley, in the East Riding of the county of York; a place famous for the residence and death of John, Archbishop of York, A. D. 721, who from this town was called [b] John of Beverley. In this town was founded by this Archbishop a monastery of monks, into which he retired after his deposition from, or resignation of, the See of York, and there ended his days.

Camdeni Britannia, p. 577, &c. So great a regard had the Northanhymbrian princes, and particularly King Athelstan, to the pious memory of this prelate, and so sacred did they esteem it, that he was accounted by them a tutelar [c] saint. To honour him therefore accordingly, this monastery, of his foundation, was endowed by them with many and great immunities, and had, in particular, granted to it the special

See History &c. of the Abbey, &c. of Faversham, p. 40, &c. privilege of a sanctuary for life, which was usually for 40 days only. So that, as Dr. Wiclif represents it, whatsoever thief or felon came to this holy house of religion, he should dwell there all his life, and no man impeach him. Accordingly, here was a stone chair, in which the criminal was to place himself at his first coming hither, with this inscription:

ſɲeoð- ɼtole, a seat of liberty.
Hæc sedes Lapidea FFREEDSTOOLL *dicitur* i. e. pacis Cathedra, *ad quam reus fugiendo perveniens omnimodam habet securitatem.*

This stone seat is called *freedstool,* or the *chair of peace,*

---

[a] Qui paucos annos habuerim.   [b] Johannis de Beverlaco.   [c] May VII.

to which any criminal coming by flight, he has all manner CHAP
of security. By this means the town became very popu- I.
lous and flourishing, to which contributed not a little their
having a water creek from the river Hull, which served
for little coasting vessels to carry on a sea trade for the
benefit and advantage of the place.

3. Here, it appears, Mr. Fisher's father, whose name Coll No. 1.
was Robert, lived, and exercised the trade of a mercer,
and in 1477 died, leaving behind him a widow and four 1477
children: of these, it is said, John was the eldest, who was
then about twelve or thirteen years old. His mother's
name was ^d Agnes, who afterwards, it is said, married a Life of Bp.
second husband, named Wright, by whom she had three Fisher by
Baily.
sons, John, Thomas, and Richard, and a daughter, named
Elizabeth, who was afterwards a nun, professed at Dart-
ford in Kent, in the diocese of Rochester, of which
Dr. Fisher, her brother, was bishop. By Mr. Fisher's
Will, it appears, that he was a person of considerable sub- Coll. No. 1.
stance, as things then were, since he gives to every alms-
house at Beverley, 20d.; to the fabric of the Collegiate
Church of St. John's at Beverley, 20d.; to the fabric of
the Cathedral Church of St. Peter's at York, 8d.; to each
house of the friars at Beverley, 3s. 4d.; to the chaplain of
St. Trinity, to pray for his soul, 13s. 4d.; to a ^e fit chaplain, to celebrate for his soul a whole year, to Robert
Kuke, Vicar of the Church of St. Mary the Virgin, 6s. 8d.;
to John Plumber, the chaplain, 6s. 8d.; to the Abbot and
Convent of Hawnby in Lincolnshire, 10s. for a trental of Hagnaby.
masses, to be there celebrated for his soul; to the fabric
of the Church of Hotoft, in the same county, where, probably, he was born, 3s. 4d., and to every one of his * four * de mea
children seven marks, or 2l. 13s. 4d., ordering, that if it propria
parte.
shall happen that either of them die before he or she is of
age, their share shall be divided among the survivors.

^d Baily calls her name Anne.

^e He had commonly a salary of ten marks, or 6l. 13s 4d for doing this.
See History, &c. of the Isle of Tenet.

CHAP.
1.

Life of Bp.
Fisher.

A.D. 1483.

Proctor's
book, MS.
A.D. 1487.
A.D. 1491.

A.D. 1494.

Life of Bp.
Fisher.

* Quære,
I rather
think there
were others
of the same
names.

4. Of this eldest son of his, John, a particular care, it seems, was taken, to give him the best education that his circumstances would allow; for this purpose, he had been, before his father's death, committed to the care of a priest of the Collegiate Church of Beverley, who was, I suppose, the master of the school for teaching the novices of the monastery. Here he learned to read, and was taught the rudiments of the grammar. Whether he had the opportunity of going to any other school, or that his friends thought this sufficient, is uncertain; but it seems as if, when he was about eighteen years old, he was admitted in the University of Cambridge. Here he was committed to the care and government of William Melton, at that time Fellow of [f]Michael House, and afterward Master of it; and as soon as he was of standing, he took his degree of Bachelor of Arts, and three years after, that of Master; soon after which he was unexpectedly chosen Fellow of the College, and senior Proctor of the University. This shews what a progress Mr. Fisher had made in his academical studies, and in how great reputation he was held there. In this space of time, it is supposed that, according to the Statutes of the House of which he was Fellow, he was ordained Priest, by the title of his fellowhip.

5. Whilst he was Proctor, he is said to have obtained letters of fraternity for * himself and his brother, * Ralph, from the Hospital of the Holy Trinity, and St. Thomas, in Villa Romana, dated May 1, which, in that age, was reckoned an instance of great piety and devotion. He

[f] This was the second endowed house in Cambridge for antiquity, being founded by Herveus de Stanton, clerk, Canon of York and Wells, &c. A.D. 1324. But King Henry VIII. dissolved it, and made it a part of Trinity College. The accurate Mr. Herne tells us, from Mr. A. Wood, that Mr. Fisher was of Christ's College, which was not founded till twenty-two years after his admission.

In Mr. Thoroton's History of Nottinghamshire, p. 159, is a certain kind of rhyming bard-like pedigree of the family of the Stauntons in that county, in which it is said, that Sir Henry Stanton, it should be Henricus de Stan-
A.D. 1324. ton, Chief Justice of the Common Pleas, 17 Edw. II. founded this House.

was likewise, during his being in that public office, sent up
to Court, which, it seems, was then at Greenwich, on the
business of the University. This was very fortunate to
Mr. Fisher, who on this occasion seems first to have been
introduced to the knowledge and [g]presence of the Lady
Margaret, the King's mother, who took such a liking to
him, as soon after to make him her Confessor, in the room
of Dr. Richard Fitz-James, who three years after this was
promoted to the see of Rochester. This was a promotion
that was not only very honourable, but exceedingly to the
worldly advantage of Mr. Fisher, or to the enriching him,
and encreasing his temporal estate. As this honourable
lady was a person of great piety and devotion, and one
who made it the whole business of her life to do good, and
employed the chief part of her noble fortune for that purpose, this her Confessor, who was a man of the same excellent spirit, soon became very dear to her, and entirely
beloved by her. Thus Mr. Fisher, a good while after,
very gratefully remembers her affection towards him. He
styles her an excellent, and, indeed, incomparable woman,
and to *him* a mistress most dear upon many accounts;
whose merits, whereby she had obliged him, were very
great. He observes of her, that she very sincerely loved
him above others, and that of this, her kindness for him,
he was very certain; that she loved him with a great and
uncommon love, and never thought she could be too kind
to him, and therefore was most munificent towards him;
for, although she conferred on him no church benefice, the
reason of which might probably be, that Mr. Fisher might
have no pretence to leave her, yet she was never wanting,

Marginal notes:

CHAP I.

A. D. 1497.
Bp Fisher's
Sermon at
the Lady
Margaret's
funeral

Epistles de-
dicatory to
Bp Fox

---

[g] Of this Mr. Fisher himself has left some intimation in the account of his
expenses in this journey, wrote with his own hand, (a very fair one, which was
somewhat remarkable for that age,) in the Proctor's book, *viz.*   s.   d

	s.	d
Pro conductu duorum equorum per xi dies	vii	0
Pro jentaculo ante transitum ad Greenwyshe	0	iii
Pro navigio illuc usque atque contra	0	iv
Pransus eram apud Dominam Matrem Regis		
Cœnatum est cum Domino Cancellario, &c	*Coll T Baker, MS.*	

CHAP.
I.
by any means, to add to, and encrease his estate, of which she gave very ample proof, not only in words, but in [h] deeds, when she came to die.

6. Being thus honourably promoted, and thereby a foundation being laid for his further advancement, Mr. Fisher commenced Doctor of Divinity, and the very same A.D. 1501. year was by the University chosen Vice-chancellor. Of this the following memorandum is entered on the senior Proctor's book of that year, *viz.*

> *Memorandum, quod* Joannes Ffysher, 5° *die Julij, in sacra Theologia creatus professor,* 15° *die Mensis ejusdem, sc. die translationis* Sti. Swythini *socio- rumque ejus Episcoporum, auctoritate et consensu Regentium feliciter eligitur in Universitatis* Cant. *Vice-cancellarium.*

This is an evidence of Mr. Fisher's growing credit and reputation in that famous University, and looks as if he took this degree at their motion, to qualify him for this dignity of their chief magistrate, next to the Chancellor.

Thos. Baily. 7. The writer of his Life tells us, that Melton, the Doctor's tutor, being promoted to the dignity of Chancellor of the Cathedral Church of York, the Mastership of Michael House became void, and that thereupon, Dr. Fisher, by a most free and willing election of all the Fellows of that House, as the most deserving of all other, was worthily promoted to this Mastership, and soon after chosen Vice-chancellor. But of this I don't find there's any certainty. Le Neve's tainty. William de Melton was indeed promoted to the Fasti, &c. dignity aforesaid about the latter end of 1495; but whether by this promotion he vacated his Mastership of this House, or who immediately succeeded him in case it was

---

[h] Quum mortem instare sibi noverit, nec posse quod destinaret perimplere, non parva me donavit pecunie summa qua in privatum meum commodum uterer. *Coll.* No. 12.

Moreri says, though without any grounds, that I can find, that *on le choisit pour précepteur du Roy* Hen. VIII. *Dictionnaire:* that he was chosen the King's preceptor.

vacated, does not appear; though, indeed, according to CHAP.
I.
the present usage of the University, it does not seem at all
likely that our Doctor should be chosen Vice-chancellor,
when he was only fellow of a college.

8. But be this as it will. During the Doctor's being
Vice-chancellor, the lady Margaret founded, by his advice,
a perpetual public [i] Lecture in Divinity in the University Preface to
of Cambridge. This her Ladyship instituted on the feast the Lady
Margaret's
of the * nativity of the Blessed Virgin, and by the original funeral
foundation, appointed our Doctor her first reader. She Sermon.
* Sept. 8,
likewise gave rules and statutes for the choice of her 1503.
reader, and for the discharge and performance of the
duties of his place, and endowed this, her lecture, with
twenty marks per annum, payable by the Abbot and Convent of Westminster, which house she had endowed with
revenues to the value of † eighty-seven pounds per annum. †about 5 or

9. The Countess seems about this time to have com- 600 pounds
a year, ac-
municated to her Confessor her design of settling on this cording to
Abbey, where she and the King, her son, intended to be the present
value of
buried, a considerable estate, for such uses as she should money.
order and appoint; some of which, very probably, would
have been, according to the superstitious mode of those
times, the performing yearly trentals and exequies, &c. for
her soul. For this purpose, she had already obtained the
King, her son's, faculty or license; but on her telling this
to Dr. Fisher, he entirely disapproved of her intentions,
and therefore advised her to let her charity run in another
channel. Accordingly, he represented to her, that the Coll. No.
Abbey of Westminster was already wealthy enough, as it 13.
was indeed the richest of all the religious houses in England, and did not therefore want any further maintenance

---

[i] Concerning this lecture there is the following entry in the junior Proctor's book, 1628-9. Quilibet in Artibus incipiens jurabit de continuatione
Lecturæ Theologicæ a Domina Margareta Regis Henrici VII. Matre fundatæ
per annum per cujuslibet Termini majorem partem, si Lector per majorem
partem legerit; neque se absentabit nisi ex rationabili causa per Vice-cancel-
larium, Lectorem, et duos procuratores et eorum singulos approbanda. *Coll.
MS. penes Rev. Alexan. Young, Rectorem de Wickham-breux in agro Cantiano.*

or support; whereas the two Universities, and especially that of Cambridge, were yet but meanly endowed; that the provisions already made for the several professors and scholars were few and small, and that colleges were yet wanting for their living and maintenance: that if, therefore, she applied her intended charity to remedy these defects and discouragements, she might thereby double it, and consequently double her reward, by contributing to the support and encouragement of both learning and virtue. As the Doctor had, by his virtuous and discreet behaviour, gained entire credit with the Countess, and was one of a very good address, and who knew the art of persuading, it is no wonder that he prevailed with her to alter her purpose and design. She therefore very graciously answered the Doctor, that she would gladly come into the measures he had advised her to take in the settling or disposal of her charity, but that she was under some ties and engagements to the King, her son, in their common designs at Westminster, so that she could not alter what she had intended without his consent, which she did not know how to ask. This, therefore, the Doctor undertook to do; and having persuaded the Countess to write to the King, he was the bearer of the letter to persuade his Majesty to give her leave to alter her former design with relation to Westminster Abbey, for which, as has been said before, she had obtained his royal license; and this he did with so much prudence and dexterity, as not only to obtain the King's consent, but to cause His Majesty to have so good an opinion of him, as hereby to lay the foundation of his future promotion by him; for, as a proof of the Doctor's success, His Majesty was graciously pleased to make him the bearer of a letter to the Countess, his mother, in answer to her's, written with his own hand. In it he tells her, that " by her Confessour, the bearer, he had received

" her good and most loving writing, and by the same had " herde, at good leisure, such credence as he would shew " unto him in her behalf, and thereuppon had sped him in

" every behalf, without delay, according to her noble peti-
" tion and desire, which rested in two principal points;
" the one, for a general pardon for all manner of causes;
" the other, to alter and change part of a license which he
" had given unto her before, for to be put into mortmain
" at Westminster, and now to be converted into the Uni-
" versity of Cambridge, for her soul's health: all which
" things His Majesty wrote, according to her desire and
" pleasure, he had with all his heart and good will given
" and granted unto her." This difficulty being thus overcome, the Countess followed her Confessor's advice, in
applying her charity to the relief of the wants of the University of Cambridge, as will be shewn by and by.

10. During the Doctor's Vice-chancellorship, he like-
wise procured from Pope Alexander VI. the grant of the
following privilege to the University of Cambridge, *viz.*
" That the Chancellor of the University and his succes-
" sors shall have license to chuse every year xii Doctors,
" Masters, or Graduates, who shall be in Priests' Orders,
" to preach throughout the whole kingdom of England,
" Scotland, and Ireland, under the common seal of the
" University, without any other license from a Bishop."
This is said, in the Bull, to have been granted to Dr.
Fisher, at the suit of Thomas Cabold, the Pope's lesser
penitentiary in the Court of Rome for the English, Scotch,
and Irish nations. Accordingly, A. D. 1505, Mr Lam-
bert and Mr. Page, the two Proctors, and *ten* others, were
chosen to be preachers under the seal of the University.
According to the form of the license, granted seventeen
years after, to one- Christopher Baily, M. A. to preach
throughout England, &c. the Pope's Bull is recited, by
which it appears, that these preachers had not an absolute
authority granted them to preach when and wheresoever
they would; since it is expressly provided, that they who
are so elected, and deputed to the office of preaching,
shall not preach in places where the Ordinaries of those
places preach, but with their consent, and that they shall

CHAP.
I.

A.D 1501

Strype's
Life of Abp
Parker, p
193.

May 31,
1522.

CHAP.
I.

have the consent of the Rectors of the churches where they preach. But the reason of the Vice-chancellor's soliciting for this privilege, might possibly be the sense he had of the want of preaching throughout the kingdom, and the backwardness of the several Bishops to encourage such useful, sound, and practical preaching, as whereby the people might be well instructed and edified. Of this

Of prelates
c. 16, MS.

Dr. Wiclif's followers often complained. " If Priests, *says* " *one of them,* wolen seye their mass, and techen the " Gospel in a Bishop's diocese, anoon he shall be for- " boden; but if he have leave of that Bishop, and he shall " pay commonly for that leave much money, or else swear " that he shall not speke against great sins of Bishops and " other priests, and their falseness; and yet it is a great " work of charity and mercy to teche men the right way

ibid. c. 42.

" to Heaven." So again, " when they, *the Prelates,* ben " unable, by ignorance and wicked life, to teche Cristen " people God's Law, they wolen not suffren true men " teche freely Christ's Gospel without their leave and " letters. They geven leave to Sathana's prechers for to " preche fables, and flattering and lesings, and to deceive " the people in faith and good works." It has been shewn

Life of Bp.
Pecock.

before what complaints were made of Archbishop Arun- del's binding the tongues of, as it were, all preachers, as his ordering them to be licensed was termed, on account of a few heretics who were suspended from preaching. Things, therefore, standing thus at this time, it is not to be wondered if the Doctor was for enlarging the number of preachers, or not suffering the power of licensing them to be wholly in the Bishops. Erasmus intimates, as will be shewn more at large hereafter, that our Doctor by no means liked the ordinary or modish way of preaching in his time, consisting of cavils about words, and a parcel of dull sophistry; but desired to have those who were de- signed for preachers exercised in true learning and sober disputations, that so they might preach the word of God gravely, and with an evangelical spirit, and recommend it

to the minds of the learned by an efficacious eloquence. CHAP
In pursuance of this good design, the Doctor seems to I.
have advised his mistress, the Lady Margaret, to found a
perpetual public preacher at Cambridge, to preach, at
least, *six* sermons every year in several churches, specified
in the Charter, in the dioceses of London, Ely, and Lincoln, which she accordingly did by her Charter, dated
October 30, 1504, appointing to the preacher a stipend of A.D. 1504.
[k] ten pounds a year, payable by the Abbot and Convent of
Westminster. So small was the number of good and able
preachers at this time, and long after, that we find frequent provisions of this kind. To mention but one or two
instances. By the Statutes of the metropolitical Church of
Canterbury, it is ordered, that " because the harvest truly cap. xxi de
" is great, and the labourers are few, therefore there shall Conciona-
" be *six* preachers added to the Canons, whose office it toribus.
" shall be to preach every one of them twenty sermons a
" year, in the country, in villages, and towns in the neigh-
" bourhood of Canterbury, or in parishes and villages
" where their Cathedral church's mannors, and estates are,
" or in their own cures, if they have any, or in the city of
" Canterbury without the Cathedral Church." Thus, long
after this, we are told, that William Bedell, afterwards
Bishop of Kilmore, in Ireland, whilst he was Fellow of Narrative
St. John's College, in Cambridge, with Mr. Abdias Ashton, of the Life
and Death
Fellow of the same House, and Mr. Thomas Gataker, for- of Mr Ga-
merly of the same College, but now Fellow of the new- taker, p 45.
founded College of Sydney-Sussex, and some others, set
on foot a design of preaching in places adjacent to the
University, even to a considerable distance, where there
were no Pastors able to instruct the people. But to return to our Doctor.

11. The same year was Dr. Fisher chosen Chancellor A D. 1504.
of the University: a place to which he was so equal, that
he was continued in it *ten* years successively, and afterwards, as will be shewn hereafter, chosen for his life

[k] This was then equal to about seventy pounds per annum now

life. Erasmus observed of him, that " during this, his " Chancellorship, he steered a middle course betwixt those " who had hitherto taught the sciences in the schools con- " fusedly and sophistically, and those who were for laying " all human learning aside, together with the schools or " Universities wherein it was taught." Du Pin adds, that

Nouvelle Biblio- theque, &c. Tom. xiv. p. 145.
it was owing to *his* care and pains, that England was fur- nished with a great number of excellent divines and pro- fessors of the languages, by which means the sciences flourished, and especially that of Divinity, in the Universi- ties of this kingdom.

CHAP. II

1. DR. Richard Fitz-James, who, as has been said before, was, from being Confessor to the Lady Margaret, promoted to the bishopric of Rochester, was, towards the latter end of 1503, translated to that of Chichester. On A.D. 1503 this occasion, the King had a mind to appoint for Fitz-James's successor in the see of Rochester, his mother's present Confessor, Dr. Fisher. But out of respect and duty to her, His Majesty first wrote to her, to acquaint her with his intentions, and to ask her leave to pursue E Regist. them. His Majesty therefore assured the lady, that his Coll. Joannis Cant. inclination to promote the Doctor to a bishopric proceeded from no other cause than the great and singular virtue which he knew and saw in him, as well in learning as in natural parts, and especially for his good and virtuous life and conversation: that by the promotion of such a man, he knew he should encourage many others to live virtuously, and to take such courses as he did, which should be a good example to many others hereafter. His Majesty added, that he had in his time promoted many a

CHAP.
II.
man unadvisedly, and that he would now make some recompense, by the promotion of some good and virtuous
men, which he doubted not would be most pleasing to
God.   He therefore besought his mother to let him know
her mind and pleasure in this matter, which, His Majesty
said, should be followed as much as God would give him
grace.   The Lady Margaret, who had so high an opinion
of her Confessor's learning, judgment, and virtue, was, no
doubt, very glad to find that her son, the King, took so
much notice of him, and had entertained the very same
thoughts of him that she had herself.   Accordingly, Dr.
Fisher was [a]nominated by the King to succeed Bishop
Fitz-James in this see of Rochester, which nomination
was confirmed by Pope Julius II's bull, dated at Rome,
Coll. No. 1. October 14, 1504.   Accordingly, he was consecrated at
Lamehithe, by Archbishop Warham, the [b]21th of the
next month, had the spiritualities restored to him by the
said Archbishop's mandate next day, and by his Proctor,
Febru. 18, Dr. Thomas Heede, whom a little before he had made his
1504.   Official, and Vicar-general, was inducted, installed, and
enthronized, April 24, 1505.

2. This promotion the Bishop himself calls a [c] sudden

[a] Notwithstanding this, and the Bishop's so frequently, and with so much
gratitude, ascribing this, his promotion, to the King, and acknowledging him
for his patron, in the Bishop's register it is entered as entirely owing to the
Pope.   Thus is the register expressed: *The register of the reverend father in
Christ and the Lord, John Fisher, S. T. P. by the grace of God, Bishop of
Rochester; seeing the most holy father in Christ and our Lord, the Lord
Julius II. by Divine Providence, Pope, has placed the aforesaid venerable father
over the aforesaid Cathedral Church of Rochester, vacant, &c. for its Bishop
and Pastor, as appears by bulls, &c.* See Coll. No. II.

[b] Qui consecratus fuit per reverendum in Christo patrem et dominum
Dom. Willielmum permissione divina Cant. Archiepiscopum totius Anglie
primatem et Apostolice sedis legatum in capella sua infra manerium suum
de Lamehith—die Dominico in festum S. Katerine Virginis, *viz.* 24° die
mensis Novembris—presentibus tunc ibidem M. Hugone Ashestone et Ri-
cardo Collect Legum doctore. *Registrum Fisher.*

[c] Meipsum, inquam, quem incredibile cunctis fuit ad Episcopatum tam
repentè promoveri. Quippe qui paucos annos habuerim, qui nunquam in
Curia obsequium præstiterim, qui nullis ante dotatus beneficiis. *Oratio ad
R. Henricum* VII.

one; since he had but few years over his head, had never
plied or solicited at Court for preferment, and had never
been beneficed before. His Lordship further observed,
that a great many thought this advancement of him was
owing to the [d] recommendation and requests of his mistress, the Lady Margaret, the King's mother, and Countess of Richmond and Derby, but, he assures us, it was
quite otherwise: that the [e] King having entertained a
good opinion of him, from the repeated commendation of
him to His Majesty, by Fox, Bishop of Winchester, the
King's Almoner and Privy Counsellor, whom His Majesty
often consulted, did of his own mere motion, without any
other application whatsoever, and without the asking of
any one, of his own accord give him the bishopric. This,
he says, the King himself more than once affirmed to *him*,
and was very well known to Bishop Fox, who was of the
King's Cabinet Council. Our Bishop therefore always
acknowledged this prelate for his patron, and accordingly
tells him, that ever since his Lordship had taken notice of
him, he had, by the breath of his favour, not only been
vehemently inflamed with the study or desire of good letters, but likewise more ardently to embrace probity of life.

3. With this promotion our Bishop expressed himself
highly pleased. Thus he wrote to his patron, Bishop
Fox. [f] " Though others may have, and enjoy greater

CHAP.
II

Vide Rof-
fensis pri-
vata Statu-
ta, MS
Coll No.
12.

Ep. dedicat

---

[d] Non desunt fortè complures quibus creditum est genetricem illius nempe
comitem Richemondiæ, Derbiæque—suis precibus a filio dictum episcopatum impetrasse mihi. Verum longè aliter sese res habet Quod et tuæ
dominationi compertissimum est qui a secretissimis consilijs ipsi regi fueras.
Ep dedicat Fox Epis. Winton.

[e] Regi Henrico septimo qui tunc habenas Regni summa prudentia mode-
rabatur—meam parvitatem commendasti, ut sola existimatione quam, te
totiès inculcante, de me concepit, et mero motu, quod aiunt, citra quodvis
aliud obsequium, citra cujusquam preces, quod et mihi non semel affirmabat,
episcopatum Roffensem, cui jam indignus præsum, ultrò donaverit. *Ibid.*

[f] Habeant licet alii proventus pinguiores Ego tamen interim pauciorum
animarum curam gero, adeo ut quum utrorumque ratio reddenda fuerit, quod
et propediem haud dubiè futurum est, nec pilo meam sortem optarim ube-
riorem

CHAP.
II.

" revenues or fatter incomes, yet I, in the mean time, have
" the care of fewer souls; so that since an account is to be
" given of *both*, which, no doubt, is daily to be expected,
" I would not give a farthing to alter my poor lot for one
" more plentiful." Accordingly, it is said, though on what

Fuller, Ec-
cles. His-
tory, lib. v.
p. 203.

authority I know not, that when King Henry VIII. would
have translated our Bishop to Lincoln or Ely, bishoprics,
at that time, treble to Rochester in revenue, he refused to

Life of Bp.
Fisher, c. 2.

accept of the Royal favour, saying, *he would not change
his poor old wife, to whom he had been so long wedded, for
the richest widow in England.*   But be this as it will, the
Bishop himself tells us, that " the excellent Princess, the
" [g] Lady Margaret, &c. after this promotion, so far favoured
" or regarded his meaness, or the smallness of his income
" or preferment, as very earnestly to desire to get for him
" a fatter bishopric," which seems to imply *his* consent;
" and, that when she found death approaching, and that
" she could not accomplish what she designed, she, by
" way of recompence, gave him a considerable sum of
" money for his own use."   He further owned, that " he
" yearly received from the bishopric of Rochester [h] abun-
" dantly sufficient to maintain the honour of a Bishop;"
which must, I think, be true, if the account given us by
a learned antiquary of the last age of the value of this
bishopric at that time, *viz.* [i] 3000*l.* a year, may be depended
on.   But I am afraid this is a mistake for 300*l.*; since,
according to the value of the benefices in England taken

---

[g] Eximia princeps domina Margareti Richmondiæ Com. usque adeo mee
exiguitati favit, ut pinguiorem episcopatum omnino studuit mihi comparasse.
Qnum ergo mortem instare sibi noverit, nec posse quod destinaret perimplere, non parvâ me donavit pecunie summâ quâ in privatum meum commodum uterer. *Roffensis, privata Statuta,* c. 1. MS.

[h] —— abunde satis ad honestum presulis victum ex episcopatu Roffensi
quotannis acceperim. *Roffensis, privata Statuta.*

[i] Libertatem autem simul ac bona redemit, datâ Regi ter mille librarum
summâ quæ integros unius Anni proventus ex episcopatu Roffensi prode-
untes valere eo tempore censebatur, si Autori Vitæ ejus fides sit habenda.
Whartoni Anglia Sacra, vol. i. p. 382.

some years after, this bishopric is thus valued : *Episcopa-*
tus Roffensis, 358*l.* 4*s* 9½*d.*

4. Our Bishop was scarce settled in his bishopric,
before he was, by the Fellows of Queen's College, in
Cambridge, chosen their [k] President, in the room of Dr.   Apr 12,
Thomas Wilkinson, who resigned this Presidentship in   1505
favour of the Bishop, being induced so to do by the in-   Coll No 2.
terest of the Lady Margaret, who likewise recommended
to them the choice of the Bishop, as not only very necessary, but much to their advantage.   This is elsewhere re-   Life of Bp
presented as a compliment paid by that College to his   Fisher.
Lordship, on account of his having no house belonging to
him as Chancellor, and his being obliged sometimes to
reside in the University, for the better execution of that
great office.   But if his Lordship was now Master of
Michael-House, he could not want a house in the University to reside in.   It seems, therefore, that if ever he was
Master of that College, he had now resigned that place,
and, that the Lady Margaret's procuring him this Presidentship, was for the conveniency of his inspecting the
works of Christ's College, the foundation of which was
laid this year.

5. In May the Bishop went down to Rochester, where,
on the 15th day following, his Lordship begun his ordinary visitation in his cathedral church.   About the same
time we meet with the abjuration of one John Moress,
alias Menes, of St. Nicholas, in Rochester, who abjured
or renounced the following odd and whimsical opinions,
which he confessed he had openly broached, as he was
accused of doing.

(1.) That as for Christ, whan he suffred a Good Ffridaye
a pon the cross, he dyed nat in perfitt charite : for as
moche as he redemed nat Lucifer, as well as he did Adam
and Eve.

(2.) That as for our blessed Lady, she is but a sakk ; and

[k] Presidens Collegii Reginalis Sanctorum Margarete et Barnardi in Can-
tebrigia

the Son of God desired the Father to come into myddel-herth to take a sakk upon his bakk.

6. It seems likewise as if, about this time, the Lady Margaret avowed and confirmed to the Bishop, " to whom " she was, she said, verely determined (as to her cheffe " trustye counselloure) to owe her obedyence in all thyngs " concernynge the well and profite of her sowle; that with " full purpos and good deliberacion, for the * well of " her synfull sowle, she did with all her herte promyse " from thensforthe the chastite of her bodye, the which " thing, she said, she had before purpassed in her lorde " her husband's dayes, and nowe eftsence fully conferred " it, as far as in her lay."

* weale.

7. It has been already intimated that our Bishop, who seems to have had much the same opinion of the religious houses, as they were called, especially of the greater sort of them, with his friend Erasmus, *viz.* " that they were more for ostentation than for the promotion of piety," had persuaded the Lady Margaret, instead of adding to their endowments, to bestow her charity on the University of Cambridge, where provisions for scholars were very few and discouraging. This, by the way, was exceeding agreeable to the sense of our Bishop's great friend and admirer, the learned Erasmus. Thus he speaks of it: " God," says he, " inspired that woman with a thought, which was by " no means a womanish one; for whereas other princesses " are wont to bequeath large estates for the building of " monasteries, this lady applied all her study to the most " holy thing of all, the instructing the people in the Gospel " philosophy. That holy heroine and the Bishop, who " was a singular example of true piety, judged right; that " there was nothing that could more contribute to amend " the people's manners, than the dispersing the seed of the " evangelical doctrine by fit and proper preachers. For," says he, " from whence is it that Christ is, as it were, ex- " tinct in the hearts of so many? Whence is it that, under " the name of Christianity, there is so much of Paganism,

"but from a dearth of faithful preachers?" Without CHAP.
Barnwell Gate, over against St. Andrew's Church, stood a ___II.___
* Maison Dieu, or hospital, founded by King Henry VI. * God's
who intended to have placed here sixty scholars, had he House
not, by his being deprived of his kingdom, and soon after of
his life, been prevented from executing this, and his other
good intentions towards this University. But instead of
sixty, there were, for lack of maintenance, never more than
four who lived here. On this hospital the Lady resolved
to bestow some of her bounty; and to fulfil the royal intentions of King Henry, to whom, as being of the Lan-
caster line, she reckoned herself a sort of heir. She
therefore obtained of the King, her son, his royal charter,
to encrease the number of students, and alter it at her
pleasure, and to change the name of this hospital from
that of Maison Dieu to Christ's College. Then she
placed in it one master, twelve fellows, and forty-seven
scholars, which made up the number of sixty, according
to King Henry's first design. For all these she provided
very well by her last Will, by which she bequeathed many
good lands to this foundation, and placed over them for
the first master, John Sickling, fellow or scholar of the old
Maison Dieu.

8. Whilst this College was thus fitting up, the Lady,
the foundress, came to Cambridge, to take a view of it,
viz. the latter end of this year, 1505. In the Proctor's A.D. 1505.
book we have the following account of the expenses of
the University on this occasion:

In expenses on the King's mother, when she   s.   d.
   was in the University   xl   v
For a present to the King's mother   xv   ii

In the same book is it entered, that the Proctor received
of her for the fabric, or towards the building of St. Mary's
Church, *ten* pounds; and that her Confessor was incor-
porated; by which must be meant, a successor of the
Bishop's in that honourable place, who was, probably, an
Oxford man.

CHAP.
II.

A. D. 1506.

9. The buildings of this college being finished the next year, statutes for the well government of it were to be provided. By one of these, so great was the regard that the foundress had to the Bishop, it is ordained, that John Bishop of Rochester, and Chancellor of the University, be Visitor of the said college so long as he lives, even although, perhaps, he should abdicate or quit the Chancellorship, and that his Lordship should have power to appoint a substitute. When, therefore, several years after, Proctors or Attorneys were substituted to interpret or explain these statutes of the college, the instrument recites, that it was done with the advice and consent, and ordination of the reverend father in Christ, the Lord John, Bishop of Rochester.

10. To grace this new foundation of his mother's, and honour the opening it with his royal presence, His Majesty was pleased the latter end of this year to accompany her to Cambridge, with the Prince, his son. On this occasion, His Majesty not only treated the whole University, but gave them [l]one hundred marks, and [m]forty pounds towards the fabric of St. Mary's church, a very generous benefaction for one of King Henry's parsimonious temper. The Proctor's book gives the following account of the expenses of the University at this time:

A. D. 1506.

	s.	d.
Paid to Robert the carpenter, for the commencement building in the church of the *Minors, five days	iv	ii
Item, for a labourer at the *Minors, in putting up the stages for the commencement	ii	0

* Minorite
Friers.

So that the commencement was now held, *coram Rege*, in the King's presence, in the church of the Franciscan Friars, St. Mary's being not yet finished. Our Bishop, as Chancellor of the University, made the King, on this solemn occasion, a very eloquent oration, which I have put in the Collection, and is to this purpose.

Coll. No. 4.

11. His Lordship observed to His Majesty, that "for

[l] Equal to 700*l.* now.   [m] Equal to about 300*l.* now.

" the most part they who were designed for great men had
" wonderful beginnings, and were exposed to great hazards
" of life, so that, unless they were preserved by the won-
" derful providence of God, they had often perished. He
" instanced in Moses, to whom he compares the King as
" being like him, wonderfully born and brought into the
" world by the most noble Princess, his mother, then pre-
" sent, who at the time of His Majesty's birth was not
" above fourteen years old, and very small of stature, as
" she was never a tall woman. That it seemed to all a
" miracle that at those years, and of so little a personage,
" any one at all should be born, much more one so tall, and
" of so fine a shape as His Majesty. As for the perils and
" hazards of His Majesty's life, the Bishop said, it would
" be almost endless to recount them; for instance, whilst
" his mother went with him, he very narrowly escaped the
" danger of the plague, of which his illustrious father died.
" His mother being thus deprived of her husband, was
" delivered of him an orphan, who was scarce weaned,
" when he was committed to the care of those who were
" involved in continual wars. The castle in which he was
" kept being besieged, he fell into the hands of his enemies,
" who yet providentially gave him an education becoming
" his noble descent; next, being sought for to be put to
" death, he was forced to fly his country, when, designing
" to go to his kinsman, the King of France, he more advan-
" tageously happened on the Duke of Bretany, by whom,
" notwithstanding, he was made a prisoner. Having made
" his peace with *him*, and intending to return into his own
" country, his fleet was driven back by a violent storm of
" wind, which was very providential, since if he had
" landed in England, he would scarce have escaped his
" enemies, who looked out very narrowly for him. After-
" wards the Duke of Bretany offered him to sale to his
" capital enemies, who desired nothing more than his life:
" the price was actually agreed on, but His Majesty escaped
" safe into France, from whence when he again attempted

CHAP.
II

Pembroke
Castle

" to come into his own country, having landed with a
" small force, he, almost as soon as he set his foot on
" shore, defeated the King that then was, with all his
" army. Being at length settled on the throne, he was
" exposed to numberless plots and treasons, murmurs and
" rebellions; all which he divinely overcame, and arrived
" at his present glory. This one thing alone, the Bishop
" said, was abundantly sufficient to prove the King's great-
" ness; so that there was no need to rehearse the distinc-
" tion of his family, from how many and most sacred kings
" and emperors he was descended, whom yet *his* nobility
" rendered no less illustrious than *their's* did him: no oc-
" casion to say any thing of the noble exercises of his
" youth in which he would be occupied, avoiding sloth
" and an unactive life as he would the plague. For the
" same reason, the Bishop told His Majesty, he omitted
" mentioning that invincible greatness of mind through
" which, in events which made others afraid, he himself
" was always without fear. His temperance in meat and
" drink, and other bodily pleasures: his prudence in the
" management of all his affairs, especially in the adminis-
" tration of his kingdom, which he had so effectually esta-
" blished in peace, and reduced to his obedience, as no
" king had ever done before him. So great and wonderful
" was his wisdom, that it was the admiration of not only
" his subjects, but of all foreign princes. The Bishop
" likewise, as he said, omitted His Majesty's speaking so
" many different languages, his eloquence, the graceful
" height of his stature, the elegancy of his mien or pre-
" sence becoming a king, his strength and courage; his
" nimbleness, agility, and dexterity, in doing whatever he
" had a mind to do: the fruitfulness of his kingdom, the
" courage of his subjects, and his great wealth. He would
" only, he said, observe, that whosoever attended to the
" Divine Providence in him, must own him to be a very
" wonderful person, and admonish His Majesty to be
" careful not to be ungrateful to so very kind a God.

" The Bishop proceeded to speak of the King's kindness
" to them of the University, which, he said, His Majesty
" exercised at a time when they had the greatest occasion
" for it. To shew this, he took notice of the antiquity of
" the University of Cambridge, and of the honours which
" had been conferred on it by the King's progenitors,
" Henry III. Edward I. II. III. and Richard II. That
" Henry III. built that house of the Friars where they
" then were; Edward III. founded King's Hall, for
" eighty scholars; Henry VI. designed another for sixty,
" and began another, to which he gave the name of King's
" College. But at that time, when His Majesty began to
" take notice of them, they, by a complication of misfor-
" tunes, were almost quite undone; but he, by his favours
" bestowed on them, had raised their dull and languishing
" spirits. His Lordship instanced in himself, who, he
" said, was promoted by His Majesty to the episcopacy,
" though he had made no application or interest at court,
" and was never before preferred to any benefice, and all
" to make students sensible, that they should not want
" encouragement, and to incite them to virtue and good
" learning. But that His Majesty had more openly shewed
" his desire to encourage them, in that the last year he
" did them the honour to come to them, and be present
" at their disputations, and that in the schools of all the
" faculties, not cursorily and perfunctorily, but for a good
" while together. Besides this, His Majesty made a public
" entertainment for the scholars, and set about finishing
" King's College, which King Henry VI. had left but in
" part built. Upon all these accounts, he tells his Ma-
" jesty, they were very much indebted to him for so great
" kindnesses done to them in their so great necessity.
" The Bishop concluded his speech with praying to God,
" that he would give the King a long, a happy, and a
" prosperous life; that his son, then present with him, an
" illustrious prince, and worthy such a father, might succeed
" him in his kingdom; that his family might be encreased,

" and he might have dutiful nobles, loving soldiers, and
" obedient subjects; that his friends might honour him,
" his enemies fear him, and his allies be constant to him;
" that he might enjoy a lasting state of health here on
" earth, and after this life, eternal happiness in heaven."

Coll. No. 5.

12. To this college, thus finished and settled by our
Bishop's care and providence, his Lordship was afterwards
himself a benefactor in the following manner. He gave
forty-three pounds to buy lands to the value of forty shillings a year, on this condition, that there shall be celebrated
an anniversary commemoration, together with a mass and
satisfactory prayer for the soul of the aforesaid Bishop of
Rochester, and for the souls of his parents and heirs;
and that on the self-same day on which this solemn commemoration is celebrated, the Master of the college shall
receive sixteen-pence, every fellow twelve-pence, and each
of the scholars, if they are Bachelors, four-pence; if under-
graduates, two-pence; which anniversary, the Bishop
ordered, if it should happen to be omitted thrice, the
lands given for it should be forfeited to St. John's College,
that the Master, and Fellows, and Scholars of that society
might observe this solemnity. To the performance of all
this, the Master, &c. of Christ's College obliged themselves, by an indenture dated February 22, A. D. 1525.

13. Having thus finished the account of the Bishop's
settling this college, I must carry the reader back again to
the year 1507, when I find the Bishop at his palace of
Bromley, where, in the parish church, an act of abjuration was read and performed before his Lordship, by one
Richard Gavell, of Westerham, in his Lordship's diocese,
on December 5. The errors and heresies, as they were
then judged and called, which he abjured, were as follows :

Reg.
Fisher.

(1.) That he affermyd, that the feaste of the holy apostle
seynt * Thomas ys nat to be sanctifyed nor to be kept holy-
daye in the churche.

* Thomas
Becket.

(2.) That it is nat necessarye to any man to take holy
water of the prestes hand.

(3.) That the oblacions and offeryng dayes that be ordenyd by the churche ar nat necessary, for they war only
lymyted and ordenyd by prestes and curates by theire
owne covetouse myndes and singular avayles.

(4.) That the corse or sentence of the churche is of
none effect, nor nothyng to be regarded or to be sett by.
Ffor the ᵇcorse of the churche is not to be sett by or
dred, but only the corse of God, which the prestes have
not in their poor. Insomyche, that when he was accursid
by the Archbishop of Canterbury, and so openly by the
curate denuncyd in the church of Westerham, he sayde,
in the presence of divers persones, *Syrs, tho' my Lorde
of Canterbury hath accorsid me, I truste yet I am not accorsid of God, and therefore, syrs, fere ye not to com-
panye or ete and drynke with me for all that.* So high
an opinion was, it seems, now conceived of the sacerdotal
powers, as to imagine, that he whom the priests blessed
was blessed, and he whom they cursed was cursed.

14. Our Bishop having now enjoyed the Presidentship
of Queen's College about three years, and the buildings
of Christ's being now all finished, he resolved to resign it.
This, his intention, his Lordship seems to have communicated to the Society, by letter, about June this year. For
thus the Fellows, in their letter to him of the 19th of this
month, tell him, that " as to what he writes to them of his
" resolution to vacate the Presidentship of their College,
" although they were wonderfully struck with that word,
" and in a consternation, and, as it were, in an ecstasy,
" yet, that they might not seem impertinent, and to no
" purpose, and unseasonably to oppose his inclination, and
" on that account less yielding to him, they submitted
" themselves in the most obsequious manner, and desired
" his Lordship to use them as he pleased, otherwise, they
" were so far from desiring to take this place from him,
" that they gave him free power of appointing for them a
" President, whomsoever he pleased, for they were cer-

ᵇ Curse

" tain he would place over them no one who was not the
" image of himself, and not like him in his virtuous quali-
" ties; and therefore whatsoever he should do in this
" affair, they would have him think it no sooner said than
" done." To the same purpose, in their letter to the Lady
Margaret, they tell her, that " for the inteer love which
" they all had of dewte unto him, the said reverent father,
" they had given hym full power to assyne and chose for
" his successour amowng them whomsoever hit wold plese
" him, that so, yf they myght not contynow with hym, at
" leyst, by his appointment, they shuld have soche on as
" somewhat shuld assemble hym and his goodly manerys."
Accordingly, the Bishop chose for his successor in this
Presidentship Dr. Robert Beakingshaw, Fellow of Michael-House, and afterward Dean of Stoke. How very
acceptable our Bishop was to this society, appears not
only by what has been already said, but by their telling
the Lady Margaret, that his Lordship " surchesed, and
" left the Presidentship of their College, to the right gret
" hevynes of them al." To the same purpose they expressed themselves in their nomination or election of his
successor. " The Bishop," they said, " was a man that,
" without flattery, was very dear to them all, not only on
" account of his ingenuous humanity, but for his excellent
" learning and prudence, who, they wished, had as great
" a desire to be their President, as they had of continuing
" him."

A. D. 1497. 15. Erasmus having been here in England, by the in-
vitation of Montjoy, who had entertained him at Calais,
as his preceptor, became, very probably, acquainted with
our Bishop; and therefore being now President of this
College, he seems to have invited him thither, and to have
allotted him an apartment in his own lodge for the prosecution of his studies; although Erasmus himself, in one of
his letters to his friend Boville, among his other friends to
whom he desired him to remember him, mentions his
landlord Gerard, the bookseller, as if, for some time, how-

ever, he lodged at *his* house when he was there. However this be, Erasmus, the very next year after the Bishop's having this Presidentship, had his grace to commence Bachelor and Doctor of Divinity at the same time, he performing his exercise, and paying the bedels. This seems owing to the favour of the Chancellor. By the same interest he seems to have been admitted *five* years afterwards to the Lady Margaret's Professorship of Divinity, which he continued to hold till A. D. 1515. By our Bishop's procurement, he was likewise made the first Greek Professor in this University; and when he quitted it in 1522, was succeeded by Richard Croke, whom the Bishop was forced to beg and entreat to accept of it. In a letter, therefore, to our Bishop, dated at Cambridge, 1510, Erasmus tells his Lordship, that "he was by him "obliged by so great offices and kindnesses, that he was "looking about to see in what manner he should express "his gratitude;" and in another, the next year, to his "friend Andrew Hammond, he tells him, "that he had "hitherto read [o] Chrysoloras's Grammar to a thin audi-"tory, but supposed he should have a better when he "began [p] Theodore's; that, perhaps, he should under-"take the Divinity Lecture, *that* being now in agitation, "though he was not moved by the profits, which were "too small to raise his ambition;" and yet, it is sure, the salary of the Divinity Lecture, *viz.* twenty marks a year, was almost equal to the pension afterward given him by Archbishop Warham, for which he was so very thankful. This, however, shews what care the Bishop took to promote good and useful learning in the University. Not above twenty years before he had any share in the government of this famous school of learning, as Erasmus observed, "there was nothing taught here but [q] Alexander,

CHAP. II.

A.D 1506.

Wood's Athenæ Oxon

[o] Manuel Chrysoloras Quæstiones Grammaticales Græce.

[p] Introductio Grammatices Græcè

[q] Alexander de Hales, called Doctor irrefragabilis Expositio in Libros Metaphysicæ Aristotelis.

" the small logicals, as they called them, and those old
" dictates of Aristotle and the stoical Questions, but that
" now good learning was revived, the mathematics were
" taught, a new Aristotle, or Aristotle renewed, was read,
" the Greek language was studied, and so many authors
" were added, that even their names were not formerly
" known, no not even to the * principals or heads of houses

* Summa-
tibus lari-
cis.

" themselves." The same learned person observed to
Mountjoy some years after this, " that the University of
" Cambridge, under the government of the Bishop of
" Rochester, flourished with all kind of ornaments:" and
again, afterwards, " that the Bishop himself had assured
" him, that in the divinity disputations, instead of sophis-
" tical arguings, there were now sober and sound ones
" used, whereby they who were present at them, were
" made not only more learned, but better men." I only
add here, that upon the College Register during our
Bishop's presidentship, are several titles for holy orders
given to several of the Fellows who were afterwards of
note: one of these, for the form's sake, I have placed in

Coll. No. 3.
e coll. MS.
T. Baker.

the Collection; it was given to William Peytoo, who was
of a good family in Warwickshire, and for that reason,
perhaps, chose to be ordained by his diocesan, the Bishop
of Worcester. He was Bachelor of Arts at Oxford, and
as such was incorporated at Cambridge, 1502-3, and proceeded Master of Arts 1505, and was afterwards made a
Cardinal.

CHAP. III.

1. *King Henry* VII. *dies, and the Bishop preaches at his Funeral.* 2. *Some account of his Sermon.* 3. *Of his Sermon at the Lady Margaret's Funeral.*

1. In the beginning of the next year died King Henry April 22, the Seventh, and in him did our Bishop lose not only a 1509. most gracious sovereign, but a very kind and faithful friend. This is very gratefully acknowledged by himself in the introduction to his Sermon at his funeral. "And "allbeit," says he, "I know well myne unworthyness and "unhabylytees to this so grete a mater, yet for my most "bounden duty, and for his gracyous favour and singuler "benefeytes exhybyte unto me in this life, I wolde now "after his deth ryght affectuously some thynge saye." Wednesday, May 9, being appointed for the bringing the King's body from Richmond, in order to its interment, it Hall's was with great reverence conveyed in a chariot to the Chron. K. Hen. VIII. Cathedral Church of Saint Paul, where it was taken out, Fo. 1. b and carried into the quire, and set under a goodly herse of wax, garnished with banners, pencelles and cushions, and next day, May 10, there was " soung a solempne dirige " and a masse, with a Sermon made by the Bishoppe of " Rochester." It is not improbable that our Bishop was made choice of to preach on this occasion at the request of the King's mother, the Countess of Richmond, &c. since it is said in the [a]printed copy of it, that " this Ser- " mon was emprynted at the specyall request of the ryght " excellent Princesse Margarete, moder unto the sayd " noble Prynce," &c.

2. On this great and solemn occasion the Bishop made

---

[a] At the end it is said to be *emprinted by Wynkyn de Worde, prynter unto the moost excellent Pryncesse mylady, the kynge's graundame* which seems to intimate, that she was a patron and supporter of this printer conformable to the sentiments of her Confessor.

choice of the first Psalm of the dirige to treat on, and proposed to observe the same order that the secular orators
have in their funeral orations. 1. To commend him who
is dead. 2. To stir the hearers to have compassion on
him. 3. To comforte them againe. His Lordship commended the King especially for these four things: 1. A
true turning of his soule from this wretched world unto the
love of Almighty God. 2. A fast hope and confidence
that he had in prayer. 3. A stedfast belief of God and
of the Sacraments of the Church. 4. A diligent asking of
mercy in the time of mercy. As to the first of these, his
Lordship told his auditory, that he " was assured by His
" Majesties Confessor, that at the beginning of Lent last
" past, the King called unto him his Confessour, and after
" his confession, made with all diligence and great repen-
" tance, he promised three things, that is to say: 1. " A
" true reformation of all them that were officers and
" ministers of his laws, to the entent that justice from
" henceforward truly and indifferently might be executed
" in all causes. 2. That the promotions of the Churche
" that were of his disposition should from thenceforth be
" disposed to able men, such as were virtuous and well-
" learned. 3. That, as touching the danger and jeopardies
" of his laws, for things done in time past, he would grant
" a pardon generally unto all his people." As a proof or
evidence of the fast hope that His Majesty alway had in
prayers, " it was not unknown," the Bishop said, " the stu-
" dious and desirous mind that he had unto prayer, which
" he procured of religious and seculers Church throughout
" his realm. In all the churches of England daily his
" collect was said for him. Besides, that diverse years
" about Lent, he sent money to be distributed for ten
" thousand masses to be said for him. Over this was, in
" his realm no virtuous man that he might be credibly in-
" formed of, but he gave him a continual remembrance
" yearly and daily to pray for him; some x mares, some
" x pounds, besides his yearly and daily alms unto the

"prisoners, and the other poor and needy." As to the
King's stedfast belief of God, and of the Sacraments of the
Church, the Bishop told his auditory, that as a proof of it,
" he received them all with marvaillous devotion, namely,
" in the Sacrament of Penance, the Sacrament of the
" Altar, and the Sacrament of Anelying. The Sacrament
" of Penance with a marvellous compassion and flowe of
" tears, that at some time he wept and sobbed by the
" space of three-quarters of an hour. The Sacrament of
" the Altar, he received at Mid-lent, and again upon
" Easter-day, with so great reverence, that all that were
" present were astonied therat; for at his first entré into
" the closet where the Sacrament was, he took off his
" bonet, and kneled downe upon his knees, and so crept
" forth devoutly tyll he came unto the place selfe where
" he receyved the Sacrament. Two dayes next before his
" depart, he was of that feblenes, that he myght not re-
" ceyve it again; yet nevertheles he desyred to se the
" Monstrant wherein it was conteyned. The good fader,
" his Confessour, in good manner, as was convenyent,
" brought it unto him. He with suche a reverence, with so
" many knockynges and betynges of his brest, with so
" quicke and lyfely a countenaunce, with so desyrous an
" herte, made his humble obeysaunce therunto, and with
" so grete humblenes and devocyon kyssed, not the selfe
" place where the blessyd body of our Lorde was con-
" teyned, but the lowest part the fote of the Monstraunt,
" that all that stode aboute hym scarsly myght conteyne
" them from teres and wepynge. The Sacrament of Ane-
" lynge, or extreme unction, whan he wel perceyved, that
" he began utterly to fayle, he desyrously asked therfore,
" and hertely prayed, that it myght be admynystred unto
" him, wherin he made redy and offred every ᵇparte of his

ᵇ By the Manuel, according to the use of Sarum, it was ordered, that
whilst the 13th Psalm was saying by the Clerk, the Priest in the mean while
should take the oil of the sick on his right thumb, and so with that thumb
touch the sick person with the oil, making the sign of the Cross on both

" body by ordre, and, as he myght for weyknes, turned
" himselfe at every tyme, and answered in the suffrages
" therof. That same day of his departynge he herde
" ᶜmasse of the gloryous Virgyn, the moder of Cryste, to
" whome alwaye in hys lyfe he had a synguler and specyal
" devotion. The ymage of the ᵈcrucyfyx many a tyme that
" daye full devoutly he dyd beholde with grete reverence,
" lyftinge up his heede as he myght, holding up his handes
" before it, and often embrasynge it in his armes, and with
" grete devotion kissynge it and betynge ofte his brest."
From hence the Bishop " concluded, that no one can
" thinke that in this manner was not perfyte faith. Lastly,
" he commends his late Majesty for a dylygent askynge
" of mercy in the tyme of mercy." Here the Bishop observed, " that tho' in *what daye* soever the synner tourn-
" eth him from hys sinne, his synne shall not noye him, yet
" moche rather than yf he do it *many dayes*, and speci-
" ally *those days* that be to Almyghty God most accept-
" able, as be the *days of* Lent, of whom the Chyrche
" redeth : this is the tyme acceptable, these be the days
" of helth and mercy. Than for all penytentes the hole
" Chyrche maketh specyall prayer. From whence his
" Lordship concluded, that it is veryly to be trusted, that
" so true a turnynge to the love of God, despysynge this

eyes, beginning at the right eye ; on the ears, lips, nostrils, hands and feet :
lastly, on the back betwixt the loins of a man, or on the navel of a woman.

But in the reformed Roman Ritual, and the *Little Missal for Priests travelling in England, it is only ordered, that the anointing shall be on the loins
or reins, and the following rubric is added : *But this anointing on the loins is
always omitted in women, and even in men who by reason of weakness, can
scarcely, or not without hazard, be moved.*

ᶜ This is one of those which the Papists call votive masses.

ᵈ By the Order of Visiting the Sick, according to the use of Sarum, it is
appointed, that when the sick person ought to be anointed, the image of the
crucifix is to be offered to him, and placed in his sight, that he may adore
his Redeemer in " the image of the crucifix, and may remember his suffer-
" ing which he underwent for the salvation of sinners;" for, as has been
shewn in the Life of Bishop Pecock, it was then believed, that a physical
presence of Christ was in this image.

" world ; so fast a hope in prayer, so ferme a byleve in
" the Sacramentes of the Chyrche, and so devout a re-
" ceyvynge of them, so many holdynge up of his handes,
" so many lyftynge up of his eyen, so many betynges and
" knockynges of his brest, so many syghes, so many teres,
" so many callynges for mercy,' *by all that gracious tyme,*
' *by all the hole Lente,* with the helpe of the hole Chyrche,
" than prayinge for hym coude not be in vayne, so that he
" doubted not a gracyous ende and conclusyon of the
" King's lyf." Such was the account which the Bishop
gave of His Majesty's behaviour during his last sickness,
and at the time of his death.

3. It was not long before his Lordship was called to do
the ᶜ same office for this King's mother, and his own dear
and kind mistress, who died at Westminster, July 29th,
this year. On this sad and mournful occasion, the Bishop
chose for his text the history of Jesus and Martha, and
observed the same method in treating of it that he used in
his sermon at the funeral of the King. In shewing her
praise and commendation, he observed, that the comparison of Martha and the Lady Margaret might be made in
four things : in nobleness of person ; in discipline of their
bodys ; in ordering of their souls to God , in hospitalytyes
kepyng and charitable dealyng to their neighbours. As
to the first, his Lordship said, that there is a nobleness of
blood, of manners, of nature, and of affinity. The Countess, he told his auditory, was noble in all these respects.
1. In blood : she was lineally descended from King Edward III. within the fourth degree ; her father being
John Duke of Somerset, and her mother called Margaret.
She was noble in manners, being bounteous and liberal to

A.D 1509

John xi.
21.—28.

1

2.

ᶜ A Mornynge Remembrance had at the Moneth Minde of the noble
Prynces Margarete Countesse of Richmonde and Darbye, Moder unto Kynge
Henry the Seventh, and Grandame to our soveraign Lorde that now is. Upon
whose soul Almightye God have mercy Compyled by the Reverent Fader in
God Johan Fisher Byshop of Rochester. Emprynted at London, in Flete-
strete, at the sygne of the Sonne, by Wynkyn de Worde

every person of her knowledge and acquaintance. She
was also very easy of access, and very courteous in her
answers, of wonderful gentleness to all folks, but especially
to her own people, whom she trusted and loved very ten-
derly. Unkind she would not be to any one, nor forgetful
of any kindness or service done to her before, which, the
Bishop said, was no small part of true nobility. She was
neither revengeful nor cruel; but soon ready to forget
and forgive injuries done to her, at the least request or
motion made to her for the same. Merciful also and compassionate she was unto such as were grieved and wrong-
fully troubled; and to those that were in poverty, sickness,
or any other misery. To God and the Church she was
very obedient and tractable, very industriously seeking his
honour and pleasure. A wariness or watching over herself, she had alway to avoid every thing that might disho-
nour any noble woman or distaine her honour in any
condition. Frivolous things, that were little to be regarded,
she would let pass by, but others that were of weight and
substance, whereby she might profit, she would not spare
for any pains or labour to obtain. She had a nobleness of
nature, having in a manner all that was praisable in a
woman, either in soul or body. She had a very good and
retentive memory, and a quick and ready conception of
even the most difficult and abstruse things. She was very
studious in books, of which she had a great number, both
in English and in French; and for her own exercise and
the profit of others, she translated several ᶠpieces of devotion out of French into English. Very often she complained, that in her youth she had not learned Latin, of
which, however, she had a little knowledge, especially of
the rubric of the Ordinal, for the saying of her service,
which she did well understand. Besides, in aspect, in
words, in gesture, in every demeanour of herself, so great

3.

ᶠ One of these was printed with the following title: *The Mirroure of
golde with the forthe booke of the followinge Jesu Chryst.* By *Rich. Pynson,*
1504, 4º.

nobleness did appear, that whatever she said or did, it
wonderfully became her. She was also noble by affinity
in her tender age, when she was not fully *nine* years old,
she being endued with so great towardness of nature, and
likelihood of inheritance, many sued to have had her in
marriage. The Duke of Suffolk, who then was a man of
great experience, very diligently endeavoured to have had
her for his son and heir : on the contrary, King Henry the
Sixth did intercede for Edmund, his brother, then Earl of
Richmond. She, doubtful in her mind what she was best
to do, asked counsel of an old gentlewoman whom she
much loved and trusted, who did advise her to commend
herself to St. [g] Nicholas, the patron and helper of all true
maidens; and to beseech him to put her in mind what she
were best to do. This counsel she followed, and often
made her prayer to this purpose, and particularly that
night when she should next day return an answer of what
she intended to do; when, as she lay in prayer, calling
upon St. Nicholas, whether sleeping or waking, she told
the Bishop she was not certain, about four o'clock in the
morning, one appeared unto her habited like a bishop,
and naming unto her Edmund, bad her take *him* for her
husband; and so by this meane she did incline her mind
unto Edmund, the King's brother, and Earl of Richmond,
by whom she became the mother of the King lately deceased, and the grandmother of the present King; so what
by lineage, what by affinitie she had thirty kings and
queens within the fourth degree of marriage unto her, besides earls, marquesses, dukes, and princes.

The Bishop having thus spoken of the Countess's nobility, proceeded, according to his proposed method, to shew
how she disciplined her body , and here he told his audi-
ence of her sober temperance in meat and drink; her
avoiding reresoupers, and joucries betwixt meals; her
observing the fasts of the Church, and especially the Holy
Lent, throughout which she confined herself to one meal

A D 1456.

[g] See the Golden Legend, *de Sancto* Nicholao

of fish on the day, besides her other peculiar fasts of devotion, as St. Anthony, St. Mary Maudelin, St. Katherine,
with others: that she had her shirts and girdles of hair,
which, when she was in health, she failed not to wear on
certain daies, sometime one, sometime the other, and that
very often her skin was pierced therewith: that, as for
chastity, though she alway continued not in her virginity,
yet in her husband's days, long before he died, she ob-

p. 14.
tained of him leave, and [h]promised to live chaste in the
hands of the Bishop of London, which promise she renewed after her husband's death into our Bishop's hands.
Next, the Bishop told his auditory how the Countess
ordered her soul to God: that she spent the whole morning, from the time of her rising, about five of the clock, to
dinner time, about ten or eleven, in prayers and devotions;
and after dinner, in going her stations to three altars every
day, saying her dirges and commendations, and her even-
songs before supper, both of the day and of our Lady,
beside many other prayers and psalters of David throughout the year: that at night, before she went to bed, she
failed not to resort unto her chapel, and there a large
quarter of an hour to occupy her devotions: that besides
all this, daily, when she was in health, she failed not to say
the Crown of our Lady, which, after the manner of Rome,

[h] These vows of celibacy or of chastity, as they were called, in the conjugal state, were now reckoned a matter of merit, and an argument of extra-

Roman
Stations in
Britain, &c.
p. 41.
ordinary devotion. In the body of the Church of Gravely, in Hertfordshire,
is a large old grave-stone, round the verge of which is this inscription, the
first word or two obliterated:

—— Eleonora *conjux virgo simulata*
Ora quod sit beatis sociata. ——

This superstitious practice is supposed to be supported by the authority of
Tertullian, who thus expressed himself: *Quot item qui consensu pari inter se*
matrimonii debitum tollunt? But it is not considered, that the great Apostle
of the Gentiles limits this defrauding one another with consent, to *a time*
that they might give themselves to prayer and fasting, and expressly orders
their *coming together again*, for this good reason, that Sathan *tempt them not*
for their incontinency. 1 Cor. vii. 5.

contains sixty-three *Aves*, and at every *Ave* to make a CHAP III
kneeling. and that as for meditation, she had several
books in French, wherewith she would employ herself
when she was weary of prayer. Her wonderful weeping,
the Bishop said, they could bear witness of, of whom there
were great numbers who had heard her confession, which
she ordinarily made every third day, and who were present
at any time when she received the holy Eucharist, which
was near a dosen times every year: these, he said, could
bear witness how at these times flouds of tears issued forth
of her eyes. His Lordship added, that, besides this, such
godly things she would take by obedience, that so all her
works might be the more acceptable, and of greater merit
in the sight of God, which obedience she promised to her
several confessors. To this account of this devout Princess, his Lordship added elsewhere, that he ingenuously Epist dedi-
owned, that when she had appointed him her monitor to cat. to Bp
Fox
hear her private confession, and instruct her life, he learnt
more from her excellent virtues for the institution of a
good life, than ever he communicated to her: to which
may be likewise added, that her epitaph informs us of her
giving stipends to three monks of the Church of Westminster, and to a *teacher of grammar, at Wymborn, in * Coll No.
Dorsetshire, which I think myself obliged in gratitude to * * 1
take especial notice of, as having received some of the
benefit of this endowment. by being in part educated
there, under the care of that excellent master the Reverend
Mr. John Moyle. Her epitaph likewise mentions her ap- A D 1686,
pointing stipends to a preacher of God's word throughout &c. See
Coll No.
all England; though, it seems, the Charter of this foun- * * 1
dation specifies the dioceses of London, Ely, and Lincoln,
as has been said before. A further instance of this lady's
piety, which, it seems, the Bishop omitted to mention Preface to
among her other acts of devotion, was her being admitted the funeral
Sermon of
into the fraternity of five several religious houses, if not Margaret
more, *viz.* Westminster, Crowland, Durham, Wynburne, Countess of
Richmond,
and the Charter-house at London, which, in the strain of &c p. xix
Lond 1708.

that age, as it entituled her to the prayers, so it gave her a share in the merits and good works of all these societies. To finish what I have to say of this charitable and munificent lady, a little before her death she had desired our Bishop to print his [1] Sermons that he had preached to her on the *seven* penitential Psalms, which accordingly were published the 12th of June this year; and were afterwards translated into Latin by one John Fen a Monteacute, who is called an English priest. Among our Bishop's other excellencies, the Lady Margaret is said to have very much admired his preaching. Of this his learned friend Erasmus took notice, that his Lordship was singularly happy in a graceful elocution or fine delivery, and upon that account *Hen.VIII. very dear to the *King's grandmother.

To thise treatise on the seven penitential Psalms, the Bishop prefixed a prologue, in which he observed, that he " of late, before the most excellent Princesse Margarete " Countesse of Richemount and Derby, &c. published " the sayinges of the holy Kinge and prophete David of " the seven penitentiall Psalmes, in the which the said " good and singuler lady much delited ; and that at her " highe commaundement and gracious exhortacion, he " had put the said sermons in writing for to be impressed." Of his preaching on these Psalms at the command of this lady, the Bishop takes notice at the beginning of his first sermon in the following manner : " Frendes, this daye " I shall not declare unto you any parte of the epistle or

[1] This treatyse concernynge the fruytfull saynges of Davyd the Kynge and prophete in the seven penytencyall Psalmes devyded in *seven* sermons, was made and compyled by the ryght reverend fader in God Johan Ffyssher, doctoure of dyvynyte and Byshop of Rochester, at the exortacyon and sterynge of the most excellent Pryncese Margarete Countesse of Rychemont and Derby, and moder to oure soverayne Lorde Kynge Henry the vii.

Emprynted at London in Fletestrete, at the sygne of the Sonne by Wynkyn de Worde, prynter unto the moost excellent Pryncesse my Lady, the Kynge's Graundame, in the yere of our Lorde God mccccc and ix the xii daye of the moneth of Juyn.

Another edition of this booke was imprinted at London in Fletestrete, at the sygne of the Pryncies armes by Thomas Marshe. Anno, M.D.L.V.

" gospell, which peradventui you do abide for to here at
" this time. But at the desire and instaunce of them
" (whome I maye not contrary in any thinge whiche is
" bothe accordinge to my dewty, and also to their soules
" healthe) I have taken upon me shortly to declare the
" fyrst penitenciall Psalme, wherin I beseche Almyghty
" God for his great mercy and pyty so to helpe me thys
" daye by his grace, that whatsoever I shall saye may first
" be to hys pleasure, to the profit of mine owne wretched
" soule, and also for the holsome comfort unto all sinners
" whiche be repentaunte for their sinnes, and hath turned
" themselfe with all their hole herte and minde unto God,
" the wai of wickednes and sinne utterly forsaken."

4. At this time was our Bishop admonished to appear
at a provincial convocation, which was now summoned to
be held. The date of the instrument is Nov. 1, 1509, and
of the Bishop of London's letters, Nov. 28. The reasons
given for the meeting of this convocation are said to be,
some men subverting the institutions of their ancestors,
and evil treating the ecclesiastics.

CHAP.
III.

Reg. Fisher.

CHAP. IV.

1. The Bishop an executor of the Lady Margaret's Will.
2. He builds and endows St. John's College in Cam-
bridge. 3. The first court of St. John's College finished.
4. The Bishop takes the profession of a Widow.

1510. 1. AMONG the ªexecutors of the Lady Margaret's
Will, our Bishop was nominated to be one, as a person in
whom she placed the greatest confidence whilst she was
alive, and whom therefore she principally trusted with the
execution of this her last testament after she was dead. A
part of this concerned the foundation of a new college in
the University of Cambridge, according to the advice which
the Bishop had given her for the disposal of her charity.
But this having been done by way of codicil, before it
could be sealed, the good lady departed this life, and
thereby left some ground for cavil and dispute, which
gave the Bishop no little trouble, and occasioned no small
expense. According to the scheme laid in the Lady Margaret's life time, it was proposed to dissolve by authority
the hospital of St. John's at Cambridge, (the Master and
Brethren of which, by their dissolute lives and prodigal
expenses in excess and riot, had exhausted all their stores
and funds, and so entirely sunk and lost their credit, that
they were almost all dispersed, and so in effect the house
abandoned) and to ingraft on the old stock a new college,
to be called by the same name, that might bring forth
better fruit. This hostell was first erected for religious
Chanons, by Nigellus, the second Bishop of Ely, and Trea-
surer to King Henry I. about the year 1134, and the
Chanons were known by the name of the Hospital and

ª King Henry VIII. Richard Bishop of Winchester, John Bishop of Rochester, Charles Somerset Lord of Herbert, Thomas Lovell, Henry Marne,
and John Seint-John, Knights, Henry Horneby, and Hugh Ashton, Clerks.
Summarie of English Chronicles.

Brethren of St. John.   But within the space of ten years
last past, they had so far wasted their revenues, and dilapidated their goods, both moveable and immoveable, that
they had sunk them from the sum of 140*l.* to that of
30*l.*; so that there was only a Prior and two Brethren
left.

2. The first thing to be done towards the dissolution of
this house, thus in a manner dissolved already, was to have
the consent of the Bishop of Ely, both as reputed founder,
and undoubted diocesan and visitor.   The next was the
obtaining the King's license.   But before these could be
had in due and legal form, the King died; and ere much
more could be done to any purpose, the Lady Margaret
herself died: and had she not lodged this trust in faithful
hands, and particularly in the Bishop's, this great and
good design must have died with her.   But a very particular account of the difficulties and discouragement which
the Bishop met with in the execution of this scheme, and
finishing and settling the new college, being entered upon
the old book in his Lordship's name, and probably by his
direction, I shall here say no more of them, but refer to
the paper itself, a copy of which will be found in the
Collection.   No. 6.

3. These difficulties, however great and troublesome,
were yet all surmounted by the Bishop's great interest and
continual application.   On which, what is now called the
first Court of the College, was finished in about six years A. D. 1516.
time by his Lordship's great care and good management;
so as to be ready to receive the scholars intended to be
placed there, when the Bishop himself came on purpose
to Cambridge to be present at the opening of it, which, as
will be shewn by and by, was done with great solemnity.

4. Among other usages that, it seems, prevailed at this
time, one was that of widows making a profession, before
the Bishop of the diocese in which they lived, of their
continuance in the state of widowhood, and not marrying
again: on which occasion they were solemnly blessed by

CHAP.
IV.
___

the Bishop, and had a ᵇmantle and ring delivered to them by him, which they wore in token of this their vow and profession. Accordingly, one Elizabeth Fitz-warren, a widow, was thus professed before our Bishop, and blessed by him, and received the mantle and ring from him on a

April 21,
1510.

Lord's day, in the parish church of Beckenham, a small distance from Bromley. The form of her profession is thus entered in the Bishop's register: "In the name of "God the Father, the Son and the Holy Goste. I Eliza- "beth a widowe, and nat weddid, ne unto no man suryd, "behote and make a vowe to God, and to ouer blessid "Ladie, and to all the companie of heven in the presence "of the reverend father in God John Bysshop of Ro- "chester for to be chaste of my bodie and trewly and "devowtly shall kepe me chaste frome this tyme, as longe "as my lyff lastith, after the rule of Saynt Powll. In "nomine patris et filii et spiritûs sancti, Amen. In cujus

* meo.

"testimonium signum crucis cum nomine *suo manu pro- "pria subscripsi.

+ Elysabeth."

Preface to
her funeral
Sermon.

Such a vow and promise of celibacy or widowhood, we have seen was *that* which the Lady Margaret is said to have taken from our Bishop's hands some years before her death.

ᵇ Wydews, and such as han taken the *mantel* and the *ryng*, deliciously fed, we wold they were wedded, for we ne can excuse hem of privy synnes. *Lollards Confession.*

CHAP. V.

1. *The Bishop is nominated to go to the Lateran Council at Rome, but did not go.* 2. *Advises the University of Cambridge to choose Cardinal Wolsey for their Chancellor.* 3. *The University follow his advice, and choose him.* 4. *Wolsey refuses the offer.* 5, 6. *The University make choice of the Bishop, and appoint him their Chancellor for his life.*

1. AMIDST these difficulties with which the Bishop was 1512. forced to encounter in the execution of his late mistress's Will, was he nominated, with the Bishop of Worcester, the Prior of St. John s, and the Abbot of Winchelcomb, to go to Rome, to sit in the Council which Pope Julius had now called to be held in the Lateran Palace, April 19, 1512. Erasmus, on this occasion, wrote to some of his friends, that he was to have accompanied the Bishop in this journey had he known of it soon enough; though afterwards he wrote, that the Bishop's [a]journey was put by all of a sudden. It is certain, that the Bishop, in order to his going to Rome on this occasion, had drawn up and sealed procuratorial letters or powers to William Fresell, Coll.No.II. Prior of Rochester, and Richard Chettham, Prior of Ledes in Kent, by which he empowered them during his absence, to collate to such benefices and offices as were of his gift, such persons as he should nominate to them, and to grant institution and induction to those which were not of his patronage. to give letters dimissory; to take care that churches and church-yards, if any of them within his diocese were by the effusion of blood, or otherwise polluted, be reconciled by some of the suffragans: to admit and license whatever pardon-mongers came into the dio-

---

[a] Ante biennium adornaram iter comes futurus R. Patri D. Joanni Epis- March 31, copo Roffensi, viro omnium episcopalium virtutum genere cumulatissimo— 1515. verum is ex itinere subito revocatus est. *Epist.* lib. 11. ep. 2.

CHAP. V.

cese with their indulgences to ask and collect the alms of those of the diocese; all which powers were to last only till the Bishop thought fit to revoke them; and the instrument itself was dated at the Bishop's manse, by Lamehith Marsh, March 10, 1514, and the eleventh year of his consecration. But notwithstanding this, and the University's recommending their affairs to him as ready to go, as will be shewn presently, the Bishop says himself, that he was disappointed of that journey; and these procuratorial powers, together with other letters recommending his Lordship to some men of note at Rome, are yet lodged among the archives of St. John's College, and shew they were never delivered. This let of the Bishop's was, however, a great advantage to the College, which must have suffered very much in its endowment had it not been for his presence, without whom nothing was done.

Feb. 6, 1513.

2. Wolsey being newly promoted to the great bishopric of Lincoln, and in very high favour with the King, the Bishop of Rochester, who had now enjoyed the honour of being Chancellor of the University ten years, and was nominated at this time to Rome, thought it would be more for the University's interest to make choice of Wolsey for their Chancellor. Accordingly, he intimated to them as much; telling them how dear Wolsey was to the King, and that he had himself wrote to Wolsey to accept this honour which was intended him. The University, in their

May 13, 1514. Coll. No. 7.

letter to the Bishop, very gratefully acknowledged this kind and friendly intimation of his, telling him, that he was continually obliging them; that they had experienced him to be not only a pastor but a father; that they were more indebted to him than to any body, who had given to them a great many ornaments; that they should unanimously have chosen him their Chancellor, had he not thought it better for them to choose another; that therefore they had chosen the Honourable Bishop of Lincoln, and were very much obliged to him, that he had by his letters solicited that prelate to accept of their choice.

They concluded, that he was never weary of serving them, CHAP.
though upon their account he had undergone immense V.
and almost intolerable labours.

3. To this letter of the University's the Bishop wrote Coll No 8
an answer, dated from London, 7 kal of June. In it May 26
he tells them, that he earnestly wished his benefactions
had been more advantageous to them, and that it was in
his power, by any study, industry, advice, recommendation, or pains to encrease or illustrate the University, that
if it was, they should plainly see that what he had hitherto
done was of very little moment, and far inferior to what
he desired to do for them. that as to their opinion of
him, in judging him fitter to be their Chancellor than any
one else, he esteemed it a greater honour to him, than the
Chancellorship itself; since, besides that Plato's philosophy does not allow any one to be ambitious of magistracy,
and that the Christian much more abhors it, experience
had fully instructed him how much emptiness is concealed
under those honours · but, that the so unanimous consent
of so many learned men, in relation to him, could not but
be above the expectation of any modest man: that, if
there could be any addition made to the obligations they
had already laid on him, they had further obliged him by
following his advice to choose the Bishop of Lincoln, as
well as consulted their own interest. for that he did not
doubt but that his Lordship would abundantly supply
with his greatness those things which his own meanness
could only wish for them, but never obtain: since he was
not wanting either in power or inclination, as doing every
thing with the King, and being a person of singular good
sense and prudence, and was said to be, and really was, of
a very generous disposition, or a most bountiful patron and
benefactor to those whom he favoured As for himself, he
told them, he could assure them of every thing that he
could do to oblige them. He concluded with praying to
God, that as their University had been of late encreased
in good learning and virtue, so likewise *they* might en-

crease in good learning and virtue; so that this their University might every day more and more flourish in Christ.

4. As the University thus notified to the Bishop their choice of Wolsey for their Chancellor, in obedience to his advice; so the very next day after they wrote to Wolsey himself, to intimate to him this their choice of him, and to desire his acceptance of it. This, it is said, was expressed in terms savouring of the most fulsome flattery, and almost servile application. But, it seems, it was all lost upon Wolsey, who, in an answer to this letter of the University's, which, under some shew of humility, sufficiently discovered a latent pride, absolutely refused to accept of this proffered honour.

5. On this unexpected repulse, the University again applied themselves to the Bishop of Rochester by letter, in which, after some compliments made to his Lordship, they tell him, that by his advice they had offered to the Bishop of Lincoln their Chancellorship, but that he had answered them, that " he would very willingly have ac- " cepted it, if he had not been so entirely taken up with " the affairs of the state; but that, however, that they " might not think themselves altogether slighted by him, " he had assured them, he would be as much their friend " as if he had accepted the honour that was offered to " him." They therefore told the Bishop, that with the same unanimity of their whole University with which they had before decreed him the Chancellorship, if he had not dissuaded them from it, they now offered it to him again, and prayed, that he would accept it, as he had done before, and suffer them, under his command and auspices, to militate and advance in good learning. They concluded with thanking his Lordship for his letter to them, and beseeching him to continue, as formerly, to assist and adorn their University.

6. In compliance with these unanimous and very earnest desires of the University, the Bishop accepted again of the

Coll. No. 9.

Chancellorship. To shew, therefore, their gratitude to his Lordship, and to induce him to be their friend and patron at Rome, whither, as has been said, he was now designed to go, they, towards the end of this year, sent his Lordship a letter by their Vice-chancellor Eccleston, in which, after their compliments made to the Bishop, as usual, they told him, that being stirred and compelled by his Lordship's more than ordinary affection for their common mother, they had conferred on him the highest honour they had to give, which was not to end but with his life. They added, that they understood his Lordship was in a short time to go to Rome, which might be an advantage to him, and to those who depended on him; wherefore they prayed and besought him, that if in any thing he could be their friend, as he could be in a great many things, since he best knew their occasions, he would be mindful of their University: and that their Vice-chancellor would explain their minds more fully to him, to whom, therefore, they desired his Lordship to give credit. They further prayed him to take care of the confirmation of their privileges, and told him they had written to several ᵇprelates of the kingdom whom they had entreated to be their friends in securing or defending them.

7. This same year, 1514, I find in the Bishop's register mention made of one William Moress, of Snodland, in his Lordship's diocese, obliged to abjure his saying, when he was demanded wherefore he received not at Easter the Sacrament of the Altar, that *he could buye* ᶜ*24 as goode*

CHAP.
V.

Feb 13,
1514

Coll. No.
10.

ᵇ Thomas Wolsey, Archbishop of York, William Warham, Archbishop of Canterbury, Richard Fox, Bishop of Winchester, Thomas Ruthall or Rowthall, Bishop of Durham. Thus are these letters placed in the University Register the letter to Wolsey being put before that to the Archbishop of Canterbury, on account, I suppose, of his being prime minister and the Pope's legate

ᶜ In Queen Elizabeth's time 2,500 of the breades then used at the H. Sacrament, though they were both broader and thicker than the wafers used in the mass, were sold for 8s and 4d which is about a half-penny a dozen *Thoresby Vicaria Leodiensis*

CHAP.
V.

as that wass for three halfpence. This sort of reflection on what the feigned Catholics call God's body we often meet with among the other sayings which were abjured about this time; *viz.* that *thirty* or *fourty* of this sort of breads or wafers were sold for a half-penny.

Bp. Gray's
Reg. 1457.

CHAP. VI.

1. Statutes, &c. provided for St. John's College. 2. The Maison Dieu at Ospringe granted to it. 3. Some account of it. 4. The Bishop consecrates the College Chapel, and opens the College. 5. Founds four Fellowships and two Scholarships in it. 6. A mistake of Erasmus's.

1. THE College being thus built and endowed by our Bishop's unwearied care and application, the executors' next care was to provide rules and statutes for this new foundation; to stock it with Fellows and Scholars, so far as the endowments would reach; and to make it, as intended, a seat of learning. But this requiring attendance, and more skill than most of them were masters of, they delegated their authority to the Bishop of Rochester, by a commission dated March 20, 1515; only, if any of their A D. 1515. number happened to be present with him, they were to have equal power.

2. It has been before observed what difficulties the Lady Margaret's executors met with in what related to the foundation and endowment of St. John's College, in Cambridge. A part of these arose from the clamours of her officers and servants, who, because they could not ^{Preface} to have all themselves, were willing to give all to the King. ^{the Lady} ^{Margaret's} Through their occasion, therefore, and the advice of some ^{funeral} powerful courtiers, and the fresh suit of the King's audi- ^{Sermon.} tors and council at law. the executors were so hard prest, and so straitly handled, that, notwithstanding all due care had been taken to secure their interest in the lands bequeathed by the foundress for the endowment of the College, by proving her Will both in the Prerogative and in the Court of Chancery, where Archbishop Warham, both as Archbishop and Chancellor, approved and allowed the Will as good; and the executors being in pos-

session of these lands, and receiving the rents and profits of them some years, they were yet forced at last to let them go. By this means, as was deposed upon oath before the Archbishop, by Dr. Nicholas Metcalfe and Richard Sharp, B. D., the College was rendered incapable of subsisting according to the foundation. The executors were therefore to look out and sue for a compensation, otherwise all was at a stand. Accordingly, there being an old decayed Maison-Dieu, or hospital, in Ospringe-street, near Faversham in Kent, worth having, this falling under the Bishop of Rochester's view, was quickly thought of by him as for their purpose: and being by devolution in the King, by the Bishop's application at Court, with the mediation of the Queen, Wolsey, and other courtiers, it was at last obtained.

Preface to the Lady Margaret's funeral Sermon, &c. History of the Abbey, &c. of Faversham.

3. This house was founded by King Henry III. about the year 1245, and consisted of a Master, who stiled himself frater *N. Magister Hospitalis Beate Marie Virginis de Ospringe*, and three Brethren, who are called *presbyteri conversi*, or Priests who were professed to be of the Order of the Holy Cross, and two secular Clerks or Capellanes, who were to celebrate for the soul of the Prince their founder, and for the souls of his royal predecessors and successors. They were likewise to be hospitable to the poor and needy pilgrims and passengers, particularly those of the Order of the Holy Cross, or of the Brethren of St. John of Jerusalem when they went beyond sea, or returned home; and to relieve poor lepers, for whom a house seems to have been provided on the other side of the way, opposite to the site of this hospital. Upon the death, &c. of the Master, the three Brethren were to choose one of their own body to be presented to the King for his consent, and afterwards to be instituted by the Archbishop. But about the year 1480, in the reign of King Edward IV., one Robert Darrell was chosen Master; soon after which two of the Brethren died, and presently after, the Master and the other Brother; on which

the two secular Priests left the house, by which means it CHAP
became dissolved, and by devolution came to the King, as _____
founder, who by his letters patent committed the guar-
dianship of it to secular persons. Thus King Henry VIII.
in the *sixth* year of his reign, committed the custody of
this hospital to John Underhill, Clerk, for his life. Of
this Bishop Fisher took notice as very proper to be appropriated by the King's grant unto the College of St.
John's, to make some compensation for the lands they had
lost. Accordingly, after long suit, that was granted, and
a Bill devised to be signed of the King for it. *But then,*
says the Bishop, in the account he has left of the difficulties he met with in settling this College, *what labor then I
hadde, what hyme that was encombent, and how long or we
cudde establishe & make it sure, both by temporal Counsell
& spirituall, and how often for this matter then I roade
both to Ospringe and to London, and to my Lord of Canterbury, or that I couthe perfor004me all thyngs for the suyrty
therof, it war to long to reherse.* But, notwithstanding,
the Bishop by his constant application and great interest
at Court, in little more than a year completed this affair.
The King enlarged the College mortmain, and made a
grant of this hospital to it, dated March 10, in the seventh A.D. 1516.
year of his reign, the next year after he had granted the
custody to John Underhill, who was prevailed with the
same day and year to resign all his claim to the said hospital to the Master, Fellows, and Scholars of the College,
on his receiving in hand 40*l.*, and having a yearly pension
of 30*l.* for his life. This grant the King, *four* years after, A D. 1520
renewed, and the Archbishop, the Prior, and Convent and
Archdeacon of Canterbury confirmed it, for their several
parts and interests. By this means, it is said, a good addition was made to the College estate, this grant having
brought with it several good estates in Kent, to the value
of 70*l.* per annum. But, according to the grant, the College had by it given to them all the lands and tenements
which belonged to the hospital of the blessed Mary, or

God's House, called *le Maison Dieu* of Ospringe. A part of these was the mannor of Elverland, in the parish of Osprindge, which, according to a terrier made of it Coll.No.*5.September 17, 1576, consisted then of a mannor house, &c. 207 acres of arable and pasture, 8 acres of wood land, and three tenements. But, besides this, the hospital was endowed with the impropriate parsonages of Ospringe and Hedcorn, and with lands lying at Lurenden in Challock, and at Hokeling, Rydemarsh, Ryde, and other places in the Isle of Shepway.

4. Before this business could be quite finished and set- A.D. 1516.tled, or, however, very soon after, our Bishop, as has been hinted before, came to Cambridge to consecrate the chapel, and to open the new College. The Bishop of Ely's license to him, empowering him to perform that sacred office by consecrating altars, vestments, and other ornaments, and administering other ecclesiastical offices pertaining thereunto, as if he himself was there present, is dated July 26, 1516. This, then, being done, the Bishop, accompanied by Dr. Hornby, another of the executors, and Master of Peter-house, made his entrance into the College, which was the more solemn on account of his being Chancellor of the University. After the usual ceremonies, a public notary, and other witnesses being called in; first, the King's license was produced in the presence of them all, sealed with green wax; the Charter of the foundation was opened and read in part, together with the Bull of Pope Julius the Second, sealed after the manner of the Court of Rome; and lastly, the Bishop of Rochester's procuratorial powers from the rest of the executors, empowering him, or such other of them as should be present, to act in the name of the rest. By virtue of these powers, the Bishop and Dr. Hornby named, elected, and ordained Alan Percy Master of the said College, and thirty-one Fellows, as the Bishop himself had before by virtue of the same power drawn statutes for the government of it, and afterwards, as he found occasion, altered

them. So the act or instrument of opening St. John's
College. But by another account we are informed, that
all the executors, by a Charter dated April 9, 1511, five
years before this, to which all their seals are affixed, did
erect, ordain, and establish a perpetual College *Unius*
magistri, &c. consisting of one Master, Fellows, and Scho-
lais, to the number of fifty, or thereabouts, Students in
Divinity, &c. and that the College so erected should be
stiled and called St. John's College, and Robert Shorton
be the first Master, with a stipend of only 20*l.* per annum,
under whose care and conduct the College was built, and
its revenues advanced and improved But, it seems, he
being promoted to wealthier preferments, voided this by
cession, and so Percy was by the Bishop, &c. chosen and
appointed in his room.

5. For this College, thus finished and settled by our
Bishop, he always retained a very great kindness: insomuch, that out of his own estate he founded heie *four*
Fellowships, and *two* Scholarships, which Scholars, and
three of the Fellows, were to be of the county of York,
where our Bishop was born, and the other Fellow of the
diocese of Rochester, of which he was Bishop. Two of
these *four* Fellows, at least, were to be Priests, and in
their masses peculiarly and satisfactorily to pray for his
soul; yet so as to commend the soul of the Lady Margaret, to whom, the Bishop said, he was obliged as to a
mother; and the soul of King Henry VII. her son, who
he gratefully remembered, without the entreaty or inter-
cession of any one, confeired on him the bishopric of Rochester. Besides these, his Lordship likewise founded here
four Examinators; one for humanity, a second for logic, a
third for mathematics, and a fourth for philosophy, who
were to have, every one of them, a salary of 40*s.* a year;
and two Lecturers, one of the Greek, for the younger students, and the other of the Hebrew tongue, for those who
were more advanced in years, to each of which he ordered
by his last statutes under seal dated July 11, 1530, a yearly

CHAP.
VI.
salary of three pounds. This foundation, together with what his Lordship paid for the mortmayning of the Maison-Dieu near Ospringe, to the College, it is said, cost the Bishop 500*l.* a sum almost equal to 4000*l.* now. He likewise, at his own expense, built a chapel, yet standing on the north side of the College chapel, into which it opens by a large wide arch near the east end. Here he intended to have had his body deposited after his death, and a monument erected to his memory, for which he had actually provided polished white marble, several pieces of which are yet lodged near this chapel. The arms of the see of Rochester, which were here engraven on a shield with the Bishop's own coat, are still remaining, though the Bishop's arms are defaced. In the College Chapel likewise, that his memory might be preserved, all the ends of the stalls had graven in them a fish and an ear of wheat, the Bishop's arms, and this motto, alluding to his name, *faciam vos fieri* piscatores *hominum.* I will make you *fishers* of men, which is now also altered. His Lordship gave likewise for the use of the chapel in plate, vestments, and other orna-

Coll.No.13.
ments, to the value of 1128*l.* 10*s.* Lastly, by a deed of gift, he gave to the College, only reserving to himself the use of them for his life, his noble library. This the Col-

Aschami
Epist. p.
293, ed.
1703.
lege, in a letter wrote by them to the Duke of Somerset, then Regent, some years after the Bishop's death, called a great treasure, and meet to have been placed among good and skilful men. In the same letter they told the Duke, that the Bishop absolutely governed the College, and that, therefore, were put in his hands the most noble ornaments which the Lady Margaret gave to it. But that his perverse doctrine deprived *him* of his life, and *them* of their riches. These things, though done at some distance of time, I chose to put altogether here, as shewing at one view how much this College is indebted and obliged to the care and munificence of the Bishop, and what returns they afterwards made.

6. The great Erasmus, through mistake, thus repre-

sents this matter. That among her other charitable bene-factions, the Lady Margaret had given to the Bishop a great summ of money for the providing preachers in seve-ral places, and endowing them with generous salaries. All which, says he, that very upright man expended either in the promotion of preachers, or relief of the needy, and was so far from reserving any of it to himself, that he made large additions to it out of his own estate But it is very certain, that the Lady Margaret founded or ap-pointed but one public preacher, unless the learned man meant all the Fellows of this College, as being obliged by the foundation to study divinity. It is as sure, that what the Lady Margaret gave to the Bishop, at the time of her death or just before it, was for his own particular use, without ordering him how he should lay it out; though, the Bishop said, he therefore remembered this generosity of her's because he would have nobody think, that he had been so great a benefactor to the College of other men's goods, but of his own.

CHAP
VI.

ingentem
pecunia-
rum vim.

non medio-
cribus sala-
riis

CHAP. VII.

1. *The Bishop desirous to learn Greek. Erasmus writes to W. Latimer to teach him.* 2. *Latimer's answer.* 3. *Erasmus's reply.*

1. THE Bishop, it seems, notwithstanding his great reputation for learning, was an utter stranger to the Greek tongue. Nor was this peculiar to him. [a]Luther, we are told, when he began to write against the Pope, knew nothing at all of Greek, and very little of Latin. The Greek and Hebrew were languages that at this time were not taught at all in the public schools. Robert Wakefield, of whom the Bishop had learned some smattering of the

A.D. 1510. Hebrew language about six or seven years since, was the first here in England, of whom we have any account, who publicly professed it, and that not till the year 1524, when he was sent down to the University of Cambridge by the

Hody de Textu Bibliorum. King for that purpose: for though by a Papal Constitution of Pope Clement V. made in the general Council of Vienna, A. D. 1310, it was provided, that in the Univer-

---

[a] Lutherus——græce nihil penitus noverat, quum ad scribendum accessit, Latinè parùm admodum; et quæ tuenda susceperat, dialectica, et argumentatiunculis tutatus est, non linguis. *Lud. Vives de disciplinis*, lib. ii. p. 74.

Marcus Censorinus Cato——rudi seculo literas Græcas ætate jam declinata didicit, ut esset hominibus documento, ea quoque percipi posse, quæ senes concupissent. *Quintilian de Instit. Orato.* lib. xii. c. 11.

Aldus Pius Manutius, a printer at Venice, observed, with no small regret, how much and how long the Greek tongue had been neglected: and therefore, in order to revive that noble language, and accustom the learned by degrees to read nothing but the originals, he resolved to publish most of his books in Greek only. This succeeded so well, that in his Preface prefixed to Aristotle's Logic, printed by him .... he observed to his readers, that now they might see many Catos, that is old men, learning Greek in their old age; and elsewhere, that Italy was not the only country where the Greek tongue was in fashion; but, that in Germany, France, Hungary, Britain, Spain, and almost every where else, where the Latin was known, not only the young, but even the old, studied Greek with the utmost eagerness and application.

sities of Paris, Oxford, Bononia, and Salamanca, there
should be public lectures read for the teaching the Students, the Hebrew, Arabic, and Chaldee languages; and
that in pursuance of this in the year 1320, in a Synod held
at Lamhith under Walter Reynolds, Archbishop of Canterbury, it was ordered, that there should be a public
Hebrew Lecturer at Oxford, and that the clergy should
pay him a salary by a tax of a farthing in the pound on all
their ecclesiastical preferment or income; yet whether
this method of paying him his stipend did not answer the
purpose, or for any other reason, we have no account of
any Hebrew lecture being read in this University till
almost two hundred years after. It was now debated, as
a disputable question, whether it was necessary to understand the Scriptures to be skilled in the original languages
in which they were written? And some there were who
were not ashamed to assert, that in some places of the
New Testament the reading in the [b] Latin version is truer
than the Greek. In opposition to this ignorant and ridiculous conceit, our Bishop's great and learned friend,
Erasmus, very strenuously maintained the necessity of understanding the original languages of the Bible. Of the
same mind was our Bishop, who therefore expressed a
very eager desire of learning Greek even in this advanced
age of his, when he was above fifty years old, that, as
Erasmus wrote to Latimer, he might study the Scriptures
with greater advantage, and a more certain judgment.
This great man had lately published the New Testament
in Greek, in which language it had never been printed
before, to which he added a Latin version and notes. By
this means the more learned and ingenuous were convinced
of the usefulness and necessity of understanding the Greek
tongue: insomuch, that Dean Colet told Erasmus, he
was sorry that he had never yet learned it, as being sen-

A. D. 1515.

---

[b] Gregory Martin, in his *Discovery of the manifold corruptions of the Holy
Scriptures by the English Sectaries*, &c calls the Vulgar Latin Bible the *true
and authentical Scripture*

sible that without it we are nothing. It is not improbable,
that the Bishop thought the same; since, in a letter wrote
by Erasmus from his Lordship's house at Rochester to
his friend Henry Boville at Cambridge, he told him, that
the Bishop both approved of his edition of the New Testament and read it, though, if the date of this letter be
right, he could only mean, I think, that his Lordship read
the Latin translation and his notes. Since, as will be
shewn presently, it was the next year when Erasmus
wrote to William Latimer to undertake the teaching the
ᶜBishop Greek.

2. This William Latimer, who in compliance with the
Bishop's desire, was pitched on by his Lordship's two
learned friends, Sir Thomas More and Erasmus, as the
properest person to be his tutor on this occasion, was
Fellow of All-Souls College in Oxford, and by travelling
into Italy, and settling for some time at Padua, had much
advanced himself in learning, especially in the Greek
tongue, of which the Italians at this time were reckoned
the greatest masters, insomuch, that about eight years
before, he was recommended as a fit person to instruct
Reginald Pole, afterwards Cardinal, and Archbishop of
Canterbury. To this learned man, Erasmus, at the
Bishop's desire, I suppose, wrote several letters on this
occasion, which, Latimer said, "shewed in him a singular
love and kindness for the Bishop, and at the same time
expressed a wonderful desire of doing honour to the
Greek language, by bringing it acquainted with so excellent a prelate, and one famous for all kind of learning."
These attempts of Erasmus to persuade Latimer to un-

ᶜ Christina, the learned Queen of Sweden, after she was Queen, learned
Greek of Freinshemius, the writer of the fine Supplement to Livy, whom
she had made her librarian at Upsal and her historiographer.—*Ista tua arte
factum est, ut eo tempore quod, intra proximum biennium —huc impendere
potuisti, jam eo processeris, ut post experimenta in Polybio, in Plutarcho facta
Platonem, at quem virum! ita legas, ut operæ meæ vix leviter egens cursim ex-
ponas eleganti latinitate, verbisque significantissimis.* Freinshemii Supplem.
Livianorum ad Christinam Regin. Decas. Holmiæ, 1649.

dertake this business, were backed by Sir Thomas Moore,
who, to induce him to it, desired him only to try a month
with the Bishop. With this Latimer acquainted Erasmus, in a letter written to him from Oxford, to which he
added, that he had given Sir Thomas an absolute denial,
because he knew he could do the Bishop no kindness in
so little a time, and that Sir Thomas had left it wholly to
him: that this was the true reason why he did not comply
with the very honourable proposal made to him by those
whose friendship he so much valued. Not that he grudged
the labour of one month, but because he knew, that in so
short a time he could never answer their's nor the Bishop's
expectation. That the learning Greek was a thing of a
complicated nature, and full of variety; and though it was
more laborious than difficult, yet it required time, however, to commit it to memorie. That he believed, as being
what he had heard from many, that the Bishop was of a
singular genius, and fit for greater things than what he
was now speaking of: that he [Erasmus] had writ to him
of his inclination, and what a strong desire he had to
learn this tongue, by which he clearly perceived also what
diligence he should meet with: from all which he might
have as a great a prospect as any one could possibly expect from a man of an excellent wit or fine parts, of the
closest application, and of an incredible desire to learn.
But still, he thought, notwithstanding all these advantages, a month was too little time to make any progress
in the study of this language: that Grocine, Linacre,
Tonstall, Pace, More, and even Erasmus himself, spent
more time about this matter, that *they* were more than
two years in learning Greek; as for himself, he was not
ashamed to own, that after *six* or *seven* years employed
about it, he was still ignorant of many things. Latimer
therefore concluded, that if Erasmus would have the
Bishop proceed, and arrive at some perfection in this language, he should procure some one from Italy who was
well skilled in these things, and who was willing to stay with

the Bishop so long as till he perceived himself so strong as not only to creep, but to get up and stand, and walk.

3. To this letter of Latimer's, Erasmus returned the following answer, that as to what he had wrote relating to the Bishop of Rochester, he was wholly of another opinion. You, said he, think it better not to attempt the matter at all, unless you could finish what you've begun; and advise, that one should be procured from Italy, who was well skilled in the Greek language. But, said Erasmus, Italy is a great way off, and has now fewer who are famous for learning than when you resided there; and, after all, it is a chance, if instead of a man learned and well skilled in the Greek tongue, there does not come some busy-body. Nor, added he, are you ignorant of the temper of the Italians, at how immense a price they demand to be hired to come to barbarians, even those of them who are but indifferent, to say nothing of their bringing with them no good manners, who do come hither skilled in good letters: and, said he, you know the Bishop's uprightness and sincerity. He added, that whilst enquiry was making for a person proper to be sent over, and a bargain was driven for his salary, and he set out on his journey, a great deal of time must be spent, and that he could not suppose that Latimer was any way of the temper of some of the vulgar, who admire nothing but what comes from far. Whoever, says he, is a good scholar, is, in my opinion, an Italian, though he was born in Ireland. He is to me a Græcian, whoso is well versed in Greek authors, though he has no beard; and that I may speak freely what I think, if I had Linacre or Tonstall, to say nothing of yourself, for my preceptor, I should not desire an Italian. He proceeded to tell Latimer, that in this he entirely agreed with him, that it was principally to be desired, that the first elements should be learned, if one could, of a very skilful artist, but if that could not be done, it was better to begin at any rate, than to continue utterly rude or ignorant, especially in this kind of know-

ledge. Since it was doing something to know the figures
of the letters, readily to pronounce them, to spell and join
them together. And so, said he, we desired of you a
month's labour, tacitly hoping for three months, though
we were ashamed to ask so much.   But if they could not
obtain that, they had a good hope, that in the mean time
some other person would be found who would build on the
foundation laid by him; and if that hope deceived them,
yet such was the force of the Bishop's genius, so [d]intent
was he on learning, that they trusted he would of himself
struggle through towards attaining some moderate skill in
the language; and that, perhaps, he was content with a
middling knowledge of it, who for no other reason thus
courted the learning Greek, but that with greater advantage, and a more sure judgment, he might study the Holy
Scriptures. Lastly, he asked, if nothing of this happened,
where would be the loss? Suppose the Bishop be never
so little advanced in these studies, yet would it be of no
little service to stir up and push forward the minds of the
youth, that so great a man learned Greek : but that, as in
all kinds of disciplines, it was requisite that we should be
entred maturely, so here, in particular, the Bishop's *age *52 years
put him in mind, that this affair should not be delayed.   at least

4. What effect this letter of Erasmus's had on Latimer,
or whether at last he consented to be the Bishop's preceptor, as he and his friends desired, does not appear.   This
is certain, the Bishop did learn somewhat of this language,
and was indifferently skilled in it, of which his Lordship
gave a specimen a few years after in the title-page of his
book in *confutation of the Lutheran Assertions,* round about
which, within a border, was printed this sentence, *Woe to
the foolish prophets who follow their own spirit and have
seen nothing,* in Hebrew, Greek, and Latin.—

[d] —— Græcas literas senex didici. Quas quidem sic avidè arripui quasi
diuturnam sitim explere cupiens. *M T Ciceronis Cato major, &c* c 8

CHAP. VIII.

*1, 2. Luther writes against the Pope's Indulgences. 3. The
Bishop fixes copies of them on School-doors at Cambridge. 4. Of Peter de Valence.*

A.D. 1515.
Thuani
Hist. lib. i.
p. 13.

1. BUT now another and more public scene, as well as
of much greater importance, was opened, in which the
Bishop acted more than a common part.   Leo X. now
Pope of Rome, by the advice of Cardinal Laurence Pucci,
his datary, a man of a very turbulent spirit, and on whom
he too much depended, that he might from all parts scrape
together an immense sum of money by diplomas or bulls,
sent into all the kingdoms of the Christian world, promised
an expiation or pardon of all offences, and eternal life to
all who purchased them, a price being set for every one
to pay in proportion to the greatness of the offence.   For
this purpose were appointed throughout the provinces,
[a]pardon-mongers and treasurers, to whom were added
preachers, who were to recommend to the people the
greatness of so noble a benefit, and immoderately to extol
its efficacy in set artificial speeches and printed books.
This was done too licentiously by the Pope's ministers
every where, but especially in Germany, where they who
had farmed these indulgences, every day shamelessly lavished and squandered away in bawdy houses and taverns,
at playing at dice, and in the vilest uses, the power they
pretended to have of delivering the souls of the deceased
out of the expiatory fire of purgatory.   This gave very
great offence; insomuch, that Martin Luther, a monk of
the Order of St. Augustine, and Professor of Divinity at
Wittenberg in Saxony, took notice of it, and wrote against
it ; and having first of all confuted, and then condemned

---

[a] These were commonly the *freres*, of whom Gardiner Bishop of Winchester thus wrote in his Answer to George Joye, 1546. *The freres served the
Devyll in retaylinge of heaven in pardons.*

the sermons of the pardon-mongers' chaplains, he at length
went so far as to call in question the power itself which
the Pope claimed as his prerogative by those diplomas
or indulgences, and at last to an examination of the doctrine on which they were grounded, which, he said, was
corrupted by the length of time. For, as Machiavel observed, however terrible and venerable the Popes became
by their censures and indulgences, they, at last, made so
ill an use of them, as quite to lose the first, so that people
stood in no manner of awe of their excommunications, and
to stand to the courtesy and discretion of others, for what
is left them of that veneration which used to be paid to
them.

2. The Popish writer of our Bishop's life thus repre- The Life,
sents this affair. " It fell out," saith he, " that Pope &c. of John
" Leo X. had granted forth a generall and free pardon, of Roches-
" commonly called indulgences, according to the ᵇ ancient Baily, D D.
" custome and tradition of the Catholique Church, to all
" christian people that were contrite through all the pro-
" vinces of Christendome, which is no otherwise than an
" application, by that ministry, of the superabundant
" merits of our blessed Saviour who shed so many, when
" the least one drop of his most precious blood was able
" to have redeemed a thousand worlds, to the souls of
" true believers." This, it seems, is called by those of
this writer's principles, *The Treasury of the Church*, in
which are pretended to be laid up the superabundance of
Christ's sufferings, and the redundancy of the superfluous
satisfactions of the Virgin Mary, and other saints, the
issuing out of which belongs almost wholly to the Pope of
Rome.

3 Certain copies of these indulgences, or pardons,

ᵇ Cœperunt indulgentiæ postquam ad purgatorii cruciatus aliquandiu tre-
pidarunt *Roffensis adv Lutherum.*

—— de indulgentiis pauca dici possunt per certitudinem, quia nec Scrip-
tura expressè de eis loquitur Sancti etiam Ambrosius, Hilarius, Augustinus,
Hieronimus, minime loquuntur de indulgentiis *Durandus in* 4 sent dist.
20, quæst 3, § 4.

granted by Pope Leo, our Bishop, we are told, as Chancellor of the University, caused to be set up in several places there, and particularly upon the School's-gate, " that so," as it is said, " the students there, as well as " others, standing in need of such a remedy, might be par- " takers of the heavenly bounty." But in the night one of the students, who, Baily says, was afterward, by his own confession, discovered to be Peter de Valence, a Norman, wrote over the pardon these words of the Psalmist, *Beatus Vir cujus est nomen Domini spes ejus, et non respexit in vanitates et insanias falsas;* to which he added the word *istas,* as applying them to the indulgence: *Blessed is the Man whose hope is in the name of the Lord, and who hath not respected those Vanities, and lying madnesses.* This was represented as adding to the book of Life, and thereby incurring the several punishments which are threatened to those who make such additions. Of this our Bishop, the Chancellor, being informed, he was, it is said, struck with horror at the no less boldness than wickedness of the fact, and accordingly endeavoured to find out the party by the knowledge of his hand-writing, but all to no purpose. Then he called a convocation, to whom he told what had happened, and shewed them the foulness of the action, interpreting to them the true meaning of the place of Scripture which he thought abused to a very wrong purpose. He likewise explained to them the meaning of the words *pardons* and *indulgences,* and justified the use of them. He further shewed them the great displeasure, both of God and the King, which they would justly incur, if they should suffer so wicked a fact to go unpunished, and put them in mind how great a reproach it would be to the University itself. Last of all, he moved the author of this fact, though unknown, to repentance and confession of his sin, that he might be forgiven, which he assured him, in God's name, he should be, if he would within the time prefixed by him make an open acknowledgment of his fault; as, on the contrary, if he did not, he threatened

him with excommunication; which sentence was accord- CHAP.
ingly inflicted, after a second and third admonition, and VIII.
the offender's not surrendering himself at the times fixed
for his appearing. The Bishop's behaviour on this occasion is thus represented by Baily. "Time," says he, "hav- Life, &c of
"ing brought on the day, there was a great multitude of John Fish-
"people, where the Chancellor, with a heavy countenance, Rochester.
"declared how that no tidings could be heard either of
"the person or his repentance. Wherefore now, seeing
"there was no other remedy, he thought it necessary and
"expedient to proceed; and so arming himself with a
"severe gravity, as well as he could, he pronounced the
"terrible sentence from the beginning to the end · which
"being done with a kinde of passionate compassion, he
"threw the Bill unto the ground, and lifting up his eyes
"to Heaven, sat downe and wept: which gesture and
"manner of behaviour, both of his mind and body," Baily
says, "struck such a fear into the hearts of all his hearers
"and spectators, that many of them were afraid the
"ground would have opened to have swallowed up the
"man, but, that they hoped he was not there." nay, as he
represents this act of the Bishop's, it had such an effect on
even Valence himself, who, Baily tells us, "became a
"domestick servant to Dr. Goodrich, Superintendent of
"Ely," so the Papists stile the Protestant Bishops, "a
man," he says, "too much taken notice of to be too great a
"favourer of Luther's doctrine;" that it made an alteration in his countenance, and he could never put the thing
out of his mind: so that, notwithstanding the endeavours
used in the family, where he was, to persuade him otherwise, "he could never be at rest till such time as with his
"own hands, in the self same place where the former sen-

---

e At the end of the Festivale printed by Caxton 1483 is the manner of ful- Modus ful-
minating this sentence. It was ordered to be done by the prelate habited in minandi
his Albe, with the cross erected, and candles burning, which, after the sen- sentenciam
tence was ended, were ordered to be put out to strike the greater terror, ad terro-
and the bells were to ring rem.

" tence was written, he had blotted out his sin, and that
" together by fixing upon the place this other sentence,
" which carried healing in every word : *Delicta juventutis*
" *meæ et ignorantias ne memineris Domine.* Remember
" not, Lord, my sinnes, nor the ignorances of my youth :
" subscribing therunto his name, Peter de Valence, wher-
" upon he was absolved and became a priest."

4. But whatever truth there may be in this relation of
our Bishop's behaviour on this occasion, what is said of
Valence seems liable to some exceptions. Goodrich, whom
Baily, in contempt, calls *superintendent* of Ely, a name
commonly given to our bishops by the Papists, was not
promoted to that bishopric till the latter end of the year

consec. Apr.
19, 1534.

1533, about eighteen years after the commission of the
fact for which Valence is said by Baily to have been excommunicated, and but a little more than a year before our
Bishop's death. On this promotion of Goodrich, Valence
was made his domestic chaplain and almoner, in which
place he continued, as he said himself, above twenty years,

Fox's Acts,
&c. vol. iii.
p. 430.
col. 1.
Strype's
Eccle. Me-
morials,
vol. ii. p.
294.

viz. A. D. 1555; when we have an account of his visiting
William Wolsey, of Well, in Cambridgeshire, and Robert
Pygot, of Wisbich, who were then prisoners in Ely gaol
for their religion, and were afterwards burnt in that city;
to whom he is said to have applied himself in the following
most friendly and compassionate manner, calling them *bre-*
thren, and telling them, that, " according to his office, he
" was come to talk with them, having been almoner there
" above 20 years: that he hoped they'd take his coming
" in good part, since he assured them he would not en-
" deavour to pull them from their faith: that, on the con-
" trary, he both required and besought them in the name
" of Jesus Christ to stand to the truth of the Gospel and
" God's word, beseeching God almighty, for his son Jesus
" Christ's sake, to preserve both *him* and *them* in the same
" unto the end: for," as he added, again calling them
brethren " he knew not himself how soon he should be at
" the same point with *them.*" But to return.—

CHAP. IX.

1. *Dean Colet's representation of the corrupt state of the Church of England. 2. The Archbishop designed to hold a provincial Council to reform it, but was prevented by Wolsey. 3. The Bishop's journey to Rome put off on this occasion. His Speech to the Bishops in this Council. 4. His Speech understood as a reflection on the Cardinal. 5. Wolsey's character. 6. The Bishop ordered to meet the Pope's Embassador.*

1. ARCHBISHOP WARHAM, for the reformation of several great enormities in his province, especially of the clergy, had designed to hold this year an ecclesiastical Council of his suffragans. Of these disorders Dean Colet had made great complaint about *seven* years before, in the sermon which he preached at the opening of the convocation which was called to meet February 6, 1511. He wished, that once remembering their name and profession, they would mind the reformation of the Church, and assured them, that there was never more need, and, that the state of the Church never more wanted their endeavours. Since the Church, the spouse of Christ, which he would have to be without spot and wrinkle, was now become filthy and deformed; and, as Esaias speaks, *the faithful City was become an harlot;* and, as Jeremiah says, *she has plaid the harlot with many lovers,* by which means she had conceived many seeds of iniquity, and daily brought forth the foulest fruits. As to particulars, the Dean observed to them how greedy and desirous the clergy of those days were of honour and dignity: how they ran from one benefice to another, from a less to a greater, from a lower to a higher, with so much speed as to run themselves as it were out of breath: that as for those who were possessed of the dignities which they so much coveted, many of them affected so haughty an ap-

*A D. 1518.
Archp
Wake's
State of the
Church,&c.
p. 391*

*Dr.
Knight's
Life of
Dean Colet,
Appendix*

pearance, that they seemed not to be placed in the humble prelacy of Christ, but in the exalted dominion of the world. Next, he observed of them, how they gave themselves to feasting and junketting, and spent their time in vaine babling, in sports and plays, in hunting and hawking, and plunging themselves into the delights of this world : that covetousness, the very foulest of plagues, had so invaded the minds of almost all priests, and so blinded the eyes of their understanding, that they seemed blind to every thing except only to these which seemed to bring them some gain : for, says he, what else do we seek in these days, in the Church, but fat benefices and promotions ? and in the preferments themselves, what else do we make any account of besides the rents and income ? Lastly, he told them, that the *fourth* secular evil which deformed the face of the Church was continual secular occupation, in which many priests and bishops at that time were so intangled, that they were rather the servants of *men* than of God, and more the souldiers of this world than of Christ; from whence, he said, it came, that the priestly dignity was dishonoured, the priesthood was despised, the hierarchical order was confounded, the laity were scandalized, priests became hypocrites, and possessed of a slavish fear, and perfectly blind and ignorant, being so blinded with the darknesses of this world, as to see nothing but earthly things. For remedy and reformation of these evils, the Dean proposed a vigorous and impartial execution of the ecclesiastical laws; for he observed there was no need to make *new laws* and constitutions, but only to observe those which were already made.

2. In order to the holding this Council, the Archbishop acquainted the King with his design, and, as he affirmed afterwards, had obtained *his* consent so to do. But Cardinal Wolsey, who now drew all things into his own hands, being angry at this, wrote a sharp letter to the Archbishop, and, as it appeared by the event, so ordered matters, as to oblige him to recal his monitions, which were

already issued out for the meeting of this Council, in expectation of a legantine one to be held by the Cardinal for the reformation of the same enormities. In pursuance of this resolution, the Cardinal by his letters summoned the several Bishops of the Church to a Synod or *a* Council at Westminster, the morrow after the nativity of the blessed Virgin. But, the pestilence raging at that time in the city, the Cardinal, by his letters, dated August 21, this year, prorogued the Council till the first Monday in Lent following, and by other letters, dated December 31, summoned the Bishops of both provinces to be present at it.

3. It is said, that, on account of the meeting of this Council, our Bishop's journey to Rome was stopped, which he bare with less uneasiness, because he hoped, that much good to the Church might happily be produced hereby. But herein, it seems, he was disappointed; for no sooner was this Council opened, according to the Cardinal's appointment, but it appeared very plainly, that this meeting of the Bishops was rather to notify to the world the extravagant pomp and authority of the Lord Legate, than for any great good to the Church, in reforming the abuses and irregularities of the clergy. Our Bishop, therefore, spoke to them, it is said, to the following purpose. That he thought, or expected, when so many learned men had been drawn together into this Body, that some good matters should have been proposed for the benefit of the Church, that so the scandal which lay so heavy on her members, might have been removed, and the distemper cured that laid hold on such advantages. But, that he observed no one yet had made the least motion to repress the ambition of those men whose pride was so offensive when their profession was humility, or to punish the incontinence of such as had vowed chastity: that it was very notorious how the Church's goods were wasted; the glebes, the tithes, and other oblations of our devout ancestors, to the great scandal of their posterity, consumed in superfluous and riotous expenses: that he could not see

CHAP IX

Septem. ix 1517.

Life of Bp. Fisher, &c.

how they could exhort their flocks to fly or avoid the
pomps and vanities of this wicked world, when themselves,
who were their bishops or overseers, minded nothing more
than that which they forbad or reproved in others. That
if they taught according as they lived, their doctrines
would sound but very absurdly in the ears of those that
heard them; and that if they taught one thing and did
another, how could they expect that any should believe
what they said? since this was no other than throwing
down with one hand what they built up with the other:
that they preached humility, sobriety, contempt of the
world, &c. and yet in the very same men who taught these
doctrines, the people saw pride and haughtiness of mind,
excesse in apparel, and a giving themselves up to all sorts
of worldly pomp and vanitie; and thus people were made
to doubt whether they should believe their own eyes
rather than their ears. His Lordship added, that he
hoped his Eminency, the Lord Legate, and the rest of
the fathers would excuse his speaking thus plainly, seeing
he blamed no man more than himself: for that for several
times when he had setled himself to visit his diocese, to
govern his Church, and to answer the enemies of Christ,
so the Bishop termed Luther and Oecolampadius, &c. to
whose books he wrote answers, suddenly there has come
a message to him from the Court, that he must attend
such a triumph or public entry, or receive such an embassador: whereas, said he, what have bishops to do with
princes' courts? If they are in love with majesty, is there
a greater excellence than him whom they serve? Do they
admire stately buildings, are there any higher roofs than
their own cathedrals? Do they affect pompous apparel,
is there any greater ornament than the habit of the priesthood? or is there any better company than the communion
of saints? Truly, he said, what this vanity in temporal
things might work *on them*, he did not know, but as for
himself, he was sure he found it to be a great impediment
to devotion. Wherefore, he thought it necessary, and

high time it was, that they who were the heads should
begin to set an example to the inferiour clergy as to these
particulars, whereby they might all become more conformable to the image of God. For that in this course of
life which they now led, neither could there be any likelihood of continuance in the same state or condition wherein
they now stood, or of safety to the clergy.

4. How this speech of the Bishop's was received by the
Cardinal and the rest of the Council we are not told. If
this be a true copy of it, it seems to have been a bold re-
primand, not only of the Court for taking the bishops so
oft out of their dioceses to serve their secular designs, but
of the Cardinal, whose foible it was to affect too much
state and magnificence. Accordingly, it is observed, that,
" after the delivery of this speech by the Bishop, the Car- Life of Bp.
" dinal's state seem'd not to become him so well." If the Fisher, &c
Cardinal thus took it, the Bishop, it is likely, was no more
in his good graces than his friend Sir Thomas Moor was,
to whom, Erasmus says, the Cardinal was not very favourable, as being one whom he rather feared than loved. It
is not improbable, that our Bishop resented Wolsey's ill
usage of the Archbishop, and therefore chose thus to try
to mortify and subdue his haughty spirit. Though this
was not the only time that the Bishop opposed this insolent prelate. It is said, that when some years after he
again insulted the Archbishop, by sending his monition to A.D. 1523.
his Grace, just after his opening the convocation of his
province, for *him*, with the prelates and clergy, to appear
before him at Westminster, and there moved for one full
moiety of the benefices of the clergy, according to their
yearly value· this extravagant demand was opposed by
the Bishop of Rochester and his patron, Fox, Bishop of
Winchester, two leading men among the clergy, and very
much revered by them, so that, very probably, the Cardinal would have been disappointed in his designs, though
it had not been observed, as it was, that this was an illegal
convention, and the acts of it therefore all null and void.

5. Wolsey being now advanced to the dignity of the Cardinalate, and of the King's prime minister, he was become so haughty and insolent, as to be perfectly intolerable to every body. Thus the great Thuanus represented him: [a] Henry VIII. says he, had at his court one Thomas Wolsey, a man of a mean and sordid birth, but of so great pride and ambition, as to be very disagreeable to the peers and nobility, and at last troublesome to even the King himself. He by the King's favour was promoted to the highest dignity, being made Archbishop of York and Bishop of Winchester, and afterwards elected into the College of Cardinals, and adorned with ample legatine powers, and did all the business of the Kingdom. The Emperor Charles, therefore, who knew how much it was his interest to preserve the friendship of the English, made it his business to gain Wolsey's favour, insomuch, that he used frequently to write to him with his own hand, and to subscribe himself his son and kinsman; and to gratify the man's vanity yet more, he gave him hopes of being elected Pope, on the death of Leo X. In like manner we are told, the Duke of Venice applied to this blind side of the Cardinal, and ascribed to him a participation of the royal power and majesty. Here, at home, the University of Oxford, in their letters to him, stiled him his most advised and most reverend majesty, which, though a title not then appropriated to sovereign princes, as it is now, yet was certainly intended as incense to

[a] Erat apud eum Thomas Wolsæus, homo vili et sordido loco natus, sed tanta ambitione et superbia præditus ut gravis proceribus ac nobilitati, postremò Regi ipsi molestus fuerit. Is ad summam dignitatem favore Regis evectus Eboraci Archiepiscopus, et Wintoniæ episcopus, dein etiam in Cardinalium Collegium cooptatus ac legatione amplissima ornatus omnia Regni negotia administrabat. Itaque Carolus qui sciret quantum sua interesset amicitiam Anglorum cum Burgundis olim initam conservare, summo studio enitebatur ut Wolsæi gratiam omni cultu et observantia demereretur; adeo ut etiam in literis quas ad eum crebras, nec alterius quam sua manu scriptas, dabat filii nomen, et cognati in subscriptionibus apponeret; et ut vanitatem hominis magis inflammaret, spem dederat fore ut, Leone x° mortuo, votis Cardinalium in pontificem eligeretur. *Histo.* lib. i.

soothe, and propitiate the vain humour of this haughty CHAP.
IX.
minister. Erasmus said of him, that he reigned more
truly than the King himself. He seems indeed to have
vied with his master in state and greatness, and to have
equalled, if not exceeded him, in the magnificence of his
public appearances. As other cardinals had one pillar
borne before them as an emblem of their being pillars of
the Church, Wolsey had two carried before him, and had
besides poll-axes, a cross, mace, purse, &c. Of this pomp Roper's
Life of Sir
Thos.Moor,
MS.
Sir Thomas Moor seems to have made a jest, when he
advised the Commons to receive him, as he expressed
himself, with all his pompe, with his maces, his pillers,
poll-axes, his crosses, his hatt, and the great seal to.
Then as to his habit, it was as rich and costly as could be
got. His chaplains, we are told, wore gowns of damask
and satin. Nay, even his master cook, went daily in velvet Stow's Sur-
vey of Lon-
don, &c. p.
136, ed. 4°.
and satin, with a chain of gold about his neck. All this
must look very ill in the eyes of so mortified and humble
a man as the Bishop; and the more so, for that he saw it
taken notice of by those who favoured the Reformation,
and made use of as an handle to expose the then established Church. It was one of the articles exhibited Art. 22.
against Dr. Barnes, that he spoke against his having pillars and poll-axes, and by ^b *the* pacifyer *of the division be-
twene the* spiritualtie *and the* temporaltie, *it* was objected
to the clergy, that they wore proud and pompous apparel,
and had many of them a love to worldly things, that
letted, and in a manner strangled, the love of God; the
former part of which charge, Sir ^c Thomas More seems to
have imputed to the Cardinal's influence and example.

6. As to what his Lordship here adds, of the bishops

^b Printed, Londini in ædibus Thomæ Bartheleti prope aquagium sitis sub
intersignio Lucretiæ Romanæ. excus. cum privilegio.

^c —— for aughte that I can see, a greate parte of the proude and pom-
pous apparaile that many priestes in yeares not longe paste were by the
pryde and oversyght of some few forced in a maner agaynst their owne
willes to weare —— I wote well it is worne out with manye whiche entende
hereafter to bye no more suche agayne. *English Works,* p. 892, col.

CHAP.
IX.

having messages from court to receive embassadors, &c. he probably meant himself, to whom, as *he* was situated in the high road from Calais to London, this must be a very great grievance, not only as to the loss of time and neglect of his diocese, but on account of expense. Thus

A.D. 1514.
Coll.No.14.

but *four* years before this, Pope Julius II. sent an embassador to the King with a consecrated sword and cap of maintenance. The embassador came by the way of Calais, and was to land at Dover. Letters were therefore sent by the Lords of the Council to the Prior of Christ Church, Canterbury, to meet the embassador between Canterbury and Dover, and to entertain him at his house at Canterbury, and from thence to accompany him in his way to London beyond Sittingborne, where, by other letters, the Bishop of Rochester was ordered to be ready, with the

* John
Young,
Clerk.

* Master of the Rolls, and Sir Thomas Boleyn, to receive him, and to entertain him at his palace at Rochester, and from thence to accompany him to London. This letter to the Bishop was dated May 12, and the 19th the embassador made his entry into London, in the company of the Bishop, &c. and on the Sunday following was the sword, &c. presented to the King with great solemnity in St. Paul's Cathedral.

Sept. 24,
1518.
Reg.Fisher.

7. In September this year, the Bishop in person celebrated a synod in his Cathedral Church of Rochester, in the presence of the Rectors, Vicars, and other Curates of his diocese, who appeared there on that occasion; when, after having sung the first mass of the Holy Ghost, the Bishop, in the chapter-house of the said church, preached before his clergy; and when sermon was ended, Mr. Ralph Mallewes, official of Rochester, at the Bishop's command, read and published to the said clergy certain provincial and legatine constitutions, which had been put forth against their having and keeping concubines. The same we find done again by our Bishop [d]*nine* years after,

―――――――――――――

[d] Octo. 8, 1527. Idem pater in Domo Capitulari ―― Robertus Johnson Officialis dicti Reverendi patris Constitutiones Legatinas contra concubinas

which looks as if the clergy, at this time, grew uneasy CHAP
under their vows of celibacy, and were seeking out ways IX.
to get rid of them.

editas coram in presencia dicti cleri Latino sermone legit et publicavit.
Reg Fisher.

CHAP. X.

1. James Faber or Smith publishes a dissertation on the three Mary Magdalens. 2. Poncher, Bishop of Paris, sends a copy of it to Bishop Fisher, who writes an answer to it. 3. The Bishop desires his friend Erasmus to get it printed at Paris; who blames the Bishop for his warm manner of writing. 4. The Bishop suspects that Erasmus was angry with him. 5. Isaac Casaubon's opinion of this controversy.

ex officina
Henrici
Stephani,
Mar. 8,
1519, 8°.
Epist. ad
Mercurinū
Gattinari-
um.

1. NOT long after this was published, at Paris, a book entituled, *de Maria Magdalena triduo Christi, et una ex tribus Maria disceptatio.* This dissertation was written by James Faber or Smith, a learned mathematician of Estaples, and of the Dominican Order, who, Erasmus said, " was master of many excellent qualifications, of an " undissembled piety, a singular judgment and prudence, " and solid learning, on which account he was very dear " to the Emperor Maximilian, who as he was a candid " fautor of all virtues, so he was an exact judge of them." Smith dedicated this little book to Francis Moline, Abbot of St. Martine, Secretary and Counsellor to Francis I. King of France. In it the learned author declared his opinion to be, that there were *three* who used to be celebrated by the name of Marie Magdalene, *viz.* that woman who had been in times past a notorious sinner in the city, but was now by the mercy of our Saviour become a saint; Marie Magdalene, the sister of Martha, and Marie Magdalene, out of whom the Lord cast seven devils. This, Faber tells us, he did in answer to the Abbot's desire to know his judgment of this matter, and published it, *ad Dei gloriam, Evangelistarum concordiam, et Annæ Mariæ, atque reliquarum sanctarum mulierum* —— &c.

2. It seems this little book was so well received, that it soon had a second edition, a copy of which Stephen

Poncher, then Bishop of Paris, and afterwards Archbishop of Sens, sent to our Bishop, and with it a letter,
desiring him to tell him his thoughts of it, and at the same
time representing to his Lordship in how great [a]danger
the Catholic Church was by such disputes, and what confusion and reproach a variety of opinions would be the
occasion of to it. This the Bishop ingenuously owns to
his readers he had not observed till he was thus put in
mind of it. He said, that indeed he had read the book,
and was offended both with the title of it, and many things
in it, but that he had so good an opinion of Faber, as not
to believe he would rashly assert any thing of which he
was not well assured, or for which he could not immediately give a reason. But having more accurately examined the matter, and turned over the Gospels with
greater diligence, he soon saw the truth, and was presently
convinced, that there was not only no difference among
the Evangelists about the only Magdalene, but, that they
were all so unanimously of this opinion, that unless any
one asserts, that there is but one, he must either make the
Evangelists liars, or acknowledge that the prediction of
Christ was frustrated. This, the Bishop says, being observed by him, he then began more carefully to examine
the particulars which Faber opposed, and found some
mistakes very unworthy of the great character which he
had long formed to himself of Faber. He observed, he
said, a great many rash assertions, and read vile reflections
made by him, not only on the modern interpreters of
Scripture, and the preachers of the present age, but on all
others also since Ambrose's time, however eminent they
were for learning and holiness. He likewise observed, he
said, and that not without concern, with what contempt
and neglect Faber treated those very grave fathers of the
Church, Gregory, Austin, Bede, and Bernard; which
made him often reflect how many incommodities would

---

[a] Stephanus Poncherius Episcopus qui tuum calamum ad hoc opus exti-
mulavit —— *Erasmi Epist. Fischero Episcopo, Apr.* 2, 1519.

CHAP.
X.
arise to the Church, if this opinion of Faber's was true: how many authors must be condemned; how many books amended, how many sermons heretofore preached to the people must be retracted; what scruples it would occasion to many; how many handles it would give to scepticism, and what a cause it would be of men's entertaining an ill suspicion of our common mother the Church, who has for many ages taught otherwise. Observing these things, and the zeal of the Bishop of Paris, who stirred him up to consider what Faber had wrote, he resolved to acquiesce in his exhortation, not trusting in his own strength, but in the patronage of the saints for whom he contended, and especially of Mary Magdalene, to whom he supposed he should not do an unacceptable thing in ascribing to her her whole prerogative, and not, as Faber had done, dividing it among three. But, as about the same time, Jodochus Clichtoveus, of Newport, had opposed this notion of there being but one Mary Magdalene, as well as Faber, the Bishop framed his answer to suit them both, and divided it into two parts, giving it the [b]title which I have transcribed in the margin.

3. When the book was finished, the Bishop sent it to his friend Erasmus, who seems to have been then at Paris, for him to get it printed: who afterwards wrote his Lordship word, that so cold and backward was the printer, that he had much ado to persuade him to undertake it. But no sooner was the book published, but it was bought up very greedily; so that, as Erasmus told the Bishop, he need not fear hereafter the printer's not printing any thing of his, there was so quick a sale of this. But as to the contents of his book, Erasmus observed to his Lordship, some were really sorry that Faber, who was now in years, a very honest man, and one who had so well de-

[b] Joannis Fischeri (Ep. Roffensis) de unica Magdalena libri duo (contra Judochum Clichtoveum Neoportuensem et Jacobum Fabrum Stapulensem) in ædibus Jodoci Badii Ascensii. Ad octavam calendas Martias 1519. Cum privilegio in biennium.

served of learning, should be so very severely used, than which nothing could be more agreeable to those who were so wedded to their old learning, as perfectly to hate any improvement of it; upon which account Faber was already on ill terms with some at Paris, especially those of his own Order. But, he added, that it could scarce be avoided, in disputes of this nature where there is an opposition, that the pen should not grow warm without our being aware of it.

4. This reproof of his friend's, though wisely tempered with so much mildness and caution, and complimenting the Bishop as Faber's superior in this controversy, yet, it seems, raised a suspicion in the Bishop, that Erasmus was angry with him for his writing this answer to Faber. But Erasmus told him, that this only shewed he did not yet know Erasmus: that in the first edition of his book many thought he joked too often, and with too much sting on the church of Faber; but that in the second edition, as the stile was more neat, so there was less passion. Only he admired, that his Lordship so anxiously laboured to drag this affair into, and make it a controversy of faith, with which Faber was very much grieved, to whom he was the more desirous to give some succour, because he both admired and reverenced his Lordship.

5. It was an observation of the learned Isaac Casaubon, which he made long after this upon another occasion, that Exercitat in Baronium. p 239, col. I. " it seem'd strange, that when formerly in better times in " such sort of philological questions as don't pertain to the " heart and marrow of the D. Word, but only to the rind " or bark, or which are not articles of faith, it was free for " any learned man both to be of the opinion which he " thought right, and modestly to publish his opinion, " there should be no room now for the same liberty attended with the like modesty, since in these questions " there is no heresy, no absolute necessity of thinking " thus or otherwise. That even about this very matter, " which was now disputed by Faber and the Bishop, the

" ancient fathers, it's plain, were divided in their opinions,
" and ascribed the accounts given by the Evangelists of
" the women who washed our Lord's feet, &c. to different
" women, to three, or at least to two; that particularly
" Basil of Seleucia, in his homily of Lazarus, seriously
" affirmed, that there are three Maries remembred in the
" Gospel." But the Bishop was apprehensive, that the
authority of the Church would suffer by this opinion; as
if the Catholic Church, or even the particular Church of
Rome, was the supreme and infallible judge of such sort
of critical questions and controversies. However, Erasmus wrote to the Bishop, that though he had only dipped
into his book, they who had read it did all own him superior throughout the whole argument; and that for his
part he perfectly envied Faber such an adversary, by
whom, though he was manifestly defeated, yet he had this
to comfort him, that he fell by the hand of the great
Æneas, and therefore he hoped his reverence would be
content with this victory, which, by the suffrages of the
learned, he was said to have got. However, it seems,
Clichtoveus had the courage to defend Faber, which drew
a reply from the Bishop, which seems never to have been
printed. Besides which, Bale mentions some *additions*,
written by the Bishop, concerning Mary Magdalene,
which, I suppose, were likewise suppressed by his Lordship.

de Script.
Brit.

CHAP. XI.

1. Dr. Luther publishes two books against the Pope. 2. An account of his book of the Babilonish Captivitie. 3. An Answer to it, written in the King's name. Bishop Fisher supposed to be one of the makers of it. 4, 5, &c. an account of it.

1. THE controversy in which Dr. Luther was engaged with the Pope and Church of Rome had now continued three years · during which time he had published several books, and particularly a small tract of the Pope's Indulgences. Against these, Eccius, Emser, and others, had written with a great deal of zeal and severity. Luther, therefore, being provoked, and heated by their urging manner of treating him, set forth two books, which were particularly remark- A D 1520 able, as very much alarming, and incensing the Pope and his dependents. One of these was in the German lan- Seckendorf guage, and written with so great liberty, that even the de Luther-anismo, § Doctor's friends reckoned it a proclamation of war. Lu- 72, 73. ther himself gave this account of it, that " he had pub- " lished a book in the vulgar tongue against the Pope " about reforming the Church, and directed it to all the " nobility of Germany; which book would give great dis- " taste to Rome, since in it was made a public discovery " of its impious contrivances and violent dealings."

2. The other book of Dr. Luther's was written in Latin, and entituled, [a] *The prelude of Dr. Martin Luther con-* D Martini *cerning the Babilonish Captivitie of the Church.* This Lutheri de Captivitate little tract he inscribed to his friend Augustus Hermannus, Babylo-nica, Anno telling him, that, " [b] whether he would or no, he was com- 1524. " pelled to be every day more and more learned, thro' the

---

[a] So Seckendorf And so Luther himself stiles it towards the end, *finem hic faciam hujus prœludy,* promising very shortly to publish the other part

[b] Velim nolim cogor indies eruditior fieri, tot tantisque magistris, &c

G

" urgings and exercisings of so many and so great mas-
" ters, who strove to outdo one another: that above two
" years since he wrote of *indulgences*, but in such a man-
" ner that he was very sorry he ever published that little
" book; for that at that time he was at a sort of stand, on
" account of a great superstition of the Roman tyranny,
" wherby he was led to conclude, that indulgences were
" not altogether to be rejected. But that afterwards, by
" the kind assistance of Sylvester and the friars, who stre-
" nuously defended them, he was made sensible, that they
" were nothing else but the mere impostures of the Roman
" flatterers, by which they wasted or destroyed both the
" faith of God, and the estates of men. He therefore
" wished, that he could obtain of the booksellers, and per-
" swade all who read them, to burn all his little books of
" Indulgences, and that, instead of all that he had written
" of them, they'd apprehend this proposition, that *indul-*
" *gences are the wanton humours of Roman flatterers.*
" Afterwards, Eccius and Emser, with their fellow conspi-
" rators, began to instruct him about the *primacy* of the
" Pope: and here also, he said, that he might not be un-
" grateful to men so learn'd, he owned that he was very
" much profited by their labours: for having admitted the
" papacy to be of human right, tho' he denied it to be of
" divine, as soon as he heard and read their most subtle
" subtilties, by which they erected their artful image, he
" knew, and was sure, that the papacy was the kingdom
" of Babylon, and the power of Nimrod the mighty
" hunter. Therefore here also, that all prosperity might
" attend his friends, he prayed the booksellers and readers,
" that, having burnt what he had published on this sub-
" ject, they would retain this proposition, that *the papacy*
" *is the mighty hunting of the Bishop of Rome: and that*
" *this is proved by the reasons of Eccius, Emser, &c.*" But
now, he said, he was trifled with in the schools about communicating in both kinds, and was to take pains about
some other matters of the greatest importance; that an

Italian friar of Cremona had written a revocation of Martin Luther to the See of Rome, and another friar, a German of Leipsic, had written against him concerning communicating in both kinds. He therefore asks Hermannus
what he thought he had else to do, but to listen with all
attention to what these writers said? He had hitherto
thought, he said, fool as he was, that it would be fine, if
in the laity's behalf it was determined by a general council,
that they should receive the Sacrament in both kinds. But
this opinion the more than most learned friar having a
mind to correct, he tells us, that neither Christ nor the
Apostles commanded nor counselled the administering the
Sacrament in both kinds to the laity; and that therefore
it is left to the judgment of the Church, whom it is necessary to obey, to determine what is to be done or omitted
in this case. But thus, he says, do they dispute, who
write against Luther, either asserting what they oppose,
or devising that which they argue against: that thus Sil-
vester, Eccius, Emser, &c. disputed with him, from whose
temper if this friar had differed, he had not written
against Luther. He therefore concludes, that this man,
and those who are his playfellows, seek through him to
get themselves a name in the world, as if they were meet
to enter the lists with Luther, but that their hopes should
be disappointed, since they should be so far despised as
never to be so much as named by him; and that he should
be content with returning this single answer to all their
books. And therefore, whilst *they* murmured at his approving the communion's being administered in both kinds,
he would, he said, proceed, and attempt to shew, that all
are profane who deny the communion in both kinds to the
laity; which, that he might do the more commodiously,
he would make a prelude of the captivity of the Church
of Rome, intending, in due time, to offer a great many
other things, when the most learned Papists had answered
and confuted this book; and this, he said, he did, that if
so he met with any pious reader he might not be offended

with those low things treated of by him, and complain very justly, that they read nothing that either cultivated or instructed their minds, or that gave any occasion to learned thoughts; for that Herman knew how ill his friends thought of his being taken up with the sordid fetches of those men, which they said were abundantly confuted in the bare reading of them, and that they expected better things from him, which Sathan, by their means, attempted to hinder him in. He, therefore, at length had resolved to take their advice, and to leave the business of brawling and invective to those wasps.

To begin, he must, he said, deny, that there are *seven* Sacraments, and, for the present, however, allow of only three, *baptism, penance,* and *bread;* all which were by the Church of Rome led into miserable captivity, and the Church spoiled of its liberty. Though, if he would speak according to the usage of Scripture, he should reckon but one Sacrament, and three sacramental signs, of which he intended to say more another time. At present he would speak of the first of all these three, the Sacrament of bread: of which, he said, being now provoked and teazed, and drawn by force into this controversy, he would freely say what he thought; *Rideant sive plorent papistæ, vel universi in unum.*

First, he said, the *sixth* chapter of St. John was wholly to be set aside, as what had not a syllable in it of the Sacrament, not only for that the Sacrament was not yet instituted, but much more, because the very consequences or contexts of the discourse and sense shew, that Christ speaks of the faith of the Word incarnate. There were therefore, he observed, two places which did very clearly treat of this matter: 1. The evangelical writing in the Supper of the Lord: 2. St. Paul, 1 Cor. xi. Matthew, Mark, and Luke, he said, all agreed together, that Christ gave to all his disciples the whole Sacrament; and it was so certain that Paul distributed both parts of it, that no one can deny it. Matthew reports, that Christ did not

say of the bread, Eat ye all of it, but of the cup, Drink ye
all of it. And Mark likewise does not say, they all eat,
but that they all drank of it, both of them placing the
note of universality not at the bread, but at the cup, as if
the Spirit foresaw this schism which forbad the communion of the cup to some, which Christ would have common
to all. But what, he said, was of the greatest force, and
did entirely conclude this matter was, that Christ said,
This is my blood, which is shed for you and for many, for
the remission of sins. Here, says he to Herman, you very
clearly see, that the blood is given for all for whose sins it
is shed. But who dares to say, that it is not shed for' the
laity? Lastly, Paul stands unconquered, and stops the
mouths of all opposers, saying, *I have received of the Lord*
that which also I delivered unto you. He does not say, I
have *permitted* to you, nor what I receive of the Lord I
give to you; but *I have received*, and *have delivered, viz.*
at the beginning of his preaching, long before this their
contention. He therefore concludes, that to deny to the
laity both the species of bread and wine in the communion
is profane and tyrannical, and out of the power of even an
angel, and much more of the Pope. The *first* captivity,
therefore, of this Sacrament is, he said, as to its substance
or integrity, which the Roman tyranny had taken from us.

The *second* captivity of this Sacrament, he said, was
more mild and gentle, so far as it concerned the conscience, but was by far the most dangerous of all to meddle
with, much more to condemn, *viz. transubstantiation.*
What was asserted without the authority of Scripture, or
an approved revelation, might, he said, be held as an opinion, but was not to be believed as a necessary article of
faith therefore, he allowed, that any one might either
hold this opinion or not, provided they did not impose
their several opinions for necessary articles of faith, and
condemn those of heresy, who did not think as they did.
Transubstantiation, he said, was neither supported by
reason nor Scripture: it was an absurd and novel exposi-

1 Corinth
XI. 23.

tion of Christ's words, that the bread should be taken for the species or accidents of bread, and the wine for the species or accidents of wine. The Church, he said, for above 1200 years believed rightly, and the holy fathers never thought of that portentous word and dream, *transubstantiation*, till Aristotle's philosophy began to invade the Church. But as for himself, if he could not comprehend how the bread is the body of Christ, he would bring his understanding into captivity to the obedience of Christ, and simply sticking to his words, firmly believe, not only that the body of Christ is in the bread, but that the bread is the body of Christ.

The *third* captivity of this Sacrament, he said, was by much the most impious abuse; by which it was brought about, that there was at that time scarce any thing more generally received in the Church, than, that the mass is a good or meritorious work, and a sacrifice; which abuse had caused an inundation of infinite other abuses, till at length the faith of the Sacrament was utterly extinguished, and of it were made mere fairs, hucksterings, and certain gainful bargains: since from hence came the participations, fraternities, suffrages, merits, anniversaries, memories, and that sort of traffic in the Church, to be bought and sold, bargained and compounded for; and that the whole maintenance of priests and monks depended in a manner on these things. He confessed, that in attempting to remove this abuse, he undertook a very hard task, and which perhaps it was impossible to perform, since it was an abuse which had been strengthened by the long use of many ages, and approved by an universal consent, and was so settled, that it was necessary to destroy the major part of the books which were then in vogue, and almost wholly to alter the face of the Church, to introduce, or rather reduce, another sort of ceremonies. But first, he observed, that in order to come safely and happily to the true and free knowledge of this Sacrament, especial care was to be taken, that all those things should be separated

from it, which by men's zeal and affections have been
added to the primitive and simple institution of it ; such
as vestments, ornaments, chauntings, prayers, organs,
lights, and all that pomp of visible things ; and that we
should turn our eyes and thoughts towards the pure institution itself alone, and not propose to ourselves any thing
else but the very words of Christ, by which he instituted,
perfected, and recommended to us the Sacrament. Now
the words of Christ are these : *After supper Jesus took
bread, &c* which words the Apostle, 1 Corinth. xi. delivers
and explains more at large, and on which we ought to rely,
and be built as on a firm rock, if we would not be carried
about with every wind of doctrine, as, he said, they had
been hitherto by the profane teachings of men averse to
the truth. Since there was nothing omitted in these words
that pertained to the integrity, use, and fruit of this Sacrament, and nothing said that was superfluous, and not
necessary for us to know. And therefore any one who
omitted these words in his meditating on, or his instructions
about the mass, would teach monsters of impiety, as was
done by those who made of it an *opus operatum,* and a
sacrifice. It should, therefore, he said, be determined in
the first place and infallibly, that the mass, or Sacrament
of the Altar, is the Testament of Christ, which, when he
died, he left behind him to be distributed to his faithful
ones. Now a testament is, without doubt, a promise of
one about to die, whereby he bequeaths his estate, and
appoints heirs to enjoy it. A testament, therefore, in-
cludes,—first, the death of the testator, and next, the
promise of an inheritance, and the appointment of the
heir · so that the mass is a promise of the remission of sins
made to us by God, and confirmed by the death of his
Son. Now a promise is of that nature, as not to be at-
tained to by any works, powers, and merits, but only by
faith : since where there is the word of God promising,
there the faith of the person who accepts of it is necessary,
that it may be clear, that faith is the beginning of our

salvation, which depends on the word and promise of God,
who without any of our study, or previous to our desire,
prevents us by his free and undeserved mercy, and offers
the word of his promise. This Luther again and again
inculcates, that man cannot any other way either covenant
or transact with God but by faith, i. e. that not man by
any works of his, but God, by his promise, is the author
of salvation; that all things may depend on, &c. the word
of his power, by which he hath begotten us, that we
James, i. should be a kind of first fruits of his creatures. He there-
18.
fore laments, that there were so many masses in the world,
and yet few or none acknowledged, considered, and apprehended these promises and riches proposed to them; but
were so mad as, through a superstitious and profane opinion, rather to reverence the words of consecration, as
they are called, as containing in them some secret, than to
believe them as the promise or testament of Christ. By
which doctrine of impious men the mass was changed into
a good work, which themselves call *opus operatum*, or a
work done, by which they presumed they could do any
thing with God: from whence they proceeded to conclude, that this good work was likewise available for
others, and on this sandy bottom founded their applica-
tions, participations, and fraternities, their anniversaries,
&c. Whereas, if we firmly held, that the mass is a divine
promise, we should be sensible of this great truth, that it
can profit no one, be applied to no one, &c. but only to
him that believes himself with his own faith. He easily
admitted, he said, that the praiers which the congregation
assembled to receive the mass poured out before God, were
good works, or benefits which they mutually imparted, applied, and communicated to, and offered for one another;
but these were not the mass, but the works of the mass, if
yet the praiers of the heart and mouth ought to be called
works, because they are done of faith, being perceived or
increased in the Sacrament. He concluded, that it was
certain the mass is not a work communicable to others,

but the object of every one's own faith, which was nou-
rished and strengthened by it.

He next proceeded to oppose the opinion, that the
mass is a sacrifice which is offered unto God This he
called another scandal, which was by much the greater
and most specious, since the words of the canon of the
mass seemed to sound to that effect, and that it was
favoured by the sayings of the fathers, so many prece-
dents, and so great a custom constantly observed throughout the world. But to all these the words and example
of Christ were, he said, to be opposed with the utmost
constancy: that we should suffer nothing to prevail against
them, even though an angel from heaven should teach it;
and that in them there was nothing of either a work or a
sacrifice: that the example of Christ was on the same
side, who in his last Supper, when he instituted this Sacrament, and made his will, did not offer himself to God
the Father, or do any good work for others, but sitting at
the table, he proposed the said will or testament to every
one there, and exhibited a sign of it. that the mass, by
how much nearer and more like it was to the first mass of
all which Christ celebrated at supper, by so much the
more christian it was; but that the mass of Christ's instituting was most simple, without any pomp of vestments,
gestures, chantings, and other ceremonies; so that if it
had been necessary that it should be offered as a sacrifice, he did not fully institute it. Not that any one ought
to reproach the universal Church for adorning and enlarging the mass with many other rites and ceremonies;
but what he meant, he said, was, that no one being deceived with the shew of ceremonies, and entangled with a
multitude of pomp, should lose the simplicity of the mass,
and in reality worship a sort of transubstantiation, as having lost the simple substance of the mass, by being stuck,
as it were, in the manifold accidents of pomp, for that
whatsoever is an addition to, or over and above the word
and example of Christ, is an accident of the mass. He

further argued, that as it was a contradiction for a testament to be distributed, or for a promise to take and sacrifice a sacrifice, so it was for the mass to be a sacrifice, since we *received that*, whereas we *gave a sacrifice;* for that the same thing cannot at the same time be both received and offered, nor be given and received together by the same person, no more than prayer and the thing prayed for can be the same, or than it can be the same thing to pray and to receive the things praied for. As to the canon of the mass, and authorities of the fathers, he said, that the priest, when after consecration he elevated the bread and wine, did not by that action shew, that he offered them to God, since then he says not one word of any sacrifice or oblation, but only uses a relique of an Hebrew rite, who used to lift up or elevate those things which they received with giving of thanks. However, he wished, that as the sign or Sacrament was plainly elevated in their sight, so the word or testament was at the same time pronounced in their ears with a plain and loud voice, and that in the vulgar tongue, that so their faith might be the more effectually exercised ; for why should it be lawful to perform the mass in Greek, and Latin, and Hebrew, and not also in German, or any other language? As to *private masses*, they were, he said, a man's making provision to communicate himself; and that a *private mass* did not at all differ from, or avail more than, a single communion of any laic received from the hand of a priest, except the prayers and his consecrating and ministring to himself. He added, that ʿin the matter itself of the mass and Sacrament, we are all equally priests and laics. He concluded, that it should not move any one, that the whole world is of a contrary opinion, and has another usage or custom: since *he* has the Gospel, which is most certain, on *his* side, and having *that*, he may easily despise the sense and opinions of men.

Dr. Luther proceeded to consider the Sacrament of

ᶜ Re ipsa Missæ et Sacramenti omnes sumus æquales sacerdotes et laici.

Baptism. And here he praised God, for that he has preserved this Sacrament in his Church unpolluted by the
constitutions of men, and has made it free for all nations
and all orders of men, and not suffered it to be oppressed
by the very worst and most impious prodigies of gain and
superstitions. But this he ascribes to God's ordaining
little children to be initiated by baptism, who are not
capable of avarice and superstition: for if this Sacrament
was to be given to adult and greater persons, it seemed
not possible that its virtue and glorie should be continued,
by reason of the tyrannie of avarice and superstition
which had supplanted all divine things. Without doubt
worldly wisdom would even here have invented its prepa-
rations and dignities, its reservations and restrictions, and
such like nets to catch money. But when Satan could not
extinguish the virtue of baptism in little ones, he yet prevailed to do it in the adult, so that now there was scarce
any one who remembered that he was baptized, much less
gloried in his being so, there were so many other ways
found for the forgiveness of sins and getting to heaven.
What gave occasion to these, he said, was that dangerous
saying of St. Jerome, either ill placed, or ill understood,
that repentance is a second plank after a shipwreck, as if
baptism was not repentance. Hence, when men have faln
into sin, they give over for lost the first plank or ship, and
begin to trust only to the second, that is, to repentance,
and from thence are sprung those endless burdens of vows,
religions, works, satisfactions, pilgrimages, indulgences,
and sects, and that ocean of books, questions, opinions,
and human traditions about them, which the whole world
now does not contain. First of all, therefore, he said, the
divine promise was to be observed in baptism; which says,
He who believes and is baptized shall be saved; which
promise is incomparably to be preferred to the universal
pomps of works, vows, religions, and whatsoever is of humane invention. Next, he observed, that it would be of
no small use or advantage, if the penitent first of all recol-

* cum fi-
ducia.

lected his baptism, and with confidence *remember'd the divine promise which he has deserted, and then confess unto the Lord, rejoycing that he is yet so secure of salvation in that he has been baptized, and detesting his profane ingratitude in falling away from the belief and truth of it. From hence, he says, we may very clearly discern the difference betwixt man who ministers Baptism, and God the author of it : and therefore we should take care not so to distinguish Baptism, as to attribute the outward Baptism to man, and the inward to God, but to ascribe both to God, and not to accept the person who confers it as any other than the vicarious instrument of God, by which the Lord who sits in heaven, plunges us into the water with his own hands, and by the mouth of a man here on earth, promises remission of sins, speaking to us by the mouth of his minister. This, he observed, the very words used by the minister in baptizing us tell us, when he says, I baptize thee in the name of the Father, and of the Son, and of the Holy Ghost ; he does not say, I baptize thee in my name ; that so we may know that we are not baptized of man, but of the Holy Trinity by man, who transacts this matter with us in his name : and hence, he adds, appears how trifling the contention is about the form of Baptism, as the words used in administring it are called. Another thing pertaining to Baptism, Dr. Luther observed, was the sign or the sacrament, which is the plunging into water, from whence it has its name. A great many, he said, suppose, that there was in the word and water some hidden spiritual vertue, which operated the grace of God on the mind of the receiver, or the person baptized. Others, in contradiction to these, determined, that there was no virtue in the Sacraments, but that grace is given by God alone, who according to his covenant is assisting to the Sacraments which he himself has instituted. But all agreed in this, that Sacraments are effectual signs of grace, to which they were moved by this only argument, that otherwise it did not appear how the Sacraments of

the new law excelled those of the old, if they only signified: and hence were they driven to attribute so much to
the Sacraments of the new law, as to determine, that they
were profitable even to those who are in mortal sin, and
that neither faith nor grace were required; but that it
was sufficient there was *no obstacle, i. e. an actual resolution of sinning again. But these things, Dr. Luther
said, were diligently to be caution'd against and avoided,
because they were impious, savouring of infidelity, contrary to the faith, and opposite to the nature of Sacraments. for it was a mistake, that the Sacraments of the
new law differ'd from those of the old; so far from it, that
with respect to the efficacy of signification, they both signified alike: for the same God who saves us by baptism
and bread, saved Abel by sacrifice, Noah by the ark, and
Abraham by circumcision, and all others by his signs. So
that a Sacrament of the old and new law is no way different as to signification, provided we call the old law
whatsoever God wrought in the patriarchs and other
fathers in the time of the law: for those signs which were
made among the patriarchs and fathers are very different
from the legal figures which Moses instituted in his law,
such as the priestly rites in habits, vessels, meats, &c.
These legal figures had not annexed to them the word of
promise which requires faith, whence they are not signs
of justification, because they are not Sacraments of faith
which alone justify. but are only Sacraments of works;
wheras ours and the fathers signs or Sacraments have annexed the word of promise, which requires faith, and can
be fulfilled by no work · whence also their whole efficacy
is faith itself, not working, and the common saying, that
not the Sacrament, but the faith of the Sacrament justifies. So that Baptism justifies no body, nor is profitable
to any one: but it is faith in the word of promise, to
which Baptism is added, that justifieth, and fulfils that
which Baptism signifies. So far was it from being true,
he said, that in the Sacraments there is an effectual virtue

* non po-
suisse obi-
cem

of justification, or that they are effectual signs of grace. Baptism, therefore, signifies two things, death and a resurrection, that is, a full and consummate justification. For that the ministers plunging the child into the water signifies death, as, on the contrary, his taking him out of it, signifies life. On which account, he wished, he said, that they who were baptized were wholly immersed or plunged into the water, as the word baptize means, and the mystery signified; not that he thought it necessary, but that it would be fair that the sign of a thing so full and perfect should also be given full and perfect, as it was without doubt instituted by Christ. Here, therefore, he observed, it was plain, that the Sacrament of Baptism, even as to the sign, was not any momentary business, but perpetual; for tho' the use of it passes away on a sudden, yet the thing itself endures till death, nay, till the resurrection at the last day. Wherfore, we should beware of those who have reduced the force of Baptism so low, as to say indeed that grace is infused in it, but that afterwards it's lost by sinning, and that then we must go to heaven another way, as if our baptism was become altogether null and void: whereas our whole lives ought to be a Baptism, and a fulfilling the sign or Sacrament of Baptism; since being freed from all other things, we are obliged to one baptism only, that is, to death and the resurrection. That this glory of our libertie, and this knowledge of baptism was now in captivity, was owing, he said, to nothing but the tyranny of the Roman pontiff, by whose means the Church was extinct by endless laws of works and ceremonies, the virtue and knowledge of Baptism was taken away, and the faith of Christ hindred. He therefore added, that neither Pope nor Bishop, nor any other man has any right of constituting one syllable over any Christian man without his consent, and that whatsoever is done otherwise, is done by a tyrannical spirit: that therefore the praiers, fastings, endowments, and whatsoever things else the Pope in all his decrees, which are as unjust as they are many, appoints and exacts, he has no right to appoint, &c. but is an offender against the liberty of the Church as often as he attempts any of these things · that the Pope's disciples assist this impious and destructive tyrannie by their wresting and depraving that saying of Christ, *He who heareth you heareth me;* whereas Christ did not say this to Peter only. Others much more impudent arrogate to the Pope a power of making laws from that in St. Matt. *Whatsoever* thou shalt bind on earth, &c.* When Christ there speaks of binding and remitting sins, not of leading captive the whole Church, and oppressing it by laws. However, he allowed, that this cursed tyrannie is to be born by Christians, according to that saying of Christ's, Whosoever shall strike thee on the right cheek turn to him the left also : but what he complained of, he said, was, that the impious Popes boasted, that they could, and did do this of right, and presumed, that by this their Babilon they consulted the Christian interest, and did what they could to persuade every body to be of this opinion. He wished therefore he could prevail to have all vows wholly taken away or avoided, whether they were of entring into religions, or of pilgrimages. or of any other works · and that we might continue in the most religious and most working liberty of baptism. He very much feared, he said, that they who took on them the vows of the religious orders were of the number of those whom the Apostle foretold, *speaking lies in hypocrisy, forbidding to marry, and abstaining from meats, which God hath created to be received with thanksgiving.* However he knew, that of them came two notable errors of the Roman pontiff: 1. That he dispensed with vows, and made as if he alone had authority so to do above all Christians; 2 That he again determines, that marriage shall be dissolved, if one, even without the consent of the other, go into a monastery before the marriage is consummated. He added, that it was exceeding ridiculous and foolish for parents to vow their children, or a girl not born, or an infant to religion or perpetual chastity,

CHAP.
XI

XVI 19.

1 Tim iv.
2, 3.

when it's certain this can fall under no vow, and seems to be a certain mocking of God, whilst they vow those things which are not at all in their power: that the more he considered the three vows of the religious, the less he understood them, and very much wondred how this exaction of vows took place; but he least of all understood at what time of life these vows might be made, in order to their being lawful and valid: that it seemed to him a foolish thing, that the term of a lawful vow should be prescribed to any one by others, who could not prescribe it to themselves; and that he did not see why a vow made at eighteen should be more valid than one at ten or twelve years old; but they might as well, he thought, determine the time, or fix the term of poverty and obedience, as if any time was to be set for a man to be sensible of his being covetous and proud.

Of the Sacrament of Penance.

Luther, in the *third* place, comes to speak of the Sacrament of *Penance*. The chief and capital mischief of this Sacrament was, he said, that they had wholly abolished the Sacrament itself, without so much as leaving the least mark of it; for wheras this Sacrament, as the other two, consists of the word of God's promise and our own faith, they have subverted both. As to the word of promise, where Christ says, Matt. xvi. 19, xviii. 18, *Whatsoever thou shalt bind on earth, &c. Whatsoever ye shall bind on earth, &c.* and John, xx. 23, *Whosoever sins ye remit, &c.* by which is provoked the faith of those who are penitent for the obtaining the remission of sins, they have accommodated it to their tyranny. For that in all their books, sermons, &c. it has been none of their business to shew what is promised to Christians in these words, what they ought to believe, and how great comfort they have from them, but how far and wide themselves may tyrannise, so far, that some have begun to lay their commands on the angels in heaven, and with incredible and most furious impietie to make their brags, that they have authority both in heaven and earth in these things, and have power to bind even in heaven. The promise and faith being thus obliterated and subverted, they had, he said, substituted in their rooms these three parts of penance, *contrition, confession,* and *satisfaction,* but so that if there was any good in either of them, they have taken it away, and put their own lust and tyrannie in its room. First, they so taught *contrition,* he said, as to make it prior to the faith of the promise, and far more vile, as what was not the work but the merit of faith, nay, they do not so much as mention that, and not at all observe, that it is faith which works *contrition* and grief of heart. Being thus grown bolder and worse, they feigned a certain *attrition,* which by vertue of the keys, a vertue they know nothing of, is made *contrition.* This they bestow on the impious and incredulous, that so all *contrition* may be abolished. He therfore cautions men against placing their confidence in their *contrition,* or attributing the forgiveness of sins to their grief. Yet, he observes, *contrition* lay less exposed to tyrannie and gain, than it did to impietie and pestilent doctrines: wheras *confession* and *satisfaction* were made the shops of power and profit. As to *confession:* it was not to be doubted but that confession of sins was necessary and commanded by God, and tho' private confession could not be proved by Scripture, yet he approved of it as useful, nay, necessary, and would not have it omitted, so far from it, that he rejoyced it was in the Church of Christ, since it is the only remedy for afflicted consciences. All that he detested was, that this *confession* is subject to the tyranny and exaction of the pontiffs, who reserve to themselves the secret things, and then command them to be disclosed to confessors named by him. But it was his opinion, he said, that if a brother or private christian confessed to a brother, it was not necessary to do it to the Church, that is, to a prelate or priest, as they interpret the word Church: that Christ's words, *Whatsoever ye shall bind upon earth,* &c. were spoken to all and singular Christians, and therefore he did not doubt but that whosoever freely confessed, or being rebuked asked pardon, and amended his fault before any brother in private, he would be absolved from his secret sins. Wherefore, he admonished those princes of Babylon, and bishops of Bethaven, to refrain from any reserved cases, and next to allow to all brothers and sisters a free liberty to hear the confession of secret sins; that the sinner may discover his sin to whom he pleases, when he is desirous of pardon and comfort, that is the word of Christ from the mouth of his neighbour. How unworthily they have treated satisfaction, he says, he has abundantly related in the causes of indulgences, where he has shewn how they have abused it to ruine Christians in both body and soul. First, they have so taught it, that the people never understand the true *satisfaction*, which is newness of life. Next, they so press it, and make it necessary, as not to leave any room for faith in Christ. But for these things, he referred to what he had said more at large of indulgences, and proceeded to attempt something of the other sacraments also, that he might not seem to have rejected them without cause.

Of Confirmation.
As for confirmation, he could not but wonder, he said, how it came into their minds to make a sacrament of it, from laying on of hands, with which we read Christ touched the little children, the Apostles gave the Holy Spirit, ordained presbyters, and cured the sick. Not that he condemned the sacraments, only he denied, that they could be proved from the Scriptures. But that now he was enquiring after sacraments of divine appointment, and he found no cause to reckon *confirmation* among *them*. And therefore he thought it was sufficient to account confirmation an ecclesiastical rite, or a sacramental ceremonie, like the other ceremonies of consecrating water and other things.

Of Matrimony.
Matrimony, he said, was taken for a sacrament, not only without any Scripture, but by the same traditions by which it was boasted to be a sacrament, it was made a

mere jest of. He therefore repeats what he had said before, that in every sacrament there was to be had the
word of God's promise, which ought to be believed by
him who receives the sign, and that the sign alone is not
a sacrament; he adds, that it is no where read, that whosoever marries a wife receives something of the grace of
God; nay, that even the sign in matrimony was not of
divine institution, nor was it any where read, that it was
instituted of God to signifie any thing, tho' all things
which are visibly transacted may be understood as figures
and allegories of things invisible : but a figure or allegorie,
he said, were not sacraments, as he spoke of sacraments.
Next, since matrimony was from the beginning of the
world, and still is among infidels, there can, he said, be
no reason for its being called a sacrament of the new
law and of the Church alone. To this, he observed, it
would be said, that the Apostle says, Ephe. v. *They two
shall be one flesh, this is a great * sacrament.* But this,
he replied, was an argument of great heedlessness, and
very careless reading. for that the whole Scripture had
not the name sacrament in that sense in which it was now
used, but to the contrary. Since it there signifies every
where not a *sign* of a holy thing, but a holy thing, secret
and hidden in the Greek *mysterie.* So in this place in the
Greek it is, they two shall be one flesh; *this is a great*
mysterie. But the translators here rendring this word
sacrament, he said, gave occasion for understanding this
to be a sacrament of the new law, which they would never
have done if they had read *mysterie*, as it is in the Greek.
So 1 Tim. III. the Apostle calls Christ a sacrament, saying, And *without controversy* or manifestly, [b]*great is the
sacrament*, i. e. the mysterie *which is manifested in the
flesh*, &c. Why have they not from hence drawn an
eighth sacrament of the new law, since they have so clear
an authority of St. Paul? for that they have been deceived

* Lat Vulg

[b] Et manifestè magnum pietatis sacramentum quod manifestatum est in
carne, &c. *Lat Vulg*

thro' their ignorance of things as well as words, and being carried away by only sounds. Christ therefore and the Church is a mysterie, that is a thing secret and great, which indeed might and ought to be figured by matrimonie as by a certain real allegorie : but matrimonie ought not from hence to be called a sacrament, since there is wanting both the institution and a divine promise, which integrate the sacrament. Having thus shewn, that matrimony is no sacrament, he next observed in what manner this kind of life, which was of divine institution, was entangled and toss'd up and down by the impious laws of men. There was, he said, a book of no little reputation, collected, like a sink, from the filth of all human traditions, which was entituled *The * Angelical Summ :* tho' it was rather a summ more than diabolical, in which, among infinite prodigies in which confessors are supposed to be instructed, eighteen impediments of matrimonie are reckoned up, which, if they are view'd with an impartial eye, we shall see the contrivers of them are of the number of those of whom the Apostle speaks, *giving heed to the spirits and doctrines of Devils, and forbidding to marry.* For what is it to forbid marrying, if this be not to invent so many impediments, and lay snares, that they may not come together, and to dissolve their marriage if they do. But by the benefit of these the Romans, he said, were become pedlers; since there was not one of these impediments but what by the intervention of Mammon might be made lawful; so that these laws of men seem'd to spring from no other cause than their being nets to catch money for covetous men and ravening Nimrods, and snares for souls. He therefore concluded, that the Pope or a Bishop, or an Official, if he shall dissolve any marriage contracted contrary to a human law, he is Antichriste, a violater of nature, and guilty of high treason against the Divine Majesty. Because the sentence, *What God has joined together let no man put asunder,* stands fast; and man has no authority to make such laws. Wherfore, that rigor of

impediments from affinity, from spiritual or legal kin and
consanguinity, ought here to give way, as far as the Scriptures permit, according to which only the second degree
of consanguinity is prohibited, and the first of affinity. So
likewise ought those baubles of godfatherhodes, godmo-
therhodes, &c. to be wholly extinct after the marriage
contract; since this spiritual kindred is nothing but the
invention of human superstition. But much vainer is the
legal kin, which yet they have set above the divine right
of matrimony. Nor should he, he said, consent to the
impediment, which they call a difference of religion, that
it should not be lawfull, neither absolutely, nor on condition of converting her to the faith, to marry a woman not
baptized. The same foolish, or rather profane rigor,
was, he said, what was called *the impediment of a crime,
viz.* when any one married a woman who had before been
polluted by adultery, or had contrived the death of another wife, that so he might be contracted to this. It was
likewise, he said, reckoned an impediment, which they
call *an impediment of the bond,* if any one be bound to
another by espousals Here they conclude, that if any
one knows the latter, the former espousals are void. This,
he said, he did not well understand; but believed, that a
man who was espoused to a former, could not with a safe
conscience cohabit with a second woman. The *impediment
of Order* also was, he said, a mere humane device, especially when they prate, that by it a contract is also dissolved, advancing their own traditions above the commandments of God. For he did not judge of the order of
priesthode as it was then, but he observed, that St. Paul
commanded, that a bishop should be the husband of one
wife, and therefore that the marriage of a deacon, priest,
bishop, or any order whatsoever, could not be dissolved.
Altho' St. Paul knew nothing of that sort of priests, and
those orders which they had then. It was equally a fiction. he said, to pretend an impediment of public honesty,
whereby to dissolve contracts. So far as he saw yet, there

was no impediment which could of right dissolve a contract, but impotency, ignorance of the man's being already
contracted, and a vow of chastity.   Yet of the vow he was
to that day so uncertain about it, that he was ignorant at
what time it was to be reckoned good, as he had said before in the sacrament of Baptism.   He concluded with
declaring, that he so abhorred a divorce, that he had
rather a man should have two wives than be divorced, tho'
whether that was lawful or not he dared not to determine.
However he wondred, that they forced a man who was
divorced from his wife to live single, and would not permit him to marry another.   He, for his part, he said, very
1 Cor. vii. much wished that of the Apostle took place here, *But if
the unbeliever depart, let him depart, a brother or sister is
not under bondage in such a case,* tho' in these matters he
defined nothing ; but if two learned and good men would
agree in the name of Christ, and pronounce in his spirit,
he should prefer their judgment to even that of councils,
however such as were then wont to be called, which had
neither learning nor holiness to recommend them, but
only numbers and authoritie.

Of Order.   The sacrament of Order, he said, the Church of Christ
knew nothing of it ; it was the invention of the Pope's
church.   But it was ridiculous to assert that for a sacrament of God which can no where be shewn to be instituted
by him.   The Church, he said, could not promise grace,
which was what pertained to God only, and therefore
could not institute a sacrament.   But that if she could do
it never so much, it would not yet presently follow, that
order is a sacrament.   Wherfore he allowed, that order
is a certain ecclesiastical rite, such as many others introduced by the fathers of the Church, as the consecration
of vessels, houses, &c. none of which does any one suppose
to be a sacrament, as having none of them in them any
promise.   To its being said, that Christ said at his last
supper, *This do in remembrance of me,* and by so saying
ordained his disciples priests, he replied, that Christ here

promises nothing, but only ordered that to be done in remembrance of him . that none of the fathers asserted, that
by these words priests were ordained. He added, that the
sacrament of order was, and is a very pretty machine for
the establishing all the prodigies which have been hitherto
done, and are yet done in the Church. But if the clergy
were forced to admit, that as many as are baptized are all
equally priests, as indeed they are, and that the ministry is
committed to them alone by their consent, they would at
the same time know, that they have not authority of command over them any farther, than they of their own accord admit them to have: and, that priests or ministers
are chosen from them to act or do things in their name ·
and that the sacrament of order is nothing else but a certain rite of electing a preacher. From hence he concluded, that he who did not preach the word when he
was called therto by the Church was not a priest, and
that they who are ordained to read hours and offer masses,
are indeed papistical, but not Christian priests; that is,
certain living idols having the name of priesthode, when
they are nothing less, but such priests as Heroboam
ordained of the meanest of the people at Bethaven, not of
the Levitical kind. But what, he said, made the captivity the greater was, the Popish clergy's distinguishing, or
separating themselves from other Christians, as if they
were profane, castrating themselves like the priests of
Cybel, and burdening themselves with a counterfeit single
life ; since it did not satisfie their hypocrisie to forbid
bigamie, or having two wives at once , but they interpreted
bigamie to mean the marrying two maids successively, or
one widow. Nay, to that degree was the most holy holiness of this most sacred sacrament carried, that he could
not be ordained a priest who had married a maid, so long
as she lived, nay, was driven from the priesthode, if he
ignorantly, and merely by an unhappy accident, married a
maid that was corrupted. But if he had had six hundred
whores, or had debauched as many matrons and virgins as

he pleased, or had maintained many Ganymedes, this was no impediment to his being made either a bishop or a cardinal, or a pope. He therefore advised young men, if they had a mind to live safely, to avoid this snare, and not to go into orders unless they had either a mind to preach, or could believe, that by this Sacrament of Order they were not made better than the laity; since among Christians all were alike priests, that is, had the same power in the word and sacraments : only it was not lawful for every one to use this power but by the consent of the community, or the calling of the majority. He concluded this head with the following observation, that since we are taught by the Scriptures that the ministry is that which we call the priesthode, he did not at all see why he who was once ordained a priest, might not agen become a laic, since a priest differed nothing from a laic but in the ministry.

Of the Sacrament of extreme Unction.

As to the rite of anointing the sick, our divines, he observed, had made two additions to it worthy of themselves. One, that they called it a sacrament; the other, that they made it the last, and that it was now the sacrament of the last anointing which ought not to be used but to those who are in the last moments of life ; tho' perhaps they made it a relative to the *first* anointing of Baptism, and the *two* following anointings of Confirmation and Order. But here, says he, they have to fling in my face, that by the authority of the Apostle James here is a promise and a sign, in which I have before said that a sacrament consists. For he says, *If any of you be sick, let him call for the Elders of the Church, and they shall pray over him, anointing him with oil in the name of the Lord, and the prayer of faith shall save the sick, and the Lord shall raise him up, and if he have committed sins they shall be forgiven him.* See, say they, the promise of forgiveness of sins, and the sign of oil ! But to this he answered, that if ever there was any dotage, it was especially shewn here. Since, not to insist on what many have with great proba-

v. 14, 15.

bility asserted, that this *epistle is not the Apostle James's, nor worthy of an apostolical spirit, altho' by custom it has obtained an authority, such an one as it is. If it was the Apostle's, he would say, that it was not lawful for an Apostle by his own authoritie to institute a sacrament, i. e. to give a divine promise with a sign added to it, since this pertains to Christ alone. that they who have made this sacrament have shewn no regard to the Apostle's words, which make this anointing to be general to all who are sick, wheras they make it singular and extreme to be used only to those who are a dying the promise of the Apostle says expressly, the *prayer of faith shall save the sick, and the Lord shall raise him up,* &c. by which its intimated, that this anointing is not to be the last; wheras the Papists say, that this anointing is to be used only to those who are a dying, i. e that they may not be healed and raised up. Agen, if that unction was a sacrament, it ought without doubt, as they say, to be an effectual sign of that which it signs and promises; but now it promises the health and restoration of the sick person: and yet who does not see, that this promise is fulfilled in few or none? for if it be the last anointing, it does not heal, but give way to the sickness: and if it does heal it, it ought not to be the last. That saying of the Apostle, he said, was therefore verified in the assertors of this sacrament, that *they would be teachers of the Law when they knew not what they said, nor wherof they affirmed:* he added, that they did not observe the Apostles order to call the elders of the Church to pray over the sick person, since scarce one little priest was now sent, when the Apostle would have many present, and that not to anoint the sick person, but to pray over him· altho' he doubted whether by elders the Apostle meant priests, or elder and graver per-

---

* This gave occasion to some of the Roman Catholic writers to report of Luther, that he denied St. James's Epistle In his preface to the first edition of his German Bible, 1526, he called it an Epistle of Straw, if compared with the Epistles of St. Paul and St. Peter *Grego Martin's Discovery, &c.*

sons in the Church. He supposed therfore, that this anointing was the same with that mentioned in the last chapter of Mark, they *anointed with oil many that were sick, and healed them: viz.* a certain rite of the primitive Church, by which miracles were done on the sick, which now for some time has ceased. However, he said, he did not condemn this their sacrament of the last anointing, but only denied, that it was prescribed by the Apostle: nor did he deny, that by extreme unction was given remission and peace; but not because it was a sacrament of divine institution, but because he who received it believed it was so done. He added, that there were besides some other things which seem'd to be capable of being reckoned among the sacraments, *viz.* all those things to which a divine promise is made, as prayer, the word, the cross. Yet if we would speak strictly, there are only two sacraments in God's Church, Baptism and Bread, since in these alone do we see the sign divinely instituted, and a promise of forgiveness of sins. For as to the Sacrament of Penance, which he had added to these two, it wanted a visible sign of divine institution, and was no other than, as he had said before, the way and return to baptism. In the conclusion he willingly and gladly offered this prelude to all devout persons who desired to know the sound meaning of Scripture and the genuine use of sacraments, and observed, that he heard there were prepared against him forthwith papistical bulls and curses, to drive him to a retractation, or declare him an heretic: which, if true, he willed, he said, this little book to be a part of his future retractation, that they might not complain of their tyrannies being blown up in vain, and intended shortly to publish such a *second* part, as the See of Rome had hitherto neither seen nor heard, as an abundant testimony of his obedience.

Dr. Luther's expectations of the Papists being throly incensed and provoked by this little book were very fully answered. They not only published their bulls and ana-

themas against him, but did all they could to expose and
blacken him by the falsest and most malicious reproaches
which their passion and desire of revenge could furnish
them with, Among these one was, that Luther should
write in this book, that *If the wife cannot or will not, let
the maid come and take her place.* Whereas there is nothing to this purpose in it. In considering the case indeed
of a woman married to an impotent man, and not willing
judicially to prove the man's impotency, and yet being
desirous of children, and not able to contain, he proposes,
that with the man's consent, who is to be considered not
as an husband, but as a single person living with her, she
should keep company with another, *being married to
him privately, and that the children should be reckoned
the reputed father's. For which he gives this reason, that
the ignorance of the man's impotency does in this case
hinder the marriage, and the tyrannie of the laws does not
admit of a divorce, and the woman is by the law of God
at liberty, and cannot be compelled to continency. However, I think, it must be owned there are some expressions
in this book which are too rude and coarse, and which can
scarce be reconciled to that purity and modesty which the
Christian religion requires: unless we are to impute this
his manner of writing to the fashion of his time, and the
Germans broad way of speaking.

3. Cardinal Wolsey, having a mind to engage the King
to act against Luther, whose opinions daily [f]spread and
got ground here in England, contrived that an answer
should be written to this book, which the King should
own for his, and be presented to the Pope in his name.
A copy of this book the Cardinal ordered to be written in
a very fair and beautiful character, and to be very splen-
didly bound, for a present to be made to the Pope, which,
when done, he brought to the King for his approbation.

CHAP.
XI

Dr. Martin
against
priests
marriage

* occulto
tamen ma-
trimonio.

[f] This was ascribed to the impression which Dr. Wiclif's books, and those
of his followers, together with their Translation of the Scriptures into
English, had made on the minds of the clergy and people.

CHAP.
XI.

The book was accordingly presented to Pope Leo by the King's ambassador at Rome, who delivered it into the Pope's own hands in a solemn assembly of the cardinals. At the same time the ambassador made a speech to his Holiness, which was immediately answered by him extempore; and to shew his most grateful acceptance of the present made him, and in testimony thereof, he gave the King the title of *Defender of the Faith.* To make this appear the more grand and important, a solemn embassy was sent by the Pope to the King, and an *Acte* in bull under lead declaring his Grace to be the *Defender of the Christian Faith,* and his successors for ever. Of this title thus conferred on him by the Pope, the King shewed himself not a little fond. For instance, in his [g]letters of privilege granted soon after for the sole printing our Bishop's book, entituled, *A Confutation of the Lutheran assertion,* His Majesty thus expressed himself: *Of which Catholic Church and Christian faith we have undertaken the defence, even as we are obliged by the surname lately given us by the late Pope Leo X. of pious memorie.* And yet it's certain this was no new title, but had been claimed and used long before by King Richard II. in the commissions granted by him for the apprehending and imprisoning those who taught or maintained the conclusions of Dr. Wiclif. Nos *zelo* fidei Catholicæ cujus sumus et esse volumus Defensores *in omnibus—commoti.* As to the book, it was soon after printed in 4° here in England, with the title prefixed which I have put in [h]the margin.

Hall's
HenryVIII.
fol. 80, b.

g —— Nos igitur hujusmodi fraudibus occurrere —— in iis præsertim promovendis operibus quæ pro Ecclesia Catholica et fide Christiana militant, cujus nos defensionem suscepimus, quemadmodum ex cognomento nobis a summo pontifice piæ Memoriæ Leone decimo nuper in ito tenemur. Ideoque Religionis et Ecclesiæ susceptum esse gaudemus patrocinium ab Antistite Roffensi.

h Assertio septem Sacramentorum adversus Martinum Lutherum edita ab invictissimo Angliæ et Franciæ Rege, et Domino Hyberniæ Henrico ejus nominis octavo, in ædibus Pynsonianis 4° Idus Julij apud inclytam urbem Londinum, 1521.

Concerning this book, it has been much disputed whether it was actually written by the King himself. On the one side, it's said, that the King, in answer to Luther's letter, which intimated, that Lee, Archbishop of York, was the compiler of it, owned it to be his: that Sir Thomas More, in a letter to Mr. Secretary Cromwell, shewed, that he knew the book was written by the King's own pen, and that in the composition of it, he was governed by his own sentiment. Erasmus, in answer to the report of *his* being the author of this book, declared, that he could never find out by whose labour the King was assisted; that the phrase was his own, and that he had a happy and ready genius for every thing; that but a few years before he wrote a theological disputation on the question, *Whether a lay-man was obliged to vocal prayer?* and took delight in the books of the school divines, and would often at meals discourse of subjects in divinity: that if the stile of the book was not unlike *his*, the reason might be, that the King, when a boy, read nothing with more pleasure and application than *his* Lucubrations, from whence perhaps he had contracted an ill way of speaking, if yet he had any thing of *his*. On the other hand it's argued, that this book was written by the King, as other books were under his name, that is, by his bishops or other learned men, of which, Erasmus observed, his court was full, or with which it was [1]crowded, and was perused perhaps, and corrected by the King: that Sir Thomas More gave this account of the book to his son-in-law Rooper, that *after it was finished, by his Grace's appointment, and consent of the makers of the same, he was only a sorter out, and placer of the principal matters therin contained,* and that this testimony of his may with much more reason be taken from this account given by one to whom he communicated his inward thoughts, than from a letter to a minister of state, where he was to speak with the vulgar · that as to

App to the History of the Reformat. vol ii p. 404. Rooper's Life of Sir Thos More

[1] —— si quid voluisset uti doctorum auxiliis, habet Aulam differtam viris disertis et eruditis.

the stile of the book, it was nothing like the King's, who did not use to write so pure and elegant Latin; but it agreed with Bishop Fisher's, which was so like his friend Erasmus's, as to be mistaken for *his*, as particularly in his answer to Faber. For proof of this, is produced a part of the King's correction of the definition of the Church, printed by the Bishop of Sarum at the end of his Addenda to vol. i. of his History of the Reformation, *viz. Cum quâ* [Ecclesia] *nec pontifex Romanus, nec quivis aliquis prælatus aut pontifex habet quicquam agere præterquam in suas Dioceses.* And therefore when Erasmus owns, that the King might have hit upon *his* stile, it's supposed to be done in mirth. But however this be,[k]

4. This book was dedicated to Pope Leo, whom the King [l]stiles his most holy Lord, and to whom he wishes perpetual felicity. In this dedication, he told the Pope, that the reason why he, who had spent his youth in warlike and political studies for the sake of the commonwealth, undertook this task, which required a life spent in learning, was, that he saw tares sown in the Lord's harvest, sects sprout, heresies in the faith spring and grow up, and so much matter of discord sown throughout the Christian world, that no one who was a sincere or sound Christian, could longer bear so great mischiefs dispersing themselves so far and near, but he must set himself to oppose them, and use his endeavours, how mean soever they are, for that purpose.

5. In the preface to the reader, he does all he can to set him against Luther, and possess him with the most vile opinion of him. For this purpose is Luther stiled an enemy, than which it's impossible for any more malignant one to arise, who, by the instinct of the Devil, pretending

---

[k] By Cardinal Bellarmine, in his book *de Scriptoribus Ecclesiasticis,* is this book ascribed to Bishop Fisher, and it is published in the Collection of his Works printed in Latin.

[l] Sanctissimo Domino nostro Domino Leoni X. pont. max: Henricus Dei gratia Rex Angliæ ac Dominus Hyberniæ, perpetuam felicitatem.

charity, is spurred up by hatred and anger, and has vo-
mited up the poison of vipers against the Church and the
Catholic faith.   Then he calls him the common enemy of
the Christian faith, a detestable trumpeter of arrogance,
contumelie and schism ; a wolf of hell, who seeks to dis-
perse the flock of Christ; a member of the Devil, who
seeks to pluck Christians, the members of Christ, from
their head : then he exclaimed, How stark naught is this
mans mind! how cursed his design! who both revives
schisms long since dead and buried, and adds new ones to
the old, and brings forth into the light, as it were, Cerberus
from hell, heresies to be covered with eternal darkness,
and reckons himself sufficient by his bare word, to direct
or rather to subvert the universal Church, treating all the
ancients with the utmost neglect.   But, as if this was not
enough, the writer further tells the readers, that he is at a
loss what to say of Luther's wickedness, which he thinks
so great, as no tongue nor pen can possibly express it.
Next, he shews himself displeased with Luther for giving
his book the title *Of the Babilonish Captivity of the
Church*, calls him an envenomed serpent, and tells his
readers, that ^mof his own head Luther wrests the Holy
Scripture against the sacraments of Christ; eludes the
ecclesiastical rites delivered down by the ancient fathers ;
shews no regard to, but makes light of, the most holy
men, the most ancient interpreters of the Holy Scriptures,
any farther than they are of his mind; calls the Holy
Roman See Babylon: the popedom tyranny; reckons the
decrees of the whole Church a captivity, and changes the
name of the Pope into Antichrist.   The writer concludes
with exhorting, praying, and, by the name of Christ, which

^m Scripturam Sacram ex suo sensu contra Christi Sacramenta detorquet,
traditos ab antiquis patribus ecclesiasticos ritus eludit; sanctissimos viros,
vetustissimos Sacrarum Literarum interpretes, nisi quatenus ipsius sensui
conveniunt et consentiunt, nihili pendit ; Sacrosanctam sedem Romanam
Babylonem appellat; summum pontificum vocat tyrannidem ; totius Ecclesiæ decreta *Captivitatem* censet, sanctissimi pontificis nomen in Antichris-
tum convertit

we profess, beseeching all faithful Christians to look into Luther's works with caution and discretion, if so be *he* be the author of the Babylonish Captivity.

6. In the book itself are set down the two following assertions, as taken from this book of Luther's which are here opposed by the writers of it.

I. Indulgencies are the frauds or tricks of the Roman flatterers.

II. The papacy is a robust hunting of the Roman pontiff.

The design of these is here said to be altogether to take away indulgences and the power of the Pope : upon which account the King reckons them impious, and no other than preparatory to the destruction of the sacraments.

7. On the *first* of these assertions it's here remarked, that as every animal is chiefly distinguished by his countenance, so it appears by this first proposition what a festered and corrupted heart *he* has whose mouth is so full of bitterness, and overflows with such filthy matter. Luther, say the makers, has not advanced in learning, as himself says, but in malice, contradicting himself, condemning indulgences wholly, and declaring they are nothing else but mere impostures, good for nothing but to spend men's money, and destroy the faith of God. It's to no purpose, say they, to talk with *him* of the means whereby we are delivered out of purgatory, who almost takes away the whole of purgatory. But however the indulgences of the Pope may be disputed, the words of Christ which he spake to Peter, to whom he committed the keys of the Church, will necessarily remain unshaken. By which words, if it be sufficiently plain, that every priest hath a power of absolving from mortal sin, and of discharging the eternity of the punishment, who will not think it absurd that the prince of all priests should have no authority over a temporal punishment?

8. To the *second* assertion, its observed, that the Pope's authority is not to be treated of as if it was any ways to be

doubted, but that the enemy of it, Luther, is so trans- ported with fury, as to destroy his own credit, and plainly to shew, that his spite will not suffer him to be consistent with himself, nor to know what he says that he cannot deny, that every Christian Church recognizes and reverences the holy see of Rome as its mother and primate, every one, at least, which is not kept from having access to it by either the distance of places, or the hazards which interpose: that even the Indians themselves, though separated from it by such large tracts of seas, lands, and deserts, yet submit themselves to the Roman pontiff: that we shall find Greece itself, though they had the empire transferred to them, yet to have yielded to the Church of Rome in the matter of the primacy. that this jurisdiction of the Pope's is so ancient, as that the rise or original of it is quite forgot, and is therefore to be reckoned legitimate.

9. It's further remarked, that Luther of *seven* sacraments leaves only *three*, and that he treats of *them* in such a manner as to leave no room for doubt, that it was his intention in time to demolish *them*. That in speaking of the Sacrament of the Altar, he alters its name, and calls it the Sacrament of Bread: that, under pretence of shewing favour to the laity, he attempts to raise in them an hatred of the priests, whom he calls impious, and represents as guilty of treason against the Gospel · that he admits nothing as proof but plain or evident Scriptures; and that if he was consistent with himself, he should therefore order the Eucharist to be received after supper. For this Luther's chief and principal argument is said to be, that there should be no violence offered to the word of God, but that, as far as possible, it should be observed in the most simple signification. But that violence is offered to the divine words, if what Christ himself calls bread, this we say is to be understood to be the accidents of bread, and what he calls wine, this we say is only the species of wine: therefore, always true bread and true wine remains on the altar, that so no force be done to Christ's words, as there must be if the species be taken for the substance.

I

To this, it's here answered, that the Evangelists, though
they speak plainly, do not yet prove any thing clearly for
Luther, but, on the contrary, that which they should
prove for him they never say: that it's acknowledged, that
they say, that Christ *took* bread and blessed, but that he
gave bread to his disciples, after he had by blessing it
made it his body; this is instantly denied, and what the
Evangelists don't say. On the contrary, in every place of
their writings, where they mention this thing, the sacrament after consecration is called only Christ's body and
blood, not bread and wine. They say Christ took bread,
that which is owned by all, but when the Apostles received it, it is not named [n] bread, but his body. But it is
not here remembered, that Christ brake the bread *after*
he had given thanks or blessed God.

10. To Luther's objection, that the Evangelists' words
are, *This* cup *is the New Testament in my blood*, not *This*
wine *is my blood*, it is answered, that it's a wonder the man
is not ashamed of so intemperate a folly. For what else
does this signifie than, that what he drank of to his disciples in the cup was his blood? To Luther's adding, that
this opinion of *transubstantiation* was not 300 years old,
it's replied, that no body will contend with him about the
word, provided he will own the thing meant by it, *viz.*
that the bread is so changed into flesh, and the wine into
blood, that nothing remains of either the bread or the
wine but the species: that after the Church has decreed
this to be true, though it should decree it so but now, yet,
if the ancients did not believe the contrary, the present
decree of the whole Church ought to be obeyed, on this
persuasion, that "*that is now, at length, revealed to the*
"*Church, which before lay hidden:*" for the spirit, as it
breathes *where* it lists, so it also breathes *when* it lists.
But that this opinion is not so new as Luther feigned;
that he ought to allow, at least, 400 years.

---

[n] This is a fallacy which imposed on Luther himself. Christ no where
says, *this bread* is my body, but only, *this thing* is my body, as Moses says,
This thing is the Lord's passover, i.e. a memorial or remembrance of it

11. Luther is next represented as a man more than ordinary sacrilegious, in that he attempted to take away the chief and only propitiatory sacrifice of God, which is continually offered for the sins of the people; and it's observed, that in this one does not know which is most to be admired, the man's impiety, or his very foolish hope, or rather his mad pride, who, when he himself sees so many obstacles in his way, does nothing to remove any of them but acts, as if he was a going to dig through rocks with a reed: since he confessed, that the opinions of the fathers, the canon of the mass, and the whole custom of all the Church, confirmed by the use of so many ages, and the consent of so many people, were all against him. His main argument is here said to be, that the Holy Eucharist is a testament, and that a testament is a promise of one going to die, wherby he bequeaths an estate, and appoints his heirs: that this sacrament is therfore no more than the testament of Christ, or a promise of an eternal inheritance to us Christians, whom he makes his heirs, adding his body and blood, as a sign of the promise being confirmed; and that from hence he infers, that the mass cannot be either a good or meritorious work or a sacrifice. In answer to this, it's said, that Christ, at that most holy supper at which he instituted that sacrament, made his body and blood out of bread and wine, and delivered them to his disciples to be eaten and drunk; that then within a few hours after he offered the same body and the same blood on the altar of the cross for a sacrifice to his father for the sins of the people; which sacrifice being finished, the testament was completed. At supper, being near unto death, he, as dying people are wont to do, declared his mind by a certain testament what he would have done in remembrance of him after he was dead. Instituting therfore the sacrament, when he had exhibited to his disciples his body and blood, he said to them, *Do ye this in remembrance of me.*

12. Luther had agen argued, as it's here said, that

homo plus-
quam sacri-
legus.

Christ at his last supper, when he instituted this sacrament, and made his Will or Testament, did not offer himself to God, but sitting at the table, declared the same Will to his disciples, and exhibited a sign. To which, arguing from Christ's example, it's here replied, that if Luther will keep us so strictly to the pattern or example of the Lord's Supper, that he will allow priests to do nothing that Christ is not read to have done, they must never themselves receive the sacrament which they consecrate. Wherfore, if he owns, that priests at mass do right in receiving what they consecrate, altho' there be no plain Scripture for it, he need not wonder if the priests offer Christ to the Father, which the Scripture clearly testifies in more places than one Christ did on the cross. To Luther's last argument, that it is inconsistent that the mass should be a sacrifice because we receive it, and the same thing cannot be both offered and received together, nor be given and taken together by the same person, it is asked, Was there ever a sacrifice under the Mosaical Law which *they* did not receive who offered it? Did not God himself eat that which was offered to him? Besides, if Christ was both the priest and the sacrifice, why could not Christ appoint, that the priest who represented the same sacrifice might both offer and receive the victim? This head is concluded with observing: 1. That Luther professedly despised the canons of the Church, and the authority of the fathers; that those very holy men saw, that as this sacrament is the chief of all the sacraments, because it contains the Lord of the sacraments; so of all the sacrifices this is the only one which alone remains in the room of so many sacrifices which were wont heretofore to be offered; and lastly, that it is by much the most salutary of all the works which can be done for the people's salvation. 2. That Luther changed the name of the sacrament for a worse; and when for so many ages past it has been called the Eucharist, or the Sacrament of Christ's body, *he*, that the same might not put the hearers in mind

of the majesty of the thing, will have it called bread.
3. Next, that the bread and wine, which the ancients
owned were turned into the body and blood of Christ,
Luther taught, that they still continued intire or un-
changed, that so by little and little he might transfer the
honour from Christ to the bread. 4. Agen, tho' he condemned not the Church for adorning and enlarging the
mass with rites and ceremonies, yet he thought it would
be much more Christian if the pomp of vestments, of
chaunting, of gestures, and all the other ceremonies was
taken away, that it might be nearer and more like the first
mass of all which Christ celebrated at his last supper with
the Apostles; but, in truth, that as little as possible might
remain of those things which move the simple minds of
the common people, and stir them up by the majesty of a
visible honour to a veneration of the invisible Deity.
5 That besides all this, Luther taught, and always incul-
cated, that the mass is not a good work, that it is neither a sacrifice nor offering, and that it is altogether
useless to the people, and that his design in this was, to
persuade the people to withdraw themselves wholly from
it, and entirely neglect it as of no use to *them*, and leave it
to the *priest* only. Lastly, that if they do at any time
communicate, all that Luther says they have to do is, to
believe that by so doing they are partakers, or have a
share, of the testament: that after teaching this brief and
compendious preparation for receiving the Eucharist, to
wit, a bare belief of the promises without any good works,
or the least examination of their consciences, he declared
his opinion how often and at what times of the year he
would have the people obliged to receive the communion,
namely, at none at all. For to what else do these things
tend, but by degrees to make the people leave off altogether the communion of this sacrament, which has already
dwindled from a daily communion to every Lord's day's,
then to a more distant time, till, at length, the fathers of
the Church, apprehending it would be wholly laid aside,

obliged people to communicate three times a year, and
threatned that they should not be accounted Christians
who did not comply with that provision. That Luther
trifled about things well known as if they were new; that
he extol'd the riches of faith, that he might make us poor
in good works, and so commended faith to us, as not only
to permit a vacation from good works, but to encourage
men to do some wicked ones: that he so magnified faith
as almost to seem to insinuate, that faith alone without the
sacrament is sufficient; and that the sacrament itself
avails nothing; that sacraments do not confer grace, nor
are not the effectual signs of grace: that he took away all
the power and authority of princes and prelates, and was
very angry with the Pope (the successor of Peter and
Vicar of Christ, to whom Christ, as to the Prince of the
Apostles, committed the keys of the Church, that others
might by him enter into it and be cast out of it) for his in-
dicting a fast and ordering of prayers.

13. The remainder of the book treats of the following
subjects, *viz.* of *Penance*, of *Contrition*, of *Confession*, of
Satisfaction, of *Confirmation*, of the Sacraments of *Matrimony*, *Order*, and *Extreme Unction*, in answer to what
Luther had said on those heads.

Of Penance *or* Repentance.

Here, it's observed agen, that it's Luther's way to propose as a new thing what is very well known to every
body: thus he asserts the necessity of our having faith in
God's promise of forgiveness of sins to the penitent, and
then inveighs against the Church for not teaching that
faith. It's therfore asked, who persuades any one to the
repentance of Judas, that he should lament what he has
done, and yet have no hopes of pardon? who ever taught
that we must pray for forgiveness, and did not teach that
forgiveness is promised to the penitent? what is preached
oftener than that God is of such immense clemency, that
he denys mercy to no one, tho' never so wicked, if he

amends his life? Has nobody but Luther ever read, *At*
whatsoever time the sinner repenteth he shall be saved?

Of Contrition.

Luther here, it's said, treats of the three parts of penance, *viz.* contrition, confession, and satisfaction, in such
a manner as to make it sufficiently plain that none of
them are enough pleasing to him. For first he is angry
at contrition, and calls the wrath of God insupportable,
because room is made for attrition, and God is believed,
in case of sorrow not vehement enough of itself, to supply
by the sacrament what is defective in man. He teaches
contrition to be a great thing, and not easily to be come
at. He bids all men to be well assured, and to believe,
without any mixture of doubting, that on account of the
word of promise, all sins shall be forgiven them, and
themselves loosed by God in heaven, after that they have
been loosed by the mouth of man on earth. In which
matter, the King observes, his assertion is either the same
with that which he finds fault with, or much more absurd: for God has promised to remit sins by repentance
either to those only who are before contrite in proportion
to the weight of their sin, or to those also who are less
contrite, or lastly, to those who have no contrition at all.
If he has not promised any farther than to those who are
contrite, so far as the greatness of the sin requires, Luther
cannot be certain, and without doubt that he is forgiven;
which yet is what he bids all others to be: for how can
he know that he obtains the promise who cannot know
that he is sufficiently contrite? and no mortal can know
how much contrition a mortal sin requires. If God has
promised pardon to those who are but a little contrite, in
proportion to the bulk of their sins, then has he promised
pardon to those whom they whom Luther opposes call
attrite, and so he agrees with those he finds fault with.
But if God has promised forgiveness to those who do not
grieve at all for their sins, much more has he promised it

to those who are attrite, i. e. to those who do grieve in
some measure, tho' not so much as the greatness of their
sins requires; wherfore, if he only admits of contrition, or
a sufficient sorrow, no body can be certain of his being
forgiven. If he allows, that to one whose sins are not
otherwise remitted on account of his lukewarm and remiss
grief, to him they are remitted by the Sacrament of Penance on his confessing himself a sinner, asking pardon,
and obtaining it by the mouth of a brother, what else does
he say, but what they think to whom he opposes himself?
who affirm that of attrition, through the sacrament's in-
tervening, is made contrition: for that the sacrament
supplys what is wanting in man. Again, says the King,
or the writers in his name, with pompous words Luther
attacks the whole Church, as if it perversely taught contrition, whilst we are taught out of a recollection and
sight of our sins to prepare contrition, when, as he says,
we ought first to be taught the beginning and causes of
contrition, to wit, the unmoveable truth of the divine promises and threats: as if such things were not every where
said to the people!

Of Confession.

This, the King says, Luther so treats, as to require
confession where there is the least occasion, *viz.* in public
crimes, which are known to the people without confession: but as to the confession of secret sins, he is so
wavering, that tho' he does not altogether reject it, he
leaves it uncertain whether it should be received or not
for a thing commanded and required. He denys, that it
can be proved by Scripture, but yet says, he is pleased
with it, and that it is profitable and necessary; tho' not to
all, but only to quiet afflicted consciences; the meaning of
which, the King thinks, is, that if any one has a conscience like his, which is secure of its own sanctity, or certain
of the word of divine promise, he has no need to confess
his secret sins: otherwise, if any one be fearful or scrupu-

lous, confession is requisite to pacify or quiet his conscience. The King proceeds to shew from Scripture the
necessity of confession of secret sins: as from Ecclesiast.
xxxviii. which, he says, does not seem to him alone to
contain the three parts of repentance. *My son, in thy
weakness do not neglect thy self, but worship the Lord,
and he will cure thee. Leave off from sin, and order thy
hands aright, and cleanse thy heart from all wickedness.*
He likewise quotes Psalm lxi, as it is numbred in the Psalm
Latine Vulgate, *Ye people pour out your heart before him.* lxii. 8
Prov. xxvi. *Be thou diligent to* know *the state of thy
flocks, and look well to thy herds.* For how, says he, can
any one *know* if it be not declared to him? Numbers, v.
*And the Lord spake unto Moses, saying, speak unto the
children of Israel, when a man or woman shall commit any
sin — then they shall confess their sin which they have
done.* Hitherto likewise appertains, he observes, that
which is in the old law of the Jews, to whom all things
were represented in figure, of those who were infected
with the leprosie being ordered to shew themselves to the
priests. For if God therfore wrote in the law, *thou shalt
not muzzle the mouth of the ox that threshes out the corn,*
that he might admonish us of the equity of *their* living of
the altar who serve the altar, there is no room for any one
to doubt, that by that bodily leprosie in that carnal law
is signified sin in the law spiritual. Into which meaning,
that Christ might by little and little lead us, he says to the
leprous persons, *Go ye, shew yourselves to the priests.*
Does not that likewise plainly make for confession which
the Lord says by Esaia, *Thou tell thine iniquities that thou* chap xliii.
mayst be justified: so it is in the Latine Vulgate, tho' in 9.
the °Hebrew it be read, *Let them bring forth their witnesses that they may be justified.* From the New Testa-

---

° This seems one proof of this book being wrote by our Bishop, who, as
Wakfeld told him, *thought himself skilled in Hebrew, and was willing to be
reckoned so by others.* Wheras the King was so far from understanding
Hebrew that he could not write good Latin.

CHAP.
XI.

ment His Majesty quoted those words of St. James, chap. v. *Confess your faults one to another;* which, he said, seem'd to him, and not to him only, a command of sacramental confession. To these authoritys from the Scripture and apocryphal writings, His Majestie added the following quotations from some of the fathers, which he supposes will have their weight with those who respect their authority. St. Ambrose, he observes, says, *No one can be justified from sin unless he shall have confessed that sin.* John Chrysostome, that *it is impossible for a man to receive the grace of God, unless he be cleansed from all sin by confession.* Lastly, St. Augustine says, *Repent as it's done in the Church; let no one say to himself I do it secretly because I do it before God. At this rate, it's said without cause,* Whatsoever ye shall lose in earth: *without cause are the keys given.* But, says the King, if there was not a word to be read of confession neither by name nor in figure, nor any thing said of it by the holy fathers, yet when I see all the people for so many ages opening their sins to the priests, when I see so much good accruing from their so doing, and no evil arising from it, I cannot believe nor think any other, than that *that* thing was not constituted and observed by any human counsel, but by a command plainly divine. Since the people could never be induced by any human authority so readily to discover to others with so great shame and peril the most secret wickednesses for which they abhorr'd themselves, and which it was so much their concern and interest to keep private and unknown. Nor could it be, when there are so great numbers of priests good and bad who hear confessions promiscuously, that they who blab every thing else, should conceal what they hear in confession, if God himself, who instituted the sacrament, did not defend so wholsome an appointment by his special grace. His Majesty adds, that Luther condemn'd the reservations of sins, by which it is interdicted, that no one priest remit all sins, but that some should require the hand of the Bishop,

and some even that of the Pope. His design in this, the
King says, is so to level all things, in order to make himself popular, as out of hatred to the Pope to reduce all
bishops to the class of the most inferiour priests. This
reservation, the King observes, was to deter the people
from sinning, by letting them see, that a pardon was not
to be obtained at any rate: but Luther, that no one might
be kept from sinning by the difficulty of penance, gives
every one a liberty of doing what they please, nay, was,
he says, arrived at that height of folly as that, tho' women
bear an ill character as touching their keeping secrets, he
would have *them* to hear men's confessions. Luther is
likewise here charged with persuading people not to take
much care to recollect their sins, which indeed, the King
says, is not very necessary when we are to confess them to
women, who have a passage so open from their ears to
their tongues. Otherwise, when the thing might be done
without any such hazard, he should not doubt to prefer
the example of the prophet to Luther's counsel, [p]*I will* Is. xxxviii.
recollect before thee all my years in bitterness, as it is in
the Latin Vulgate; but in the Hebrew, *I shall go softly
all my years in the bitterness of my soul.*

Of Satisfaction.

Whether Luther satisfies any one about satisfaction, the
King says he does not know; to him, it seems, as if rather
than say nothing, he had used abundance of words to no
manner of purpose. For, first of all, what he says, that
the Church does so teach satisfaction that the people do
not understand the true satisfaction, which is newness of
life, it's a mere calumny. Who has taught Luther that
the Church does not teach that men's lives ought to be renewed? *He* has not gone all over the Church, nor been

[p] So the makers of this book read this text. But in the several editions
of the Latin Vulgate, 1532-1549, it is *Recogitabo omnes annos meos in amari-
tudine* animæ meæ . and in that of 1543, 8°. *Recogitabo tibi* —— and in the
margin *Tristis incedam*

present at all confessions, to be an ear-witness of this ignorance of the priests.   He must needs therfore either have
the Holy Spirit in his bosom, or some devil in his heart
to inspire him with this falshood.   For who was ever such
a blockhead, as to enjoin works satisfactory for sins past,
on purpose to give indulgence to the commission of them
for the time to come ?   Who does not constantly, when he
gives absolution, repeat those words of Christ, *Go, and sin
no more ;* and that passage of Saint Paul, *As ye have
yielded your members servants to uncleanness, and to iniquity unto iniquity, even so now yield your members servants to righteousness unto holiness ?*   Who does not read
that of St. Gregory, *we cannot worthily repent unless we
also know the measure of that repentance.*   For that to repent is to bewail our sins, and not again to perpetrate what
we have bewailed.   The King next observes, that Luther
very loudly declaims against the Roman See in the following manner.   What monsters do we owe to thee, O See
of Rome! and to thy murdering laws and rites, by which
thou hast brought the world to this pass, that they fancy
they can make satisfaction to God for sins by works, when
he is to be satisfied by the faith alone of a contrite heart!
which faith thou by these tumults dost not only cause to
be suppressed, but also oppressest, only that thou mayst
have thy insatiable blood-sucking desire, and make a sale
of sins ?   But first of all, says the King, how ridiculous is
this exclamation of his against the See of Rome? as if at
Rome only, and not in every church throughout the
whole world, works of satisfaction were exacted, and penance enjoined ; or as if the laws, which he calls murdering ones, were not many of them published long ago by
the ancient fathers, and the public consent of Christians
in synods and general councils.   Then when he says, that
satisfaction is not made to God by works but by faith
alone, if his meaning be, that God is not satisfied by works
alone without faith, he foolishly inveighs against the See
of Rome, in which no one was ever so foolish as to say

that works without faith will satisfie; since nobody is
ignorant of that of St. Paul, *Whatsoever is not of faith is*
sin. But if he thinks works superfluous, and, that faith
alone is sufficient, whatever the works are, then he says
something, and truly dissents from the Roman See, which
believes St. James, that *faith without works is dead.* But
indeed, says the King, it's Luther's real opinion, that faith
is alwaies sufficient to salvation without good works. That
these are his thoughts is plain, as from many other places,
so from that where he says, *God cares not for works, nor*
needs them, but he wants to be reckoned by us faithful in
that he has promised. By which words, adds his Majesty,
what Luther means let him look to it. I do certainly believe that God cares for or regards both our faith and our
works, tho' he stands in need of neither of them. But
because Luther seems to aim at this, that the penitent of
himself may enter on a new life, altho' he neglect to receive penance from a priest for satisfaction of the sins he
has committed, let us hear what Saint Augustine says to
this purpose. *It is not enough,* says he, *to amend our*
manners, and to depart from the evils that are past, unless
also satisfaction be made to the Lord for those things
which we have done, by a penitential sorrow, an humble
lamentation, and the sacrifice of a contrite heart, accom-
panied with fasting and prayer. And elsewhere, *Let the*
penitent, says he, *put himself entirely under the judgment*
and power of the priest, reserving nothing of himself to
himself, that he may be ready, at his command, to do every
thing for saving the life of his soul, which he would do to
prevent the death of his body. Agen, *The priests,* says he,
bind also when they impose the satisfaction of penance on
those who confess to them, and lose when they dismiss them
from it, or discharge them from any part of it. For they
do a work of justice on sinners when they bind them in a
just punishment, and a work of mercy to them when they
relax any thing of it. His Majesty concludes with saying, that he trusts he has plainly shewn how rashly

Luther calumniates the Church, and thro' every part of
penance what foolish, impious, and absurd things he has
maintained, contrary to the Holy Scripture, to the public faith of the Church, to the consent of so many ages
and people, and almost to even common sense: that he
was not content even with this, but having long owned
penance to be a sacrament, at the end of his book he begins to repent of there being any thing of truth in it, and
therefore changing his opinion for the worse, according to
custom, he absolutely denies that penance is a sacrament.
The King therfore wishes, that Luther may repent of his
treating so ill of repentance, all the parts of which he endeavoured to destroy; that he may hereafter comply with
all the parts of it, be contrite for his malice, publicly
confess his errors, submitting himself to the judgment of
the Church, which he has offended with so many blasphe-
mies, and recompense with the best satisfaction he can
make whatsoever he has hitherto committed.

Of Confirmation.

Confirmation, the King says, Luther is so far from
owning to be a sacrament, that he even wonders how it
ever came into the Church's head to make it one, and, a
trifling fellow as he is, jests and sports with so sacred a
matter, asking why they did not likewise make *three* sacraments of bread, since they might have had some handle
for it from the Scriptures. He likewise said, that confirmation no way operates towards our salvation, and is
supported by no promise of Christ: on which, the King
observes, that this is all affirmation without any proof, and
is a denial of every thing. But when Luther himself
produces some places of Scripture from whence the Sacrament of Confirmation, however Luther derides it, may not
absurdly have its original, why does he, says the King, so
malignantly judge of the whole Church as rashly receiving it for a sacrament, because in those places he reads
of no word of promise? as if Christ has promised, said

and done nothing but what the Evangelists report. At
this rate, if there was only extant the gospel of St. John,
he might deny the institution of the Sacrament in the
Lord's Supper, because that Evangelist writes nothing of
it. By the same D. counsel have all of them omitted
many other things which Jesus did, which, this Evange-
list says, *if they should be written every one, he supposes,* John xxi.
*that even the world itself could not contain the books that
should be written,* some of which things were told to the
faithful by the Apostles, and preserved afterwards by the
perpetual faith of the Catholic Church. Why, therfore,
says the King to Luther, should you not believe the
Church in some things, though they are not read in the
Gospels, when, as Augustine says, if it was not for tradition, you could not know which were the Gospels. Otherwise, if a man will receive nothing but what is so plainly
read in the Gospels, as to leave no room for dispute, how
does he believe, (if so be *he* believes who scarce believes
any thing) the perpetual virginity of Mary, about which
Helvidius was so far from finding any thing in Scripture,
that from the words of Scripture he took a handle to determine the contrary? Nor was there any thing produced
in opposition to him but the faith of the whole Church,
which is no where greater, or of more force than in the
sacraments. I truly, says the King, cannot think, that
there is any one who has the least spark of faith, that can
be persuaded, that Christ who prayed for Peter, that his
faith might not fail, and has placed his Church upon a
firm rock, would suffer her universally for so many ages
to be obliged by an erroneous trust in empty signs of
bodily things, as in divine sacraments. Certainly, if any
one consider the name and minister of this sacrament, and
the virtue which it promises, he must be sensible, that it
is not such a matter as the Church can be believed to
have received rashly. From the chrism used in it, as
Hugo de Sancto Victore says, has Christ his name; from
Christ comes the name of Christian. Nor are we anointed

with this chrism but by the bishops. unless in cases of necessity, that they may sign or seal the Christian, and give him the Holy Spirit. As to the fruit or virtue of this sacrament, the same Hugo declares, that as we are baptized for the remission of sins, so by the laying on of hands is the Holy Ghost given. In *that* is grace conferred for the remission of sins, in *this* is it given for confirmation. The King then quotes St. Hierome, as saying, that the Bishop, if he lays on his hands, he lays them on those who are baptized in the right faith: that if any one ask why he who is baptized in the Church does not receive the Holy Spirit but by the hands of the Bishop, this observation or usage is derived from this authority, that after our Lord's Ascension the Holy Spirit descended unto the Apostles. To this opinion, His Majesty says, many places of Scripture bear witness, but most clearly *that* in the Acts, which declares, that the people who were before baptized in Samaria, after that Peter and John came down to them, had their hands laid on them, and received the Holy Ghost. Luther, therfore, adds the King, should leave off to despise the Sacrament of Confirmation, that is recommended by the dignity of its minister, the authority of the Church, and the usefulness of the sacrament itself.

Of the Sacrament of Matrimony.

This, the King says, Luther denied to be a sacrament, least any hereafter should think the conjugal faith deserving any regard; and when, says His Majesty, he has so taken away the other sacraments, as to deny in one any instituted sign, and in another any promise of grace, in this of matrimony he denys both. Matrimony, he says, was among the patriarchs and Gentiles, and yet with neither was it a sacrament, tho' among both it was as true matrimony as it is among *us*. But, said the King, as for the fathers who were under the law, and before the law, I by no means agree with Luther, but do really think, that matrimony was to them a sacrament as much as circumcision. As to the Gentiles the case is somewhat different, altho' there are not wanting some who, contrary to Luther, think, that even among the Gentiles matrimony was a sacrament · among whom His Majesty reckons Augustine and Hugo aforementioned. The King proceeds to give some reasons why the matrimony of the faithful is a sacrament rather than that of unbelievers. 1. He says, Christ consecrated matrimony by an indissoluble bond of society (except in case of fornication) betwixt those whom God hath rightly joined together, and that the Apostle Paul calls it a ᵠsacrament. 2. The words of Adam concerning Eve were a prophecy of Christ and his Church. 3. The Apostle to the Ephesians admonishes those who are joined together in matrimony so to carry themselves one towards another, as to render their matrimony a fit and very resembling sacrament of so holy a thing of which it is the sacrament. Then His Majesty shews, that matrimony confers grace, for which he gives these reasons: 1. Marriage is honourable and the bed undefiled. 2. Matrimony would not have a bed undefiled, was it not that grace, which is infused on marriage, turned that into good which otherwise would be sin. 3. The unbelieving husband is sanctified by the believing wife, &c. 4. God, when he joined together our first parents in marriage, consecrated their matrimony by his benediction. 5. Christ not only honoured matrimony with his presence, but ennobled it with a miracle.

Of the Sacrament of Order.

In the Sacrament of Order Luther proceeds, the King says, without any order, but picking here and there, he emptys all the treasures of his malice, and shews a mind well inclined to doing mischief, if he had it but in his power. Of Order, therfore, because he proceeds in no

---

ᵠ According to the Latin Vulgate, St. Paul writing to the Ephesians, c v about marriage, says, *Sacramentum hoc magnum est* But in the original Greek it is, *This is a great mystery*

order, we shall collect here and there his opinions, that the reader may have at once before him that heap of evils, and we may be saved the labour of arguing with a man, whose impious doctrine every one sees directly tends to pervert the whole faith of Christ, and to establish infidelity. For what else can he design who determines, that among the clergy and laity there is no distinction of priesthode? that all are priests alike, have all the same power in every sacrament? That priests have not the ministry of the sacraments but by the consent of the people: that the Sacrament of Order can be nothing else but a certain rite of choosing a preacher in a Church: that whoso does not preach, he is not a priest but equivocally, as the picture of a man is a man· that he who is a priest may agen become a lay-man, for that the character is nothing: that order itself, by which men are ordained clergy-men, who know not how to preach, is a mere whimsy or figment of people who understand nothing of ecclesiastical matters, of the priesthode, of the ministry of the word, or of the sacrament: last of all, says the King, that holy Priest (that he may leave others to guess how chast he himself is) lays it down as a principal error, an utter blindness, and the greatest bondage, that priests oblige themselves to a chast celibacy. Of all these pernicious opinions, the King observes, that Luther's denying order to be a sacrament is the spring or fountain head. This sacrament, says he, Luther says, the Church of Christ knows nothing of; it was the invention of the Pope's Church; which few words, His Majesty observes, contain no small heap of falshood and absurditie; since he distinguishes betwixt the Pope's Church and the Church of Christ, when the Pope is high-priest of the same Church of which Christ is the high-priest. The King proceeds to shew, that the Church cannot err in receiving the sacraments of the faith, no more than it can err in receiving the Scriptures, in which Luther himself owns it cannot be misled: that if nothing be to be reckoned certain but what is confirmed

by the Scriptures, and those very plain ones, we must not
only not assert the perpetual virginity of the Virgin Mary,
but there will be suggested an unexhausted fund of matter
for opposing the faith, if at any time a man has a mind
either to form new sects or to revive old ones. The King
next undertakes to enquire whether the Scriptures be indeed altogether so silent as is pretended touching this
sacrament. For this purpose, he observes, that nobody
but Luther denys, that the Apostles were ordained priests
at the Lord's Supper, when it's plain they had then power
given them to make the body of Christ, which none but a
priest can do. But that Luther's objection to it is, that it
was no sacrament, because there was no promise of grace
made to them. But, says His Majesty, how does Luther
know this? because he does not read so! This is his
familiar consequence, it is not written in the Gospel, therfore it was not done by Christ, But, says the King, let us
come a little nearer to Luther: he grants the Eucharist
to be a sacrament, and he'd be mad if he did not. But
where does he find in Scripture grace promised in that
sacrament? for he is concluded by nothing but texts of
Scripture, and those very plain or express ones. Let him
read the places where the Lord's Supper is mentioned,
and he will not find either in the Evangelists or in St.
Paul's Epistle any promise of grace in receiving this
sacrament. Therfore. as it is sufficient that we read in
the Gospel, that a power of making the sacrament was
given to those in whose places priests succeed: so it is
enough that we read that the Apostle advised Timothy to
lay hands suddenly on no man, &c. which places plainly
shew, that the ordering of priests is not made by the consent of the community, but by the sole ordination of the
bishop, and that by a certain imposition of hands, in which
by an outward sign God infused an inward grace. His
Majesty therfore wonders, that any one should be so weak
as to any wise doubt whether grace be conferr'd on the
priests of the Gospel at their ordination, when every where

are read so many things which seem to signify, that grace was conferr'd even on the priests of the old law. For, says God, thou shalt anoint Aaron and his sons, and consecrate them, and sanctifie them, that they may minister unto me in the priest's office. For otherwise to what purpose was this outward sanctification for the worship of God, if God did not likewise pour upon them the inward or spiritual grace by which they were sanctified inwardly, and that also by Christ, the faith of whom to come might add strength and force to the preceding sacraments, as it made the Jewish people capable of sometime obtaining eternal salvation. In the Acts of the Apostles, when Paul and Barnabas were separated for the work wherunto the Holy Ghost had called them, they were not dismissed before they were ordained by the laying on of hands. But why did the Apostles lay their hands on them? only, that they might rap the body with an idle touch, and no way assist the soul with spiritual grace? But, says the King, Luther says, orders are never called a sacrament by the ancient doctors, except by Dionysius. To which, His Majesty replys, that this is truly a fine reason of Luther's, but that it is notoriously false; and if it were true it is good for nothing: for if the ancients had writ nothing at all of a thing which, perhaps, was not controverted in their time, or when they did write any thing of it, they called it by its proper name, and not by the common name of a sacrament; it would not necessarily follow from thence, that either orders were not at all, or, that they were not a sacrament. For if any one should call *baptism, baptism,* and not add the word sacrament, should he therefore be said not to have accounted baptism for a sacrament? But not only Dionysius, but also Gregory and Augustine held orders to be a sacrament. Besides, the indelible character of which Luther makes such a jest, tho' it be not called by that name, is yet in reality plainly described by Jerome in the Sacrament of Baptism, and an account taken of it by St. Augustine in both that sacrament, and the Sacrament of

Order. This character the King thus describes. It is,
says he, that quality of soul which God imprints as known
to *him*, tho' not thought of by *us*, for a mark to distinguish
his flock from strangers : which mark, tho' they who have
it defile it by their vices, and make it of white, black, of
whole, maimed, and of being most pure, impure, yet they
can never so deface it, but that they, who being imprinted
with this mark of the character, are marked to whose
flock they belong, and continue still to be knowable to the
whole world at the day of judgment, Nor is it for any
other reason, that it is the constant usage of the Church,
that when it so often repeats the other sacraments, it
never allows baptism, confirmation, and orders to be repeated. For in those sacraments the Church has been
taught by the Holy Spirit, that the mark of the character
is conferred, which, since it cannot be deleted, ought not
to be repeated. But, that it may plainly appear, that
order in this respect is on a level with baptism, let us hear
what Gregory says · Your asserting, says he, that he who
is ordained should be ordained again, is very ridiculous ·
for, as he who is once baptized ought not to be baptized
agen, so he who is once consecrated cannot be consecrated
agen in the same order : you see the Church no more
allows the Sacrament of Order to be repeated than it
does that of Baptism, which thing, as I said, depends on
its indelible character. Concerning which matter, that
we may stop Luther's mouth, that he don't agen gabble
that the character is a fiction, and that Dionysius alone of
all the ancients called order a sacrament, we will subjoin,
as we promised, St. Augustine's opinion of this matter.
He then, speaking of Baptism and Order, thus writes :
Both are sacraments, and both are given to man with a
certain consecration. Therfore, in the Catholic Church is
neither of them to be repeated ; for if at any time hære-
tical bishops for the sake of peace are received into the
Church, tho' they are permitted to perform the same
offices which they used to perform, they are not re-or-

CHAP.
XI

dained, because the fault was in their schism not in the sacraments, which, wheresoever they are, are sacraments. But notwithstanding, the King says, Luther, in opposition to the reasons, the authority, and the faith of all, defends himself with one argument. We are all priests, says he, according to that of Peter, *Ye are a royal priesthode, and a priestly kingdome.* But one cannot be more a priest than another, no more than one can be more a man than another. Therfore, they who are called priests are nothing else but certain lay-men chosen to preach either by the consent of the people alone, or by the calling of the bishop, but not without the people. We have, says the King, not only faithfully reported his argument, but have also freely added what tends to support it: and yet who can help laughing at the shrewd dulness of this theologant? for if therefore there is no order of priesthode, because every Christian is a priest, by the same reason it will follow, that Christ had nothing above, or was no way superiour to Saul; because even of Saul, David said, *I have sinned in stretching forth my hand against the Lord's Christ.* In whatever sense all Christians are priests, in the same sense are they all kings. For it is not only said, *Ye are a royal priesthode,* but it is also said, *Ye are a priestly kingdome.* As for Luther's saying, that they who do not preach are not priests, this, says the King, is to contradict the Apostle Paul, who writing to Timothy, says, *Let the elders that rule well be counted worthy of double honour, especially they who labour in the word and doctrine.* The Apostle plainly asserts, that altho' they are especially worthy of double honour who being priests do labour in the word and doctrine, yet, that they who do not thus labour are not only priests, but may *rule well,* and also deserve *double honour:* otherwise he would not have said, *especially they who labour,* but *they only who labour,* &c. Further, that Luther mayn't say, that which he does say, that the priestly office consists in nothing but preaching, that, I say, this may appear how false it is, let us

1 Epist. ii.

1 Sam
XXIV.

1 Epist v.

agen hear the Apostle. *Every high priest*, says he, *taken from among men, is ordained for men in things pertaining to God, that he may offer both gifts and sacrifices for sins.*

Heb. v.

Does not the Apostle plainly declare, that it is the office of even an high priest to offer sacrifice to God for the sins of men? which since he wrote to Hebrews who were Christians, and whom he would not have to judaize, it's plain he speaks of an high priest of either law, and so does twice, or in more respects than one, oppose Luther with his testimony. For he instructs us, both, that the mass is a sacrifice, and to be offered for the people, since the Church offers none other; and, that the office of offering is the chief part of the high priest's employment. If every lay-man has an equal power with the priest in every sacrament, and the order of priesthode is nothing, why does the Apostle write thus to Timothy: *Neglect not* 1 Epist. iv. *the gift that is in thee, which was given thee by prophecy, with the laying on of the hands of the presbyterie. I ad-* 2 Epist. i. *monish thee to stir up the gift of God, which is in thee by the laying on of my hands: lay hands suddenly on no man, neither be a partaker of other men's sins.* Lastly, the Apostle writes to Titus in this manner. *For this cause* ch. i. *left I thee in Crete, that thou shouldst set in order the things that are wanting, and ordain elders in every city as I had appointed thee.* Those who Luther says were made by the consent of the people, Paul shews were made by the Bishop, whom, he says, he left at Crete for this very purpose, that he should ordain elders in every town, yet not rashly, but as he himself when present had ordered him. It's likewise plain, that priests were made by laying on of hands. And that here may be no doubt but, that at the same time grace is conferred, we see that collated by the laying on of hands. *Stir up*, saith he, *the gift of God, which is in thee by the putting on of my hands; neglect not the gift that is in thee which was given thee by prophecy, with the laying on of the hands of the presbytery; in these things exercise thyself.* I wonder, therfore, Luther is not ashamed to deny the Sacrament of Order, since he cannot be ignorant, that the words of St. Paul are in every bodie's hands : which words instruct us, that a priest is not made but by a priest, and, that he is not made without consecration, in which is exhibited both a bodily sign, and so much of spiritual grace is infused, that he who is consecrated does not only receive the Holy Ghost himself, but likewise a power of conferring it on others.

Of the Sacrament of extreme Unction.

In the Sacrament of extreme Unction, the King says, Luther scoffs at the Church on these two accounts. *First,* that divines, as he says, call this *unction* a sacrament; as if they only whom he calls divines so termed it. *Secondly,* that they call it *extreme,* which is therefore so called because it is the *extreme* or last of the *four* sacraments. That Luther may shew this to be no sacrament, he first objects to himself, that he sees every one will be ready to oppose the words of St. James, *Is any one sick among you? let him call for, or bring in the priestes of the Church, and let them praie over him, anoiling with oile in the name of our Lord, and the praier of faith shall save the sick, and our Lord shall lift him up : and if he be in sinnes they shall be remitted him.* These words, which, according to his own definition, very plainly declare this unction to be a sacrament, and, that it neither wants a visible sign nor a promise of grace, Luther, the King says, is so impudent as to elude, as if they had no force in them. But, says he, I say, if ever there was any idle talk, we have in this place a special instance of it. " I omit, that many " affirm, with great probability, that this Epistle is not " St. James's, being unworthy of an apostolical spirit, " tho' by use it has obtained authority, such as it is. " But if it was the Apostle's, I might say, that an Apostle " might not by his own authority institute a sacrament, " that is, give a divine promise with a sign joined to it : " this pertains to Christ alone. So Paul says, that he

" received of the Lord the Sacrament of the Eucharist,
" and was sent not to baptize but to preach the Gospel.
" But the Sacrament of this extreme Unction is never read
" of in the Gospel." Thus, says the King, does Luther
endeavour two ways to enervate or destroy the force of
the Apostle's words. *First*, by affirming, that the Epistle
is not the Apostle's: next, that if it was the Apostle's, yet
he had no authority to institute sacraments. If he had
said, that it has sometime been doubted whose Epistle
this was, he had said true. For the Church has not received any thing rashly, but has diligently examined all
things. But when he says, that many affirm, that this
Epistle is unworthy of the apostolical spirit, and that they
don't only assert it, but assert it with probability, it is probable that he cannot prove *that*. But as yet he has not
produced so much as one of those many. I will, therfore,
says the King, vouch one who ought to be reckoned sufficient to oppose a great many. It is St. Hierome, than
whom no one was ever more learned in the Scriptures, nor
by a more exact and judicious censure distinguished the
true and genuine from the doubtful. He, then, when for
some time he had doubted of an Epistle of Paul's, but at
a time when the thing was not confirmed by the full consent of the Church, yet pronounced without the least
hesitation of the Epistle which is ascribed to James, that
it is his. Thus he writes, James, Peter, Jude, and John,
published seven Epistles, &c. If indeed Luther had given
any reasons why it was not St. James's Epistle, but another's, who wrote by the same spirit, it might in some
measure have been born. But now, he says, it is probable, that therfore the Epistle is not his, because it is
unworthy the apostolical spirit. In which matter, says the
King, I will oppose no one to Luther but Luther himself,
for indeed no one almost contradicts Luther oftner or
more to the purpose, than Luther. He then on the Sacrament of Order saith, that the Church hath this gift
bestowed on it, that it can discern betwixt the words of

CHAP.
XI.

God and the words of men.   How then does he now say,
that the Epistle is unworthy an apostolical spirit, which
the Church, whose judgment, he says, cannot be deceived,
has judged to be full of an apostolical spirit? Wherefore
now he has on all sides so hampered himself by his own
wisdom, as either to be forced to allow, that the Epistle is
the Apostle's, the contrary to which he said was probable,
or to say, that the Church in judging of Holy Scripture
may be deceived, which he had denied it could be.   As to
his saying, that tho' the Epistle be the Apostle's, yet it is
not lawful for an Apostle by his own authority to institute
a sacrament, because this pertains to Christ alone, the
King says, he will not at present dispute whether an
Apostle has authority to institute a sacrament or no ; but
since it plainly appears, that the Apostle delivers that
unction for a sacrament, he makes no doubt of its being
truly a sacrament, and that the Apostle was not so profanely arrogant as to deliver that to the people for a sacrament which was not so.   But if *he* had no power to make
a sacrament, yet why might not Christ will something to
be taught by the Apostle James as received from him, as
well as by the Evangelists and St. Paul? Luther, says
the King, having thus with all his might opposed the
Apostle, he now applys himself to ridicule the Church,
which, he says, perverts the Apostle's words, in that it
does not minister this unction, but to those who are sick
unto death, wheras James says, *If any one be sick*, not *If
any one die*.   As if the Church is therfore wrong because it does not administer so great a thing as a sacrament in every slight fever, which, perhaps, a man has got
by drinking too much, or by a sacrament desire a miracle
should be wrought in a distemper which may be cured by
a little sleep or abstinence.   All the prayers that are said
over the sick person, which no body doubts are very ancient, and not a new invention of those whom Luther calls
divines, shew that this sacrament is not to be ministred
but to those who are very dangerously sick : and yet, as

they who minister it don't promise certain health of body, so neither do they despair of the sick person's recovery, or come to them as to folks who are just a dying: for it would be impertinent to use so many prayers for the sick person's health or recovery, if they were certainly assured of his death. The Church therfore does not intend this to be the last anointing, tho' it be called extreme unction, but that it should not be the last, and that the sick person should recover. But if God otherwise disposes of the sick person, so that he does not recover his bodily health, that does not yet evacuate the force and virtue of the sacrament, whose principal effect is not on the body but on the soul. The reasoning of Luther concerning the efficacy of the sign has neither reason nor strength. " If," says he, " that unction be a sacrament, it ought without " doubt to be, as they say, an effectual sign of that which " it signs and promises. But now it promises the health " and recovery of the sick person, as the plain words are, " *the praier of faith shall save the sick.* But who is not " sensible that this promise is fulfilled in few? What then " shall we say? either that the Apostle lies in this pro- " mise, or that that unction is not a sacrament; for that a " sacramental promise is certain, wheras this for the most " part fails." But, says the King, even from this argu- ment it may appear, that Luther no way cares how noto- rious the calumnies are which he broaches, so he can but impose on the unwary by some appearance of truth, and that he is not ashamed to produce against the divines things as if they were said by them which they no where say. " A sacrament is," says he, " as they say an effec- " tual sign of that which it promises." But now divines do not say *that*, but, that it is an effectual sign of grace. For thus they define it: a sacrament is a visible sign of an invisible grace; they don't say of bodily health, which may be given even without grace. Wherfore, as to what, he says, follows, that if this unction was a sacrament the Apostle would lie, Luther lies himself. For a sacrament,

as it is a sacrament, does not promise bodily health, but
the health of the soul by bodily signs. Since then the
Apostle says, that he who is sick is to be healed by unction and prayer, and Christ tells us, that *these signs shall
follow them that believe, they shall lay hands on the sick,
and they shall recover*, who does not see, that these are
things so done sometimes as yet not to be done always?
Luther's opinion, that if unction be a sacrament, it always
cures that, so it be not an ineffectual sign, tends to this,
that it cannot be a sacrament unless it makes the body
immortal; which yet he himself promises may be done by
prayer made by good men nothing doubting. For, says
he, it is not at all to be doubted but that at this day there
might so be cured as many as we would, or desired. For
since these things may be done by faith, not only sometimes but continually, provided it be a faith that nothing
doubts, it's probable, that if any one has such a faith, Luther has it in the greatest perfection, who is a man so
much addicted to faith, as in favour of it to lay aside or
oppose good works. I wonder, therfore, says the King,
if he says true, that he himself does not cure some dying
people. In the mean time, whilst we daily hear reports
from Germany of even those who were buried being raised
again, we yet are so far from hearing of any cures performed, that on the contrary we are told of good and in-
nocent priests being slain and cruelly murdered for his
sake by some of his followers, that he may teach by example that order is nothing, that the character is a fiction,
and David a coward, who repented of his touching the
Lord's anointed. What follows is all such satyr and de-
clamation, which therfore I do not transcribe.

14. With the treatment of him in this book thus written
in the King's name, Luther was so provoked, that he
wrote and published a most bitter answer to it, in which
he declared, that in defence of the cause in which he was
engaged, he valued no man's person or honour. But as
the publication of this book was not till about two years

after this, I must defer giving an account of it till then, CHAP.
and in the mean time take notice of what was done fur- XI.
ther in relation to him, in part of which our Bishop was
concerned.

CHAP. XII.

*1. Pope Leo condemns one and forty Propositions, taken
out of the two before-mentioned books, as heretical and
erroneous, and summons Luther to retract them. 2. An
account of those Propositions. 3. Luther answers the
Pope's Bull. 4, 5, &c. an account of it. 13. The Bishop
replies to it.*

Maimburg,
Histor. Lu-
theranismi.

1. THE Pope being informed of Luther's publishing
the two before-mentioned books by his legates and by
Eccius, who took a journey to Rome on purpose to acquaint him with it, resolved to descend to the utmost rigor,

A.D. 1520. and therefore published a Constitution, by which [a] one
and fourty conclusions or propositions, said to be taken
out of these two books, were condemned as partly manifestly heretical, and partly rash and scandalous; and
Luther himself had prescribed to him *sixty* days, within
which he was to send to Rome a retractation in an approved form, or to bring it thither himself, having letters
of safe conduct granted to him. But if he neglected to do
this, and did not keep the time set, he was declared excommunicate, and all persons whosoever were prohibited
protecting him, on pain of incurring the same censures,
and losing all offices and dignities.

2. The propositions thus condemned were as follows:

I. It is an heretical, tho' a common, opinion, that the
sacraments of the new law do give grace to them who do
not bar against or withstand it.

II. To deny, that sin remains in a child after baptism is
to trample under foot both Paul and Christ.

Fomes pec-
cati.

III. The fewel of sin, or original sin, altho' there be no
actual sin, stayeth the soul when it's going out of the body
from its entring into heaven.

[a] Mr. Strype, by a mistake in making *two* of one of these conclusions,
reckons them to be *two* and *fourty*. *Memori. Eccles.* vol. i. p. 37.

IV. The imperfect charity of a dying person carrieth with it necessarily great fear, which fear by itself alone is sufficient to make the pain of purgatory, and hindreth entrance into the kingdom.

V. That there are three parts of repentance, *viz.* contrition, confession, and satisfaction is not founded in the Holy Scripture, nor in the ancient holy Christian doctors.

VI. Contrition, which is made or framed by examination, recollection, and detestation of sins, by which any one looks back on his time spent, or thinks over again the years he has lived, in the bitterness of his soul weighing the greatness, the multitude, and the baseness of his sins, the loss of eternal happiness, and the acquisition of everlasting damnation, this contrition makes a hypocrite, nay, a greater sinner.

VII. Its a very true proverb, and better than all the doctrine hitherto delivered concerning contrition, which says, *A new life,* or to do so no more, *is the best repentance.* de cætero non facere.

VIII. By no means presume to confess venial sins, nor yet all your mortal ones, because it is impossible you should know all your mortal sins; wherfore in the primitive church they confessed those mortal sins, which were notorious.

IX. Whilst we desire to confess purely all our sins, we do nothing else but desire, that nothing may be left to the mercy of God to pardon.

X. Sins are not remitted to any one, unless he believes they are remitted to him when the priest remits them; so far from it, that the sin would still remain if he did not believe it remitted. For remission of sins, and the donation of grace is not sufficient, but it is also necessary to believe, that sin is remitted.

XI. By no means depend on your being absolved on account of your contrition, but on account of the word of God, *whatsoever thou shalt lose.* Here, I say, place thy confidence; if thou shalt obtain the priest's absolution, and firmly believe *that*, thou art absolved, whatever becomes of thy contrition.

XII. If through an impossibility a contrite person should not be confessed, or if the priest absolve him, not in earnest but in jest, if yet he believes himself absolved, he is most truly absolved.

XIII. In the sacrament of penance, and the remission of a fault, the Pope or a bishop does no more than an inferiour priest, nay, than every Christian does, where there is no priest to be had, tho' it be a woman or a child.

XIV. No one ought to answer the priest that he is contrite, nor ought the priest to ask or require it.

XV. It is a great error of those who come to the sacrament of the Eucharist trusting or depending upon this, that they are confessed, that they are not conscious to themselves of any mortal sin, and have premised prayers and preparation. All those eat and drink judgment to themselves. But if they believe and trust, that they shall there obtain grace, this faith alone makes them pure and worthy.

XVI. It seemeth adviseable, that the Church should ordain in a general council, that the laity ought to receive the communion in both kinds, and that the Bohemians, who do thus communicate, are not heretics and schismatics.

XVII. The treasures of the Church, out of which the Pope granteth indulgences, are not the merits of Christ and the saints.

XVIII. Indulgences are the pious frauds of the faithful, and the remissions of good works, and are to be reckoned among those things which are lawful but not expedient.

XIX. Indulgences don't avail to those who truly obtain them for the remission of the pain due by divine justice for actual sins.

XX. They are seduced, who believe that indulgences are salutary, and useful to bring forth the fruits of the spirit.

XXI. Indulgences are necessary for public crimes only, and are properly granted to such as are hardned and impenitent.

XXII. To six sorts of men are indulgences neither
necessary nor useful, *viz.* 1. To those who are dead or a dying. 2. To sick people. 3. To those who labour under a lawful impediment. 4. To those who have committed no crimes at all. 5. To those who have committed crimes, but no public ones. 6. To those who amend their lives.

XXIII. Excommunications are only outward punishments, nor do they deprive a man of the common spiritual prayers of the Church.

XXIV. Christians are to be taught rather to love excommunication than to fear it.

XXV. The Bishop of Rome is not the successor of Peter, nor is he instituted by Christ himself in St. Peter the Vicar of Christ over all the churches of all the world.

XXVI. Christ's saying to Peter, *Whatsoever thou shalt bind upon earth,* &c. extends only to the sins which are bound by Peter.

XXVII. It is certain, that it is not at all in the power of the Church or of the Pope to decree or appoint articles of faith, no nor yet laws of manners, or of good works.

XXVIII. If the Pope with a great part of the Church should think so or so, and also should not err, or be mistaken, yet is it not a sin or heresy to be of a contrary opinion, especially in a thing not necessary to salvation, untill by a general council the one be rejected and the other approved.

XXIX. A way is opened for us to * weaken the authority of councils, and freely to contradict their acts, and judge their decrees, and boldly to own or confess the truth, whether it be approved or rejected by any council.

* enervandi. Mr. Strype read enarrandi.

XXX. Some articles of John Huss condemned in the Council of Constance are most Christian, most true and evangelical, which even the universal Church cannot condemn.

XXXI. In every good work the just man sinneth.

XXXII. A good work very well done is a venial sin.

L

XXXIII. To burn heretics is against the will of the Spirit.

XXXIV. To go to war against the Turks is to resist God, who by them visits or punishes our sins.

XXXV. No one is sure, that he does not always sin mortally, by reason of the most hidden vice of pride.

XXXVI. Free will after sin is a thing in name or title only, and whilst it does what is in its power, sinneth mortally.

XXXVII. Purgatory cannot be proved from holy Scripture, which is in the canon.

XXXVIII. The souls in purgatory are not secure of their salvation, at least not all of them; nor is it proved by either any reasons or Scriptures, that they are out of a state of deserving or of increasing charity.

XXXIX. The souls in purgatory sin without intermission as long as they seek for rest, and abhor, or are frightned at, punishments.

XL. The souls delivered out of purgatory by the prayers of the living, are less happy than if they had made satisfaction themselves.

omnes sac-
cos mendi-
citatis.
XLI. Ecclesiastical prelates and secular princes would not do ill if they destroyed all the sacks of beggary, or the begging friers.

3. To this bull of the Pope's, Luther wrote an answer in two books, which are both dated December 1, 1520. The first of these is entituled, *Against the cursed Bull of Antichrist:* and is directed to the Christian reader, whom he tells, that he had heard a report, that a certain bull against *him* was dispersed almost thro'out all the world before it came to him who was alone concerned in it, and to whom therfore it ought especially to have been delivered: that, perhaps, the reason of this is, that the daughter of night and darkness was afraid of the light of *his* countenance; but that by the help of some friends he had, at length, seen the night owl in its own shape: that neither the stile nor process of the Roman court is observed

in it, and what is more, it condemns articles which are
plainly and manifestly most Christian, so that it seemed to
him to be the production of that monster John Eccius, a
man made up of lies, hypocrisies, errors, and heresies.
What added to the suspicion was, that the same Eccius
was said to be the Roman messenger of such a bull, and
that there could not be any messenger more fit to be sent
on such a message. But that, whoever was the author of
this bull, he took him for Antichrist, and wrote these
things against Antichrist, designing to redeem the truth
of Christ, which *he* endeavoured to extinguish.

  4. And first of all, says he, that he may get nothing of
me of all that he desires, I protest before God and our
Lord Jesu Christ and his holy angels, and all the world,
that I do from my heart dissent from the damnation pronounced by this bull, which also I accuse and curse as the
sacrilegious and blasphemous adversary of Christ the Son
of God and our Lord, Amen. Next, I assert and embrace with all sincerity the articles condemned by this
bull, and pronounce, that they ought to be asserted by all
Christians on pain of eternal damnation; and, that they
are to be accounted Antichrist's whosoever consent to the
bull, whom also, in conjunction with the spirit of all who
know and worship Christ in purity, I reckon and avoid as
heathen men, according to the precept of our Lord Jesu
Christ. Amen.

  5. Having made this protestation, to which he desires
his readers to be witnesses, he proceeds to confute the
bull by some arguments by way of prelude. The first of
these is taken from the ignorance of this Antichrist. The
Apostle Peter commands us to be ready always to give an
answer to every man that asketh us a reason of the hope
that is in us with meekness and fear. And Paul orders a
bishop to be apt to teach, or able to exhort in sound doctrine, and to instruct those that oppose or contradict
them; and this, says he, is what these three years I have
earnestly desired and looked for from Rome; but when I

CHAP.
XII.

1 Epist iii.

expected grapes, that they would inform me with testimonies of Holy Scripture, behold they brought forth wild grapes, condemning me with their bare words, when I had defended my writings with so many Scriptures.

6. Nor, says he, does impiety less manifest itself; since that notable bull decrees in the openest and most barefaced words, that also those books of mine should be burnt in which there are no errors, that my memory may be entirely destroyed. The same men add, as they are very pleasant and facetious, what is perfectly ridiculous, *viz.* that over and above the immense favours conferred upon me, they have offered me money to bear my charges in a journey to Rome. But I know whose notable lie this is. Cardinal Cajetan, born and formed for composing lies, having successfully discharged his legateship, and being now secure at Rome, pretends he promised me money: when at Ausburgh he was so very poor as to be afraid his family would perish for want. But it is meet the bull should be a bull, void of truth and wisdom.

7. Our bull likewise, says he, produces new Latin: for Augustine having said, that he would not believe the Gospel if he was not moved to it by the authority of the Church; forthwith this notable bull makes this Catholic Church to be some of the most reverend cardinals, the priors of the regular orders, the masters of divinity, and doctors of law. See then the madness of the Papists. The Catholic or universal Church, according to them, is a few cardinals, priors, and doctors, perhaps scarce twenty men, when it's possible not one of them is a member of any one chapel or altar; but, since the Church is the communion of saints, as we profess in the creed, whosoever are not of the number of these twenty men, they must be excluded the communion of saints, i. e. the universal Church. But to all their temerity, says Luther, I constantly oppose the unconquered Paul, 1 Cor. xiv. *If any thing be revealed to another that sitteth by, let the first hold his peace.* Here, it's plain, that the Pope and any

other superiour ought to hold his peace, if any thing be revealed to another inferiour in the Church. Relying on this authority, and despising the rashness of the bull, with confidence I undertake a defence of the articles, not regarding the bare condemnation of any one, tho' it were the Pope with the whole Church, unless he informs me by the Scriptures.

8. Accordingly, in this book he defends the *six* first articles. The two first of these he owns for his; but of the third, he says, he had hitherto defined nothing, tho' he had copiously enough disputed of the probability of it. The fourth article, he observes, follows from the preceding one, but that he had no more asserted it, than he had the other. The two others he undertakes the proof of, but concludes, that there's no occasion for his proving them all, since there are extant little books of his in which he has abundantly given an account of them.

9. However, Luther soon after published another book, which he entituled, *An Assertion of all the Articles of Martin Luther condemned by the late Bull of Leo X.* This he dedicated to Fabian Feilitsch, a German knight, and dated it at Wirtembergh, the very same day with the former in December 1, 1520. But tho' dated now, it was not finished till some time after, since in it he speaks of A D 1520. his burning the decretals, which, it's plain, was not done till the *tenth* of this month. In this book he particularly explained and defended the one and fourty articles condemned by the bull, and that with so much learning and force of argument, that even Maimbourg here acknowledges his gifts of learning and ingenuity.

10 He begins with his usual protestation, that he would not be concluded by the authority of any father, tho' never so holy, any farther than what he said was proved by the judgment of Holy Scripture. This, he says, he knows the Papists will take very ill, and will say as usual, that the Holy Scriptures are not to be interpreted by a *private spirit: when yet they themselves, in direct * proprio Spiritu.

opposition to this opinion of their's, never interpret the Scriptures but by their own spirit. From whence it comes, that the Holy Scriptures are set aside, and men immersed in the commentaries of men only, not enquiring what the Holy Scriptures say, but what men's opinions of them are; till at last they attributed to one man, the Bishop of Rome alone, the authority of interpreting Holy Scripture, fabling that the Church, i. e. the Pope, cannot err in the faith.

11. Of this, he said, it's useful to say somewhat. First of all, if it be not lawful for any one to interpret Holy Scriptures by his own spirit; why then do they not observe, that it is not lawful for Augustine, nor any other of the fathers to do so? and that he who understands the Holy Scriptures according to St. Augustine, and not rather St. Augustine according to the Holy Scriptures, does certainly understand them according to a man, and a private spirit. But if it be not lawful to understand the Scriptures according to our own spirit, it is much less lawful so to understand Augustine; for who shall assure us that we rightly understand him? Besides, since we believe the Holy Catholic Church has the same spirit of faith which it once received in its beginning, why is it not as lawful now either alone or chiefly to study the Holy Scriptures, as it was for the primitive Church so to do? for they did not read Augustine or Thomas. Agen, who shall judge if the sayings of the fathers contradict one another? The Scripture ought to be the judge; but how can that be except we allow it the principal place in every thing which is ascribed to the fathers, that is, that it be in itself most certain, easy, and plain, an interpreter of its self, trying all the things of all men, judging and enlightening, as it is written, Psal. cxix. ? Luther then observes, how great errors are to be found in the writings of all the fathers; how often they fight against and dissent from one another; that there are none of them but very often wrest the Scriptures; that Augustine often only disputes,

and concludes nothing; that Hierome in his commentaries
scarce asserts any thing, &c. He concludes, that the first
principles of Christians are no other than the divine
words; that the words of men are conclusions drawn from
hence, and to be referr'd back again thither, and by them
to be tried. These things being premised, he comes to
the articles themselves.

12. *Article* I. He proves by the Scriptures, saying,
The just man shall live by his faith, not by the sacraments: *He who believeth and is baptized shall be saved,*
&c. for it is not baptism that saves but the faith of baptism: *With the heart man believeth unto righteousness;*
the Apostle does not say with the body sacraments
are received unto righteousness. Lastly, *Abraham believed God, and it was imputed to him for righteousness.*
By reason he proves it thus. Because in every sacrament
there is a word of divine promise which affirmatively promises and exhibits the grace of God to him who receives
the sacrament. But now wheresoever God promises
there is required the faith of the hearer, that so he may
not make God a liar by his unbelief. Wherfore in receiving the sacraments, the faith of the receiver is necessary to believe that which is promised.

Article II. Paul says, *I had not known lust except the
law had said, Thou shalt not covet.* Here, it's without
doubt plain, that lust or concupiscence is sin. But what
man is there who is not sensible of lust after he is adult,
tho' he be baptized, when this most holy Apostle, notwithstanding his being baptized, finds fault with his lust?
Whence then is this sin, but from the fleshly birth remaining even after baptism? And, that no one may imagine that the Apostle speaks in the person of others, he
says, Galat. v. to those who lived after the Spirit, *If we
live in the Spirit, let us also walk in the Spirit.* What
occasion was there to bid those to walk in the Spirit who
live in the Spirit, if there be no sin of the flesh remaining
for them to crucifie? This he further confirms by other

texts of Scripture, by the lives of the saints, the sayings of
the fathers, &c.

Article III. he says, he does not now dispute, but
assert, since he sees nothing produced against it by any
adversary.

Article IV. he likewise asserts, and infers and proves
it from the foregoing articles.

Article V. he says the Papists have maliciously contrived.
For he never denied contrition and confession; yet, as
the article sounds, they would seem to insinuate that he
had denied them. But indeed he had opposed satisfaction, such as *they* teach, which will not be difficult for him
to justifie. Let them, says he, shew, if they can, where
in all the Scripture there is one word or tittle of our being
obliged to make seven years satisfaction for one mortal sin.

Article VI. altho' Cassian teaches it, and every one's
common sense experiences it, so that it is superfluous to
prove it, yet, that the mouth of his adversaries may be
stop'd, he says he will consult the Scriptures of God.

Article VII. Nothing, he says, is truer than common
proverbs. So that even the Holy Scripture very often
cites proverbs as very true. Wherfore he wonders what
has happened to his adversaries, that, contrary to the
sense and opinion of all men, they should dare to condemn
it. Besides, that opinion, he observes, is not his alone,
and therfore he leaves the defence of it to all. But he
here defends what he added, in shewing, that *that* proverb
is agreeable to Scripture.

Article VIII. He would be glad, he says, to be taught
for what reason the things contained in it are deemed
false and condemned, for as for himself he cannot think
why they should be so judged. Tell me, says he, where
the precept is for confessing venial sins to a priest? Don't
they themselves unanimously say, that venial sins do not
pertain to confession? why then do they condemn their
own sayings for my sake?

Article IX. Let those bullarian penitents go, says he,

and confess all things purely, and leave nothing to the
divine mercy to pardon, and let them answer me when
they'll have peace of conscience, and what way they'll
take to escape the judgment of God.   Let them make
David a liar when he says, *Enter not into judgment with
thy servant;* and agen, *Who knows his errors.*   Let *them*
run on judgment, and know *all* their errors, that they alone
may be true men.   *We* shall willingly be reckoned liars
by them with David, and always assert, that we cannot
purely know nor confess all our faults, but must leave a
remnant to the Divine Mercy to pardon, saying, *Cleanse
me, O Lord, from my secret faults.*

Article X.   From the condemnation of this article, Luther observes, it follows: 1. That he who is a going to be
confessed ought not to believe, that he is absolved, or that
his sin is remitted to him.   2. That Christ lied, when he
said, *Whatsoever thou shalt lose is losed.*   But, says he, I
have proved my assertions thus: Christ absolved the
woman who was a sinner on account of her faith: *Thy
faith hath saved thee, go in peace.*   And to the paralytic,
he said before he absolved him, *Believe, thy sins are forgiven thee.*   Since then in every absolution of a sinner the
divine sentence is pronounced, faith is necessarily required
for the belief of this sentence, without which faith, absolution, and all repentance are to no manner of purpose.

Article XI. he says, follows from the preceding one,
because the word of Christ, *Whatsoever thou shalt lose,*
requires the faith of the penitent, as is sufficiently clear,
since it's a word of promise, and cannot therefore be fulfilled without faith.

Article XII. likewise flows, he says, from the preceding
article; for faith, as I said, is required in the word of a
divine promise, which, in whatsoever manner it be heard,
if it be received by faith, justifies.

Article XIII. Since it's plain from the foregoing articles, that not the power or authority of the minister, but
the faith of the penitent, operates the remission of sins,

I'd fain, says he, be taught by these bull merchants, how the Pope does more than any other priest; since he can no more give faith than any other priest, nor absolve by any other word than *that, Whatsoever thou shalt lose,* by which every priest absolves.

Article XIV. I therefore, says he, said this, because this matter depends on the judgment of God. For Paul says, *I know nothing by myself, yet am I not hereby justified:* and *not he that commendeth himself is approved.*

1 Cor. iv.
2 Cor. x.

Article XV. Here, says he, Paul is on my side, who says, *I know nothing by myself, yet am I not hereby justified.* See, he rejects every thing except faith only, of which, he says, that a man is justified by faith. Wherfore, I still say, if you exclude faith, all that you do is deceit and sin.

Article XVI. he says, he has revoked in his book of the *Babilonish Captivity,* and does agen by these writings revoke it.

Article XVII. he says, he has thus proved, because the merits of Christ are things living, spiritual, and sacred, which justifie the heart, As to *their* saying, that the merits of Christ are to be taken two ways, one in the way of satisfaction, another in the way of justification. What, says he, have I to do with those fancies? I know that now adaies the merits of Christ are also taken in the way of money.

Article XVIII. I confess, says he, I was mistaken when I said, indulgences are the pious frauds of the faithful. So I had heard it said by many by way of proverb, whom I then imitated. I revoke it therfore and say, that indulgences are the most impious frauds and impostures of the wickedest of the popes, by which they cheat both the souls and estates of the faithful. But this proposition, with the foregoing one, and the four following, I have revoked in the book of the *Babilonish Captivity.*

Articles XIX. XX. XXI. XXII. he says again he has before revoked, and has begged, and does the same now, of all booksellers and readers, that they would burn what has been disputed and written by him of indulgences. For he did not then know when he laboured about them, that the Pope was Antichrist, who by these and the like workings of error, destroyed the Christian world under the empire of Sathan.

Article XXIII. he says, he has strongly enough proved in a sermon of excommunication; nay, by their own words, where the Pope says, that excommunication is me- lib. vi. de
sent ex-
commu dicinal, and not mortal nor eradicating. But if it deprives men of the common spiritual good things, certainly it is mortal, because it separates the soul from God.

Article XXIV. he says, is proved, because the Pope himself says it is medicinal, not mortal but disciplining. But that which is medicinal and enlivening no body ought to fear but those who composed this bull, &c.

Article XXV. he says, he very easily proves by experience or fact. For the Bishop of Rome never was over all the churches of the whole world, nor is not yet, nor, as he hopes, ever will be.

Article XXVI. First, says he, I deny that Christ's word to Peter, *Whatsoever thou shalt lose,* &c. was said to Peter only. Nor did I ever say this; for he asked all his disciples, *Whom do men say that I am?* And Peter answered in the name of all of them, *Thou art the Christ.* So also in the name or person of them all he received the keys.

Article XXVII. This article, says he, I prove thus: *Other foundation can no man lay than that is laid, which is Jesus Christ.* Here you have a foundation laid by the Apostles. But every article of faith is a part of this foundation, wherfore no other article can be laid than what is laid.

Article XXVIII. These things, he says, he wrote of indulgences at a time when he was less skill'd in things. For, adds he, I spoke foolishly: I condemn the article myself. For since in it the question turns on things not necessary, I ought not to have attributed so much power to the Pope, or to a council, as to allow that they can make necessary what is unnecessary. But so I ought to have said as I now say; If the Pope and a council have been such fools as to spend their time and study in determining things not necessary to salvation, they are to be taken and despised for fools and madmen, with all their masquerade determinations. Since there are many things necessary to salvation which alone ought to be treated of.

Article XXIX. How spitefully and treacherously, says he, does that most holy Vicar of Christ take my words? for thus he represents this article, as if I would, that any one might oppose councils as he listed. Wheras I have taught, that we should dissent from, and oppose councils, if at any time they determined things contrary to Scripture or themselves. My mind, I say, is, that Scripture should be the judge of councils.

Article XXX. I have been mistaken, says he, as to this article, and have revoked it, and do now revoke it as to what I've said, that some articles of John Huss are evangelical. Wherfore now I say thus: that not *some* but *all* the articles of John Huss were condemned at Constance by Antichrist and his Apostles in that synagogue of Sathan composed of the most cursed sophists.

Article XXXI. This article, says he, I have so copiously defended in my Sermons on the Epistle to the Galatians, and afterwards in my *Resolutions* against the doctrinal condemners and incendiaries of Lovain, that I see nothing else in the incredulous adversaries of it, but the *ears of a deaf adder stopping his hearing*, or, as the Apostle says, their being *turned unto fables* from hearing the truth.

Article XXXII. he says, plainly follows from the former, unless that it is to be added which he has elsewhere more copiously affirmed, that this venial sin is not such in its own nature, but by the mercy of God.

Article XXXIII. I prove this, says he, *first* by the example of the whole Church, which from its beginning

until now burnt no heretic, nor would at any time burn
any.　Now it's a wonder, if it was the will of the Spirit,
that heretics should be burnt, that in so many ages some
were not burnt.　But they'll say, at Constance John Huss
and Jerome of Prague were burnt.　I answer, I speak of
heretics, whereas John Huss and Jerome were Catholics,
and were burnt by heretics and apostates and the disciples of Antichrist. *Secondly*, from Scripture, Esai. ii.
They shall beat their swords into plowshares, and their
spears into pruning hooks. Esai. xi. *They shall not hurt*
nor destroy in all my holy mountain. Christ gave his
Apostles no arms, nor imposed any other penalty than
that *he who did not hear the Church should be accounted*
as an heathen man, Matt. xviii.　The Apostle, Tit. iii.
teaches, that an heretic should be avoided; he does not
command him to be killed with fire and sword.　And to
the Corinthians he says, *there must be * heresies that they* * sects.
who are approved may be made manifest. When the
disciples would have fetch'd fire from heaven to destroy
the Samaritans, Christ restrained them, saying, *Ye know*
not what spirit ye are of.　The Son of Man came not to
destroy men's lives but to save them. This is that which I
also said, and do still say, that, according to Christ our
master, they who persecute men with fire are not the
children of a good spirit.　Of what spirit then? of an evil
spirit, who was a murderer from the beginning.

Article XXXIV. he says, he also proves by our own
unhappy experience.　In that hitherto we have had no
success against the Turk; and his force and empire are
immensely increased by our wars with him, and we have
suffered ourselves for so many years to be gull'd by impostors and Roman legates, so often devouring our money
and estates by the most impudent sale of indulgences and
faculties for the Turkish war.

Article XXXV.　If what has been said in the XXXI.
and XXXII. articles be true, this article is likewise true.
For if the good work of a righteous man be a mortal sin

CHAP
XII.

when referr'd to the judgment of God, how much more is the whole mortal life if it be not succoured by the Divine Mercy? Briefly, this article, says he, is not mine but Job's, ix. *b Though I were perfect, yet should not my soul know it.*

Article XXXVI. is grounded, he says, on the saying of Augustine. *Free will without grace avails nothing, unless it be to sin.* But I pin not my faith on Augustine: let us hear the Scriptures. Christ says, *Without me ye can do nothing.* What is this nothing that fice will does without Christ?

de spiritu
et litera ca.
iv.
John xv.

Article XXXVII. About the matter of this article, says Luther, the sophisters trifle ridiculously enough, quoting that passage of the Psalmist, *We went thro' fire and water, and* c *thou hast brought us out into refreshment.* For they have not brains, wit, or thought enough to see, that if this be said of purgatory, all the martyrs and the whole Church went into purgatory. Since these things are said in the name of the martyrs and all the afflicted, for whom they themselves know it is an injury to pray.

Psal lxv
apud Vulg

Articles XXXVIII. XXXIX. XL. he says he has disputed, and has protested, that he was ignorant of the things contained in them, and that he has not yet found any proof or certainty of them.

Article XLI. and the last, Luther calls a very elegant, rhetorical, artificial, proprial, and truly papal conclusion of these Articles, really worthy of the most holy Vicar of God to invent. By a metaphor, says he, it is said to blot out the sacks of beggary, because sacks are as writing tables, or as writings or pictures which may be blotted out. But I don't remember I said a tittle of prelates or princes, but only, that I wished there were no orders of mendicants or beggars, to obtain which wish there is no need of the

---

b The Latine Vulgate reads, *Etiam si simplex fuero, hoc ipsum ignorabit anima mea,* which the Doway translators thus render *Although I shal be simple, the self same shal my soul be ignorant of*

c ——— et eduxisti nos in refrigerium.

assistance of princes or prelates, but only of every one's understanding christianity.

13. To this book of Luther's, in his own defence, our Bishop wrote an answer, which he called *A Confutation of the Lutheran Assertions*, of which I shall hereafter give a particular account. I must now divert a little to the Bishop's perfecting the settlement and endowment of St. John's College.

CHAP. XIII.

1. *The Bishop petitions the King for his license to dissolve the two Nunneries of Higham and Bromhall, and to appropriate their estate to the College of St. John's. 2, 3, 4, 5, 6. Some account of these Nunneries and their dissolution. 7, 8, 9, 10. What has been said in excuse of these proceedings.*

1. NOTWITHSTANDING the Bishop had pretty well got over the difficulties he met with about the site and building of the College of St. John's, and that it was opened for the reception of the scholars and students for whom it was intended; yet still there was wanting a sufficient endowment to maintain so many as the foundress designed should be here educated. For a part of this purpose, I've already shewn the Bishop had obtained a grant of the dissolved Maison Dieu at Ospringe, and that the several lands, impropriate parsonages, &c. belonging to that hospital should be appropriated to the College of St. John's. But this, it seems, was not sufficient to answer the expenses of this new foundation. The Bishop therefore resolved to petition the King for his license to dissolve a couple of nunneries in which was dissolute living, which could not by the ordinaries be regulated, and to appropriate their estates to this newly-founded college.

2. One of these nunneries was in the Bishop's own diocese, at a little village called Higham, about four miles from Rochester. It was founded by King Stephen, who placed in it a prioress and sixteen nuns, who were profest of the Order of St. Benedict, or black nuns, and made his daughter Mary the first Prioress of it. The King's two sons, William and Eustache, were likewise great benefactors to it. Of this nunnery the Bishop of Rochester, as diocesan, was the Visitor. Thus in the beginning of the reign of King Edward III., Hamon of Heth, at that time

Lambard's Perambulation of Kent, p. 487, ed. 1596, 4°.

Bishop of Rochester, confirmed the election of Mawde of CHAP. Colchester to be Prioress of this house: and about four- XIII. teen years after he visited both the Prioress and whole society of nuns. The situation of this nunnery being in a lonely place, remote from houses, and far from neigh-bours, this proved a temptation to the nuns to indulge their wanton and sensual inclinations, and to admit people of the same lewd and vicious dispositions, especially priests, with whom they imagined they might be familiar without scandal or suspicion, to resort to and frequent their house. By this loose and infamous course of life, the nuns not only became very scandalous, so that women of any virtue or principle would not continue in the house, or be pro-fest of it: by which means the number of nuns was de-creased from sixteen to three or four at the most; but they had so far, through their carelessness and misma-nagement, and expensive living, wasted and dilapidated their estate, that when our Bishop came to the See, he found the nunnery itself much gone to ruin, and only the Prioress, one Anchoreta Ungothorpe, and *three* nuns be-longing to it· upon which his Lordship visited the nun-nery, and there being no money to put it into repair, the Bishop not only advanced a good deal himself towards repairing the dilapidated buildings, but by his care and industry procured large contributions from others for the same purpose. He likewise encreased the number of nuns by adding two more, not finding, I suppose, a maintenance for a greater number.   But it was not long before it was 1511. discovered, that three of these were too familiar with Sir Edward Sterop, Priest and Vicar of Higham, and that two of them, Elizabeth Penney and Godlife Laurence, were actually with child by Sterop. Upon this the Bishop went to the nunnery, and finding things to be as they were re-ported, ordered these lewd nuns to do penance.

3. In this posture the affairs of this nunnery seem to have continued some time after. So far as appears, not a thought was entertained hitherto of the dissolution of it,

but only its reformation and restoring endeavoured. It seems scarce probable, that the Bishop should be at so great an expense himself, and take so much pains to procure the charitable contributions of others, to repair the site and buildings of this nunnery, had he then resolved to get them all demolished and the society dissolved. But the Bishop being entrusted with others to dispose of Lady Margaret's bounty in building and endowing St. John's College in Cambridge, and wanting to augment it's estate for the better subsistence and encouragement of the great number of fellows and scholars intended to be placed there by the foundress, had now fixed his eyes on the estate of this nunnery, among other estates, as proper for this purpose. Application was therefore made by him to the new king, Henry VIII. as founder, and the state of the nunnery represented to him as follows · that the number of the nuns was decreased to three, and that these were become very infamous for their lewdness and unchaste manner of living; that by these means their estate was wasted, and the buildings of the nunnery gone to decay; and the ends of their first institution not at all answered, since divine worship, regular observance, hospitality, alms, and other works of piety which ought to be there done, and had used to be done, were now manifestly lessened and gone to decay. It was further shewn to His Majesty, that the most noble woman the Lady Margaret, late Countess of Richmond and Derby, and his Grace's grandmother, after that she had founded a certain college, which she called by the name of Christ's, and had begun to build the college now called St. John's the Evangelist, in which she designed for ever to maintain fifty students, before she could bring this her purpose to effect went the way of all flesh, and so left her good design unfinished. His Majesty was therefore petitioned to grant his royal license for the dissolution of this nunnery, and appropriating the estate belonging to it to the Master and Fellows of this college. To this His Majesty assented, prudently

considering the divine displeasure arising from the cor-
ruption of manners and dissolute lives of the nuns, and
very much desiring, that the Christian faith should be encreased and propagated, and being somewhat moved by a
love of good learning, and especially of that which is
divine.

4. The King's license being thus obtained, his Lordship, as diocesan and Visitor of the nunnery, orders a 1521.
process to be made and executed, for examining witnesses
on the several interrogatories put to them, to prove the
common fame of the ill reputation of the house, and the
dissoluteness of the nuns, and the dilapidation of the house,
and decay of the nunnery's estate. These witnesses were
John James of Strode, near Rochester, who had formerly
been a servant of the Prioress and convent at Higham
John Standeanought, Priest of the hospital of Strode,
Elianor Smyth, of Clif, widow, a midwife, and one Richard
Danyell, of Clif. These all agreed in their evidence, that
this nunnery had a very ill name and reputation for lewdness in the city of Rochester, the parishes of Clif, Mepham,
Higham, Gravisende, Chetham, Strode, and other neighbouring places, and that it still laboured under the same.
James and Standeanought swear, that two of the three
nuns, ᵃElizabeth Penny and ᵃGodlife Laurence, were both
impregnated, and had children by ᵃEdward Sterop, Priest,
Vicar of Higham, Smyth, the midwife, swears, that she
delivered Penny of a male child; and James, that he saw
her in the priory when he waited on the Bishop thither,
sitting and bewailing herself. But there's no such evidence of Laurence's having a child. James only swears,
that the Prioress ᵃAnchoret Ungothorpe told him she

ᵃ Jan. 26, 1506. In ecclesia conventuali de Higham sue dioc Anchoret
Ungethorpe de consensu domine Agnetis Swayne monialis ejusdem monasterij fecit expresse profiteri et quandam cedulam professionis sue ibidem
peripsam aliis lectam crucis signo signavit et eidem reverendo patri realiter
tunc tradidit, presentibus, &c.

Penultimo die mensis Maij, A.D 1508, idem reverendus pater in palacio

CHAP.
XIII.

was with child by Sterop as well as Penney, and Standea-nought says no more than, that she as well as Penney was impregnated by Steropp, and was delivered of a child; but there's no evidence to prove what child, or when and where she had it, as is attested of Penney. Of the other nun, dame Agnes Swayne, I don't observe any accusation in the fore-mentioned answers, and therefore, I presume, she suffered for the crimes of others rather than for her own. However this be, she first made her resignation and renunciation into the holy hands of the reverend father in God [b] John Busshoppe of Rochester, her Ordinary, as it is exprest in the form, of all her ryght, tytle, interest, and possession that she had in the monastery, and from them departed for ever by those presents. This resignation was made before John Bere, notary, who formally attests it, on the eighteenth of December, 1521. Penny's resignation is dated December 21, and Laurence's January 3, being expressed in much the same form with that of Swayne's. The Prioress Ungothorpe was dead, and no other chosen in her room, for want, I suppose, of a sufficient number of nuns to proceed to an election. Of all this an Act was made sometime after, which was authorised, ratified, and confirmed by the Bishop's pontifical authority, and by the Prior, and Chapter, and [c] Arch-

Coll. No.
XXII.

suo Roffensi admisit Dominum Edwardum Sterop cap[m]. ad vicariam perpetuam de Higham.

Godliva Laurence, Elisabetha Penney admissæ moniales de Higham, Mar. 21, 1508. Margeria Hilgerden priorissa. Penney was, after the dissolution of the nunnery of Higham, removed to that of St. Sepulchre's without the walls of Canterbury, for which an annuity of 26s. 6d. during her natural life, was paid by the College of St. John's to Joan the Prioress of this house.

Anno Regis
Hen. VIII.
Sexto de-
cimo.
A. D. 1525.

[b] In the Bishop's register is the following entry concerning the dissolution of the Abbey of Lesnes or Lesues, in Eryth, in this diocese, by Cardinal Wolsey. Dissolucio monasterij de Lesons per Card. Wolsey, ordinis Sancti Augustini, de expresso consensu et voluntate D. Willielmi Tischurste tunc Abbatis dicti monasterij, in consulto reverendo patre Johanne Roffe Episcopo loci Ordinario, 1524.

[c] Nicholas Metcalfe, S. T. P. who was presented by the Bishop of Rochester to the rectory of Sturmouth, in the diocese of Canterbury, Octob. 8, 1509, and promoted to the archdeaconry of Rochester, A. D. 1512.

deacon of Rochester, by their several instruments for that
purpose.

5. The other nunnery was likewise of black nuns, and seated at a place called Bromhall, near Windsor, in Barkshire. This, I suppose, was likewise of royal foundation; and the nuns having misbehaved themselves as the nuns of Higham had done, application was made by the Bishop to the King for his license to dissolve the nunnery, and apply their estate to the College of St. John's. Accordingly, the King granted his letters patent to the Bishop of Sarum, their Ordinary and Visitor, in which he required him to execute his pastoral authority in excluding or expelling the Prioress and nuns, and bestowing or placing them in other virtuous houses of religion. Upon this, I presume, the like process was issued by the Bishop of Sarum against these nuns, as we've seen was executed against the nuns of Higham. However this be, the Prioress and nuns all resigned their right, &c. and their estate was all appropriated to the college. The resignation of Joan Rawlins, the Prioress of this nunnery, bears date August 9, 1521.

6. To make all these proceedings the more effectual, the Bishop obtained of Pope Clement VII. his bull, to ratify and confirm the dissolution of these two nunneries, and the King's grant and appropriation of their estates to the college. This bull is dated October 1, 1524, and is to the following effect: "That wheras in a petition exhibited Coll No.
XXIII.
" to him it was shewed, that the late prioresses and nuns of
" the nunnery monasteries of Bromehall and Higham, of the
" Order of St. Benedict, and the dioceses of Salisbury and
" Rochester, to which the parish churches of Higham,
" Sonynghill, Allworth, and Rokland, in the dioceses of
" Rochester, Salisbury, and Norwich, were perpetually
" united, incorporated, and annexed, for certain just and
" lawful causes were summoned before the Ordinaries
" of the places, their faults and demerits so requiring, and
" were by the ordinary authority deprived of and removed

" from the said monasteries, their governments, and admi-
" nistrations, and the monasteries themselves were reduced
" as it were to profane uses, and that no nun inhabited
" them · and that the King had given, applied, and ap-
" propriated for ever the moveable and immoveable goods,
" and whatsoever rights pertained to the said nunneries of
" Higham and Bromhall, and the churches aforesaid, to
" the college, for the decent sustenance of the Master,
" Fellows, and Scholars, for the time being; that therfore
" he was humbly supplicated on the part of the said
" Master and Fellows, &c. who asserted, that the rents,
" income, and profits of the goods and properties of the
" aforesaid monasteries and churches, did not exceed the
" yearly value of twenty gold ducats of the chamber, ac-
" cording to common estimation, that he would vouchsafe
" to add the force of apostolical confirmation to this dona-
" tion, application, and appropriation of the King's for
" their subsistence, and in them wholly to suppress and
" extinguish the names of the monasteries, their prioris-
" sals, dignities, order, and conventuality, and anew for
" ever to apply and appropriate to the foresaid college
" the goods, propertys, and endowments of these monas-
" teries and churches aforesaid; and that accordingly he
" did by these presents approve and confirm, by the apos-
" tolic authoritie, the application and appropriation afore-
" said, and decree, that they should obtain the force of a
" perpetual confirmation. Thus were these two nunneries
" both dissolved, and their estates claimed by the King, as
" devolved and rightfully belonging to him as founder, by
" reason of there being no nuns living in them, given and
" appropriated to this college. And so, it's observed, these
" nunneries fell, a lasting monument to all future ages,
" and to all charitable and religious foundations not to
" neglect the rules, or abuse the institutions of their
" founders, lest they incur the same sentence."

7. In excuse of these proceedings, it was said, that the
nuns placed in these two houses of religion were, by reason

of their heinous wickednesses and very depraved manners, a
perfect scandal and disgrace to christianity, and that they
never could by the Ordinaries be brought to good order.
But it seems as if the Ordinaries had but little authority
over these houses, if they had no power to redress their
disorders, and to oblige the nuns to live according to the
rules of their profession. However this be, the Bishop
fairly owned, that he and the other executors of the Lady
Margaret were advised by their counsel to make suyte to
the King to have some hospital, or religious house or benefice, to be appropriated by the King's grant to the
college, and that in pursuit of this advice they petitioned
the King for the grant of these two nunneries: so that
had these religious houses been reformed by the power of
the Ordinaries, it would not have answered *their* purpose
who wanted their estates.

8. It has likewise been suggested, that the dissolution of
these two houses was a leading case to Cardinal Wolsey's
design at Christ Church in Oxford, and the King's general
dissolution of the other religious houses afterwards. But
it's plain this was not the first precedent of this kind. If
we look some years backward, we shall find, that Archbishop Chichely, about A. D. 1438, procured a license for
the dissolution of the priories of New Romney, in Kent, Historia et
and Wedon Pinkney, in Northamptonshire, and of several Antiq
Oxon.
cells, and appropriating their estates to his College of All
Soul's in Oxford. About ten years after William Patten,
alias Wainflet, Bishop of Winchester, obtained the like
license of the King for the dissolution of the hospital of
St. John's in Oxford, and appropriating all its mannors,
lands, and possessions, spiritual and temporal, to the College of St. Marie Magdalen, which he founded in Oxford.
As to the general dissolution of either the lesser or greater
religious houses, this was not till twelve or fourteen years
after the suppression of these two nunneries, and could
not therefore, one would think, be so much as thought of
now. And therefore, however the Cardinal's zeal to serve

the Bishop, and forward his suit in this matter, might be
owing to his intention to promote the like suit himself on
the like occasion, which accordingly he did in less than
three years after, the King's readiness to comply with the
Bishop's desires could never be owing to any design *he*
had formed, to suppress all the houses of religion, and
apply their estates to other uses. Had not His Majesty
fallen out with the Pope, as thinking himself ill used
by him, it's not at all improbable, that there had been
no general dissolution of the religious houses in his
reign.

9. A late writer of what he calls, very improperly, an
ecclesiastical History, &c. is very solicitous to defend the
suppression of these two houses from the charge of sacrilege, a charge almost constantly brought against the dissolution of the other religious houses by the King and
Parliament, without a word being said in vindication of
their so doing. Thus he pleads in *his* way: "That this
Collier's
Ecclesi.
Hist. vol.ii. " dissolving of religious houses, and alienating their reve-
p. 19, &c. " nues to serve other purposes, was according to the prin-
" ciples of that age, and justified by the then received
" doctrines: that the supremacy of the Papal See, and
" the plenitude of its power, inferr'd an authority in the
" Pope of transferring the lands and revenues of the
" Church to what uses he thought fit: that the Popes had
" formerly given instances of their authority in this kind :
" that they had given leave sometimes to monks, who had
" been dedicated to holy purposes, to return to the world
" and revoke their dedication: What, therfore, should
" hinder them from altering the settlement of lands and
" recalling *their* separation? Lastly, that in settling the
" estates of these houses on colleges in the universities,
" they were not really alienated from the service of reli-
" gion, but only altered in the disposal, these academical
" societies being expressly dedicated to the honour of
" God Almighty." And it does indeed appear by Pope
Benedict XII. statues or constitutions concerning the

black monks, that [d]with the Pope's license, not only their estates might be mortgaged or sold, but the monasteries and priories themselves be alienated or transferred to others. And therefore Sir Thomas More very truly observed, that " there was not so precise provision made " against all sale of their lands, but, that they might be " aliened for cause reasonable approved by the advice and " counsell of their chief head ; and, that many a man was " there in the realme that had lands given or solde out of " abbyes and bishoprics both." But however this may justifie the sale or transfer of the temporalities belonging to these houses, I don't see how it defends the appropriating to them the spiritualties which they had: since if the detaining the tithes and offerings from those who minister in things pertaining unto God be a robbing of God, the principles of that or any other age can't make the alienation of these to be any other than sacrilege. As therefore these were, at first, unlawfully appropriated to these houses, so when they were dissolved, they should have been restored to the Church, and employed, according to their first institution, for the maintenance of those who ministred in holy things, and laboured in the word and doctrine. But of these consisted, at this time, a great part of the revenues of many an abbey and monastery, and they were too good a prey to be let go by the new impropriators. As to the mannors, granges, and other revenues of these houses, which are called their temporalties, they were not properly the estate of the Church but of the State, and therefore might certainly be alienated or transferred to another use, without the Pope's leave, by those whose estate it was, when it was found to be to

CHAP. XIII.

English Works, p. 332, col. 2

---

d Decernimus, insuper, quod cum civitas, castrum, villa, vel jurisdictio alicujus eorum feodum solempne aut grangia seu magnum teritorium vel magnus possessionum aut terrarum numerus vendenda vel obliganda, seu monasteria, prioratus vel ecclesia, a jure permisso alienacionis titulo, alienanda, vel in alios transferenda extiterint, vendiciones seu alienaciones aut translaciones hujuslibet fieri nequeant ni eciam prius consulto Romano pontifice ac ejus super hijs petita licencia et optenta, c. 12, MS

their damage and prejudice to let them continue as they
were. If it was according to the principles of this age, as
has been shewn before, that the abbey lands, &c. might
be mortgaged and sold to the laity by the monks themselves, without the guilt of sacrilege, it must certainly be
as lawful for the King and estates of the realm, who first
gave these lands, to resume them when they found their
good intention abused, without incurring that crime. Since
if the civil powers have a right to prohibit their subjects
giving away their lands to monasteries, &c. as being * in-
commodious to the public and inconsistent with its safety
and welfare, they have certainly a right, for the same
reason, to resume the estates which are already so given.
But indeed the humour of building and endowing what
they called religious houses, which was very violent, and
lasted a long while, seems now to have pretty well spent

English
Works, p
333, col 1

itself; insomuch, that Sir Thomas More observed, that
" at this time, as for abbies or such other great founda-
" tions there were not many made, nor had been of a good
" while, except somewhat done in the Universities," meaning, I suppose, the College of Corpus Christi in Oxford,
now founded by Bishop Fox, and the two colleges of
Christ's and St. John's at Cambridge, and these, Sir
Thomas said, " the substance of them were not all founded
" upon temporal lands anew taken out of the temporal
" hands into the Church, but of such as the Church had
" long before, which were now translated from one place
" to another."

* Non quod nefas sit —— ubi immensa opum vis et ad luxum usque re-
dundans copia (et erat in monasterijs copia et excrevit in immensum)
demere de acervo aliquid tam conjesto et cumulato ——dum eorum menti
ne fiat fraus qui Deo hæc solenni ritu dedicarunt, &c. *Ep. Andrews ad
Bellarmini Apolo responsio.*

CHAP. *XIII.

1. *Wolsey calls in Luther's books, and orders the Pope's Bulls which condemned them to be fixed on the doors of the Churches. 2. Luther's books are burnt at Paul's Cross, and the Bishop of Rochester preaches on that occasion. 3. An account of his Sermon. 4. W. Tyndal's reflections on it.*

1. ON Luther's being thus condemned by the Pope at Rome, Cardinal Wolsey, as the Pope's legate *de latere* here in England, and to complement the King on his new title of *Defender of the Faith*, directed his ᵃletters, dated May 13, 1521, to the bishops of every diocese throughout the kingdom, wherein he recites the fore-mentioned bull of the Pope's, and the articles condemned by it, and orders them to enquire after Luther's books, many of which had been translated into English and dispersed here, that so they might be delivered up to them or their commissaries within fifteen days, and that upon pain of the greater excommunication, &c. By the same letters the Pope's bull, to which were annexed the forty-one articles of Luther's just now mentioned as condemned by it, was ordered to be fixed to the folding doors or other public places of every cathedral, collegiate, or parish church.

2. It seems as if on the publication of this injunction of the Lord Legate's, several of Luther's books were brought unto the bishops and their commissaries: since we find that by his order some of them were burnt this year at St. Paul's. On this occasion the Bishop of Rochester preached a sermon there, which was afterwards printed

A D. 1521.

ᵃ June 4, 1521. Rev. pater in manerio suo de Halling recepit quasdam literas Reverendissimi in Christo patris D. Dom. Thome Cardi Eboraci ad denunciandum Martinum Lutherum Herereticum. *Reg. Fisher.*

both in ᵇEnglish and ᶜLatin.   Nicholas Wilson, the pub-
lisher of it in Latin, tells us, that it was established by a
decree of the fathers of the Church, that Luther should
be taken for or deemed an heretic, and his books committed to the fire · and that when this was done at London, and there was present a great multitude of the clergy
and laity, our Bishop preached this sermon.

3. His Lordship, on this occasion, chose for his text
those words of our Lord to his disciples, John xv. *When
the Comforter is come, whom I will send unto you from the
father, even the Spirit of Truth who proceedeth from the
Father, he shall testifie of me:* which words, he observed,
offered to us *four* notable instructions, as against all perilous whirlwinds of heresies whensoever they arise; so
especially against that most pernicious tempest which
Martin Luther had raised in their time.

First, he observed, that in these words is promised to
us the Spirit of Truth, to comfort us in all doubtful opinions which may arise in Christ's Church.   And here he
took occasion to explain three things: 1. That the instructions of this holy Gospel pertain to the universal
Church of Christ. 2. That the Pope is *jure divino* head
of the universal Church. 3. That Martin Luther, who
separates himself from this head, has not in him the Spirit
of Truth.   The *first*, his Lordship says, Luther cannot
deny: since in his book of the *Babilonish Captivity*, he

ᵇ A Sermon very notable, fruitful, and godlie made at Paule's Cross in
London, Anno Dom. 1521, within the octaves of the Ascension, by that
famous and great clerke John Fisher, Bishop of Rochester, concerning the
heresies of Martin Luther, &c.

ᶜ Contio quam Anglicè habuit Reverendus pater Joannes Roffensis Episcopus in celeberrimo nobilium conventu Londini eo die quo Martini Lutheri
Scripta publico apparatu in ignem conjecta sunt, versa in latinum per Rich-
ardum Pacæum a serenissimi Regis Angliæ secretis, Virum Græcè et Latinè
peritissimum   Cum gratia et privilegio.

At the end

Excudebatur in præclara Cantabrigiensi Accademia per Joannem Siberch,
Aᵒ M D XXI.

observes, that ^d if we grant that any one Epistle of Paul's, or any one place of any Epistle of his does not pertain to the universal Church, the whole authority of Paul is made void. Now, says the Bishop, if this be true of the words of Saint Paul, it is much more true of the Gospels of Christ, and of the several places contained in them. As to the *second*, the Bishop asserts, that the Jews were the shadow of Christians; that Moses and Aaron, who were their heads, were the shadows of Christ and his vicar St. Peter, who under Christ was the head of the Christian people. To prove this, he makes the following comparison. Moses and Aaron were both priests; Moses was chosen by God, and Aaron by Moses at God's command, and to him, in Moses's absence, was committed the care of the Jews. Likewise Christ and Peter were priests of the new law: Christ indeed was chosen by All: God his father, and Peter by Christ, and to him, when he was absent, he committed the care of his people, saying, *pasce oves meos, pasce, pasce*—feed my sheep, feed, feed. Next, Moses went betwixt All· God and Aaron in the people's causes, and Aaron betwixt Moses and the people in God's causes, as the Scripture shews us in the *fourth* of Exodus, v 16. where God speaks to Moses of Aaron in these words: *He shall be thy spokesman unto the people; and he shall be to thee instead of a mouth, and thou shalt be to him instead of a God.* Now you shall see how Christ was Peter's mouth unto God; for he said unto Peter, *Symon, Symon, behold Sathan hath desire to have you, that he may sift you as wheat: but I have prayed for thee, that thy faith fail not; and when thou art converted, strengthen thy brethren.* Is it not plain from hence that Christ was the mouth of Peter, pleading his cause with God the Father, and praying that his faith failed not? On the contrary, was not Peter the mouth of Christ, when being converted

---

^d Quod si demus unam epistolam aliquam Pauli, aut unum alicujus locum, non ad Universalem Ecclesiam pertinere, jam evacuata est tota Pauli autoritas

he strengthened his brethren? Last of all, Moses went up into the mount to speak unto God, and Aaron remained to instruct the people. Has not Christ likewise ascended to God the Father into the high mountain of heaven? and did not Peter remain to instruct the people committed to his care? This figure, the Bishop confirms by Christ's paying the tribute money, Matt. xvii. This *tribute, he says, was a poll-tax levied on them who were reckoned the heads of families, and Christ ordered it, that it should be paid for no others than himself and Peter, for thus the rest were exempted. If, adds the Bishop, we join this fact of the Gospel with the figure mentioned before, what is more evident to prove that Peter under Christ was the head of his universal familie? But Luther, the Bishop says, objects here, that he does not understand how there can be two chiefs; which, says his Lordship, I do indeed wonder at; since it is manifest in Scripture, that Aaron was called chief, and that Moses was not under him. Whence it's necessary to conclude, that they were both chief, one under the other, in respect of the people. As Paul makes many heads, when he says, The head of the woman is the man, the head of the man is Christ, and the head of Christ is God. See, the woman has these three heads, God, Christ, and her husband, and besides all these, has her own head, which nature gave her. The Bishop concludes this his *first* instruction with telling his auditory, that by this means they understand after what manner the Spirit of Truth abideth for ever in the universal Church of Christ, and that the Pope under Christ is the head of the Church; and that from hence it will be briefly demonstrated, that the Spirit of Truth is not in Luther.

* This tribute was half a shekel, paid every year by every Jew above twenty years old to the Temple. This was demanded of Christ and Peter at Capernaum, where they both dwelt, Matt. viii. 14, and Christ accordingly makes provision for the payment of it for himself and Peter, it being demanded now of none of the rest, who lived elsewhere.

To the *second* instruction, the Bishop says, relate those
words which immediately follow, *He shall testifie or bear
witness of me.* And that the tendency of it is, to subvert
one great foundation of Luther's, that *faith alone without
works justifies a sinner.* On which foundation he builds
many other erroneous opinions; and chiefly *that*, that *the
sacraments of the Church do not justifie, but faith alone.*
He concludes, that from what he has said, it is plain, that
faith alone is not sufficient, but that love also and works
are required for the justification of our souls.

For the *third* instruction, it follows in the Gospel, *And
ye shall bear witness, because ye have been with me from
the beginning.* From these words, and others before recited, the Bishop says, it will appear, and be made plain,
that there is other testimony to be admitted for sufficient
authority besides that contained in the Bible; which, he
says, if he can explain and establish, it will subvert a
great part of the opinions of Luther. To shew this,
therfore, he proposes it to be considered, that altho' the
labour of these three persons which this Gospel mentions
be individual, and that one is not separable from the
other, but all things are connected; yet the Scripture
assigns to them certain times wherein they instructed man-
kind touching the truth necessarily to be believed. And
first, God the Father instructed our ancestors by the
Prophets; next, the second person, the Son of God,
Christ our Saviour, was sent by the Father into this world
to instruct man both by himself, and by his Apostles, who
were from the beginning with him. These holy Apostles
have left us many things by word of mouth, which are not
written in the Bible. Last of all, the third person in the
Trinity, i. e. the Spirit of Truth, was sent to continue with
us for ever; and that he might be our perpetual comforter
in the Church of Christ as oft as the winds and storms of
heresies arise; and that he may open to us the pure truth
in which we ought to stand in every doubtful opinion.
But by whom, I pray, does he speak to us? By whom

does he teach us any thing of the truth? Truly, by none other than the holy fathers and doctors of the Church; according to that, *It is not ye that speak, but the Holy Ghost that speaketh in you.* When St. Basil was baptized, a wonderful light was seen shining about him; and it is not to be doubted but that thing was a sensible sign of the Holy Ghost. So whilst Ambrose wrote the xliiid. Psalm, a like light stood over his head in the form of a shield; which was what likewise happened to other holy fathers also. Wherfore it is not to be doubted but that the Holy Spirit spake in these bishops and doctors of the Church; but by far more amply in general councils, when many being gathered together assembled in one place. If there was in the Trinity any *fourth* person, or another spirit sent to us by Almighty God, we might somewhat doubt whether Martin Luther had met him in his travels, and led him away, and taken him from us. But since we are sure there are no more than three persons in the Deity, and that every one of them diligently teaches us the truth; and lastly, that there is no other holy Spirit but the Spirit of Truth, who shall for ever remain with us and declare to us the truth, it ought to be no wise doubted by us, that Martin Luther has not this Spirit of Truth; since he is one who teaches things contrary to this truth which the Spirit has here taught us. For he clean takes away the traditions of the Apostles, he rejects general councils, despises the doctrines of the holy fathers and doctors of the Church, and with his whole strength labours to subvert all the ordinances of the Church, and especially the seven Sacraments. He takes away free will, and asserts, contrary to all the doctrine of the Church of Christ, that all things come to pass of absolute necessity. Wherefore, it is plain, that he hath another wretched spirit, i. e. the spirit of error, and not of truth. But here Luther, says the Bishop, as he is one of a shrewd wit, will oppose us, and say, that general councils sometimes err, and as they err in one place they may do so in another, and for that reason he is not bound to pin his faith on any of them. But to this it may be answered, that the Prophets being sometimes left to themselves, that is, being mere men, erred from the truth : for the spirit of prophecy did not always enlighten the minds of the prophets. For example; King David, when he had resolved to build a 2 Sam. vii. temple to Almighty God, consulted the prophet Nathan whether he should do what he had resolved on: and Nathan approved the King's purpose, saying to him, *Go, do all that is in thine heart; for the Lord is with thee.* But Nathan was deceived, for he said not true. Will therfore this deception make, that we should believe nothing else that Nathan prophesied? God forbid. The same is to be said of the Apostles. For Peter, when he said to Christ, *Thou art Christ the Son of the living God,* spake by revelation, and Christ our Saviour commended him, saying, *Blessed art thou, Barjona.* But a little after he dissuaded Christ from his passion, saying, *Far be it from thee, O Lord:* and here he spake ill. Shall we not therfore believe what he said first, because he erred in the second place? This is certainly contrary to reason. In the same manner, I say, that the doctors of the Church are not therfore totally to be rejected because they have sometime erred, that we might be sensible they also were men and left to themselves. In like manner, altho' some of the latest general councils have not, perhaps, been called together with that piety and charity as was meet, which yet, the Bishop says, he does not affirm, and by permission have erred in some particular article, it would be very unreasonable for us therfore to condemn all the rest.

The *fourth*, and last instruction, the Bishop observes, overthrows the arguments by which Luther's followers defend him. This defence, his Lordship says, consists of these three particulars. First, they say, that Martin Luther is notably skilled in the Holy Scriptures, and proves all his opinions by their authority: that he lives a religious

N

life, and by his doctrine and other virtues has got him many followers. Next, they affirm, that he has his mind fixed on God, and is so far from sparing the authority of any when it comes in competition with the truth, that he has excommunicated the Pope, who arrogates so much to himself by his own authority as not to believe those are of the Catholic Church who do not embrace his opinions. Lastly, they say, he has a wonderfully fervent zeal towards God, by which he is stirred up to labour with all his might to bring the whole world to be of his opinion, as thinking, that whilst he does this, he offers to God a special sacrifice. These things, the Bishop says, when they are heard by a weak mind, forthwith it is in peril, as being inclined to believe these things, and to distrust the doctrine of the Church; for who can think any other than that such a man walks in the way of ᶠtruth? But the words of the Gospel, which remain and follow, plainly answer these things offered in Luther's vindication. *These things have I spoken unto you, that ye should not be offended. They shall put you out of the synagogues: yea, the time cometh that whosoever killeth you will think that he doeth God service.* But some may think, that these words pertain only to the time of the Jews, who cast the Apostles out of their synagogues, or to the times of the tyrants, who put to death great numbers of Christians at the beginning of the Church. But if this were so, they would not contain a general instruction to the Catholic Church, as, he says, he collected at the beginning of his discourse. Wherfore they much more belong to the times of the heretics, and are rather to be understood of their persecution, than of any others. Wherfore, O Christian! when thou hearest that Luther is a man of great learning, and skilful in the

---

ᶠ On the other hand Ludovicus Vives, who was our Bishop's contemporary, tells us, that Luther's learning was made by some an argument against learning, as if it was the seminary of errors. *At docti sunt Græci ac Latini sermonis Lutherani et Lutherus ipse quos pontifex Romanus et Academiarum consensus damnavit.* De cau. corrup. Artium, lib. ii. p. 74.

Holy Scriptures; that he is one of virtuous endowments,
and has many followers, think with thyself that there have
been many others before him in the Church of Christ
who by their learning and perverse interpretation of the
divine words have raised the like storms. Foɩ with what
a tempest did that famous heretic Arrius harass the
Church of Christ? How many souls did he destroy?
Was not *he* a man of gɩeat learning, of singular eloquence,
and, as far as appeared, of a holy life? Did not he confirm his opinions by the holy Scripture? St. Augustine De Hæresi-
mentions fifty-seven capital heresies. But now the authors Quodvult-
of them every one proved their several opinions by the deum.
authoritie of the Scriptures; and a great many of them
were men of a very subtle wit, of deep learning, acute in
finding out strong reasons, and who made pretensions to a
virtuous and holy life; and had that peculiar faculty of
applying and wresting the Scriptures in such a manner as
that they seemed to confirm their erroneous opinions.
Lastly, such was their life, their learning and explanation
of the Scriptures, that they got themselves many followers
and fautors, as well bishops as emperors, and other Christian princes, whom they abused in a wonderful manner.
Wherfore it was necessary, that our Saviour Jesus Christ
should leave an instruction and admonition to all Christian
people and the universal Church of this persecution; and
so he did, saying, *These things have I spoken unto you,
that ye be not offended.* Agen, when thou shalt hear, that
Martin Luther has a constant mind and fixed on God, &c.
thou mayst depend upon it, that other heretics also have
all of them so behaved themselves. Notwithstanding, the
Church of Christ is but one, holy Catholic and Apostolic
Chuɩch. It is one, having one head, that is the Pope,
who is the Vicar of Christ, from whom it is called One.
And tho' there are in this Church many sinners, yet, on
account of the holy sacraments which remain, and daily
restoɩe sinners, and also by reason of the Holy Spirit,
which continually abɩdes in it, it is called Holy. And

CHAP.
*XIII.
because it is not assigned or limited to any one certain nation or people, but is common to all, it is called Catholic, that is, universal. Lastly, because it is derived from the Apostles, and especially from the prince of the Apostles, St. Peter, it is called Apostolic. This Church alone is the spouse of Christ; the residue are not, but are synagogues of Satan, and councils of devils. Wherfore, O Christian! be not astonished when they excommunicate and separate true Christians from their synagogues. Lastly, when thou shalt hear, that Martin Luther has a fervent zeal towards God, and thinks himself bound in conscience to do as he does, &c. be thou yet here also strong in thy faith, and take notice, that thy Saviour has admonished thee of this also, saying, *But the hour will come, &c.* But if the other heretics, Luther's predecessors, have not done the same, then think with thyself that Luther is somewhat. Did not the Arrians the same? Did they not furiously rail against the catholic bishops and presbyters ; and not only murder men's souls by their pestilent heresies, but cruelly kill great numbers of the bodys of Christians ? Did not the Donatists do the same ? Did not the disciples of Wiclif do the same ? For altho', out of fear of the laws of the land, they did not dare to kill any one, yet they delivered a paper of articles to the secular lords, in which they exhorted them to take their adversaries out of the way. And what do you think Martin Luther and his followers would do, if he had the Pope and his fautors in his power, whom he so often calls by way of reproach, Papists, Papastres, and Papens. He would not, I verily believe, have treated them more courteously than he has treated their books, that is, the Decretals which he burnt.

4. In this manner did the Bishop think fit on this occasion to harangue this great assembly : forgetting in the meanwhile, that tho' he judged or condemned them who did such things, he did the same. For if Luther's burning the Pope's Decretals was a specimen of the treatment

which he would give the Pope himself if he had him in his
power, what must be thought of the burning Luther's
books? Has not *that* the same appearance? Agen, are
the terms Papists, &c. more odious and reproachful than
the name of Heretics? Or have they who boast of their
being of the Holy Catholic Church, been at all wanting in
their invectives against excommunications, persecutions,
&c. of those who have differed from them?

5. On this sermon of the Bishop's, William Tyndal Obedience
of a Chris-
tian man
afterward reflected in the following manner. He observed,
that the Bishop proved by a shadow of the Olde Testament, i. e. by Moses and Aaron, that Sathan and Antichrist, our most holy father the Pope, is Christ's vicar and
head of Christe's congregation. Moses, saith he, signifieth Christ, and Aaron the Pope. And yet the Epistle
to the Hebrews proveth, that the high priest of the old
law signifieth Christ, &c. Next, he says, that the Bishop,
a little after the beginning of his sermon, alledgeth a saying of Martin Luther's, that " if we affirm that any one
" Epistle of Paul, or any one place of his Epistles per-
" taineth not unto the universal Church, we take away all
" Saint Paul's authority," and thus reflects on it, that if it
be thus of the words of St. Paul, much rather is it true of
the Gospels of Christ, and of every place of *them*. This,
Tindal remarks, savours both of ignorance and malice: of
ignorance, because he understood by this word Gospel no
more than the four Evangelists, wheras the Gospel, which
signifies glad tidings, consists not only of them, but of the
Acts and Epistles of the Apostles : of *malice*, because his
Lordship craftily takes away the authority of Paul by insi-
nuating, that the Gospels are truer than that which Paul
wrote ; wheras, if it be so then is it not one Gospel which
the Evangelists and Paul preached, nor one Spirit that
taught them. Agen, Rochester, says Tindal, alledgeth
the beginning of the *tenth* chapter to the Hebrews, *The
law hath but a shadow of things to come :* and immediately expoundeth the figure clean contrary unto the

chapter following, and to all the whole Epistle, making Aaron a figure of the Pope, whom the Epistle maketh a figure of Christ. So he quotes halfe a texte of Paul, 1 Tim. iv. *In the latter dayes some shall depart from the faith, giving heed unto spirits of error, and devilish doctrine:* but it follows in the text, *giving attendance or heed unto the devilish doctrine of them which speak false thorow hypocrisy, and have their consciences marked with a hot iron, forbidding to marry, and commaunding to abstain from meates which God hath created to be received with giving thanks:* which two things who ever did, save the Pope, Rochester's god, making sin in the creatures which God hath created for man's use to be received with thanks. He alledgeth another texte of Paul, 2 Thess. ii. *Erit dissessio primum,* i. e. saith Rochester, before the coming of Antichrist, there shall be a notable departing from the faith. And Paul saith, *The Lord cometh not except there be a departing first.* Paul's meaning is, that the last day cometh not so shortly, but that Antichrist shall come first, and destroy the faith, and sit in the temple of God, and make all men worship him, and believe in him, as the Pope doth, and then shall God's word come to light again, as it doth at this time, and destroy him, and utter his jugling, and then cometh Christ unto judgment. What say ye of this crafty conveyer? would *he* spare, suppose ye, to alleage and to wrest other doctors pestilently, who feareth not for to juggle with the Holy Scripture of God, expounding that unto Antichrist which Paul speaketh of Christ? He alleageth for the Pope's authoritie St. Cyprian, St. Augustine, Ambrose, Jerome, and Origen, of which never one knew of any authoritie that one bishop should have above another. And St. Gregory, alleageth he, who would receive no such authoritie above his brethren when it was profered him. I would he would tell how Hierome, Augustine, Bede, Origene, and other doctors expound this texte, *Upon this rocke I will builde my congregation:* and how they interpret

the keyes also. Therto *pasce, pasce, pasce,* which Rochester leaveth without any English, signifieth not, *pole,*
shere, shave. Upon which texte beholde the faithfull exposition of Bede. Note also how craftily he would
enfeoffe the Apostles of Christ with their wicked traditions and false ceremonies which they themselves have
fayned, alleaging Paul, 2 Thess. ii. wheras Paul taught
by mouth such things as he wrote in his Epistles, and his
traditions were the Gospell of Christ, and honest manners
and living, and such a good order as becometh the doctrine of Christ. In the end of his first instruction, intending to prove, that we are justified through holy
workes, he alleageth halfe a text of Paul, Galat. v. *Fides*
per dilectionem operans; which he thus englisheth, *Faith*
which is wrought by love, and maketh a verb passive of a
verb deponent. Rochester will have love to go before,
and faith to spring out of love. Lastly, because all the
worlde knoweth, that Martin Luther slayeth no man, but
killeth onely with the spiritual sword, the word of God;
neither persecuteth, but suffereth persecution: yet Rochester, with a goodly argument, proveth, that he would
do it if he could. Martin Luther hath burned the Pope's
Decretals, a manifest sign, saith he, that he would have
burnt the Pope's Holiness also, if he had had him. A
like argument, says Tyndal, I make: Rochester and his
holy brethren have burnt Christ's Testament; an evident
sign verily, that they would have burnt Christ himselfe
also if they had had him.

CHAP. XIV.

*1. Of Luther's answering the King's Book.   2. The con-
tents of his Answer.*

1. IT has been already said, that to the book of the
King's before mentioned, Luther wrote a very warm and
violent answer. This was now published, being dated
A. D. 1522. from Wittemberg, July 12, 1522, and dedicated to Sebas-
tian Schlick, a Bohemian count, who favoured the Reformation. The reason of this dedication was, that the King,
among other things, had objected to Luther, or rather
reproached him, that he was preparing to make his escape
out of Germany into Bohemia. The King of England,
multa sali- says he, in this book, talks like a driveler, or prates till he
va blaterat. fomes at the mouth agen, of my running away into Bohemia, and fancys, that therfore is his book victorious and
well written, if Luther make his escape to the Bohemians :
so weak and womanish is the foolish King's spite! But,
says Luther to the Count, I write this to you, that I might
make the beginning of this flight with you, and thro' you
and your dominions proceed to all Bohemia. The King,
a lay-man, has written to his most holy Pontiff; and I,
who was lately by the Pope's mercy a clerk, ought to
write to a most Christian laic.

2. In the beginning of the book itself, he takes notice,
that among the Papists there is a most vicious kind of
disputing, which is called begging the question : so that,
says he, when I cry, the Gospel, the Gospel, Christ,
Christ! they answer, the fathers, the fathers, custom, custom, statutes, statutes. Such is this book of the King of
England, who does nothing but argue from the traditions
of men, the glosses of the fathers, and the use of the
several ages. Not content with my allowing these, provided they are left free, this new god makes necessary
articles of faith of whatever he finds said or done by men ;

which articles, unless I believe, in what a passion is he!
treating me as an heretic, and I know not what monster.
But, that I may not seem to treat the name of so great a
king with contempt, and may answer a fool according to
his folly, I shall very briefly make his folly manifest in this
little book, so far as my other employments will allow,
deferring till another time the handling it more largely.
For that almost every body's believing that this is none of
the King's book I am no ways affected with. I would have
it to be the King's, and would act against the foolish
King, who has suffered knaves to abuse his feigned name,
and fill a whole book with so great lies and virulence.
One of these, Luther supposed, was Edward Lee, afterward Archbishop of York, and well known by his disputes with Erasmus. He therfore adds, that the King
should not blame him, if he was treated by him harder
and more roughly than ordinary ; since he had not written
like a king, but rather like a slave, and used language very
unbecoming his princely dignity: that he was to be pardoned if he had only mistaken as men are apt to do ; but
that now, since he had knowingly and willingly told lies
against the majesty of his heavenly King, *he* had a right
in his sovereign's defence to bespatter even his English
Majesty with his own dirt and dung, and to trample under
his feet that crown which was so blasphemous against
Christ. Besides, since its plain, that the Thomists are so
stupid, and even a lethargic kind of sophisters, that nothing in nature was ever produced more gross and dull;
and that our King Henry affects in this book to be
thought an excellent ªThomist, whilst among other things
he dreams and snores of the character, and of the sacramental virtue in the waters, (prodigies which even the
companions of the sophist in the universities cannot endure
any longer,) it seems necessary that he should be twitch'd
with rough language to raise him, if possible, from this
most profound lethargy, that he may hear his own dreams.

ª ―― totum Thomistam qui nihil probet

But before I come to the thing itself, I shall, first of all,
purge or clear myself of two crimes objected to me. The
first is, that I often contradict myself. The other is, that
I slander the Church and the Pope, i. e. the bawd and
procurer and seat of Sathan, whose defender he himself is
lately declared to be with indulgences. That therfore I
may confute his impudent lie thro'out the world, it is fit I
should here relate in order the things of which I have
written. Of these there are two sorts: I. Those which
are taught in the Holy Scriptures, *viz.* Faith, Charity,
Hope, Works, Sufferings, Baptism, Repentance, the Lord's
Supper, the Law, Sins, Death, Free Will, Grace, Christ,
God, the Last Judgment, Heaven, Hell, the Church, and
such like · for these are heads of things which a Christian
ought to know, and which are even necessary to salvation.
These things I have so treated, that no one can say, I
ever treated them otherwise than I did from the beginning. I never contradicted myself, but have always continued of the same opinion from the first, and like myself;
witness my books which are extant, and all they who have
read them, and even the self-condemned conscience of the
lying King. Besides, who would believe, that so great a
King should not only dare to lie thus in charging me with
contradicting myself, but likewise openly to assert, that I
have so taught faith as to make good works needless, nay,
to affirm, that they are evil? as if there was nobody living who had read my works, and could prove *him* a liar!

The other sort of things of which Luther said he had
written, are those which are out of the Scripture, or foreign
to it, *viz.* Of the Papacy, Decrees of Councils, Doctors,
Indulgences, Purgatory, the Mass, Universities, monastical
Vows, idol Bishops, the Traditions of men, the worship
of Saints, new Sacraments, and such like, which are tares
sown by Sathan thro'out the Lord's field, and which the
Church cannot only be very well without, but also can't
indeed well subsist unless it be without them, or use them
at its free discretion; for nothing more pestilent can be

taught in the Church than the necessity of those things
which are not necessary. Since by this tyranny are consciences ensnared, and the liberty of faith is extinguished;
a lie is worshipped instead of the truth, an idol for God,
and abomination for holiness. If the King means, that I
am not consistent with myself in these things, because, at
first, I modestly dissented from them, and afterwards
utterly condemned them, who does not see the folly and
stupidity of this? If this be to be inconsistent with one's
self to think otherwise than he did before he knew the
truth and revoked his error, who, I pray, of the wisest
and best of men was ever consistent with himself?

As to the other crime alledged against him, *viz.* that of
slander, first of all, he says, it behoves the King to prove
his bitterness, and the Papacy's innocence. Otherwise,
why does Christ himself with so much vehemence inveigh
against the Scribes and Pharisees, and call them hypocrites, blind, fools, full of uncleaness and hypocrisie, and
man-killers? But let us come to the thing itself. The
chief, general, and only strength of Henry's wisdom in so
kingly a book is, not the authority of Scripture, or any
urgent reason, but that [h] Thomistical way of disputing, *It
seems so to me, I so think, I so believe.* Thus when I in
my book of the *Babilonish Captivity* had chiefly attacked
this Thomistical general principle, and set up the Holy
Scriptures against rite, use, custom, and humane authority, yet our lord King answers nothing, but *so it must be,*
it is the use, it has been long accustomed to be so, I so believe, the fathers have so written, and the Church has so
ordained. But if I say, how do you prove this use and
humane authority? it is answered, it must be so; it seems
so to me; so I believe: are you alone more learned than
every body else? This therfore is my general answer, and

[h] —— videns quæ esset Ecclesia quæ hoc determinasset, nempe Thomis-
tica hoc est Aristotelica. *Lutheri de Captivitate Babilonica.*

Quid hic dicemus, quando Aristotelem et humanas doctrinas facimus tam
sublimium et divinarum rerum censores. *Ibid.*

I divide it into two parts. If he alleges use or humane authority in manifest opposition to the Scriptures, let use, authority, the King, Thomist, sophist, Satan, yea, even an angel from heaven, be anathema: for nothing ought to prevail against, but every thing to be for the Scriptures. Such is that which the foolish King produces concerning the other part of the sacrament, contending, that use in not giving the wine to the people is valid against a very plain text of Scripture. But if he alleges use or human authority, which does not clash with the Scriptures, I am so far from condemning it, that I would have it tolerated, only with this proviso, that Christian liberty be safe, and that it be in our power to follow, hold, and change it when, where, and how we please. Wheras, if they will take from us this liberty, and attempt to make or decree necessary articles of faith, I again say, let him be anathema who presumes to do this, whether he be a foolish Thomist, or a stupid Papist, a King or a Pope. Such is our lord the King's urging for articles of faith, his sacraments of confirmation, matrimony, order, and unction, and the mixture of water with the wine, &c. But there are on our side more than two powerful divine thunderbolts against these Thomistical straws; as where Christ determines of all humane traditions, saying, *In rain do they worship me, teaching for doctrines the commandments of men.* Paul establishes it by a great authority, that our faith ought to stand on the words of God, when he saith, *My speech and my preaching was not with enticing words of man's wisdom, but in demonstration of the Spirit and of power; that your faith should not stand in the wisdom of men, but in the power of God.* We therfore adhere to the defender of our Church who saith, *I will build my Church,* not on the length of time, nor on the multitude of men, nor on it must be so, nor on use, or the saying of the saints; lastly, not upon John the Baptist, nor on Elias, Esaiah, Jeremiah, or any of the Prophets, but on the alone and solid *rock,* on Christ the Son of God. This is

Matt. xv.

1 Cor. ii.

the strength of our faith; we are here safe against the gates of hell.

Let us now come to the particulars of our Henry, and see how happily his Thomistical wisdom fits his principles to his conclusions. First of all, the King touches indulgences, which I had affirmed to be the impostures of Roman fraud. These he thus defends: if indulgences are impostures, not only the preceding popes will be impostors, but even Leo the Tenth himself, whom yet Luther much commends. But if Luther be of so great authority as to be believed by so great a King when he commends Leo X. why does he not give credit to him when he condemns indulgences? especially when here he is guarded by the Scriptures, by reasons and by facts; wheras the other is only a civility, or an act of complaisance to a man. He next defends the Papacy, which I had confuted by powerful texts of Scripture. To these he says not a word, but thus proves the Papacy· it must be so, because I have heard that India is subject to the Pope of Rome, as likewise Græce; St. Jerome also owns the Church of Rome for the mother-church. What will Luther dare to say against reasonings so notable and Thomistical?

Hitherto the King of England seems in jest; now he puts on a serious look, and applys himself to the business he has undertaken, to assert *seven* sacraments, beginning with the Sacrament of the Altar, in which I had reprehended *three* tyrannical acts. I. That one part of it was taken away from Christians. II. That Christians are urged to believe it a necessary article of faith, that the bread and wine are no more bread and wine after consecration. III. That they have made it a work of merit and a sacrifice. Here I have to do not with ignorance and stupidity, but with the shameless wickedness of Henry. He not only lies here as a most frothy buffoon, but in these serious matters he sometimes feigns, sometimes depraves and wrests things, saying and concealing whatsoever

he pleases.   Read my book of the *Babylonish Captivity*,
and you'll see I say true.   I have proved, that one part of
the sacrament is impiously taken away from the Christian
laity by seven arguments, which even then overcame me,
but now do perfectly triumph over me, since the most
glorious defender of the Papists with a royal fortitude
passes them over untouched.   But that speechless defender in things necessary, let us see how full of tongue he
is in his trifles.   The Church, says he, received the sacrament in the morning which Christ administred at night:
we mix water with the wine, of which yet the Scripture
says nothing.   Wherfore, if the Church could here make
alterations, and do or institute another thing, it could also
take away a part of the sacrament.   But this is to prove
by an impertinent fact, that the Scripture is to be abro-
gated : for to mix water with the wine is no more contrary
to either part of the sacrament, than to the Creation, or
the Nativity of Christ.   If therfore the King rightly
argues, wine is mixed with water without the Scripture :
therfore the Scripture touching one part of the sacrament
is to be deserted ; even that syllogism will be good, wine
is mixed with water, &c. therfore the Scripture relating to
the Creation, &c. is to be laid aside.   But what have
these people to do with Scripture ?   Whence is it proved
that the mass is necessarily to be celebrated in the morning ? or how is this contrary to Christ's institution, if that
be celebrated in the morning which he did in the evening ? I ask the same of mixing water with the wine.   Who
made this an article of faith ? who dares to say it is a sin
to celebrate without water ?   We reckon, that the communion of the sacrament is free ; or, that we are at liberty
to receive it either by day or by night, in the morning or
in the evening.   We are at our liberty as to seasons,
hours, places, vestments, and rites relating to it.   With us,
he does not sin who eats or drinks moderately before the
communion.   Christ, when he instituted the communion
at night, did not institute either morning or evening for

the communion: he says not a word of the time, persons, places, nor habits. Otherwise, if the particularitie of time was an article of faith, the particularitie or circumstance of age, of persons, of places, and of habit, would be likewise articles: and so it would not be lawful for any other then males of the age of manhode, as the Apostles were, to partake of that supper, and they too in lay habits. Lastly, we might not give it to women, not even to virgins, since the Scripture does not say, that they then partook of it. But now the other part of the sacrament is quite another thing: for Christ has not left *that* free or at liberty, but has instituted both it and the use of it in plain words, and that admit of no doubt: and in my opinion it were better and safer not to mix water with the wine at all, seeing it is a mere human invention, and has a perverse, nay, the worst signification: for it does not signifie our incorporation with Christ, since such a sign is not to be found in Scripture, but that which Esaiah mentions, *Thy wine is mixed with water*, i. e. the most pure Scripture of God is corrupted by humane traditions. Not that I condemn the custom of communicating in the morning and in sacred places, but we reject the necessity of so doing: for tho' the Church cannot be altogether without rites and ceremonies, it yet does not make of them laws and snares of souls.

When I had demonstrated, that it is not necessary to believe, that the bread and wine are transubstantiated, the Thomist King attacks me with two engines; of which the first is a saying of St. Ambrose, the other that Thomistical battering ram called, *It must be so.* But is a saying of Ambrose a necessary article of faith? Be it so, that he was of opinion, that the bread and wine do not remain after consecration: I would say, let Ambrose abound in his own sense. But sure that holy man never intended by this saying to oblige the conscience of any one as to an article of faith, since he could not demonstrate it from the

Scripture, but as he himself freely thought in this manner, so he allowed others to think otherwise.

Another argument of the King's is, that the words of Christ are plain, who says, *This is my body,* not with this or in this is my body, as if it was *in* the bread, or together *with* the bread, but *this is my body,* to wit plainly declaring, that all that which he held out to them was his body. But here I agen accuse the King, not of stupidity, but of fraud; since he so mangles the words of Christ, and royally skips over my argument, as if he had authority to plunder the words of God, and dispose of them as he pleases. He, according to the rude and asinine philosophy of the Thomists, fits the pronoun *this* to the predicate *my body,* and in the mean time craftily conceals the weight of my argument. For what I aimed at in the whole dispute was this, that the pronoun *this* could not relate to *my body* in that place. I did not want to be told, that there was nothing but body there if the pronoun *this* demonstrated, that there was nothing but body. But first he ought to have shewn, that the pronoun *this* does appertain to the predicate, and answered my reasons against it. It's nothing to the purpose, that Christ did not say *in* this, or *with* this, but *this* is my body. May not I likewise say, Christ did not say the bread is transubstantiated into the body? But the King labours here to shew, from the context, that the pronoun *this* relates to the bread, and that the words plainly sound thus, *This is my body,* &c. i. e. this bread is my body. For the text runs thus, He took bread, he blessed, broke, and said, this is my body, &c. You see that all those words, he took, blessed, broke, are said of the bread: and the pronoun *this* demonstrates the same, because that very thing which he took, blessed, broke, *this,* I say, being taken, blessed and broken is meant. When it's said, *this is my body,* not the predicate but the subject is demonstrated; for he did not take, bless, and break his body, but bread: ther-

fore it does not demonstrate the body, but bread. These CHAP.
are plain words, which the King conceals, and urges that XIV
naked proposition, *this is my body*, and fits the pronoun
this to body.

Hitherto the King has acted the part of a philosopher,
it is now proper to see how he acts the divine. When I
had produced those words of the Apostle, where he so
expressly calls this sacrament *bread, the* bread *which we
break, is it not the communion of the body of Christ?* He
does not say, *the body which we break.* To this answer is
made, that the Holy Scripture is wont sometime to call
the thing itself that which it has been, or to which it is
like: as Exod. vii. Aaron's rod devoured the magician's
rod, i. e. the dragon, which was Aaron's rod, or into which
Aaron's rod had been turned. But what a door has the
King opened to all hæretics and enemies of the faith? If
it be once admitted, that the authority of the Scriptures
rests on uncertain and fallacious words, what then may
not all the masters of all sects prove, disprove, maintain,
and defend? But supposing it true, that the rod is called
a dragon which was a rod, how will it follow, that here
that is called bread which is not bread, but was so once?
But, says the King, if Luther so rigorously takes the
words of Scripture, he will say, that Christ is even
wheaten bread in heaven, because he says, *I am the bread
which came down from heaven.* Likewise, that he is a
natural vine, since he says, *I am the true vine.* But what
child does not laugh at this? for the very consequence of
the words, the absurdity of the things, the contradiction
to common sense, as well as Christ's own explanation of
them, do all oblige us to understand him as speaking of
spiritual bread, as he says, *My words are spirit and life.*
There is nothing of this in the words of Paul speaking of
the bread of the sacrament, so far from it, that every thing
shews, that Paul is to be understood of wheaten bread.

But the chief and capital part of Henrie's assertion
is, that the mass is a good or meritorious work, and a

o

sacrifice. To prove this, the King argues thus: if the mass
weie not a good work, suiely the laity would never give
the clergy any temporal benefice for it. For the same
reason, if the laity did not dispose of their wealth to the
priests, the mass would not be a good work. It's not less
madness which follows, where he protests against medling
with my chief argument from Christ's own words, that the
mass is a testament and a promise, therfore it cannot be
said to be a work, or a sacrifice.

Next, the King proceeds to answer my reasons, and
first, he Thomisticates in this manner. '" He who cuts
" wood does a work, therfore he who consecrates does a
" work ; wherfore the mass also will be a work. But if it
" be a work, it is not a bad work but a good one." But
this is a new definition of the mass, and a new instance.
For if the mass be to consecrate, it may likewise be to cry,
to chaunt, to incense, to light wax tapers, &c. We own,
therfore, that at this rate the mass is a work. But the
mass is truly and properly, as we speak of it, the word of
promise, with a sign of bread and wine added to it. For
if every thing else be wanting, and you believe these words
of Christ, *This is my body which is given for you,* you
have indeed the whole mass. Next, if you receive the
sign with the same faith, you have the use and fruit of
the mass. From whence it is most manifest, that the mass
is not any thing of *our* work or word, but of Christ's alone,
as he is the giver of the word of promise, and of the sign
solum in in the bread and wine, and that it's use cannot consist in
recipiendo
et patiendo. offering or doing it, but only in receiving and suffering.

Next, in defence of the mass's being a sacrifice. the
King thus Thomisticates. " Be it so, says he, that the
" mass is a promise, it does not hence follow, that it is not
" at the same time a sacrifice; since in the old law there
" were sacrifices which were also promises." But the King

ᶜ Mirabimur profectò si cum is opus faciat qui imaginem facit ex ligno,
Christus nullum prorsus opus fecerit cum carnem suam fecerit ex pane.
Assertio 7 Sacramento. &c

should have produced one instance, however, of this assertion. For it's a manifest error to say, that in the old law
sacrifices were promises; unless the King has a mind to
speak figuratively, as if sacrifices did promise, i. e. did
signifie things to come in Christ. But this is not to assert
sacraments, but to play and trifle with words. He also
dares to affirm, that it is plain, that the priests do not only
that which Christ did in the supper, but that which he
also did on the cross. But I on the contrary say, that it's
plain, that the priests in the mass leave undone that which
Christ did at supper, and do that which the Jews did to
Christ on the cross. Nor do I only say this, but I prove
it also. For he who perverts and destroys the word of
God, he truly crucifies the Son of God. This is that
which all doe who of a promise make the mass a work,
since this is indeed to change the truth of God into a lie.
Next, he urges me with that canon of the mass, in which
the mass is called a sacrifice; by the authority of which
he would therfore have me obliged, because I have made
use of its words. For those words, *As often as ye shall do
this*, &c. are not to be found, he says, in the Gospel, but
those, *Do this;* but in Paul there are other words: as if it
was necessary that the Evangelists should agree in every
syllable, and appoint that form of the sacrament which the
Papists have imposed upon us as so immutable and necessary, that they make him guilty of mortal sin, and deliver
him to hell who shall omit that little word *for*. But I have
rejected, and do reject the canon, because, in direct contradiction to the Gospel, it terms those things sacrifices
which are signs added to God's promises, offered to us, to
be received by us, and not by us to be offered. Wheras, I
had written, that a sacrifice and the mass are inconsistent,
since a sacrifice is offered, and the mass is received, the
King appeals to the Bible, saying, Where in the old law
was there ever any sacrifice which was not both offered
and received? and boasts and triumphs as overthrowing
my principal argument: I answer, This is not my principal

argument, but that which above he has graciously yielded to me, *viz.* that the mass is a testament and promise. This, I say, is my capital argument. Yet, that I may say something to the triumpher, if he had only once opened and look'd into the Bible, nay, if he had but remembred Psalm li. which he read when he was a boy, he would not thus have triumphed; since there he would have read, that a whole burnt sacrifice, than which there was no sacrifice in the law greater and more celebrated, was all of it offered to God, and nothing of it received. But I would ask, where in the law is there any sacrifice that was received, and not all of it wholly offered? Will he make a sacrifice of the shoulders, breasts, &c. which were for the use of the priests? or will the King call that being offered which was brought by the people and the priests out of the fields and set before the Lord? At this rate, to bring and to offer must be the same thing. I for my part think it sufficient, that under the law whatever was offered in sacrifice to God was all burnt. What was not burnt, but was distributed, partly to the priest and partly to the people, was not offered, but was separated from the things that were offered and eaten. Last of all, he introduces the sayings of the fathers for the sacrifice of the mass, and wonders at my folly, who would seem to be wiser than every body else. But he is forc'd to own, that his fathers have very often been mistaken, and that his ancient use does not make an article of faith. As for me, I set against the sayings of the fathers, of men, of angels, and of devils, not antient use, not a multitude of men, but the word of the one eternal Majesty, the Gospel, which they themselves are forced to approve, in which the mass is evidently shewn to be a sign and testament of God, in which he promises us, and by a sign certifies us of, his grace. His rage, wherwith he inveighs against me as teaching, that faith without works is the best preparation for the sacrament, and that Christians ought not to be obliged by laws to receive it, I despise: for they are the words of a

man who thinks men may be made good before God by
the laws, and who knows little what faith and works are,
and how far the laws work on the consciences of evil persons.   But at the end of this head, it's worth while to
observe, with what anxiety he toils to establish the necessity of humane traditions in opposition to my opinion,
which is, that nothing ought to be determined that is not
contained in the Scriptures, or if there be, that it ought to
be accounted free and not necessary.   The King argues
thus: if nothing is to be observed but what is delivered
in the Scriptures, since it is not written that the sacrament
was received by Christ, it will follow, that neither may
priests receive it.   But this is begging the question.   The
King ought to have proved first, that it is necessary, on
pain of mortal sin, for priests to receive the sacrament; for
I say they are at liberty to receive or not: the necessity
of their doing it is all owing to human tradition and common use.   2. The King argues, Christ, not the Apostles,
consecrated the sacrament, therfor may not the Apostles
or priests consecrate.   But Christ instituted the use of
receiving when he said, *Take ye and eat:* and the office
of consecrating, when he says, *Do this:* for to do is to
imitate all that he himself then did.   The King quotes the
saying of Augustin, *I would not believe the Gospel, if the
authority of the Church did not move me to it.*   This saying is therfor wrested and depraved, that the Church,
i. e. the Roman harlot, who has nothing of the Church or
christianity but the title, may have ascribed to it the authority of making laws.   To this the King adds a saying
of mine, that the Church has authority to judge in matters
of faith.   But the King, like a child, wants to be taught
words; as if this authority of judging was the same with
an authority to make and establish laws.   Briefly, if Augustine had in so many words roundly asserted, that any
one in the Church has a power to make laws, who is
Augustine? by what authority is his saying an article of
faith?   This authority of making laws is to be proved by

CHAP.
XIV.

extraScrip-
turas.

a divine, not an humane edict. But Augustine speaks of the Church diffused thro'out the world, whose right it is to judge of opinions. *They* ascribe this to the Pope, whom they themselves own to have been often a member of the devil, and in a mistake. Nor do they only allow him a right of judging, but likewise of making a law, &c. It appertains to all and every Christian to know and judge of doctrine, and it so pertains to them, that he is accursed who in the least prejudices this right; since Christ himself has established this right by several and invincible proofs.

Matt. vii. *Beware of false prophets which come to you in sheeps' clothing.* Certainly, he speaks this to the people against the doctors, and commands them to avoid their false opinions. But how can they avoid them unless they know them? and how can they know them, if they have no power to judge of them? To the same purpose all the prophets admonish the people not to give credit to false prophets. But what is this admonition but a declaration and confirmation of the people's right of knowing and judging? Let us

John, x   come to the new law. Christ says, *My sheep hear my voice, but the voice of strangers do they not hear, but fly from them.* Does he not here make the sheep judges, and transfer the right of knowing to the hearers? And Paul,

1 Cor. xiv. when he says, *Let one speak, and the rest judge,* &c. does he not mean that here the judgment should be in the hearer? So whatsoever Christ says, Mat. xxiv. and elsewhere of false doctors; whatsoever Peter and Paul say of false Apostles and masters, and John of proving the spirits, all tends to shew, that the authority of judging, proving, and condemning is in the people, and that most justly. For every one believes rightly or falsly at his own peril, and therfore ought every one to take care of his own self that he believe rightly. So that even common sense, and the necessity of salvation urges, that the judging of doctrine should necessarily appertain to the hearer. We have therfore without controversy an authority of knowing and judging of doctrines. But it does not from hence

follow, that we have likewise an authority to make laws.
This is the property of God alone : it is our part to know
his law and word, to prove and judge it, and to distinguish
it from all other laws.

But here it will be said, if it be every one's right to
judge and prove, what method must be taken if the judges
disagree, and every one judges according to his own capacity ? Wherfore it is necessary there should be one to
whose judgment all others should be content to stand,
that so the unity of the Church be preserved. I answer,
what is done now where all stand to the judgment of one
Pope ? where is the unity preserved here ? Is this to
keep the unity safe, to be united in the outward name of a
Pope ? Where remains the unity of minds ? who is certain in his conscience that the Pope judges rightly ? But
unless there be certainty there can be no unity. Therfore
under the Pope there is indeed the appearance of an outward unity, but within there is nothing but a most confused Babylon. We must therfore enquire after another
way of the Church's unity.• This is that which Christ
lays down, John vi. *They shall be all taught of God,
every one who has heard of the Father cometh unto me.*
That inward spirit, I say, alone maketh men of one mind
in an house. This teacheth them to relish the same
thing, to judge, know, prove, profess, and embrace the
same. Where he is not, it's impossible there should be
unity ; and if there be any, it is outward and pretended.
This is sufficient for my defence of the first sacrament, in
the asserting of which the King has most of all laboured,
as not being ignorant that in it was placed the principal
safety of the papistical kingdom. The others I am forced
to defer till another time, being overwhelmed as it were
with many other businesses, but especially with ᵈtranslat-
ing the Bible, a very necessary work !

ᵈ He first mentioned his design of translating the New Testament in a
letter to Langus, 1521. In January, 1522, he thus wrote to Nicholas Ams-
dorff I will translate the Bible, altho' I have undertaken a load too great

Nor is there much labour required to refute the foolish Thomists in the other *six* sacraments, since thro'out them all, they offer nothing worthy of an answer, except that one thing of the Sacrament of Order, *viz.* Paul's commanding Titus to ordain presbyters in every church. But the Thomistical masque does not see either what I say, or what he himself answers. I denied order to be a sacrament, i. e. a promise and a sign of grace added, such an one as is baptism and the bread. I never denied, so far from it that I have asserted it, that order is a calling and institution of a minister and preacher; whether this be done by the authority of an apostle or a bishop alone, or of the people choosing and consenting together with him, it matters not: tho' it's done more rightly by the people's choice and consent, as the Apostles instituted the seven deacons. For however Paul bids Titus ordain presbyters, it does not yet follow, that Titus alone by his authority did so, but, after the example of the Apostles, he instituted them by the suffrages of the people. But as for those things, which from the laying on of hands he draws to this Sacrament of Order, children see that they no ways pertain to it. Laying on of hands was then a visible donation of the Holy Ghost. But what shall I say? He will not understand even the name of a sacrament, which he plainly shews when he treats of that place of St. Paul, Ephes. v. as relating to matrimony, which Paul lays down of Christ and the Church, saying, *This is a great sacrament, but I speak of Christ and the Church.* For the Scripture no wise allows matrimony to be called a sacrament; since a sacrament is used thro'out the whole Scripture to signifie a thing secret and hidden, which you can attain to by faith alone: wheras matrimony is so far from being a thing hidden and perceived by faith, that unless

for my strength to bear, but it is a work that is great and worthy. Accordingly, he was the whole summer, 1521, learning Hebrew and Greek, that being a master of those languages he might be equal to this great undertaking. *Seckendorf, Hist. Luth.* § 125.

it be done openly before your face, it cannot be matrimony.

Luther concludes this his answer to the King's book
with telling his readers, that if his rough usage of the King
offend any one, he has this to answer for himself: that in
this book he has to do with senseless monsters, who have
despised all his best and modest writings, and even his
most humble submission, and have been hardned by his
modesty: that, however, he has abstained from virulence
and lies, of which the King's book was very full: that it
is not much if he does treat with contempt, and lash an
earthly king, when he himself is no way afraid in his writings to blaspheme, and by the most virulent lies to profane
the King of Heaven. Seckendorf observes, that, not only Com. de
in the judgment of Erasmus, who was master of a cautious Lutheran.
civility and a fawning obsequiousness, but according to § 114.
the opinion of more sincere friends, Luther here exceeded
all bounds. But that he himself was not insensible of it,
as appears by what has been already said, and by other
writings of his. Thus, in a letter to Spalatinus, he tells
him, that he knew he should give many offence by thus
writing against the King of England, and treating him as
a foolish and virulent Thomist, but it was my pleasure so
to do, and it was necessary for many reasons. To the
same purpose in a letter to another of his friends: " The
" Elector, my prince, and other friends have often ad-
" vised me to write more softly, but I always answered,
" and do now also answer, that I would not; that my
" cause was not to be reckoned among indifferent things,
" in which one might yield and dissemble, as I have
" hitherto foolishly done: and in the book itself," he says,
" they have provoked me to war, therfore shall they have
" war: they have despised peace when offered, therfore
" shall they have no peace. Let it be tryed who will be
" weary first, the Pope or Luther." Maimbourg represents Luther as treating the King as a fool and one of the
mob, in a stile that's insolent, beastly, and furiously impu-

CHAP.
XIV.
_____
Histo. Lu-
theranismi.
dent. But to this Seckendorf answers, that the King was
the agressor ; that let any one who has leisure compare
both writings, and only remember, that the King, [e]laying
aside the state of a king, personates a Thomist monk, and
is not afraid to enter the lists with a man that was a
foreigner, who he knew was of a very free temper and
speech, and to provoke him with reproaches, and particularly with that of inconstancy. The laws of his sect ought
to have restrain'd the King from this temerity. However,
Luther owned, that this book of the King's was written in
ferè omni- almost the best Latin of all the books that were written
um latinis-
simus. against him, and about two years after wrote, as it's said,
Septem. 1,
1525. a very submissive letter to the King, wherin he excused
himself as guilty of rashness and folly, and being more
governed by the advice of those who did not favour His
Majesty, than by his own inclination : to which he added,
that he had learnt from unquestionable witnesses, that the
book which he answered, tho' appearing under His Majestie's name, was not yet the King of England's, but that
he was very much ashamed, and afraid even to lift up his
eyes before His Majesty, for suffering himself to be moved
to use so much levity towards such and so great a King,
especially when he was a worm which deserved to be
overcome with contempt alone. The inconsistency of the
excuse he here makes, that he was *more governed by
others' advice than his own inclination,* with what he elsewhere says, is very obvious. King Henry therfore, in
answer to it, upbraided him with levity and inconstancy,
and assured him, that many of greater credit than *his*
creditable witnesses, knew, that the book which he published against him was his own ; that it was approved by a
great consent of good and learned men, and in particular
Sleidan's
Hist. of the
Reforma. by the honourable vote of the [f]See of Rome. When Lu-

[e] Vulgò et verè dicitur; hoc scio pro certo, quod si cum stercore certo,
Vinco vel Vincor, semper ego maculor. *Luther, de Captivitate Babilonica.*

[f] In a private letter that Pope Leo wrote to the King, he among other
things told him, *Ut Spiritum affuisse Sanctum apparcat,* that it appeared by

ther had read this answer, and found inconstancy objected
to him, as if he had changed his opinion in matters of religion, which he look'd upon not only as a private injury
done to himself, but also to the reformed religion, it much
troubled him, he said, that to gratifie his friends, he had
written so submissively to the King: that the King of
Denmark had put him in hopes, that Henry being gently
dealt with would receive the reformed religion, but that
now he was sensible of his error: that he had been just so
served by Cardinal Cajetan, George Duke of Saxony, and
Erasmus of Roterdam, to whom, at the desire of others,
he had written affectionately, but that all he got by it,
was to render them more fierce and untractable: that it
was a foolish thing for him to imagin to find godliness in
the courts of princes, to look for Christ where Sathan bore
rule, and to enquire after John Baptist among courtiers
who were clad in purple: that therfore since he could do
no good by that gentle and loving way of writing, he would
take another course for the future. A very strange resolution! but thus easily are men led to indulge their own
inclinations.

I've here put all these things together, that the reader
who is qualified to judge of such matters may see what
was said by the principal advocates on each side of the
questions debated by them. Since I thought it unfair, and
no way like a faithful and impartial historian, to give an
extract of the ᵍKing's book, of which I was obliged to
take notice, on account of the Bishop's being concerned
in it, and to pass over the book which occasioned it, and
the answer made to it in utter silence.—

his writing, that the Holy Spirit was present with, or assisted him in writing it.

ᵍ Mr. Collier gives us large, tho' partial, extracts, from the book called
the King's, without taking any manner of notice of any more of Luther's
reply than his indecent language, and yet he determines for his readers, that
the King seems to have the better of the controversy, and, generally speaking, to be the sounder divine. However, he owns, that the King gives rough
language sometimes, treats Luther with contempt, and drives his invective
pretty strong upon him *Eccle. Histo.* vol II.

CHAP. XV.

*1. The Bishop of Rochester answers Luther's book against
the Pope's Bull. 2. An abstract of this Answer.*

A. D. 1523. 1. THE next year the Bishop published an answer to
Luther's book before mentioned which he wrote against
the Pope's bull.[a] This he entituled *A Confutation of the
Lutheran Assertion.* In his epistle to the reader, he tells
him, that he would not have him think that he has written
so much against Luther because he was confident that it
was in his power to reclaim him; for if he had had but
the least hopes of *that,* he would sooner have sent this
work to the press; but he perfectly despaired of Luther's
ever returning to the Church: that, according to St. Paul,
whosoever is an heretic, and much more, whoso is the
author or leader of sects or heresies, after he has been a
second time admonished of his error, and he does not repent, there is then no manner of hope of his amendment,
but he ought to be avoided by all Christians, and to be accounted perverse or obstinate indeed, since he is self-condemned, or condemned by his own judgment: that all
this agrees exactly to Luther, who if he be not an heretic,
there never was an heretic; since he attempts to establish
his opinions in opposition to the sentiments of all the
orthodox fathers: and what else is this but introducing a
sect and heresy? for *choice* is by the Greeks stiled αἵρεσις,

---

[a] Assertionis Lutheranæ confutatio per reverendum patrem Joannem
Roffensem Episcopum Academiæ Cantabrigiensis Cancellarium.
Cum privilegio Imperiali   Privilegium serenissimi
      in triennium   Regis Angliæ reperies in proxima pagina.
Apud inclytam Antwerpiam in ædibus honesti viri Michaelis Hilflenij,
An. M.D.XXIII. postridie Calend. Januar.
Round this title is printed, within a border of pictures, in Hebrew, Greek,
and Latin, this sentence, *Woe to the foolish prophets who follow their own
spirit and have seen nothing.* On the next page, as is intimated here, is the
King's privilege to John Addison, B.D. the Bishop's chaplain, for the sole
printing it for *three* years.

heresy, and therfore whosoever chooses to teach what
differs from the common sense of the whole Church, he is
deservedly reckoned an heretic, and an author or leader
of sects or heresies, for he cuts himself off by his own
choice from the orthodox, that is, fiom those who think
rightly with the Church. The Bishop closes this address
of his to the reader with telling him, that he has in this
book so discussed in order the articles which Luther has
not been ashamed to assert in opposition to the Pope's
bull, that he judges there is nothing which Luther has
produced in asserting them, but what he has throughly
confuted.

2. At the beginning of his preface to this *Confutation*,
the Bishop observed, that since, at length, as fiom other
books, so especially from two which Luther had published, *viz.* one of the *Babylonish Captivity*, the other of
the *Assertion of all his Articles*, he had discovered himself to be a manifest or open heretic, and a common enemy
of the whole Catholic Church, he judged it to belong to
all christians to oppose his heresies with what arguments
they can: that the former book King Henry had opposed,
and not only so, but quite defeated, conquered, and over-
thrown it: that the latter he had now undertaken to demolish. Since he, who was a Bishop, such an one as he
was, was ashamed to turn a deaf ear to so many injuries
and affronts every where offered by a little frier, not only
to the Pope the Vicar of Christ, but likewise to the Holy
Scriptures, which were foully wrested by him, and to the
general councils of the most holy fathers, which he had in
the utmost contempt: who likewise had affronted the interpreters of the Scriptures, men most famous for their
learning and holy life whome he despised; the venerable
sacraments of the Church which he most basely mangled,
and the apostolical traditions and usages of the Church
received for so many ages, all which he set at nought. He
was ashamed, his Lordship said, to enjoy the satisfactions
acquired by a learned idleness, when he saw his most

illustrious King, for the avenging these injuries, so power-
fully in his own person engaging in this war.

3. His Lordship comes next to what he calls his
proeme, in which he lays down these *ten* conclusions, which
he calls truths, and which he undertakes to maintain.

I. It's very plain, that in the interpretation of the Holy
Scriptures, a great many have foully erred by having a
[b]confidence in their own parts.

II. The very same thing may likewise be done at this
day, so that if any one in interpreting the Scriptures [b]de-
pends on his own spirit, he may easily be led into error.

III. Where any controversie arises about the Holy
Scriptures, or any truth relating to the Catholic Church, it
is convenient that the dispute should be decided or determined by some judge.

IV. Every controversy so raised cannot always be determined by the sole aid of the Holy Scriptures.

V. Therfore was the Holy Spirit sent, that he might
always continue in the Church to make it more certain of
the truth when such errors arise.

VI. That Holy Spirit has hitherto used, and will always
do so, the tongues of the orthodox fathers for the extirpa-
tion of heresies, and the full instruction of the Church in
doubtful matters.

VII. Whosoever does not receive the orthodox fathers,
it is manifest, that he despises the doctrine of the Holy
Spirit, and has not that Spirit.

VIII. If the Holy Spirit has spoken by the mouths of
particular fathers for the instruction of the Church, he is
to be thought to have done so much more in the general
councils of the fathers.

IX. The apostolical traditions, altho' they are not delivered in Holy Scripture, are nevertheless to be observed
by true Christians.

X. But besides traditions, the customs also that are

[b] This was what Bishop Pecock was charged with.

received by the universal Church, are by no Christian
man to be rejected.

These, his Lordship tells Luther, are the Christian
arms or weapons, which he shall make use of against the
public enemies of the Church, and that *he* can reject none
of them if he will suffer himself to be called a Christian:
that he shall think it sufficient to produce the public usage
of the Church, or an apostolical tradition, or some general
council of the fathers, or some approved interpreter; and
that with these, where texts of Scripture are wanting, he
was to be assaulted. Thus does the Bishop begin his
confutation of Luther's proeme, tho' he could not but
know, that these authorities Luther had declared to be of
no weight with *him*, and that the insisting on them was
only a begging of the question. His Lordship proceeded
in charging Luther with inconstancy and retractation, in
that here he declared, that he regarded the authority of
no father any farther, than it was proved by the sentence
or declaration of Holy Scripture: wheras when he first
offered his conclusions to be disputed, he protested he
would hold and say nothing but what is and may be had,
first of all, in and from the Holy Scripture, next of the
Church fathers received by the Roman Church, and
hitherto observed by it, and of the Pope's canons and decretals. He next observed, how perilous it is for any one
to expound the Scripture by reason without authority:
that Luther's term *own spirit* is doubtful or uncertain: proprio spi-
that one may by those words understand either spirit of ritu.
Scripture, or the spirit of an interpreter: that he, the
Bishop, has hitherto spoken of the spirit of an interpreter: and that the Spirit of the Scriptures is no other
than the Holy Ghost. But his Lordship allowed, that
the Scriptures might have light given to them by men,
and that the fathers were sometimes mistaken, since they
were men as well as we; but that where they agreed
there was the true sense of the Holy Spirit.

These things being premised, the Bishop proceeded to a particular confutation of the several articles.

Article I. Concerning the sacraments, whether they confer grace or not, says the Bishop to Luther, because the King has dealt so largely with you, I will say nothing: but shall only answer to what you have offered in behalf of your opinion. But first of all, that error is to be combated which has taken too much hold of you, *viz. that* about faith; to which you ascribe every thing, and leave nothing to good works. For you think, that grace is conferr'd on men by faith alone, without any outward work. He next finds fault with Luther's definition of faith, *viz.* faith is nothing else but to believe that which God says or promises. If faith be nothing else but a belief of the promises and sayings of God, what Christian will not be reckoned to have faith, altho' he has no works, if so be he believes whatsoever is contained in both testaments to be true? The Bishop, therfore, shews, that Peter instructs us, that besides faith there are a great many other things necessary to justification: that justifying faith is fruitful of good works; that the ᶜjust or righteous man is said to be only initiated by faith, but not consummated; that so far he agrees with Luther, that without faith no body can be justified; as in infants he thinks that faith is divinely infused into them by the regeneration of baptism, tho' yet it is not any act of believing, as Luther's opinion, he says, is of faith, who denys, that faith is a certain habit quiescent in the mind, and asserts it to be a most lively act, which it cannot be in infants. To Luther's quotations from the Epistle to the Romans and the prophet Habacuk, *The just shall live by his faith,* he does not say, the just shall live of the sacraments, the Bishop observes, that neither

2 Ep. 1.

ᶜ On this Tyndal thus reflects, that now cometh my Lord of Rochester, with a little and vain distinction invented of his owne brayne —— if works do make justification perfite, then are not St. Paul's words true. *Works,* p. 237.

of these places prove, that grace is not conferr'd by the
sacraments: that Paul, it's plain, uses the word faith for
hope and confidence, rather than for bare credulity. As
for the text in the last of St. Marc, *He who believeth and
is baptized,* &c. the Bishop answers, that salvation and
justification are promised to him who is baptized and believeth, and that it's his opinion, that if any one believes
as much as it's possible, and yet shall refuse baptism, he
shall nevertheless not be justified: that not faith alone,
but faith with the receiving of the sacrament, justifies the
receiver. To Luther's argument from the Apostle's
words, Rom. x. *With the heart many believes unto righteousness,* he does not say, with the body the sacraments
are received unto righteousness, the Bishop replys, that it
does not follow from *he does not say so,* that it is not so.
He does not say, say you, *the just shall live of the sacraments,* therefore the sacraments do not give life. To
Rom. iv. and Gen. xv. *Abraham believed God,* &c. he answers, that Abraham did not want works whereby his faith
might be rendred more consummate.

Luther's arguments from reason the Bishop thus answered: first, by denying, that in every sacrament there is
a word of divine promise, which affirmatively promises
and exhibits God's grace to him who receives the sacrament. For a sacrament, he says, contains the word and
element, and these two are sufficient for a complete ratio
of a sacrament. As to Luther's instances in penance and
the Eucharist, he denys, that any one is absolved by virtue
of those words, *Whatsoever thou shalt lose,* &c. but rather
by virtue of them, *Whosoever sins ye remit,* &c. and yet even
they are not the words by which the grace of absolution is
performed, but others, *viz. I absolve thee in the name of
the Father,* &c. Luther's calling the holy Eucharist the
Sacrament of Bread, the Bishop tells him, is to establish
his heresy of the substance of the bread's remaining: but
that as Aaron's rod, tho' truly a serpent, is yet called a
rod, according to its former denomination, so in the

sacrament of the Altar, that which is truly the body of Christ goes by the name of bread, on account of its being like bread, and called so before it was changed or turned into Christ's body. As to Luther's concluding, that faith is necessary to those who are going to receive the sacrament, by which they may believe they shall obtain that which the sacrament promises and confers, the Bishop answers, that nobody denys faith to be necessary to those who receive the sacrament, but that he does not believe, that a man shall receive no grace from the sacrament, unless he has an explicit faith in the particular word of promise relating to the sacrament the very moment that he receives it.

This opinion of Luther's, that we are justified by [d] faith only, seems to have been a common handle to his adversaries to abuse and reproach him, as if he thought all good works, or a holy life, perfectly unnecessary. Thus, in the King's book, he himself observed, that he was inveighed against as holding, that faith without works is the best preparation to the sacrament, which he rejects with the highest indignation, as a very gross calumny. To the same purpose, the Bishop here insinuates, as if Luther's justifying faith was no wise fruitful of good works. But thus did that reformer defend himself, and this opinion of his. Where pure faith, saith he, is taught, works will come of their own accord, and without any hazard, whilst they learn that a greater stress, nay, the whole, is placed on the faith which doeth works. But now the Church is so filled with the boasting of external works, that one would think Christ spake of our time when he said, *When the Son of Man cometh shall he find faith upon the earth?* In short, since faith is a right and good opinion of God, and every opinion does of itself put

Seckendorf, comment. § 60.

[d] Bishop Gardiner compares it to the doctrine of *indulgences.* Now, says he, the devil perceyveth it can no longer be borne to bye and sell heaven, he hath excogitate to offre heaven without workes, for it so frely that men shal not nede for heaven to worke at all. *Answer to George Joye.*

men on working, it is not to be doubted but that he who
has faith will do all works.   For if an opinion and love of
a woman does not suffer a man to be idle, but, on the contrary, without either law or master, he does even more
than is required of him to do, how much more shall faith
influence and affect us? Is the world governed by its
opinions, and shall not faith alone be able to rule or direct
Christians? By this, I think, it's very plain how unde-
servedly Luther was reproached for this opinion, as if he
subverted all true piety.

Article II. Here the Bishop remarks, that the word *sin*
is used by Paul in many senses. 1. For original sin.
2. For the impure motions of the flesh. 3. For the consent of the mind to those motions: and then charges
Luther with gross ignorance or malice in attempting to
confound so various acceptations of the word in one.
The words of St. Paul, Rom. vii. he calls obscure ones,
but denys not, that concupiscencies remain in the body of
one that is baptized, only, he says, they are not to be
reckoned sins, according to the proper and peculiar ratio
of sin.   He affirms, that by baptism the guilt of original
sin is taken away from little ones; that they neither have
original sin, nor as yet the use of reason, so as to admit of
actual sin; so that they are wholly without sin: that
* original sin is not sin, according to the true ratio of sin : * fomes
that the guilt which, St. Augustine says, passes away in peccati.
baptism, is properly called sin, but that the concupiscence,
which remains after the guilt is removed, is by no means
to be called by that name.

Article III. The Bishop thinks something wanting
here to perfect the sense. For how, says he, does original sin retard the soul from the body, and from its entrance
into heaven? But he speaks of the soul after its separation from the body, which he thinks to be retarded by its per fomi-
sinful inclination from its entrance into heaven. But tem.
altho', says the Bishop, there are various opinions among
the schoolmen concerning original sin, yet I willingly follow

Augustine, who seems every where to say, guilt is taken away by baptism, that lust or concupiscence which remains in the flesh may not any more be properly called sin. For if it raise any motion in the mind, provided the mind do not consent to that motion, that motion will not be imputed to it for sin. His Lordship concludes, that in original sin there is the *guilt* and the *fomes* or inclination to sin: that the guilt being washed away by baptism, there yet remains the *fomes* or sinful inclination, which by a continual mortification of the flesh will at length be removed. But that from this it no way follows, that this inclination or incentive to sin, is properly sin, nor that it retards the soul from its entrance into heaven, if it's guilt has been before washed away by baptism.

Article IV. The Bishop charges Luther with maintaining elsewhere, that no body who goes from hence has perfect charity: from whence, he says, it will follow, that heaven gate is open to no body after death, unless he has first suffered the pains of purgatory; which is indeed ᵉmost absurd. To Luther's saying, that holy Scripture has nothing concerning the universal state of the souls of the saints after death, nor yet of purgatory, the Bishop answers, that by this he shew'd himself what he was, that his design was to make his Germans have an ill opinion of purgatory, that they might more easily be brought to despise indulgences. But that if purgatory be truly to be believed, and the holy Scriptures are defective in the proof of it, arguments for it must be fetched elsewhere, *viz.* from apostolical traditions, the usage of the Church, from the sacred interpreters, &c.

Article V. The Bishop observed, that many things were delivered by Christ and the Apostles by word of

---

ᵉ By the council of Florence, A. D. 1105, it was decreed, that *the souls of the saints are forthwith received into heaven.* But Dr. Stapleton owned, that this was directly contrary to the opinion of a great many celebrated ancient fathers, who thought, that the souls of the righteous did not enjoy the vision of God before the day of judgment. *Staplet. defens. autori. Eccle.* lib. 1. c. 2.

mouth. which were yet never committed by them to writing : that yet he did not doubt but that every one of these
parts of penance may be grounded on Scripture; but
since Luther own'd the two former parts, contrition and
confession, he had no occasion to dispute with him about
any other than satisfaction: that the common opinion of
the Catholic Church is, that after the guilt of sins is pardoned, there are still some remains in the minds of men to
be expiated by satisfaction, especially in those in whom
so great contrition has not preceded as was sufficient,
with the working together of D Grace, wholly to cleanse
the mind thro'out. The Bishop therfore undertakes to
prove these two things: 1. That after absolution there
remain for the most part the reliques of sins. 2. That
these reliques are to be expiated by some troubles to be
undergone or endured by us: that there are none of the
interpreters who have otherwise understood those words,
Matt. iii. *Bring forth fruits meet for repentance,* than as
meaning the bitterness of repentance · that if there be no
particular mention in holy Scripture of a septennial satisfaction, it does not therfore follow, that satisfaction is not
a third part of repentance : that he can easily imagine,
that Luther hates the word satisfaction : but that 'tis not
so much for the sake of the word. as on account of the
court of Rome, that he prosecutes it with so clownish a
malice.

Article VI. Contrition may be procured two ways, i. e.
by fear or love.   Luther, the Bishop says, rejecting *fear,*
would have contrition sought for by sinners by *love* alone ;
which opinion is widely different not only from the fathers,
but also from the Scriptures. As to Luther's saying, that
Cassian teaches this conclusion, and the common sense of
all men experiences it, the Bishop says, that this is a wonderful boldness, not to say rashness, thus to pronounce so
generally of the common sense of all men: that he wished
he had quoted the place of Cassian to which he refers,
since *he* can find no such thing said by him : that there is

not one way only of calling sinners, but that some are called by *fear*, others by *love;* and that *fear* is more necessary for this purpose than *love.*

Article VII. The falseness of this article, the Bishop says, appears from what he has said on the *fifth* article: for it takes away all satisfaction, which is so necessary to the penitent, that unless he before hand make satisfaction for the sins he has committed, he cannot have admission into heaven. The ancient fathers certainly thought, that nobody could rightly or duly begin a new life except he repented of his old one, and very severely was revenged on himself for former faults. That there are a great many proverbs which are not always very true, altho' this proverb may be true in some sense, as if we speak of those penitents who frequently begin repentance, but never finish it: that Luther misunderstood what Paul says, Gal vi. that *in Christ Jesus neither circumcision nor uncircumcision availeth any thing,* &c. as in the other text quoted by him, *If I have not charity I am nothing,* since in both places Paul's meaning is, that they are nothing, i. e. of no account, so far as relates to the obtaining of heavenly glory, but this is not to be altogether nothing. To Luther's saying, that the Blessed Virgin was disturbed at the entrance of the Angel, and by this very disturbance was impelled to a high love of virginity, the Bishop answers, that the Gospel no where asserts, that the Blessed Virgin was disturbed at the infusion of grace: that, however, the case is very different as to sinners, in whom there are great obstacles of grace, which are first to be shaken off by fear: and the mind so to be prepared and habilitated for the reception of grace. Whosoever therfore condemns this preparation, and concludes, that whatsoever goes before charity is a hurtful thing, he takes away from sinners all endeavours to rise again, and withall the disposition of amending themselves.

Article VIII. The Bishop thinks no one so blind and mad as, on account of Luther's opinion alone, wilfully to expose himself to so great peril, as not to open to the priest those sins which he either knows or doubts are mortal or deadly; especially when he understands, that the most antient, as well as most learned fathers have asserted, that there is so great a necessity of confession, that whoever shall sin mortally, it behoves them to disclose their sins either privately to the priest, or publickly before all the people.

Article IX. The proofs which Luther brings, the Bishop observes, relate to hidden or unknown faults, which if he had mentioned in the article, nobody, he thinks, would have condemned it. But because he pronounced after that manner, that he might be understood of sins, if any occurred to the memory of the person who confessed, therfore they rightly condemned it. For, says the Bishop to Luther, What should move you, when you was not ignorant that all the orthodox prescribe that sinners should disclose to the priest every sin which they can on the most diligent search remember, to order that they should not presume to confess their sins particularly? How this article follows from the former, the Bishop adds, he does not see.

Article X. This article, the Bishop says, at first sight, seems to have some appearance of truth; but when one looks nearer into it, it's nothing but the mere error of darkness. For Luther attempts to attribute to faith the whole cause of justification, and nothing to the Sacrament of Absolution. To Luther's argument, that Christ absolved Mary Magdalen for her faith, the Bishop replys, that he should read the Gospel more truly, and he would find, that first, Mary Magdalen's sins were forgiven for her love, *Her many sins are forgiven her, for she loved much.* But because faith was the beginning of this love, therfore Christ subjoins to the woman, *Thy faith hath saved thee.* To Luther's instancing in the paralytic, the Bishop observes, that it is his opinion, that faith is every where necessary for receiving the sacraments, and that also **Christ** required it of the paralytic, or the man sick of the palsy: that accordingly he believed on Christ without the least doubting, and did not any ways hesitate about his words or promise; but that it is much otherwise as to a priest: since of Christ it was no wise lawful to doubt whether he was Christ, and had authority to forgive sins; wheras of a priest who hears confession, nobody can be so secure that he is a priest, and that he has sufficient authority to absolve, as to leave no room for scruple.

Article XI. the Bishop says, contains in it no harm, according to the outward appearance of the words, nor is there any thing in it but what the orthodox assert. Since no one can be certain of his contrition that it is altogether sufficient: nor do our people require contrition from him who is a going to confession, but only attrition. Yet forasmuch as under the words of this article, Luther conceals a certain sinister opinion, therfore, the Bishop adds, that it is deservedly condemned with the rest.

Article XII. the Bishop says, that he fancied when he read it, that he understood it sufficiently; but that it has a far different sense with it from what at first sight it appears to have. For, according to Luther, it is not sufficient to believe at any rate; but a man must believe after this manner with such and so great a faith as may produce contrition and grace in the soul, otherwise he is not absolved. The Bishop adds, that the whole effect, *viz.* remission of sins, ought not to be imputed to faith alone, but partly to faith, partly to the Sacrament of Absolution: and that priests have a power of remitting sins and yet are not idols, nor don't seek to turn away the people from the living God, or so to establish their power as to condemn the faith of the word of God.

Article XIII. The former part of this article, the Bishop says, he does not eagerly oppose, but as for the other part of it, he is so far from approving it, that he does not doubt to call the assertor of it an hæretic. Luther, he says, takes a handle for this assertion from hence, that

he thinks he has collected from the immediately foregoing CHAP.
article, that the whole force or vertue of blotting out a ___ XV
fault is not in the minister, but in the faith of the believer,
and that the effect of remission is to be attributed, not to
the power of the ministers, but to faith, wherby we believe
in the word of God. Wherfore he presently adds, that if
even a woman or a child pronounce these words, the
sinner hearing and believing them is forthwith absolved.
But here his Lordship asks Luther, What if the sinner
himself should with a loud voice, so that he might be
heard by himself, pronounce the same words to which he
might apply his faith, would he think he was absolved?
If he denys, that by them absolution may be given, it will
be plain, that besides faith, the office of the priest is also
necessary, and that neither faith nor the words alone, whether read or otherwise heard, is sufficient. His Lordship
adds, that the absolving priest is not a bare reciter of the
word, but an executor of it, so that unless he give sentence
according to it, he does nothing. that it is not sufficient
for the priest to rehearse what Christ says, *Whose sins ye
remit they are remitted unto them;* but he is to execute
the authority which Christ has granted him, and to say in
his own person, *I absolve thee,* otherwise Christ said it to
his Apostles to no purpose : that Christ has made all priests
equal, but not in releasing punishments; that from the
jurisdiction of the chief priest no one is exempted, since
Christ committed to Peter the care of all his fold in general, and of all his sheep. As to Luther's argument, he
who is baptized hath the Spirit of Christ, but where the
Spirit of Christ is, there is liberty, the Bishop answers,
that it abounds with many errors. 1. That tho' he who is
baptized hath received the Spirit, it is not therfore enough
evident whether he has not since lost that same Spirit.
2. If no one can absolve but he who has the Spirit of
Christ, and even a priest very often wants it, how can we
with safety be confident that we are absolved? 3. If there

be the power of all where the Spirit of Christ is, Christ has in vain given some Apostles, some Prophets, and others Evangelists, pastors and teachers : for why does he establish such a variety of orders in the Church, since a certain One can do all ?

Article XIV. Here the Bishop repeats an observation he had made before, that Luther is wont to confound the word *contrition*, and sometimes to take it for the grief which goes before absolution, and at other times for that which accompanys it, and is formed by grace ; and by this confusion for the most part imposes on and deceives both his reader and hearer. As to Luther's saying, that this matter depends on the judgment of God, the Bishop grants it, he says, if we speak of the sufficiency of grief ; but that no body enquires after *that ;* for the priest asks him who confesses whether he is *truly* sorry for his having sinned, not whether he is *worthily* or *sufficiently* sorry : that as to the Scriptures produced by him, they prove nothing, unless we understand by a *contrite* one him who has sufficient and worthy repentance for his sins. Since he who confesses may affirm that he is sorry, altho' he does not judge or assert, that he is justified, nay, altho' many things which he has done do not occur to his me-mory. The Bishop adds, that ignorance of sins is no hindrance to one's being truly contrite : that the words of St. Paul, 2 Cor. *Examine yourselves whether ye be in the faith,* &c. are nothing to Luther's purpose, if he has a mind to conclude from thence, that faith formed, may be perceived in the heart : for the form of faith may be de-stroyed, faith itself remaining unformed.

Article XV. If Luther, says the Bishop, would have this article understood of a formed faith, nobody will oppose him, however so far as pertains to the last part of it. For he who has such a faith does not need confession, but has grace already, and is of a broken and contrite heart, and fit to be a partaker of this sacrament. But if

he speaks here of an unformed faith, he has so many
adversaries as there are orthodox interpreters of the Holy
Scripture.

Article XVI. This article, the Bishop observes, consists of two parts. I. That Luther thinks it would be
adviseable, that the Church in a general council should
decree, that the laity should be communicated in both
kinds. II. That the Bohemians for their thus communicating should not be reckoned heretics and schismatics.
As to the *first*, the Bishop undertakes to shew, that the
Church has done nothing in this matter but what it was
lawful for it to do, nay, but what it was fit for it to decree;
and that it is by all means to be believed, that this sanc-
tion was not without the instinct of the Holy Ghost. If   1.
the Church might make alterations in what is greater, it
might likewise do so in what is less, but it has made no
scruple to alter the institution of Christ in a matter of
much greater moment. For when Christ had commanded
the form of baptism to be ministred unto all in the name
of the Father, and of the Son, and of the Holy Ghost, and
that too in almost the last words which he spake to his
Apostles, the Church, depending on its own authority, has
changed that form, and f willed all to be baptized in the
name of Christ. Next, it became the Church to decree,   2.
that in administering this sacrament one species should be
taken from the laity. Christ himself, the Bishop says,
gave his body to some of the laity under the one species
of bread, without any wine. Luke tells us, that Jesus ac- ch.xxiv 15.
companied two of his disciples who were going to the
Castel of Emaus, whose eyes were held that they did not

---

f The Bishop seems here to allude to Acts ii where Peter is said to have
ordered the Jewish converts to be baptized in the name of Jesus · though
this means no more than, that they should, according to the form of baptism
appointed by Christ, be made his disciples. And so the Church of England
plainly understood it, since, according to the Salisbury Manual, every parish
priest is ordered to instruct his parishioners in this form of baptism, and to
use it without any addition, alteration, putting of one word for another, &c.

CHAP.
XV.
____

know Christ till, he entring into the house, sat down at meat with them. For then, having tasted the bread, which he had before blessed with his hands and broke and gave to them, their eyes were opened, &c. You see here, says the Bishop to Luther, that they received the body of Christ under the one species of bread, no mention being made of wine. And Paul in his voiage not only blessed bread, but with his own hand gave it to Luke and the rest of his disciples. In which places, his Lordship said, it very plainly appears, that Christ gave to his disciples the sacrament of bread, not of wine, and that Paul like-wise on ship-board did the same. To shew, that it is to be believed, that the Church instituted this by the instinct of the Holy Spirit, the Bishop said, he thought no one was so stupid as not to see, that it behoveth there should be some rule and standard delivered to Christians to which they should conform themselves in all things which they are to believe. For since differences very often arise about the Scriptures, even among the most learned, it is neces-sary to fix another butt or mark to be aim'd at in all those controversies, and that butt is none other than the consent and decree of the whole Church. It was therfore fit, that as oft as any dispute about articles of faith arose among Christians, the bishops of every Christian nation should forthwith meet together to determine that dispute, to whom, says the Bishop, we have certain confidence the inspiration of the Holy Spirit will never be wanting; since Christ for that very reason, *viz.* that the Spirit himself might teach all truth, has promised he should always abide in the Church so long as it continued.

Acts, xxvii.
35.

3.

Article XVII. There is no difference, the Bishop says, betwixt Luther's opinion of ᵍ indulgences and *his*, except that Luther thinks the punishment due to former sins is

ᵍ Indulgences are, in effect, but a commutation of penances, that is, a milder and less severe satisfaction is accepted (for still some penance must be done to gain the indulgence) instead of the great and many rigors en-joyned by the canons. *Dialogue of Contrition and Attrition, &c.*

pardoned together with the fault, and that either by faith, or
the absolution of some priest, wheras *he* with the Church
believes, that for the most part after the fault is blotted out
or pardoned, there remains in the sinner a certain obligation to the punishment due for old sins, which obligation
may be removed or cancelled by the Pope's pardon. For
his Lordship supposed, that there are innumerable persons
who have endured much more grievous troubles than
were sufficient for the expiation of their own sins, and because they have not assigned the fruit of their satisfaction
to any particular persons, therfore it is that it is applied to
the common profit of the whole Church, and is called the
common treasure of the Church, that from thence may be
paid whatever is wanting of a just satisfaction to the rest:
and that the dispensation or management of this treasury
especially pertains to him who is the head of the whole
Church, and to whom also Christ promised the keys of
the kingdom of heaven.

Article XVIII. Perhaps, says the Bishop, it is what
moves many not to place very much trust in those indulgences, because the use of them in the Church seems to
be more fresh or modern, and but very lately found out
among Christians: to which he says, that it is not indeed
certain by whom indulgences first began to be granted;
but that yet there was some use of them among the most
ancient Romans, as appears from the stations: that, it's
said, Gregory I. granted some in his time; and that it's
plain to every body, that by later wits many things out of
the Gospels, as well as the rest of the Scriptures, are now
more plainly discovered and better understood than they
were before. He adds, as an instance of it, that now no
orthodox person doubts whether there be a purgatory, of
which yet among the ancients there is very little or no
notice taken, and which even to that day the Greeks did
not believe. And as long as there was no regard had to
a purgatory, no body enquired after indulgences, all the

A. D. 590.

value of which depending on *that :* since if you take away purgatory, to what purpose are indulgences?

Article XIX. Luther, the Bishop says, often confounds the three texts of the Gospel, Matt. xvi. 19.—xviii. 18. John, xx. 23; as if they were but one : wheras, if he was not very much mistaken, they were very different, and insinuated far different powers in the Church.

Article XX. It is false, the Bishop says, that they are seduced who believe indulgences are wholsom and profitable for the fruits of the Spirit : for they very much conduce to all salutary fruit of it.

Article XXI. We, says the Bishop, do not doubt but that indulgences are necessary for all sinners who are debtors to punishment; much less do we doubt of their being necessary to public or notorious criminals, to those who are entangled in public crimes, and are of an hardned and intolerable disposition.

Article XXII. The Bishop here observes with how evil and depraved a mind Luther revoked this article. For before he paid some deference to indulgences, asserting them to be necessary to certain persons : wheras now he made them altogether of no consequence, and peremptorily asserted them to be useless to every body.

Article XXIII. For the proof of this article Luther referr'd to his Sermon of Excommunication, in which, the Bishop says, he distinguished the communion of the faithful into two sorts, one of which he call'd internal and spiritual, the other he termed outward and corporal. The former, Luther said, consisted of faith, hope, and charity, or the love of God; the other in a participation of the sacraments, which he called the signs of faith, &c. and extended to a communion or fellowship in the use of common things, as conversation, habitation, and other corporal commerce. Next, the Bishop says, he asserted, that as no creature can either admit the soul to a fellowship with that former spiritual communion, or reconcile the excom-

municate to it, since this is a power that pertains to God CHAP.
only: so neither can any one take away that spiritual com- XV.
munion, or excommunicate any one, unless a man do it
himself by his own sin. And so, says the Bishop, at length
he collects from these principles, that ecclesiastical ex⸍
communication is only a privation of external communion,
i. e. of the sacraments, funeral, sepulture, common prayer,
&c. This, says his Lordship, is the summ of his whole
argument, which to me seems to have a great deal of craft
in it, but very little of solid truth. For what if no body
can take away from any man faith, hope, and charity, unless he himself by sin takes them away, or deprives himself of them; are there not other things besides to be
taken away by excommunication? We do not deny but
that a person may sometimes be unworthily excommunicated, and that then he suffers no loss by it; but we speak
of one who is justly excommunicated; of which sort are
they who for the most part retain faith with the loss of
charity; such an one, for instance, as that Corinthian
whom Paul delivered to Satan. Was not *he*, after the
delivery and excommunication which Paul inflicted on
him, more in the power of Satan than he was before?
The Bishop concludes with observing, that the proud and
contumacious are killed with the spiritual sword when
they are cast out of the Church. For they are not able to
live out of it, since the house of God is one, and no one
can be saved unless he be in the Church.

Article XXIV. To Luther's saying, that Christians are
to be taught rather to love excommunication than to fear
it, the Bishop replys, that this truly would be a new kind
of teaching which we don't read that any of the sacred
and orthodox authors have hitherto used: that it may
indeed be the occasion to some of their repenting, and
that so far it is medicinal, but to the contumacious, and
those who persist in their wickedness, such as Luther
seem'd to him to be, it is really deadly and mortal.

Article XXV. Here, the Bishop says, he'll endeavour

to perform what he has before so often promised, namely, to shew, that the Pope is head of the whole Church. This he trys to do these two ways: I. By the Scriptures, in which many prerogatives are ascribed to Peter. II. By the testimonies of all the orthodox fathers who are most noted.

1.

Among the prerogatives of Peter, which are not a few, the *first* in order is, Christ's changing his name, and calling him Cephas, or Peter, when his name before was Simon. The change of a name was always a token of some higher mystery, as is plain from even the Old Testament, where we read of the names of Abraham, Sarah, Israel, being changed: so that we are to think it was not without a great mystery that Christ gave this Apostle a new name. For Christ, as Paul witnesseth, was a rock, and therfore from Christ, the rock, is Simon called [h] Peter, a rock, that by this derivation of his name Christ might præsage to us, that to Peter was his place and especial

2.

authority to be committed. The *second* prerogative is, that altho' Peter was not the *first* as to his calling, yet the

3.

Gospels every where ascribe the first place to him. On account of that excellent confession of Christ's divinity, or his being the Son of the living God, it was said by Christ to Peter, *Blessed art thou, Simon Barjona, because flesh and blood has not revealed it unto thee, but my Father who is in heaven. And I say unto thee that thou art Peter, and on this rock will I build my Church, and the gates of hell shall not prevail against it.* These things, the Bishop said, it is plain were said not to the rest of the Apostles, but unto Peter alone; since none of the others but Peter only was called Barjona: and this, as a notable preroga-

[h] Xavier thus misrepresents Christ's words, Matt. xvi. *Thou art Peter*, i.e. the rock on which the building of my Church shall be firm; and in his History of St. Peter, observes, that he begun at St. Peter when he washed his disciples' feet. So in his History of Christ, he tells us, that Christ baptized Peter only, and washed his feet with deep humility, and clemency of heart, &c.

tive of Peter, have all interpreters unanimously noted.
To Peter alone by name did Christ promise the keys of
the kingdom of the heavens. The rest indeed received   4.
the power of binding and losing, but in heaven in the singular number; but Peter had this power in the heavens
in the plural number. The promise of Christ to Peter
was of the keys not of *one* heaven, but of the heavens.
In the payment of the tribute money Christ joined Peter   5.
with himself, exclusive of the other Apostles, as his equal;
which thing was so plain a token of a certain pre-eminence
which Peter was to have, that immediately on it a question arose among the rest, *Who should be greatest in the
kingdom of the heavens?* On this dispute concerning   6.
who of them should be the greater, Christ by his example
teaches them after what manner he should behave himself
who should be the greater among them; and forthwith
turning to Simon, he saith, SIMON, SIMON, *behold Satan
hath desired you to sift you as wheat, but I have prayed
for* thee, *that* thy *faith fail not; and* thou *when* thou *art
converted strengthen thy brethren.* The angel sent the   7
women to Peter by name, to tell him and the rest of the
Apostles, that Christ was risen. Peter was the *first* who   8.
went into Christ's sepulchre. Peter first entred into the
place of Christ, who after Christ was to be the *first* in the
Church. Christ committed to Peter by name above all   9
the rest the care of his sheep. After all this, Christ said   10
particularly to him, *Follow thou me.* Thus far out of the
Gospels. His Lordship next observed by what tokens
these prerogatives of St. Peter may be demonstrated from
the acts of the Apostles, and those things which Peter did
after Christ's ascension. When Peter judged it proper   1
and reasonable, that some one should be chosen into the
place of Judas, to fill up the sacred duodenary, he preached
the sermon on that occasion to the Christians then present. When at the day of Pentecost some ascribed the   2.
miraculous descent of the Holy Ghost on the Apostles,
and their speaking divers languages, as the Spirit gave

CHAP.
XV

3

them utterance, to their being filled with new wine, Peter alone, as the prince and head of the rest of the Apostles, confuted out of the Scripture this foolish conceit of theirs'. Tho' John was with Peter when they went together up to the temple, yet Peter only healed the lame man, and made that sermon to the people by which he converted five

4. thousand. *He* severely animadverted on the fraud of Ana-

5. nias and Sapphira. When the other Apostles did publicly among the people many signs and wonders, yet of none of them by name, besides Peter only, has the Scripture de-

6. clared this. This prerogative of St. Peter occurs in con-

7. stituting the *seven* deacons. It appears likewise from the

8. acts done by him in Samaria, and from the vision he had of a great sheet tied at the four corners being let down to him from heaven, in which sheet were all sorts of four-footed things, beasts and reptiles, and a voice saying to him, *Rise, Peter, kill and eat :* by which Peter was com-manded to kill them first, i. e. by the word of God to shed the foul blood of sin, and then to eat, i. e. after the manner of meat, to convey them into the body of the Church, and incorporate them into Christ. Do not these things shew,

9. that Peter was head of the whole Church? When, long after this, a synod was held on occasion of a question being raised about some legal observances, Peter in this synod is reported to have delivered his opinion 'first, as

10 the prince and head of the rest. Lastly, Paul writes to the Galatians, that after *three* years he came to Jerusalem to see Peter, and abode with him fifteen days. To these instances out of the Scriptures, the Bishop adds the testi-monies or authorities of the fathers, Hilary, Ambrose, Leo, &c.

Article XXVI. Peter, the Bishop said, could bind no body to sin, but he could lose as many as came to him, as

---

¹ If one was to judge of this by modern usage, which is, for the juniors to deliver their opinion first, this should be an argument of Peter's being infe-riour to the rest of that assembly, however to James, who gives sentence or judgment.

well from the guilt of sin, as from the punishment due to
it. Wherfore these words, *Whatsoever thou shalt lose
upon earth,* &c. are extended not only to the things bound
by Peter, but also to those which he never bound.   To
Luther's saying, that Peter received the keys in the person of all the Apostles, the Bishop replied, that it's probable it was not revealed to them all that Christ was the
Son of God, and was the more likely in that Christ con-
gratulated Peter alone when he said, *Blessed art thou,
Barjona,* &c. and that for this confession of his faith he
gave him the keys of the kingdom of the heavens.

Article XXVII. Here the Bishop reports the opinion
of Scotus, whose acumen, he says, he highly approves,
that *the Church cannot constitute truth or falshood just as
it pleases.*   But his Lordship adds, that tho' the Pope,
together with a council, i. e. the Catholic Church, cannot
make any thing true or false, and consequently cannot
make new articles of faith, yet whatsoever these shall deliver to us as an article of faith, all who are truly Christians are obliged to believe no otherwise than as a certain
article of faith.   To Luther's saying, that there is nothing
of faith and good manners but what is abundantly explained in the Holy Scriptures, the Bishop replys, that he
had before observed, that there are things both to be believed and practised by Christians which are no where
mentioned in the H. Scriptures: that Luther would seem
to be a patron of Christian liberty when he was nothing
less; that his liberty was mere slavery, since it was a
liberty to Christians, to despise the sacraments of the
Church, and to obey no other laws of the Church than
what are plainly delivered in the Gospels and the Epistles
of the Apostles; and which overturned all the order of
ceremonies, and would at length introduce the greatest
confusion in the Church of God.

Article XXVIII. Here the Bishop charges Luther
with being inconsistent with himself.   In the last article,
says he, you were displeased with there being so great a

CHAP.
XV.

variety of ceremonies in the Church: but now in this article you are not at all displeased with a variety of opinions in it. And which of these, I pray, do you think most unbecoming Christians, to dissent or differ in their opinions, or in rites or ceremonies? To Luther's saying, that he ought not to have ascribed to the Pope or a council so great an authority, as to make of an unnecessary thing a thing necessary, the Bishop answers, that if the Pope treated with a council of things no way pertaining to salvation, at the same time dismissing more useful ones, he should no way approve of it. But very often a thing may seem necessary to one, which perhaps by another is judged needless: and therfore there ought among Christians to be some one constituted in the place of a judge, whose decrees it is fit all the rest should obey. For, adds he, I am very fully persuaded, that the Church cannot err in those things which appertain to the substance of faith, and at the same time do believe, that the Scriptures fully intend it should be so, especially when a general council agrees with a very approved Pope. For there is no doubt but that the Pope, together with a council, represents the universal Church. To Luther's adding, that whether the Pope apart, or together with a council, thinks so or so, it ought to prejudice nobody, but every one should abound in his own sense as to those things which are necessary to salvation, the Bishop replys, that the things which the Pope with a council declares to be necessary to salvation, cannot but be so necessary. Not that the popes make them so, but because they were so before, therfore the Pope, being instructed by the Spirit, defines them to be of necessity to salvation.

Article XXIX. A more pestilent article than this, the Bishop says, no one could possibly contrive. Since it destroys all the power of the universal Church, and moreover renders the minds of Christians altogether uncertain whom they ought chiefly to believe. For if we may not with security believe a general council, whose authority

shall we believe? To Luther's saying, he would have the
Scripture be the judge of councils, the Bishop answers, so
would he, provided not an heretic, but an orthodox man,
interpreted it. If the Scripture knew how to speak of
itself, or if the Spirit of Truth speaking in the Scripture
could be heard, it would then be the best interpreter of
itself: but heretics do very often so draw and wrest the
Scriptures to their own sense, that, being depraved by
them, they seem to be opposite to the councils, when
otherwise they would exactly square or agree with them.

Article XXX. It's sufficient for us, the Bishop says,
that Husse's articles were condemned by the council of
Constance, in which there were the most famous men of
all Christendome, both for learning and probity of life.
To Luther's saying, that his adversaries did not do him
justice in calling him a Hussite, since Huss was not of the
same opinion with him, the Bishop replys, that this is
what he himself had observed a little before, that no one
of them agreed with the rest, which was a most manifest
token of error and falshood. You, says he to Luther,
altho' you think most wretchedly of the other sacraments,
yet don't deny but that in the Eucharist is contain'd the
true body of Christ, which John Wiclif your grandsire
altogether denied.

Article XXXI. Here, the Bishop says, he thinks it of
very great consequence, whether we assert, that no just
person is without sin, or that a just person sins in every
work of his: that Luther's quotation from Isaiah lxiv. *We
are all as an unclean thing,* &c. makes nothing for his
purpose: that in citing Eccles. vii. he omits the note of
causality, *for* by which it is plainly shewn, that this Scripture was introduced for the proof of quite another thing,
viz. of this, *Wisdom * comforted,* or *the wise man above* * strength-
the ten princes of the city; the reason of which is given ened.
consequently: *For,* says she, *there is not a just man on
earth that doth good and sinneth not.* The meaning therfore is, that Wisdom, which is Christ, or the grace of

Christ, will comfort or strengthen the wise man more than any principality.   Because without the help of wisdom, or Christ's grace, no one, although he be a just man, can avoid sin by his own strength.   In conclusion, the Bishop thus states the difference betwixt Luther and him on this head.   You, says he, say, that there is no man without sin, but that it is possible there should be one; wheras, on the contrary, I allow to you what you have denied, that by the grace of God there is a man without sin, and yet that of himself he cannot be so.

Article XXXII. If, says the Bishop, a just man may do any work and not sin in it, it forthwith follows, that the work is very well done, and is not a venial sin.   David, when Psal. cxliii. he says, *in God's sight no man living shall be justified,* does not say, *no work* of a living man, but *no man living* shall be justified.   Luther can't produce so much as one man who thinks with him, that a work very well done is sin; and when he says this, he not only gives to sinners a great handle for their sinning, but also for excusing their sin.

Article XXXIII. Of this article of Luther's, wherin he maintained, that to burn heretics is contrary to the will of the Spirit, the Bishop observes, that this is no new heresy, since it is what has vexed the Church many years.   For heretics desire nothing more than, that they may with impunity infect the Christian people, whom they more greedily desire to devour with their pestilent opinions than wolves do the sheep; for which reason Christ in the Gospel calls them wolves.   Now who is so unwise as to trust wolves with the sheep? or who will not rather drive them from the sheep-folds?   But, you'll say, it is one thing to drive them away, another to destroy them.   It is lawful to drive them away, because Christ has allowed it, but it is not lawful to kill them.   To this the Bishop answers, that he indeed is of opinion, that they are even to be destroyed or killed where you cannot otherwise save the flock: that even Christ himself seems to have intimated this plainly enough, since he calls them devouring wolves. For who, when he is afraid of his flock, will not rather kill a devouring wolf, than let his sheep be butchered by him? To Luther's plea, that from the beginning of Christianity to this time the Church never burnt any for heresy, the Bishop replys, that Ananias and Sapphira were punished with death for their fraud about [k] *a little money;* that if Luther will give a reason why at the beginning of the growing Church, so severe a revenge was taken by the Holy Spirit, and *for so small a matter,* he will likewise give a reason why at length, after a course of so many years, it has pleased the Spirit, that heretics should be so severely punished. Heretics in a matter of much greater moment than money, i. e. in the orthodox faith of Christians, deceive and miserably destroy the minds of Christians, which ought to seem to any Christian incomparably more grievous than the cheating any of even the greatest summ of money. Next, the Bishop remembers St. Augustine's answer to the Donatists in his letter to Boniface. They had objected, that the Apostles never addressed the kings or emperors of the world to offer violence to heretics: to which the father reply'd : " What emperor " did then believe in Christ, who according to his duty or " devotion might serve him in putting his or their laws in " execution against impiety? But after that began to be " fulfilled which is written, *All kings shall fall down be-* " *fore him,* &c. who of any sobriety would say to kings, " do not take any care by whom the Church of your Lord " is defended or opposed? It does not belong to you in " your kingdoms to see what any one has a mind to be, " whether religious or sacrilegious, chast or debauched :" that heretics [l] compelled the Church to invent many medi-

---

[k] St. Peter represents Ananias and Sapphira's crime to be *lying to the Holy Ghost,* and *tempting the Spirit of the Lord,* which is not a *small matter* or a *little money* matter. *Acts,* v 3, 9.

[l] Mea primitus sententia erat, neminem ad unitatem Christi esse cogendum, verbo esse agendum, disputatione pugnandum, ratione vincendum, ne

cines as the experiments of many distempers; so that
when milder remedies did no good, necessity forc'd the
Church to make use of rougher ones.   Heretics were first
punished with the loss of their money, then with banish-
ment and confiscation of all their goods.   But still this
poison crept among Christians, and no remedy was found
to avail any thing so long as the heretic was suffered to
live: wherfore there was a necessity either by the punishment of death to remove the heretics, or to bear with innumerable and daily slaughters of souls.   To the places
of Scripture quoted by Luther, the Bishop thus replys:

chap. ii.
the words of Isaiah, *They shall beat their swords into
plowshares,* &c. he says, signifie that long peace which
was made at the time of our Saviour's birth.   The same

chap. xi.
prophet's saying, *They shall not hurt nor destroy in all my
holy mountain,* is no prohibition of the burning of heretics,
but ought to be understood of the serpent and asp, and

Matt. x. 9.
other poisoned and wild creatures.   Christ's giving his

Luke, xxii.
35.
disciples no weapons, nor appointing them to inflict any
punishment, besides accounting him for an heathen who
does not hear the Church, the Bishop calls a negative
argument, which proves nothing.   For what if Christ has
not ordered heretics to be burnt, should therfore a vigi-
lant pastor suffer them to devour the flock of Christ with
impunity?   But Christ has permitted or allowed many
things to be done by his Church of which he himself had
before said nothing.   To Luther's observing, that tho'
St. Paul directed that an heretic should be avoided, he
did not command him to be put to death by fire and
sword, the Bishop replys, that neither has Paul ordered

fictos Catholicos haberemus quos apertos Hæreticos noveramus. Sed hæc
opinio mea non contradicentium verbis, sed demonstrantium superabatur
exemplis —— Quam multi putabant veram Ecclesiam esse partem Donati,
quia eos ad cognoscendam Catholicam Veritatem *securitas* torpidos, fasti-
diosos, pigrosque faciebat? —— Quam multi, nihil interesse credentes in
qua quisque parte Christianus sit, ideò manebant in parte Donati quia ibi
nati erant, et eos inde discedere atque ad Catholicam nemo transire cogebat.
Augustini Epist. 93

thieves to be hanged; and yet unless by the laws theft
was thus punished, there would be no secure or safe living in towns or cities. As for his telling the Corinthians, that *there must be heresies or sects*, &c. which was another text cited by Luther, the Bishop allows, that it cannot be avoided but there must be heresies: since as no one can wholly clear his garden of weeds, so neither can any one quite root out of the Church all heresie. But then he adds, that as by these words Paul does not command, that heresies should be taken away, so neither was it his mind, that heretics are to be left to their own humour. For thus Hierome enlarges on this place · the Apostle, says he, does not say this because there ought to be heresies, but because the Corinthians had divisions among them, therfore, he says, this must be, and it is necessary that there be sects. As if you should say, he who drinks so much must necessarily be drunk, so Paul also says, because you are so disposed, or have such conditions, you must of necessity come at last to have even sects or heresies among you. To the instance produced by Luther of Christ's restraining the disciples when they would have had fire from heaven to destroy the Samaritans, &c. and telling them, that they did not know what spirit they were of, the Bishop replys, that James and John were on this occasion lawfully reproved by Christ, because they asked this out of a desire of revenge, not for the salvation of souls. But magistrates are not so to be reproved who punish heretics with the only view that the salvation of many souls may not be hazarded. Nor has what Christ there objected any place here, *The Son of Man came not to destroy men's souls*, &c. since this way a no small number of souls is saved, which otherwise, it's certain, would perish. To Luther's saying, that they who persecute men with fire, are not the children of a good spirit, but of an evil one, who was a murderer from the beginning, the Bishop replys by asking, what of an evil spirit was in Christ when he whipt the money changers out of the

temple, and beat the sellers of doves? None at all, says he; but rather he was acted by an excellent charity. What evil spirit was in Peter when he inflicted the punishment of death on Ananias and Sapphira? Nothing at all of malice, but a desire of another's salvation. Thus it is in magistrates, who out of a regard to the public peace hang malefactors; and in those who cut off a gangrened limb, by which the whole body is endangered, when there are no hopes of curing it. Luther had said, that Christ would not have men compelled to the faith by force and by fire, and, that therfore he gave the sword of the Spirit, that they who were the children of the spirit might fight with it, and that this sword of the Spirit is the word of God. To this, the Bishop reply'd, that it was not fit at the first beginning of a growing Church to use force and violence, when the wise were to be converted by fools, and the strong were to be drawn to the faith by the weak; but that now they who are converted to the faith are to be compelled to continue in it. That Christ gave indeed this sword of the Spirit to fight with against unbelievers, but that it is time to sound a retreat, when it's plain that we are no way gainers by this kind of fighting, but that rather we injure even the heretics themselves and our own people by it. His Lordship concludes, that he thinks it sufficiently plain from what he has said, that it is lawful for the bishops to deliver up to the secular arm those who have been convicted of heresy after their abjuration of it.

Article XXXIV. Here the Bishop tells Luther, that he seems to *him* to differ very much from himself, in that a little after he declares his opinion to be, that all things come to pass by mere necessity, when yet here he disswades from going to war with the Turcs. But, he says, he knows what Luther means; that his intention is not so much to persuade men against going to war with the Turcs, as to hinder the raising of money on his Germans, on pretence of a Turkish war: that this is what makes a war with the Turks so odious to him. But, says his

Lordship, so far as I hear, there are a great many at Rome, men conspicuous both for learning and holiness, to whom, whatever error there may be in the Court, this war, and levying money under pretence of it, is no less uneasy than it is to Luther.

Article XXXV. How this article agrees with the XI. in which Luther asserts, that *every one is absolved from his sins who believes that he is absolved,* the Bishop says he does not apprehend; since here he says, that no one is sure he does not sin mortally because of the most secret vice of pride. To Luther's citation from Job, *Though I* chap. ix. *were perfect, yet shall my soul not know it,* the Bishop answers, that Luther's article has nothing like this saying: that Job in these words does only not own his simplicity or perfection; as if he had said, it is not my desire that my mind should be sensible of my perfection: if I have any I would think more humbly of myself than to allow any thing of that nature of myself. To his quotation from David, that in God's *sight shall no man living be justified,* Psal. cxliii. the Bishop replys, that he has fully enough answered it in Article XXXII. and that the prophet says not *every work of a living man,* but [m] *no man living.* To Paul's saying, *That every mouth may be stopped, and all the world become* Rom. iii. *guilty before God,* and that *God hath concluded them all* xi. *in unbelief, that he might have mercy upon all,* the Bishop replys, that Luther does not rightly infer from it, that in every work we sin mortally: that Paul never intended this, but that we are all sinners, and that there is no one who is altogether without sin that his other saying of God's, *concluding them all in unbelief,* &c. makes no more for Luther, unless his meaning is, that we are all still in unbelief.

Article XXXVI. This article, the Bishop observes, has *two* parts: 1. That free will is a thing merely titular. de solo titulo.

[m] *Non justificabitur in conspectu tuo omnis vivens.* Sciebat enim cunctos pari retinendos punitionis vinculo nisi Deus in quibus vellet misericordiam fecisse, superexaltaret judicio. *Fulgent. ad Monimum,* lib. 1.

2. That when free will doth what is in its power, it sinneth mortally. As to the former, his Lordship says, free will has always been as it were a rock to the presumptuous, and more audacious wits of heretics, on which they have split, and suffered a very grievous shipwreck: that the Manichees, first of all, made two minds in a man, a good and a bad; that these two they asserted have a mutual conflict with each other in men, the flesh lusting against the spirit, and the spirit against the flesh: that, on the contrary, the Jovinianists widely differ'd from them, since they denied, that any one could sin after baptism: that after these arose the Pelagians, whose heresy it was, that free will by its own strength may avoid any sin, and stands in no need of grace to do good, or to perform it the more easily: that at last came Wiclif, whose followers asserted, that all things come to pass by a sort of [n]necessity, and will have it, that Judas and other sinners, whatsoever they have done, they have done it by mere [o]necessity, and not by a spontaneous liberty. But the orthodox, neither declining to the right nor left, keep the middle way, and own, that free will does some things by its own strength alone, and some by the assistance of Divine Grace. To Luther's proof

John, xv.

from the words of Christ, *Without me ye can do nothing*, the Bishop answers, that in the Scriptures of the New Testament very often that is said to be *nothing* which is *of no merit*, as to the reward of eternal life. After this manner therfore ought what Christ said to be understood, *Without me ye can do nothing*, i. e. no merit or fruit without

[n] Bishop Gardiner is pleased to affirm, that no conclusion is by Luther more stoutly affirmed than this, that all things come to passe by an absolute necessitie, and so mannes lyfe, death, mannours, behaviour, state, condicion, and every thing is fixed and fastned in his place appoynted with nayles ryveted and clenched with meere necessite. *Answer to George Joye*, fol. 21.

[o] In the same manner Huetius reproaches Beza and all the reformed: *Propositionem hanc*, Quidquid fit a nobis sive boni sive mali mera necessitate fit, *approbare studet Theodor. Beza in lib. Quæsti. Christian: et in annotati: major. in N. Testamentum, quam a Wiclefo et Luthero traditam, et a Calvino propagatam hausit.* Ad Origen comment. observ. et notæ, p. 59, col. ii.

me. When therfore Luther asks, What is this *nothing* that free will doth without Christ? we answer: free will without Christ, if by Christ you mean the grace of Christ, which we call *gratum facientem*, can do many things both good and bad. It can also prepare itself by certain good works, which tho' they are *nothing*, according to the Scriptures' way of speaking, yet they are not simply nothing. To the words of Solomon, *The Lord hath made* Prov xvi. *all things for himself, yea, even the wicked for the day of evil*, the Bishop observes, that the orthodox fathers abominated nothing more than that God should be thought the author of sin. By the *wicked* therfore in this place Hierome understood the Devil, whom he denied to have been made wicked by God, but to have become so of his own accord, because he voluntarily forsaking the good in which he was created, of his own will became evil and wicked. To Rom. i. *God gave them over to a reprobate mind*, the Bishop replys, that the soul is placed in the middle as it were betwixt the flesh and spirit, so as to have it in its liberty either to obey the admonitions of the Spirit, or to acquiesce in the lusts of the flesh. The soul therfore which deserts the instinct of the Spirit, having followed the lusts of the flesh, if it persists in so doing, and will not by any admonitions be persuaded to return, is at last deservedly left or forsaken of God: and being so forsaken is said to be given up to a reprobate sense to do those things which are not convenient, as all the orthodox fathers to a man interpret it. His Lordship concludes, that in thus pleading Scripture, Luther does not degenerate from former hæretics, who always arrogated to themselves the knowledge of the Scriptures. But that as for himself he was abundantly satisfied to be wise with the fathers, against whose common sense, unless he was altogether raving, he could not admit of any figments of Luther's brain concerning understanding the Scriptures.

Article XXXVII. Of this article, the Bishop observes, 1. That tho' purgatory may not be proved by the Scriptures, the truth of it is nevertheless to be believed by all Christians, and especially since by the most ancient usage of the Church a special commemoration has been made by the priests at mass for the souls of the deceased, which are believed to be in purgatory. 2. That this article seems not to square with the others: for it follows from it, that other proofs are to be sought for by us besides the Holy Scripture, which yet elsewhere is stiffly denied. 3. Since purgatory is affirmed by so many fathers, as well Greek as Latin, it is not unlikely but that its truth appeared to them by fit proofs. 4. It is not credible, that purgatory cannot be proved by Holy Scripture when it is a thing so necessary to be known by all Christians. For the knowledge of it is useful, not only, that of charity we may desire to help their souls who are detained in those punishments; but as it strikes us with fear of our easily admitting lighter faults, since we are certain for them to suffer grievous pains in those fires, and not to be admitted into heaven till we have been very well purged from them by the bitter torments of purgatory. It likewise contributes to our hope, that we may not altogether despair as if some grievous and deadly distemper had suddenly seized us, thinking that all, even our smallest sins, for which we have not made satisfaction here, ought to be punished in hell. To Luther's objections to the places of Scripture usually urged in behalf of purgatory, the Bishop replys: to the words of the Psalmist, *We went thro' fire and water, and thou broughtest us out into a cool place*, his Lordship observes, that Luther seems to him a much more trifling sophist than they who urge this text, in concluding, that because he thinks he has confuted a place or two of Scripture impertinently urged by them, therfore the truth of purgatory is not to be evidenced from Scripture. To the words of the Apostle,—*the day of the Lord*

Psal. lxv.
ed. Vulg.

1 Cor. iii.

shall declare it, because it shall be revealed by fire—he CHAP.
himself shall be saved, yet so as by fire, the Bishop says, XV.
that the Greek has not that word Lord, but it is there
only *the day shall declare,* &c. that this place not only the $\dot{\eta}\,\gamma\grave{\alpha}\rho\,\dot{\eta}\mu\epsilon\rho\alpha$
Latins, but some of the Greeks will have to be under- $\delta\eta\lambda\acute{\omega}\sigma\epsilon\iota.$
stood of purgatory; but he will only produce two of them,
viz. Origen and Austin. So when the same Apostle says,
The Lord Jesus shall be revealed from heaven with his 2 Thess. i.
mighty angels in flaming fire, &c. the Bishop observes,
that Paul speaks of a fire of conflagration, of which David
also prophesied, *a fire shall devour before him,* &c. But Psal. l.
that there is no necessity that he should here speak of the
same fire which he mentioned to the Corinthians, and
especially since there he said not one word of *the day of
the Lord,* but absolutely, *the day shall declare it,* which
may very well be understood of a day of tryal of every
one who goes hence. To Luther's asking, what occasion
there is for making such a noise about purgatory, unless
the papistical Church is afraid of losing the inestimable
gain which it draws from purgatory, the Bishop replys,
by putting this question, Whether ought most to be
blamed, the Pope, if for his advantage he would have purgatory believed by others which he also believes himself,
or Luther, who, only that he may oppose this gain, endeavours to suppress the belief of purgatory, of the being of
which he yet no wise doubts?

Article XXXVIII. This article, the Bishop says, has
two parts: one, that the souls in purgatory are not sure of
their salvation, at least not all; another, that it is not
proved by either reason or Scripture, that they are placed
out of a condition of deserving or increasing charity. As
to the first, his Lordship says, it's probable, that every
soul before it is cast into purgatory shall give an account
of its particular thoughts, words, and deeds; which if it
be done, it can't be that the souls which are sent to purgatory should not know the state of their salvation. As
to the other part, the Bishop says, Luther's want of pro-

bity is very much to be wondred at, in his so impudently
asserting it, when by so many very plain texts of Scripture, of which he himself is not ignorant, this thing is so
solidly proved, that it can scarce be asserted by any other
John, ix. words. Does not Christ say, *I must work the works of him
that sent me while it is day: the night cometh when no man
can work?* Which words, unless any one be very obstinate, cannot otherwise be taken than for the time following after death, when there is no more or farther opportunity of meriting. For since it is certain by the Holy
Scriptures, that neither the souls of the blessed or the
damned are altogether idle, and no one can doubt but
that Christ said true in these words, it's necessarily inferred, that he spake only of meritorious work, and of
the time of this present life.

Article XXXIX. It may be clear, the Bishop observes,
from what he has already said, that the souls in purgatory
do not sin: for since they are sure of their future salvation, they are warm'd with so great a desire of enjoying
that glory, as not willingly to commit what may any wise
retard their possession of it.

Article XL. the Bishop says, may be understood two
ways, either for the satisfaction which might be made by
the souls in purgatory in this life, or for the satisfaction in
purgatory itself. For betwixt these satisfactions there is
this difference, that the former, if it were made in this life
and in grace, carrys also something of merit with it, besides the blotting out of the fault; but the other which is
made in purgatory gains nothing of merit, but only expiates
the spots contracted. To Luther's saying, he had disputed these three articles with a protestation of his ignorance of the matter of them, the Bishop replys, that if he
be indeed ignorant of these things as he now professes,
why would he publicly dispute of them at the peril of his
hearers?

Article XLI. and the last, Luther denied to be his, and
therfore the Bishop thinks it not worth while to waste

woids upon it. Only Luther defended the metaphor of *deleting the sacks of beggary* from the like expression, Gen. ʋɪ. in the Latine Vulgate *Delebo hominem quem creavi.* To Luther's saying, that there is no body who is not displeased with the beggary of the laity, and therfore much moɪe with the begging of the clergy, the Bishop replys, that he did not know what he meant by these words. For a thing might displease any one either out of hatred or pity. If beggary therfore did so displease him as that he wished there weɪe no such peɪsons as beggars, his displeasure was a wicked displeasure; and that he, perhaps, if he had lived in the Apostles' times, would not have been moved with compassion towaɪds them, as *they* weɪe, but ratheɪ would have exhorted Christians to reject these poor people For that with Luther, fastings, watchings, prayers, and other things of that kind, in which *they* exercised themselves day and night to the very great pɪofit of the whole Chuɪch, weɪe of no great moment. But, adds the Bishop, perhaps Luther is only displeased, that the friers beg and ask from door to door. But if that be not lawful, why did Chɪist send his own disciples to preach almost destitute of every thing but cloaths? for they lay under a necessity of discovering their poverty to others, and of ᴾbegging of them what they wanted. Unless, therfore, Luther condemns this, the Bishop says he does not see why the orders of the begging friers are by any to be condemned. His Lordship therfore concludes, that if there be any among these friers who do not live according to the truth of their rule, if Luther would reform them, he would have no opposer. But since there are

Saccos
mendicita-
tis delerent.

ᴾ Christ himself sets this matter in another light. He consider'd his disciples as so many *labourers* sent into his vineyard, and therfore gives this reason why he ordered them to *provide neither gold, nor silver,* &c that the *workman* was worthy of his meat, and the *labourer* of his hire, Matt. x. Luke x Wheras the begging friers are represented as begging for the maintenance of pride, laziness, &c. *See Dɪ. Wiclif's Life.*

CHAP.
XV.

many of these orders who are very useful to christian people, both by their example of life and their word of doctrine, for their living happily, he who would have all these orders quite taken away, did not, in his opinion, act either prudently or piously.

CHAP. XVI.

1. Ulrich Velene writes a book to shew, that St. Peter was never at Rome. 2. Some account of this controversy. 3. Who Velene was, and the contents of his book. 4. The Bishop's answer to it, which was replied to by Simon Hess.

1. SOME months after the Bishop had answered these articles and assertions of Luther's, he had lent him, he tells his readers, by Tunstall, then Bishop of London elect, a little book of one Ulrichus Velenus, (so, the Bishop A. D. 1523. says, he calls himself, as if he suspected this was a feigned name,) than which, he says, he never read one more impudent: since, in opposition to every body else, he with a shameless forehead contended, that Peter was never at Rome. The Bishop therfore says, he was very much concerned, that this book of his in answer to it was so long kept from the press, (tho' on the other hand he was glad, that it did not go out of his hands before he had an opportunity of rooting out this error,) lest, perhaps, it having taken root in the minds of those who read it, less credit upon that account would be given to his collections. He therfore promises to endeavour, according to his ability, as briefly as possible, to confute this error which Velenus has attempted to establish with all his might by many and immoderate calumnies. Nor does he doubt, he says, but he shall make it very plainly appear by the greatest and most noted authors which he shall produce, that Peter sat long at Rome. This, he says, he takes to be a thing so notorious, that it is indeed a wonder that any one should be so impudent as not to be ashamed to maintain the contrary. But so great is the madness and malice of the Lutherans, that there is nothing so false which they do not dare to assert, so that it be but against

the power of the Bishop of Rome, that so they may have some colour for their heresies, insomuch, that he was afraid, lest in a little time some one would come forth who would even deny that Christ has suffered.

Pearson de
Successi-
one primo-
rum Romæ
Episco. ch.
vi. § 5.

2. It's observed, that there have not been wanting learned men, who have openly denied, that St. Peter fix'd his See at Rome, or ordained any one there, or was ever in that city. For since in the Acts of the Apostles there is no intimation of the coming of this Apostle to Rome, and some things are produced elsewhere which seem to contradict his coming thither, they have not been afraid to deny, that Peter was ever at Rome. It's therfore granted, that it cannot be proved from Holy Scripture, that St. Peter ever saw Rome, which even St. Jerome seems to allow, when in his commentary on the second chapter of the Epistle to the Galatians, he says, *Last of all, we have received that Peter was the first Bishop of the Church of Antioch, and was from thence translated to Rome, which thing Luke has altogether omitted.* But this, it's said, is no wonder: since neither has Luke ever remembred Titus, St. Paul's companion, whom the Apostle himself has so often remembred in his Epistles. And therfore, tho' it be yielded, that it cannot be proved from Scripture that St. Peter was ever at Rome, it is thought that it cannot be proved from thence that he never was there: that here the faith of [a] history, tho' not divine, and reasoning from circumstances, taken from the eldest antiquity, may have place;

[a] Many have argued St. Peter to have never been at Rome; which opinion I shall not avow, as bearing a more civil respect to ancient testimonies and traditions; altho' many false and fabulous relations of that kind having crept into history and common vogue; many doubtful reports having passed concerning him; many notorious forgeries having been vented about his travels and acts (all that is reported of him out of Scripture having a smack of the legend) would tempt a man to suspect any thing touching him, which is grounded only upon human tradition; so that the forger of his Epistle to St James might well introduce him, saying, *If while I do yet survive, men dare to feign such things of me, how much more will they dare to do so after my decease?* Barrow of the Pope's Supremacy.

tho' yet as to the times and [b]years which are commonly attributed to Peter's sitting at Antioch and Rome, they are
inconsistent with the Scripture, and not sufficiently
grounded on any convincing testimony of the ancient
Church.

3. This Urich Velene was a learned minister of the
Lutheran Church at Minden in Germany; and the design of this [c]tract of his was to defend the opinion just
now mentioned, that St. Peter was so far from being
Bishop of Rome, that he never was there, nor did not
there end his life: and that therfore the Pope, or present
Bishop of Rome, does idly and rashly enough boast and
call himself the successor of Peter. This book he divided
into two parts, the former of which contains XVIII. arguments, to prove, that Peter after Christ's passion was never
at Rome, and that he suffered not at Rome, but at Jerusalem. The *second* part contains VII. objections or cavils
as he calls them, by which the court of Rome has used to
answer these arguments, to which Velene makes VII.
replys.

Westpha-
lia.

Velen's *first* argument is, that the Holy Scripture is
silent about Peter's coming to Rome after Christ's passion:
that history disagrees with itself; and that the doctors of
the Church deserve no credit to be given to them here,
because they so oppose one another. He instances in the
different opinions about Peter's successor at Rome. His
second argument is, that they who say that Peter came to
Rome at the beginning, or in the [d]2d or 4th of Claudius
Cæsar's reign, i. e. the 8th or *9th year after Christ's passion, *their* opinion confutes who assert, that Peter staid in
the East *five*, or according to others *seven* years, when

I.

II.

*12th.

b There remain only xi years in which he, Peter, could possibly be at
Rome. *History of the Propagat. of Christianity*, vol. 1 p. 279.

c Ulrichi Veleni tractatus quo asseritur Petrum Apostolum nunquam
Romæ fuisse. 1524

d St Peter came to Rome in the 2d year of the Emperor Claudius, Anno
Christi 42. St. Paul writ to the Romans, A. D. 57. *Shortest Way*, &c.
p 84

CHAP.
XVI.
___

* 4th.

III.

IV.

A. D. 53.

ch. i. 18, ii.
1.

V.

diverting to Antioch he sat there *seven* years, and made some stay in Pontus, Galatia, Bythinia, and the adjacent provinces: that they of this opinion are favoured by what Luke says, Acts, xv. and that if this be so, that Peter did not come to Rome till the *7th or 8th of Claudius, and was bishop there 'twenty-five years, he did not suffer martyrdome under Nero, but under Vespasian rather, which nobody ever said or wrote. His *third* argument is, that Peter could not come thither in the 9th of Claudius, Suetonius proves in his life: since there he tells us, that the Christians at that time were banished from Rome, which is confirmed by the Acts of the Apostles. To shew that Peter could not come to Rome the 20th year after Christ's passion, Velenus says, it's certain, that all those seventeen years which immediately succeeded Christ's ascension, Peter was at Jerusalem, and in the neighbouring countries, and never went to Rome: this he proves from the Epistle to the Galatians, where 'St. Paul says, *After* three *years I went up to Jerusalem—then* fourteen *years after I went up to Jerusalem:*—that afterwards Peter went to Antioch, where Paul met him, and chid him for his dissimulation: and that all this time, from the ascension of Christ to this chiding of Peter by Paul at Antioch, makes more than twenty years. That Peter was not at Rome

---

e In Chronico Eusebiano habetur 25 culpâ typographorum, aut MSS. codicum quos sequuti sunt. Nam ex annorum ratione, et consensu Scriptorum qui illum sequi videntur, legendum esset 7 tantum. *Reynolds adv. Hart.* cap. vi § 3.

f De his alibi disputaturus contra vulgarem Romanorum sententiam, eamque fortioribus argumentis refutaturus, hîc tantummodo sententiam nostram expromere statui, et quidem verbis Theodori Bezæ accurati admodum Scriptoris, qui ad illa verba S. Petri, *Salutat vos Ecclesia quæ est in Babylone collecta,* hæc annotat, *quod traditum est de 25 illis annis quibus Petrus Romæ sederit, partim ex Pauli epistolis Româ scriptis probabiliter refellitur, partim etiam necessarijs argumentis demonstratur ex temporum supputatione; etiamsi Romam illum venisse, ibique pro Christi nomine trucidatum fuisse, non invitus concedam.* Pearson de Success. primo. Romæ Episco.

g Additis 14 annis quibus Hierosolymam revenerat ad annos 3 quibus proximè post conversionem suam [Paulus] visitaverat Hierosolymam 17 anni proveniunt. *Veleni Tractatus,* &c.

when Paul wrote to the Romans, the Epistle itself is an
evidence, at the close of which he bids the Romans to
salute many of the brethren by name, who by his means
had sometime since believed in Christ, and were then the
chief and elders of that church, as Narcissus, Andronicus,
Julian, Priscilla, and Aquila. How then could it be, if
Paul believed that Peter was then at Rome, that he did not
salute *him?* But to shew further, that Peter was not at
Rome when Paul sent his letter thither, St. Ambrose on
the Epistle to the Romans saith, he had read in some ancient books, that Narcissus, whose houshold the Apostle
orders the Romans to salute in his name, was then a presbyter of Rome.   Now in the primitive Church there were
only two ecclesiastical orders, *viz.* presbyters and deacons;
therfore we are here to understand by Narcissus being a
presbyter or elder, that he was Bishop of the Roman
Church, of which he not only took care, but likewise of
the churches in the neighbourhode.   Besides, Andronicus
and Julias, two of the seventy disciples, according to Origen, were then at Rome, and Priscilla and Aquila, according to Ambrose, did not come to Rome out of devotion,
but were sent thither to confirm the Romans.   What
occasion therfore there was for Peter's being at Rome,
who was now old and decayed, no one can suppose.   The
Apostle, in his letter to the Galatians, tells them, that the
Gospel of the uncircumcision was comitted to *him*, as that
of the circumcision was to Peter.   How then could Peter
so soon forget this compact, and usurp another's province,
since Rome at that time was the mother of all paganism?
Besides, if he was the Apostle of the circumcision, how
comes it to pass that he had no correspondence with the
Jews at Rome for so many years, *viz.* till the coming of
Paul thither?   For, as Luke reports it, on Paul's coming
thither, the Jews said to him, " as concerning this sect we
" know that it is every where spoken against, we therfore
" desire to hear of thee what thou thinkest; for we have
" neither received letters concerning thee, neither have

CHAP.
XVI.

VI.
Anno Ne-
ronis 3.
Æræ Vulg.
57

VII.

ch. xxviii.

CHAP.
XVI.

VIII.

A.D.58,or
after
Christ's
Ascens. 25.

"any of the brethren that came out of Judea shewed or "spake any harm of thee," &c. What then did Peter do at Rome in so [h]great a space of time, if those things which the Jews heard of Paul seemed to them new, and were not heard of by them before? for they declared, that none of them had heard of the rites and institutes of the Christian sect or heresie before *he* told them of them. Paul being compelled by the Jews appealed unto Cæsar, and was carried to Rome, where he lived in a hired house of his own a whole two years, whither the Jews daily resorted, and whom he received without making any distinction, preaching to all that came to him the kingdom of God, &c. During this [i]imprisonment he wrote several letters to the Philippians, Galatians, &c. in the latter of which he several times mentions Peter, but says not a word of him whether he then had him for his colleague at Rome, or if he would subscribe to what *he* had written. So far from it, that he does not even salute those to whom he writes in Peter's name, which yet one would have expected he should have done, if Peter had been then at Rome, that they being moved more easily by the name of so eminent an apostle, might repent and be brought off from the strange doctrine which they were so much inclined to embrace. But the Apostle did nothing of this; which is a very great argument that neither at that time was Peter at Rome, when yet it was now twenty-five, or, according to some, twenty-seven years, after Christ's ascension. But neither in his letter to the [k]Ephesians, which he likewise wrote at Rome, does he mention Peter, when yet at other times it's his usual way to salute believers in the name of

[h] From A.D. 44 to A.D. 63, *viz.* 19 years.

[i] The Epistle to the Galatians was written, according to Bishop Pearson, Neronis 1[mo]. or A.D. 55 ; according to others, A.D. 57 ; wheras, according to the Bishop, St. Paul was not brought a prisoner to Rome till the *seventh* of Nero, or A.D. 61, and according to others, A.D. 63.

[k] St. Paul, according to Bishop Pearson, wrote this Epistle and that to the Philippians, A.D. 62, or the 8th of Nero.

his colleagues. The letters which the Apostle Paul sent
by Epaphroditus to the Philippians, are an argument that
Peter was not at Rome in Paul's time; since in them he
advises the Philippians of many things, and explains what
was done to him at that time, but especially what progress
he had made in propagating the Gospel, that through his
occasion the Gospel was preached at Rome by all with
the same zeal, tho' with a different intention. *Notwithstanding every way, whether in pretence or in truth, Christ
is preached, and I therin do rejoyce, yea, and will rejoyce,
for I know that this shall turn to my salvation,* &c. and I
had rather die with the propagation of the Gospel, than
live without it.   A marvellous thing indeed! if Peter was
then at Rome (as he ought to have been there many from 2
years.) That Rome should hear so uneasily from Paul Claudius,
the name of Christ, that even a great many deceitful men 8 Nero,
should be suborned for the purpose under pretence of A. D. 63.
preaching Christ, to seek the ruine of the Apostle! Did
Peter hide himself up there, and continue idle so many
years, and conceal the faith of Christ, for fear of the
tyrant's cruelty? For if *he* had preached the Gospel at
Rome every year for so many years as he is supposed to
have lived there, Paul ought not to have been afraid of it,
since Rome had so long before very patiently heard it
from Peter.   Besides, Paul adds at the end of this Epistle, *All the saints salute you, chiefly they that are of
Cæsar's houshold;* he ought rather to have said, *chiefly
Peter, who is as it were the chief of us all.* Paul, writing to
the Colossians by Tychicus and Onesimus, adds in the
close of the letter, *Aristarchus my fellow prisoner saluteth
you, and Marcus sister's son to Barnabas, and Jesus, who
is called Justus, who are of the circumcision. These only
are my fellow workers unto the kingdom of God, who have
been a comfort unto me   Luke the beloved physician, and
Demas greet you.* See how he reckons up all by name
who were then with him, and were his fellow workers in
the kingdom of God, that is, in the Church of Christ. He

CHAP.
XVI.

says, that *these only* are his fellow workers, &c. What was become then of Peter? Had he, like an old and discharged souldier, betaken himself to an idle life, so as not to be a *fellow labourer in the kingdom of Christ?* This be far from Peter; he therfore was not then at Rome.

XI.

Onesimus, whom some think to have been a Phrygian by birth, was a slave of Philemon's, a Colossian. He having stol'n some things from his master run away from him, and went to Rome, where hearing Paul preach, he became a Christian, and was baptized: and, that nothing of the blot of his past life might remain, he opened his conscience to the Apostle, and confessed the injury he had done his master. Paul, having a kindness for him for this his ingenuity, resolved to try to reconcile his master to him. For this purpose, he wrote him a letter in Onesimus's behalf, requesting him to receive him as he would receive himself, and telling him, that if he had wronged him, or owed him any thing, he would repay it. In the beginning of this letter he salutes Philemon, Apphia his wife, and Archippus, Bishop of the Church of Coloss, and, that, as St. Chrysostome thinks, he might the more easily obtain his request, he adds Timothie's name, saying, *Paul a prisoner of Jesus Christ, and Timothy our brother*, &c. Why does Paul suppress Peter's name in the salutation, when he adds that of Timothy? since Philemon might, perhaps, more easily have been moved by the name of so great a preacher of the Gospel to forgive Onesimus his offence. What could so plainly shew that Peter was not then at Rome, as this letter sent by Onesimus to Philemon from Rome? At the end of the letter Paul adds, *There salute thee Epaphras, my fellow prisoner in Christ Jesus: Marcus, Aristarchus, Demas, Lucas, my fellow labourers.* O unhappy Peter! if he was then at Rome, and left Paul

XII.

destitute in this his most honourable employment. Two years being now past, and many at Rome being converted to christianity, and letters sent from thence to the churches of several places, at length Nero set Paul at liberty, as he himself tells Timothy, saying, *I was delivered out of the* *mouth of the lion.* But [1] *ten* years after Paul is again committed to prison, and treated [m] worse than ever. Of this first imprisonment he takes notice in his *second* Epistle to Timothy, *At my first answer*, says he, *no man stood with me, but all men forsook me,* &c. Where was Peter then? certainly not at Rome. It is known, that Luke the Evangelist, and historiographer of the Apostles' acts, was the inseparable companion of Paul in all his travels, and that his history reaches to the time when Paul was carried a prisoner from Jerusalem to Rome, where he was guarded by a souldier in his own hired house. Of this Luke makes a copious mention in his last chapter, where he shews how Paul was conveyed to Rome from Malta; that the *brethren who were then at Rome, when they heard of his coming came to meet him as far as *Appij forum*, &c. and that after three days he called the Jews to him, and discoursed with them, and confuted them, and dwelt there two years. Notwithstanding all this punctuality, Luke no where makes any mention of Peter, whether he met him, or in this whole two years vouchsafed to see Paul, or what he did at Rome whilst Paul preached there very fervently the word of God: and yet it's believed, that this history was then written when Luke fearlessly attended on Paul a prisoner at Rome. Thus Hierome: from whence he concludes, that the vision of Paul and Tecla, and the whole fable of Leo's baptism, is to be reckoned among the apochryphal writings. Is it not then, not only apochryphal, but more than very false, that Peter came to Rome the *second* year of Claudius, and held the bishopric twenty-five years, of whom Luke in so very excellent and accurate a history does not make the least mention as being there? About the 27th year after Christ's ascension, and the 4th or 5th

CHAP.
XVI.

XIII.

* Christians.

XIV.
A.D. 60.

---

[1] *Six* years according to Bishop Pearson, *viz.* 13 Nero, and A D. 67.

[m] —— in carcerem conjicitur et arctâ custodiâ tenetur, non ut antea in domo conductâ omnibus notâ · unde Onesiphorus non nisi *postquam sollicitè quæsivisset, invenit eum.* Pearson, Annales Paulini.

CHAP.
XVI.

of Nero, it is as plain as it can be, that Peter was not yet at Rome. And that he could neither come thither in the last of Nero, i. e. the 31st after Christ's ascension, is thus deduced, or from hence inferred. Paul being escaped out of the hands of Nero set out on his journey to Spain and the western parts: this, it's certain, the Apostle intended

*6.

when he wrote to the Romans. Having spent *ten years, he again fell into the hands of Nero, and seeing his death approaching, he in a letter tells Timothy, that taking with him Mark, he should come to Rome, because he had no colleague with him but Luke. But how could this be, if Peter was *perpetually resident* there from the 2nd year of Claudius to the end of Nero's reign? In the same letter to Timothy he writes, *The Lord give mercy unto the house of Onesiphorus; for he oft refreshed me, and was not ashamed of my chain, but when he was at Rome he sought me out very diligently, and found me. The Lord grant unto him that he may find mercy of the Lord in that day.* It is plain enough from these words how grateful the Apostle was to those who did him any good office. Onesiphorus surely might have been informed by Peter, if he had been then at Rome, where Paul was, and so have been freed from that very anxious solicitude which he shewed in finding Paul out. So grateful as the Apostle was to his friends, so as to omit the remembrance of no one who did him any kindness, it's a wonder he should never mention Peter's visiting him in prison. Wherfore it's very true, that Peter was not at Rome the last year of

XV.

Nero. Besides the letters of Paul before mentioned, there are some others of his more familiarly written to Seneca, Nero's præceptor, which are supposed to be written when Paul was a second time brought before Nero. In these letters neither Paul nor Seneca take any notice of Peter; but in the *third* of Seneca's letters to Paul we read, that Nero was angry with the Apostle, that being formerly a pharisee, he had not only himself departed from the rites and antient sect of the Jews, but persuaded others to do

so too: which Peter ought certainly to have done before
Paul, if he had resided at Rome so many years before
Paul's coming to that city. That Peter and Paul did
suffer at Rome the same day, in one and the same place,
is the common opinion of the whole Church of Rome,
which on their solemnity thus chaunts, *Glorious princes of
the land, as in their lives they loved one another, so in their
deaths they were not divided.* But that all this is false is
shewn by their passions forged under the name of the
disciples of Paul, which neither agree with this account,
nor with one another. For as to what is here said, that
they suffered both on one day, Linus positively denys it,
and Dionysius affirms it. As to their suffering both in
the same place, some agree with the chaunting of the
Roman Church, but Linus writes, that Peter was fastened
to a cross with his head downwards, in a place called
Naumachia, but says not a word in what place Paul lost
his head. But by this one thing he sufficiently evidences,
that he had no mind to say, they both suffered in one
place, since he assigns to each of them different apparitors
and executioners, and spectators of their death. Besides,
Dionysius in express words varies from their opinion; for
he says, when they were led unto death, they were separated one from the other, and Paul said unto Peter, *Peace
be with thee, thou foundation of the churches, and shepherd
of Christ's sheep and lambs.* Next, there is no agreement
about both of them being sentenced to die by Nero's
edict. For when all pronounce Nero the author of that
fact, Linus alone testifies, that Peter was put to death by
Agrippa's command. Thus he writes. that whilst Peter
lived at Rome many of the female sex by Peter's admonition renounced the enticements of luxury, among whom
were four concubines of Agrippa's, whose continency made
him so angry, that he ordered Peter to be crucified. Further, it is to be admired, that Josephus himself, who was
carried to Rome by Vespasian after the taking of Jerusalem, and continued there till near the end of Domitian's

CHAP.
XVI.

reign, and there wrote the *History of the Jewish War,* which he dedicated to Vespasian and his son Titus by name, and in it mentions those who were put to death by Nero, as elsewhere in his Antiquities, yet says nothing of Peter and Paul; when yet he was very favourable to the Christians, and was wont on occasion to speak honourably
Antiq. lib.
xviii., xx.
of them, as of John the Baptist beheaded in the castle of Macheron, and of James the Apostle, the brother of Jesus Christ, and a presbyter at Jerusalem. Lastly, it's contrary to reason, that Peter should be put to death the same day with Paul. Since when he was called by Christ he had a wife and children, and a wife's mother, and was accounted the most aged of all the Apostles: and yet he so long executed the evangelical function that, writing to his be-

XVII.

loved disciples, he owns he was worn out with age. That Paul a second time escaped the violence of Nero is very probable, and that both he and Peter suffered at Jerusalem is plain by irrefragable testimonies. First, the words of Christ himself, who tells the scribes and pharisees, and even Jerusalem itself, that they filled the measure of their fathers, and would kill, &c. the prophets, &c. which he sent to them; which words John Chrysostome expounds, not of the prophets of the old law, but of the Apostles. To the same purpose Jerome and Nicholas Lyra. Velenus concludes this part with accounting for the general reception of this error, that Peter was Bishop of Rome, &c. This he does by observing, that others as gross as this have been, and still are believed by the common people as articles of faith; particularly, the Pope's primacy, and the donation of Constantine, made to Pope Sylvester, in direct contradiction to all the writers of history.

I.

In the other part of his book Velenus proposes to answer seven *cavils,* as he calls them, of the Papists, against what he had offered in the former part. The *first* of these relates to his *fourth* argument, that Paul when in his letter to the Galatians he remembers his *two* journeys to Jerusalem, would have it understood, that he took them in

fourteen years after his conversion, and not in seventeen as
Velenus his opinion was, and that this is confirmed by the
testimony of Nicholas Lyra. To this Velenus answers,
that Lyra's exposition would be thought pretty, if he did
not in it dissent from so many good authors, to whom he
was not worthy to hold a candle : that one Jerome is to be
preferred to many Lyras, and that he in his exposition of
the Galatians often mentions these seventeen years. It is
next pretended, that Peter in his catholic Epistle says himself, that he was at Rome, *The Church,* says he, *which is at*
[n] *Babylon, saluteth you.* Now both Jerome and Lyra understand this of Rome, and say, that Rome is figuratively
designed by the name of Babylon. To this Velenus replys, that we learn from the cosmographers, that there
were two Babylons, one in Asia, and another not far from
Egypt, called Egyptian Babylon; but Strabo shews, that
it was rather situated in Arabia than in the provinces of
Egypt. Whence in the Arabian language they call it
Chayr, which is the same with Babylon in our tongue.
And thus it's very plain, that Peter wrote this Epistle
from this Babylon or Chayre. It's objected further, that
if there was nothing else, this alone would be a good argument, that Peter was at Rome before Paul's first coming

II.

III.

---

[n] This Bishop Pearson calls a new and very specious argument : but he is
no way satisfied with that figurative interpretation, which shews, that Rome
ought to be understood by Babylon. He allows, that Peter was at Babylon
when he wrote his letter to the dispersed Jews; but that this Babylon was
neither Rome nor that in Asia, which was a long way from Judea, but Babylon in Egypt; *Argumentum totius Epistolæ Petri in qua* Babylonis *mentio
fit, et nonnulla quæ ex eadem particulatim deduci possunt,* Babylonem *illam
longissime a Judæa sitam potiùs aspernantur, et huic propinquiori melius conveniunt.* De Successione, &c. cap. viii.

—— tantopere orarunt ut Petrus quoque exiverit, et ex urbe egressus sit.
At nondum terminos urbis egressus fuerat, quum D. Jesus ipsi apparuit
cruce super humeros pergens ad Urbem. S. Petrus eum agnovit et dixit:
Domine noster quo cogitas ? Respondit ei et dixit, Romam eo, ut vice alia
crucifigar. hoc dixit, et ex oculis ejus delituit. *Historia S. Petri contaminata
Persice.*

See *Beausobrès Histoire de Manichee,* &c. tom. i. p. 395, 396.

thither; that when Paul was brought bound thither from Jerusalem under a guard, the brethren met him at the Appian-forum, whom when Paul saw he thanked God. For by what monitor or teacher had *they* believed in Christ, if Peter was absent from Rome, or had never been there? Velenus replys, that Orosius, Tertullian, Platina, nay, even an enemy to the Christians, Suetonius Tranquillus, do all testifie, that there were Christians at Rome immediately after Christ's passion, and not only when Paul came thither. Wherfore, none ought to wonder, that so many brethren were at Rome to meet Paul when he came thither. Nor were they without presbyters, as Narcissus, Andronicus, Julias, &c. It was farther objected, that the apostolical disciples, and they who flourished next after the Apostles, to whom this matter ought to be best known, have undoubtedly delivered to us, that Peter and Paul suffered at Rome. Velenus replys, that these passions of Peter and Paul were not written by their disciples, and are very different from and inconsistent with one another: that learned men are persuaded, that even in the Apostle's life-time many things were published under the name of the Christian profession which were repugnant to it: that Origen tells us a letter was directed to the Thessalonians under the name of Paul, that they might the more easily be deceived by the false Apostles; and that the Apostle, on discovering the fraud, wrote to the Thessalonians to advise them *not to be soon shaken in mind*, or be troubled, neither by spirit, nor by word, nor by letter as from *him*. Lastly, that the passions of Peter and Paul, published under the name of Linus, have so much falshood mixed with them, that they not only contradict Christ and Paul's letters, but even the sayings of Peter himself. Agen, it is objected, that the Church of Rome yearly chaunts words taken from Linus's acts of Peter's passion, &c. which it would never do, if it did not know that it was genuine: that among other things in this passion are these words, *But as soon as Peter had deter-*

IV.

2 Ep. ii.

V.

mined to go out of the city gate, he saw Christ coming to
meet him, and adoring him he saith, Lord, whither goest
thou? Christ answered him, *I am come to Rome to be*
again crucified, &c. And that this may appear the more
credible, there is yet remaining a chapel built in the very
place where those words were spoken. Velenus replys,
that the Holy Catholic Church does not chaunt this lie;
since the eastern churches, and many Christians in the
west, do not receive it; but as for the Church of Rome,
what should hinder *that* from approving, professing, and
chaunting lies? that we no where read in the Scriptures,
that Christ after his ascension appeared to any of the
saints in that habit or dress in which after his resurrection
he conversed with his disciples forty days, and spake to
them of the kingdom of God; nay, being instructed by the
catholic faith, we believe he will not at any time appear
before the day of judgment come: that as for the chapel,
built for confirmation of this lie, he could copiously prove,
that for some hundreds of years after Christ's ascension,
there was neither chapel nor church built at Rome, or the
places adjacent; but that the Christians there were wont
to assemble in private places and subterranean caves either
to shew forth the Lord's death, or by hymns and prayers
to obtain Christ's suffrage, and the divine grace for themselves. A *sixth* objection was, that Mark the evangelist,   VI.
a disciple of Peter's, by his master's advice, wrote the
Gospel at Rome, which Gospel °Peter, when he had
heard and approved it, published by his authority to be
read to the Church; and that Peter in his Epistle speaks
of this Mark. Velenus replys, that there were two Marks,
viz. John Mark, and Mark Aristarchus, and that the
Gospel was written by the latter, who was not a disciple
of Peter's, but a fellow labourer and disciple of Paul's.
The *seventh* and last objection mentioned by Velenus is,   VII.
that Philo, the Jew, a man of excellent learning, being

° Irenæus is positive that St. Marc and St. Luke wrote their Gospels after
the death of Peter and Paul. *Lib.* iii. c 1.

CHAP.
XVI.

sent to Rome by his countrymen in the reign of Caligula, and agen a second time in the reign of Claudius, and in some danger there, conferr'd with the Apostle Peter about some affairs, and made so strict a friendship with him, that at length in his books he commended the Christians so far as it was safe for him to do, and wrote a whole book of the praises of John Marc. Velenus answers, that these are trifles fit to be replied to only with laughter. For how could Philo meet Peter at Rome, &c. when it's plain Peter was never at Rome? But if on that account Philo is thought to have commended the Christians because of the friendship he had contracted with Peter, it's more probable *that* was done in Judæa where Peter spent his whole life in preaching Christ, and where he died.

4. To this book of Velenus's the Bishop, as has been said, wrote an answer, which he called, [p] *A Confutation of the Calumnies of Ulrich Velenus of Minden, in which it's cavilled, that Peter was never at Rome.* To Velene's first

1.

argument, the Bishop answers, that at this rate a great many things which are delivered by historians, and they too very likely to be true, may very easily be convicted of falshood: since nothing is more wanting among historians than an agreement in dates: that any one, tho' never so exact, may easily mistake in counting the time, as may abundantly be made to appear not only in profane, but even in sacred histories. But that since of so many writers all unanimously assert, that Peter was at Rome, and sat there a great many years, it would be very impudent, because there is some difference among them in counting them, to dare to affirm, that Peter was never at

II.

Rome. The *second* calumny, the Bishop says, destroys itself. For since no one has hitherto written or said, that Peter lived beyond Nero's time, but all agree, that he suffered under [q] Nero, and that he held the bishopric of

[p] —— Convulsio Calumniarum Ulrichi Veleni Minhoniensis *quibus Petrum nunquam Romæ fuisse* cavillatum.

[q] Anno regni 13.

Rome twenty-five years, it necessarily follows, that he
came to Rome before the 9th of Claudius, since from the
9th of Claudius to the very last of Nero there are no more
than nineteen years. To Velenus's *third* argument, the
Bishop says, that this calumny is of no manner of moment,
and that upon many accounts. 1. Because it might be,
that altho' there was an edict to banish the Jews and
Christians from Rome promulgated, yet Peter, either by
the favour of friends, or because he did not fear death,
might still stay there. 2. The words of *Tranquillus
seem to import no more than that Claudius banished the
ʳJews from Rome, who were continually raising tumults,
† being set on by Chrest. But Peter was none of those
who were thus tumultuous, nor he whom Christ would
have banished from the city, rather on the contrary he
would have him continue there to preach the Gospel.
3. If Priscilla and Aquila did go out of Rome for fear of
Claudius, it does not therfore follow, that all the rest of
the Christians or Jews had the like fear, and that none at
all of them remained there. Lastly, granting that Peter
was banished from Rome with the other Jews, yet this
nicety does not hinder but that he might come to Rome
ˢbefore the 9th of Claudius. To the *fourth* argument the
Bishop answers : 1. That betwixt the conversion of Paul
and his going to Jerusalem the second time could not be
more than fourteen years, tho' Velenus reckon'd it seventeen. So that no one ought to count also those latter fourteen years which Paul mentions to the Galatians as altogether distinct from the former three years : that Paul
freely owns he met Peter twice, once when he did not stay

CHAP.
XVI.

III.

* Sueto-
nius

† impulsore
Chresto.

IV.

ʳ In Augustus's time, according to Josephus, there were of the Jews at
Rome above 8,000 *Antiq.* lib xvii. c 13.

ˢ Sub Claudio nondum Petrum Romam pervenisse sentio *Pearson. de
Successi.*

La tradition générale est que S. Pierre alla à Rome l'an quatre de Claude
——Mais comme cette tradition—se trouve evidemment fausse, plusieurs
modernes reconnoissent que S. Pierre n'alla à Rome que vers le commencement du règne de Neron. *Beausobre, Dissert. sur les Adamites,* Partie ii.

with him above fifteen days, and a second time when he conferr'd with him of the Gospel which he had preach'd to the Gentiles fourteen years before: that it therfore follows, if it be to be depended on, as all unanimously agree, that Peter sat at Rome twenty-five years, that the council held at Jerusalem could not be at above fourteen years distance from the conversion of Paul, unless any one will say, that Peter, after he had staid some time at Rome, returned to Jerusalem to be present at the council. It is plain therfore, that this calumny is of no force, whether the computation be right or wrong, since if the reckoning be right, it is no wise contrary to the Scriptures, that

V.
Peter returned from Rome to Jerusalem. To the *fifth* argument, the Bishop says, it is not the Apostle's custom in his other Epistles to order the presbyters of the churches to be saluted by name: that he wonders that Rome should

** St. Paul calls y^m his *kinsmen,* men eminent among the Apostles.
have such prelates as *Julian or *Junian, the wife of Andronicus, and Priscilla, the wife of Aquila, when elsewhere Paul commands, that women should not speak in the Church: that there may be other reasons why Paul in his letters to the Romans did not salute Peter, as Peter might possibly be absent on some business; or perhaps Paul wrote private letters to him: for who, after a course of so many years, can give any certain account of this

VII.
matter? To Velenus's *seventh* argument, the Bishop replys, that granting in the first place, that Narcissus, &c. were Paul's coadjutors and the disciples of Christ, nay, if you will, presbyters and bishops, Rome had not for that reason no occasion for Peter: as if Paul was of no use to the Ephesians because they had Timothy for their bishop, or that he could do the Corinthians no good, because Apollos and Peter presided among them. But why did Paul promise to come to Rome, that he might impart to them some spiritual gift, when he knew such excellent preceptors and bishops were there? If Paul's presence was necessary to the Romans, altho' they had such presbyters, why not likewise that of Peter? You'll say, Peter

was then aged and decayed. But his senses did not fail
him, nor the Spirit which spake in him, and by which he
did so many wonderful works, especially in that ᵗconflict
in which he subdued Simon Magus. As to Narcissus,
the Bishop says, he believes he was a presbyter; but, as
Ambrose says, not a fix'd one, but one who performed the
office of a pilgrim, often going out of the city to confirm
believers in the faith by his exhortations; and that therfore it is not true, that Narcissus was Bishop of the city of
Rome, nor has any one hitherto so called him. As to Velenus's supposing Andronicus and Julian to be of the
number of the seventy disciples, and quoting Origen as
favouring that opinion, it is certain, that Origen does not
affirm it, but only says, that so it was possible to be, and
that perhaps it might be : but that if Velenus would know
who they were, he should read Athanasius, who asserts,
that * Julian or Junian was a ᵘwoman; but it's very plain * So the
there was no woman among the seventy. To the *seventh* Lat. Vulg.
and some
argument, the Bishop answers, that the two places of Gr. copies.
Scripture on which this calumny seems to be grounded, if VII.
any one had a mind to retort them on the adversary, would
more strongly attack *him* than those whom he opposes.
For if Peter was the Apostle of the ˣcircumcision, and

ᵗ This romance we have at large in the contaminated History of St Peter,
written in Persic, as is supposed, by Xavier There we are told, that Peter's
hearing how famous Simon was at Rome, was the occasion of his going thither. that S. Peter and S. Paul both joined in detecting his frauds, and un-
deceiving Cæsar, who was much præjudiced in his favour, so that he
reckoned him as his God, and thought that on him depended the preservation of the world, &c P. 65, 66, 67, 68

ᵘ So Theophylact on the place, καὶ ταῦτα γυναῖκα ἔσαν τὴν Ἰουνίαν.

ˣ Occulta hic oritur quæstio, Quid igitur Petrus si invenisset ex gentibus
non eos adducebat ad fidem ? aut Paulus si ex circumcisione aliquos repe-
risset, non eos ad Christi baptismum provocabat ? Quæ ita solvetur, ut dica-
mus principale singulis in Judæos et Gentes fuisse mandatum, ut qui
defendebant legem haberent quem sequerentur; qui Legi Gratiam præfere-
bant, non deesset eis Doctor et prævius In commune verò hoc eos habuisse
propositi ut Christo ex cunctis gentibus Ecclesiam congregarent Hieron.
ap. *Pearson de Success.*

there was no small number of the circumcised at Rome, it ought to be of right that Peter betook himself to Rome according to the agreement; and especially since he had left James at Jerusalem, Euodius at Antioch, and knew that Barnabas was at Cyprus, and John in Asia, and was not ignorant, that Paul was very diligently travailing over all the adjacent countries. Besides, the argument taken from the compact makes no less against Paul than against Peter: for why was *he* so soon unmindful of this agreement as every where to enter into the Jews [y] synagogues? The Bishop adds, that even the latter place makes nothing against *him*. For what if some of the chief of the Jews who lived at Rome did not believe in Christ, did not Paul find such every where? So that it is not by any to be wondred at, that Peter had not converted all who were at Rome. But the adversarie, the Bishop says, affirms there what is directly false, *viz.* that the Jews whom Paul caused to be called together said, that they had never before heard any one who had declared to them the rites and institutions of that sect. Nothing like it is to be met with in the Acts. They denied that they had received any letters from Judea concerning Paul's conduct or behaviour there, or that any one coming from thence had reported to them any thing ill of him, but of the sect of the Christians, because they knew it was every where spoken against they said, they desired to hear of Paul what *he* thought of it. Not that they had heard nothing of it before from any body, but that they hoped to hear from Paul something new, and perhaps what might confute that sect.

VIII.　To the *eighth* argument, the Bishop says, it is not easy for us, after a run of so many ages, to tell the reason why Paul in his Epistles sometimes remembers his colleagues, and at others says nothing of them. It's therfore weakly argued from thence, that [z] Peter was not at Rome because

[y] Legimus enim et a S. Petro Gentilem baptizatum fuisse Cornelium, et a Paulo in Synagoga Judæorum Christum sæpissimè prædicatum. *Hieronimus ut supra.*

[z] See Whitby's Preface to his Comment on the first Epistle of Peter.

Paul writing from thence makes no mention of him in his
letters: since we see the same Paul writing to the Ephesians, and not taking the least notice of Timothy that he
was there present. To the *ninth* argument, the Bishop
answers, that there's no inconsistency in Peter's, together
with others, preaching the Gospel at Rome long before
Paul came thither, and the same men's being stirred by
the presence of Paul to do it with more zeal and fervour
than they did before. To the *tenth* argument, the Bishop
answers, if there were not more fellow labourers in the
kingdom of God than those which Paul has here reckoned
up, where were James, John the evangelist, Barnabas,
and the rest of the Apostles? You'll say, these were not
at Rome. But what if they were not at Rome? they yet
laboured in the kingdom of God. You'll say, Paul means
those who laboured at Rome : but that he did not mean,
or is not to be understood of, *all* those is plain from what
Velenus himself has observed, that Paul says, that on his
account the Gospel of Christ was every where preached
at Rome by all. Thus, he says, Paul wrote to the Philippians. But Paul does not only say, that these alone were
his *fellow labourers unto the kingdom of God,* but he
added, *who have been a comfort unto me.* Paul therfore
does not absolutely deny, that he had any other fellow
labourers, &c. but that of no others who laboured with
him, he had so great comfort. This therfore makes nothing against Peter's being then at Rome ; rather it's an
argument *for* his being there; that in the same Epistle,
Paul mentions Mark, sister's son to Barnabas, who was
very dear to Peter, and whom in his first Epistle he calls
his son, and who historians every where say was at Rome
with Peter, and there wrote the Gospel which is now
called Mark's. To the *eleventh* argument, the Bishop
says, that no one can now tell what Paul's design was in
mentioning Timothy's name in his letters to the Philippians, Colossians, and Philemon, and omitting it in his
letter to the Ephesians, when they were all written at the

CHAP.
XVI.

IX

X.

Coloss. iv.

1 Peter, v.

XI.

same time, and Timothy was present when they were all dictated. But since what Paul desired of Philemon was not of so great moment, and that it does not sufficiently appear what acquaintance Peter had before with Phile-mon, there seems no reason why Peter's name should have been added in this letter. To the *twelfth* argument, the Bishop replys, that when Paul complains of his being for-saken by all, he is to be understood either of those whom he brought with him out of **Judæa**, or of others whom he was accustomed to use with familiarity in his own parti-cular affairs, but not of **Peter**, since he was never wont to adhere to *him:* that he said, or used the word *all*, accord-ing to his usual way of speaking, since it's certain, that not *all* did forsake him: that Peter had his own business to mind, that he took care of his flock, and now saw, per-haps, that the time was at hand when they ought to be especially confirmed in the faith, least they should be struck with fear, and make a defection from christianity on their hearing, that Paul himself, that great Apostle, was convened before Cæsar's tribunal. Add, that Peter had sufficient experience of Paul's eloquence, and nothing doubted of his constancy, but was fully persuaded, that the Spirit would not be wanting to him: that being moved by these or the like reasons, he thought it would be more advantageous not to leave his flock, which Christ had so earnestly recommended to him, than out of love to Paul, whom he knew perhaps by the Spirit that he should die for Christ, to suffer his flock to be in danger. To the *thirteenth* argument, the Bishop says, if this calumny was of any force, Velenus might with equal facility collect, that there are a great many other things never done, which yet were really fact. For what does Luke remember of those things which Paul did all those *two* years, but summarily, and in the very fewest words? When therfore he reads in Luke's last chapter of the brethren going out to meet Paul, when they heard of his coming, so far as the Ap-pian forum, &c. how does he know that Peter was not

XII.

XIII.

among them? especially since all used then to be called
brethren indifferently, or without making any disinction.
To the *fourteenth* argument, the Bishop answers, that
Velenus goes on with his usual logic, endeavouring to
infer, that since Paul in his letters to Timothy saluted
some brethren there named by him, and said nothing of
Peter, therfore Peter was not then at Rome; but this
trifling logic, he says, he had often before confuted. That
in this Epistle Paul remembred Onesiphorus rather than
Peter, the reason was because *he* at that time dwelt at
Ephesus, where Timothy resided, and was very intimate
with them both. Besides, we are in the dark as to Timothy, whether *he* was known to Peter, since he was not circumcised before Peter left Judæa. As to the former part
of this calumny, where the adversarie reports, that Paul
said, that besides Luke, he had no colleague left with him
at Rome, Paul does not say any such thing, but *only Luke
is with me :* by which words he does not mean, that there
were no other Christians at Rome besides himself and
Luke, nor does he by them exclude certain more modern
companions, since he testifies in the same letter, that he
had then with him, Eubulus, Pudens, Linus, and other
brethren; but when he says, *only Luke is with me*, he
must be understood to speak of his old acquaintance or
companions, whom he named before, saying, *Demas hath
forsaken me, and is gone into Thessalonica, Crescens into
Galatia, Titus into Dalmatia, only Luke is with me.* To
the *fifteenth* argument, the Bishop says, that in the opinion of the [a] learned these Epistles were not written by
Paul and Seneca. This is attested in the first place by
Erasmus, whose single judgment in this matter, his lordship says, would be sufficient to him against a thousand

---

[a] Quod post Baronium ad A C. 66 num. 13. Raynaudus cumque secutus
Claudius Frassenius, p. 73 disquisit. Bibli et alij putant ex *fabulosis hisce
Acus* petitam esse occasionem fingendarum ejusmodi Epistolarum, mihi
neutiquam verisimile apparet. Neque enim illius vel antiquitatis vel autori-
tatis fuere illa commentitia Acta. *Fabricij Codex Apochry N. Testa.*

CHAP.
XVI.

others. But suppose it was otherwise, and that these Epistles were their's, what is there in them that is repugnant to our purpose? If Nero was angry with Paul, because having been a pharisee, he left the pharisaical sect, must he therfore be angry also with Peter, who was not a pharisee, nor ever professed himself an admirer of that sect? But how does it appear that Nero had not conceived the like displeasure against Peter? does Seneca's Epistle deny it? so far from it, that it does not say, that Nero was angry with Paul. To the *sixteenth* argument,

XVI.

the Bishop replys, that this calumny contains in it various sophisms, to which he shall answer in order. As to the disagreement of writers, he thinks he has abundantly shewn before, that however they may vary as to the time, place, and judge, they have no difference as to the Apostles Peter and Paul dying at Rome, and do all therfore agree, that they were there. If the variation of writers for one day can derogate from the credit of a thing done, Christ himself shall not be believed to be crucified: for some of the ancients, among whom are Tertullian, Chrysostome, and Cyril, assert it was done the seventh of the calends of April; but Nicetas, and he a Greek author, says it was on the 10th: Theophilus Cæsariensis on the 11th; Victorinus Lenionicensis on the 7th; wheras Roger Bacon places it on none of the calends of April, but on the 3d day. But, his Lordship says, he shall not grant, that among authors there is so great a controversie about this matter of Peter's dying at Rome, as Velenus pretends; that he has read the lives of both the Apostles written by [b] Linus, and translated into Latin by Faber,

---

[b] *de passione Petri et Pauli.* Latinè primus vulgavit Jacobus Faber ad calcem sui in Epistolas Paulinas commentarij Paris. 1512, fol. Neque hic e græco in latinum illos transtulit, ut tradit Ulrichus Velenus libro quod Petrus Romæ non fuerit, *persuasione* 16, sed quales in Codice Bibliothecæ Majoris Monasterij in Gallia invenit latinè protulit. *Fabricij Codex Apochry. N. Testamenti*, p. 776.

Hi vero qui publicè extant, omnium propemode confessione, fabulosi supposititij, et Episcopo Romano ejus ætatis cujus Paulus, 2 Tim. iv. 21, memi-

and found no difference betwixt him and Ambrose, except
about the judge; for as to the day, whatever Faber has
said in the preface, he finds no variation in Linus himself,
no, nor yet as to the place. But allow, says he, that there
were different particular places, yet this is not inconsistent
with Ambrose, who speaks of a general place, *viz.* Rome.
As to the judge, what hinders Peter's being condemned to
suffer death by Agrippa, and yet that being done by an
edict of Nero's? Neither does Dyonisius any thing contradict the rest. For what if he does remember some
words said by the Apostles to one another, which others
say nothing of, shall *he* therfore be contrary to them?
As to Josephus, tho' he does take notice of two that belonged to Christ, he says nothing of Stephen, and the
other James, and a great many besides. And what he
does say of their being stoned is nothing to Peter, who
suffered the death of the cross, as it is read every where
in books, and seen also in pictures; to which we may add,
that Peter, by the evidence of all, outlived James seven
years. To the *seventeenth* and last argument of Vele- XVII.
nus's, and his conclusion of this *first* part, the Bishop answers, that this is a mere calumnie and sophism every
body must be sensible who has at any time turn'd over
Hierome and Lyra. For that the adversarie very plainly
refers to these authors contrary to their meaning. As to
what a great many believe of the Pope's primacy and
*Constantine's donation, whether it be an error or not, the * See Bp.
Bishop says, it's not his present design to discuss, it re- Peacock's
quiring a larger volume; however he thinks, that in his Life.
Confutation of Luther's Articles, he has entirely answered
what Luther has urged against the Pope's primacy: and
as to Peter's See, he does not apprehend why that should
be called a fiction which has the most grave and eminent
vouchers, and they next to the Apostles' times, and who

nerit plane indigni, ut, paucis quibusdam Jac. Fabro, Sixto Senensi, Salme-
rone, Coccio, &c. qui judicio suo usi non sunt, exceptis, agnoscunt plerique
omnes, etiam e Pontificiis, &c. *Ibidem*

CHAP.
XVI.
can no wise be suspected of inventing such a thing, such as Tertullian, Cyprian, Ambrose, Leo, Hierome, Bede, Eutropius, Orosius, besides more modern writers, as Platina, Sabellicus, Volateranus, John Baptist Mantua; insomuch, that no one yet before Velenus has been so impudent as to deny, that Peter was some time at Rome.

de excidio
Hierosolymæ, lib.
iii. c. 2.
The Bishop then quotes Ægesippus, as next the Apostles' times, relating Peter's magnificent gests with Simon Magus at Rome, &c. *Eusebius's Eccles. History*, lib. ii. c. 14; to which he adds, that Eusebius reports from Papias, that Peter in his first letter remembred Mark, and tropically named ᶜRome Babylon, when he says, *The Church which is in Babylon saluteth you, and Mark my son.* Eusebius also in his Chronicles testifieth, that Peter came to Rome the *second* of Claudius, and there sat twenty-five years, and died there gloriously the last of Nero's reign. Ire-

adv. Hære.
lib. iii.
næus also digesting the succession of the bishops of the city of Rome, asserts, that Peter and Paul were at Rome. To these we add Chrysostome and Theophylact, who say, that Linus was the second Bishop of the Church of Rome after Peter. These unanimously affirm, that Peter was the *first* Bishop of Rome.

I.
In answer to the other part of Velenus's book, the Bishop says, that in his confutation of Velenus's *second* argument, he has shewn, that Hierome's computation is manifestly opposite to, and cannot possibly agree with, that reckoning which Velenus has collected under his *fifth* argument: that, according to his own account, the fourteen years of St. Paul's travels are to be reckoned from his conversion; that Lyra is not the only author of this reckoning, since Bede, who is a most exact computer of times,

---

ᶜ That Babylon is figuratively here put for Rome is an opinion so early delivered by Papias, and which afterwards so generally obtained, that I subscribe to the note at the end of this Epistle, that *it was written from Rome. Whitby in locum.*

See Spanhemij F. F. operum, tom. ii. col. 331-338. *Turretin Theologia elenctica,* vol. iii.

does not only say thus, but proves by irrevincible arguments, that those fourteen years are to be counted from
the conversion of Paul, and that the 14th makes the 4th
year of Claudius, and not the 2nd, as Eusebius and Jerome
reckon it. But whether the council of Jerusalem was celebrated the 14th year, or after fourteen years, it is plain,
that neither Eusebius nor Jerome agree, that it was held,
seventeen years after, since both say, that Peter came to
Rome the 2nd of Claudius, and there sate twenty-five
years. To Velenus's answer to the *second* objection, the   II.
Bishop says, that there need not many words to explode
it, especially since he brings no evidence, either from the
Scriptures, or any of the sacred interpreters to support it,
but only the figment of his own brain, void of all reason.
For what if there was a Babylon near Egypt, will it therefore follow, that from that place Peter wrote that his
catholic Epistle? Were the fathers of the Church ignorant of this, from whom it has been delivered down to us,
that Peter wrote this Epistle at Rome, and that in it
Rome is by him called Babylon tropically? To Velenus's
answer to the *third* objection, the Bishop replys, that the   III.
adversary here objects to himself, what he supposes no
one else would object to him. For that no one can from
hence argue, that Peter was at Rome, because there was
no more necessity of *his* being there than of any other
Christians. Besides, it's credible, that those brethren who
went to meet Paul, had some acquaintance with him before, and were not first of all converted to Christianity at
Rome. It's therfore a weak objection: nor does the adversary attempt to confute it by a reason much stronger: .
for what if in Tiberius's reign some brethren did go to
Rome, was therfore the presence of Peter there unnecessary? Don't we read in the Acts, that when the Apostles
heard that Samaria had received the word of God, they
sent to them Peter and John? To Velenus's answer to
the *fourth* objection, the Bishop says, that it would be   IV.
easy, at this rate, to reject any writers, if for such cavils

CHAP.
XVI.
as these they were to be reckoned of no authority. For what if under Paul's name there was an Epistle forged to the Thessalonians, ought we therfore to have his other Epistles in less esteem? God forbid. Velenus should shew, if he can, for what reason any of the heretics should feign, that Peter was at Rome, or whose heresy would by this opinion be in the least promoted. To this very day no one is to be found, except Velenus alone, and he a capital foe to the Roman Church, who ever denied that Peter was at Rome. As to the Apostle's dying at Rome, suppose there is some variety as to the year or day when they were put to death, this ought not to be an argument that they were not put to death at Rome, no more than we ought to doubt of Christ's death at Jerusalem, when yet there is no little controversie among writers, not only about the year, but also about the day when he was crucified. As to Velenus's stiling what is ascribed to Linus concerning the passions of Peter and Paul, inventions and lies, he has, the Bishop says, no reason for it : since the things he quotes from Paul are not inconsistent, but relating to different times, which the adversary either orders preposterously, or very odly confounds. But should he grant to the adversary, that these *three* books of Linus, Dyonisius, and Hegesippus, were forged, there are innumerable writers besides, and so many monuments of that matter extant, that he must be a very impudent man who should attempt to contradict it : besides a most constant fame,

V.
which Jerome and others call the law of history. To the answer to the *fifth* objection, the Bishop observes, that Velenus attempts here to prove, that Christ never spake the foresaid words to Peter. But, says he, for what reason? To wit, because Christ never has descended from heaven since he ascended thither; nor ever will come again from thence before the day of judgment; which he attempts to prove from Scripture, and particularly from

Acts, iii.
the words of Peter himself, *Whom the heaven must receive till the time of restitution of all things,* &c. But, says the

Bishop, from this Scripture nothing more can be collected than that Christ is perpetually to remain in heaven till he come to judgment; and this no wise contradicts the former story of his appearing to Peter: since Christ may by his miraculous power exhibit himself corporally present on earth, and yet nevertheless continue in heaven at the right hand of the father inconvulsibly. His Lordship adds, that there is nothing in this story of Peter unlike the colloquy or conversation which Christ had with Paul when he appeared to him in his way to Damascus; and that there is more than one witness of this story of Peter, as Eusebius, Linus, Ægesippus, and Ambrose. To Velenus's answer to the *sixth* objection, the Bishop says, VI. there is no one called in the Holy Scriptures Mark Aristarchus, as they are two persons in the Epistle to the Colossians, so they are also in that to Philemon: that the adversary owns, that this Mark, whom Paul remembers to Philemon, wrote the Gospel according to Mark, and therfore he cannot deny, that he was called by Peter his son: now that he whom Peter called his son was the cousin of Barnabas is plain from the Acts. His Lordship adds, that since in the Acts, Aristarchus is often mentioned, but never called Mark, it's by no means probable either, that in the Epistle to Philemon he was called Mark Aristarchus, or that in those two Epistles to the Colossians and Philemon, Paul should mention two called by the name of Mark. To the answer to the last objection, the Bishop VII. replys, that the reader here sees what fetches the adversary uses: for when he ought to have answered the testimony of Jerome, he does not do it; but, avoiding the dart, he pretends, that he has proved, by very powerful reasons, that Peter *was never at Rome*, which is nothing else but to shew himself conquered. For he cannot deny, that Philo was some time at Rome, so great is the consent of writers in this affair; and therfore by way of subterfuge, he betakes himself to the fiction of Philo's rather contracting friendship with Peter in Judæa. But that 'tis plain the adversary has done nothing by this cavil of his, since it no wise hinders Peter's being at Rome, as Eusebius and Jerome, no inconsiderable authors, constantly affirm. And indeed if the adversary had not cast away all shame, he would by these proofs be so restrained, as no longer to bark against Peter's pontificate at Rome: shame, if he was not a man of the most brazen forehead, would restrain him from affirming so extraordinary a lie. But all the Lutherans have imbibed so much malice against the See of Peter, that, as a rotten ^dclose-stool always sends forth nothing but a pestilent vapour, so *they* don't cease to vomit out against the Pope and his See what lies and calumnies they are able to invent. The Bishop thus concludes his *Confutation*, &c. He thinks it plain, he says, from this answer of his, by what foolish pratings, frivolous sophisms, and most trifling trifles the adversary has attempted to shew, that Peter was never at Rome; and, on the contrary, by what effectual reasons, by what solid subscriptions of authors, and by what more evident tokens *he* has demonstrated that Peter was at Rome, so that he believes the reader desires nothing more to be said for this cause. But notwithstanding, *ex abundanti*, he shall endeavour agen to shew how these things in the Gospel which suit this matter, serve to the purpose. For the

* See Barrow of the supremacy.

present he shall only remember *three*. I. That Peter, tho' he was not the *first* * called by Christ, was yet by Christ constituted the *first* among the Apostles. II. That Peter was called by Christ Petra, the rock, upon which the structure of his Church should be raised. III. That it was said to him by Christ, *I have prayed for thee, Peter, that thy faith fail not.* These things the Bishop thought so

---

^d In much such a cleanly manner does our Bishop's great friend, Sir Thomas Moore, treat Luther. *Hæc est domini doctoris posterioristice, qui quum sibi jam priùs fas esse scripserit coronam regiam conspergere et conspurcare stercoribus; an non nobis fas erit posterius hujus posterioristice linguam stercoratam pronunciare dignissimam ut vel meientis mulæ posteriora lingat suis prioribus donec rectius ex prioribus didicerit posteriores concludere propositionibus. Responsio ad convitia M. Lutheri,* fol. 72, b. col. 1.

plain, that they could not be denied by any but those who are perfectly shameless; and therfore he refers it to the reader to consider with himself, whether it does not most fitly agree to the *first* of these : that when the whole world was to be converted to christianity, *that* city which is accounted the *first* should by divine appointment fall to the lot of no other for a seat than of him who was the *first* among the Apostles. As to the *second,* who, says the Bishop, does not know, that the Church which we now have, proceeded from no other Apostle than Peter only ? Who therfore does not see how agreeable it is to those words of Christ that Peter sometime sat at Rome? since from the Roman Church, as from the chief fountain, the light of the true faith shines to the rest of the churches which are dispersed thro' Christendome. Lastly, the Bishop observes, that if we consider what has been said in the *third* place of the faith of Peter, we shall plainly perceive, that it's by no means fit that Peter should have for his principal seat any of the churches which are now in the possession of the darkness of infidelity, as Antioch, &c. but that he should have that part of the world in which the evangelical faith should not be extinguished, that which, the Bishop adds, he scarce dares to assert has happened to any other of the Apostles.

In this manner did the Bishop assert the certainty of the Apostle Peter's being at Rome, in order to support the opinion of his being bishop of that place: an opinion which, however it may serve the purpose of his supposed successors there, is so far from being to the honour of the Apostle, that it rather lessens and degrades him, and, to use the words of a learned writer, is a *disparagement to the apostolical majesty.* So much superior is the office of an Apostle to that of a particular bishop. But however this be, it has been observed, that the time which old tradition assigns of St. Peter's going to Rome is rejected by divers learned men, even of the Roman party, and by others asserted to be not till a long time after the 44th

Barrow of the Supremacy

Scal. in Euseb.

Onuph. apud Bellar —

Vales. in Euseb.

year of Christ, or the 2nd of Claudius Cæsar. But whether Peter was ever at Rome or not, it's plain, as was said
before, no argument on either side of the question can be
had from the Scripture, but must be deduced from profane history. This being observed by Velenus, and that
there was a great variety and disagreement among the
writers in setling the time when Peter came to Rome;
observing likewise the shameless practice of the Romanists
in forging fables to serve their cause, as in the pretended
donation of Constantine, and being sensible that a fraud of
the same nature was in those monuments which they have
left concerning Peter, as is that fable of Linus about his
death : and lastly, having found, that St. Peter's martyrdome is remembred by Jerome and Lyra, as if he was
crucified by the scribes and pharisees, he was led by those
and the like reasons into an opinion, that Peter was never
at Rome. But in this, as he is acknowledged to be very
singular, so it seems as if he was mistaken, since all the
fathers do with one mouth declare that he was at Rome.
Accordingly, it has been observed, that none of all the
Protestants who have been employed in compiling histories and chronicles, excepting Bale, however they may
have spoken doubtfully of it, and as what is no article of
our faith, have ever ᵉdenied, that Peter was at Rome, but
only, that he did not go thither till a long time after the
44th year of Christ, or the 3rd of Claudius. But however
this be, in July this year was published an answer to this
book of the Bishop's, of which I've not been able to come
at the sight of any more than the title. It was written by
Simon Hess, and had this title præfixed to it. ᶠ*An Apology against the Lord of Rochester, an English bishop, on*

Summa
Colloquij
Joannis
Rainoldi
cum Jo-
anne Harto
de Capite et
fide Eccle-
siæ.
cap. vi. §3.

ᵉ See a Discourse of Peter's Lyfe, Peregrination and Death, wherin is
plainly proved, by the order of time and place, that Peter was never at
Rome, by Christo: Carlile, Rector of Hackney, London, 1582.

ᶠ Apologia Simonis Hessi adversus dominum Roffensem Episcopum An-
glicanum super concertatione ejus cum Ulrico Veleno, An Petrus fuerit
Romæ, et quid de primatu Romani Pontificis sit censendum. Addita est

his dispute with Ulric Velenus, whether Peter was ever at
Rome, *and what is to be thought of the primacy of the*
Roman pontiff. In it, I suppose, was Velenus's opinion
defended, but I don't find that any notice was ever taken
of it by the Bishop.

5. Cardinal Wolsey at this time summoned a convocation of the clergy, to consider of, and provide for the
reformation of their lives.   His mandate for this purpose
is entred in our Bishop's register, and dated at his palace
at Westminster, May 7, 1523. The monastery, or nunnery
of Higham, was likewise now appropriated to the college
of St. John the Evangelist, in Cambridge, the instrument
of this union and annexing is dated May 19, 1523. There
is likewise entred in our Bishop's register the abjuration
of one Thomas Batman, heremyte, and late keper of the
chapel of St. Williams, in the parishe of St. Margaret's
next Rochester.

Epistola eruditissima de Ecclesiasticorum pastorum autoritate et officiis in
subditos et subditorum in superiores obedientia

Versa pagina, Lector, conspicies libelli summam.

At the end, *Julii Mense Anni* M D. XXIIJ. 12 leaves, in large 4°.

CHAP. XVII.

*1. Of the Bishop's ill state of health. 2. His desiring
Erasmus to write a treatise of the manner of Preaching.*

1. THESE severe studies and labours of the Bishop
seem to have had a very ill effect on his health, insomuch, that in a letter wrote by him about this time to
his dear friend, Erasmus, he intimated to him, that he
very much doubted whether his book, which Erasmus was
then compiling, and which the Bishop hastened him to
finish, would find him alive. This intimation was yet further explained to Erasmus by the Bishop's servant who
brought him this letter, who assured him, that his lord was
afflicted with a very ill state of health. Erasmus, therfore,
in his answer to this letter of his Lordship's, dated from
A. D. 1524. Basil, September 4, 1524, tells the Bishop, that he no
way indulged his thin body: that he suspected that a
great part of his illness proceeded from the place, and that
therfore, if he'd give him leave, he'd act the part of a
physician to him: that it was near the sea, and the slub,
being every now and then left bare by the tide, exasper-
ated the air; that he had a study which was glass windows
on every side of it, which thro' their chinks transmitted a
subtile, and, as the physicians speak, a percolated air,
which was pestilential to thin and weak bodies: that he
was very sensible how much the Bishop was in his study,
which was a paradise to him, or in which he took the
greatest pleasure; but that if *he* was to stay in such a
place but three hours he should be sick: that therfore a
chamber would be more convenient for him with a boarded
floor and wainscotted walls, since bricks and lime produce
a noxious steam: that he knew, that to those who live a
devout life, death is not formidable; but that the whole
Church has an interest in the life of such a bishop, when

there is so great a scarcity of good ones. Tho' as for Erasmus, it was not much matter how he did.

2. The book mentioned to Erasmus by the Bishop seems to have been, *Of the manner of preaching*, about which his Lordship desired this great man to compose a discourse. Erasmus himself intimated in the Epistle De- Basil, Aug. dicatory to what he calls a Miscellany, rather than a just 6, 1535 treatise on this subject, that the Bishop pressed him very much to set about this work; and that tho' he did not actually promise his Lordship, he yet intended to oblige him with this book. To induce him to undertake and finish such a performance, Erasmus tells us, his Lordship signified to him, that he had then the care of *three* col- Queen's, leges in the most celebrated University of Cambridge, of alias Coll which he was likewise Chancellor, from whence his aim retæ et was, that there should come forth divines, not so much Christ's furnished with weapons to maintain a fight about words, Coll. St. as instructed soberly to preach the word of God. By what has been said before, it appears how sensible the Bishop always was of the necessity and usefulness of sober, serious, and affectionate preaching. But it's not at all improbable, that now he had a better opinion of it than ever, since he saw how much, thro' the neglect of it, the Reformation gained ground, the patrons of which did all they could to recommend themselves by it. Whatever has been said to soften and palliate this fact of there being but few sermons in the time of popery, it's very notorious, that as there was then very little preaching, so what there was of it was far enough from being to the edification of the hearers. The preachers of those times were generally of the orders of the begging friers, who were the Pope's questors or pardon-mongers, and whose business it was in their sermons, instead of preaching the Gospel, and promoting the power of godliness, by pleasant flattering and lying words, to get people together Ricardi about them only that they might have, and eat, and devour Confessitheir worldly things, insomuch, that they became the very 85, b.

See Chau-
cer, &c.
Of the Or-
der of
Priesthode,
MS.

scorn and jest of the poets. As for the parish priests, or they who had the cures of souls, who were not always in priest's orders, a writer of those times tells us, " they " were so unkunning, that men ᵃscorned them in saying of " their service, in reading of their Epistle and Gospel." To the same purpose Archbishop Peccam had observed before, that the people were plunged into error thro' the ignorance of the priests, and therfore he made a constitution, requiring every parish priest to read to his parishioners four times a year, or once a quarter, the explanation of the fourteen Articles of faith, the Ten Commandments, &c. which he there gave them. But, alas! this signified little, the explanation itself needing explaining to men so ignorant as not to understand plain Latin. Thoresby,

Vicaria
Leodien-
sis, App.

Archbishop of York, therfore translated into English this explanation for the use of the clergy of his diocese, for which his Grace gave the following reason. " For thi " that mikel folke now in yis world ne is noght wele ynogh " lered to knawe God almighten, ne love him, ne serve " him als thai suld do—and peraventure ye defaitor in " thaime that has thaire saules to kepe, and suld teche " thame als prelates, parsons, vikers, and priestes."—We

Diction:
Theolog:
MS.
Oratio ad
Clerum.
1511.

therfore need not wonder at Dr. Gascoigne's complaint afterwards, that there were but few good preachers of God's word, and Dean Colet's observation about our Bishop's time, that the vicars and parish priests were foolish and unmeet. Our Bishop's friend, Erasmus, agen

Episto. Li-
ber. xxvii.
ep. iv. lib.
xxix. ep.
64.

and agen takes notice, that the people at this time seldom heard evangelical preachers, or those who preached the Gospel, and yet seldomer fit or proper ones: that in country villages, and even in some towns, they never, or very rarely, heard the word of God, or the Gospel of Christ. He intimates the same in his Epistle dedicatory before this book of the manner of preaching, which he intended for the Bishop, if he had not been prevented by

ᵃ A. S. ſceaᴒn, dung, dregs.

his untimely death. He observed, that nothing contributes more to the amendment of people's manners, than
the scattering abroad the seed of the Gospel by fit
preachers. For, says he, whence is it, that in the hearts
of a great many Christ is so cold, not to say quite extinct?
whence is it, that under the Christian name there is so
much real paganism, but from the scarcity of faithful
preachers?

CHAP. XVIII.

1. *The Bishop writes a Defence of the Christian Priest-hode, in answer to Luther.* 2. *Some account of this book.*

1. NOTWITHSTANDING the regard shewed by the Bishop to the friendship of Erasmus, it seems his advice had not that effect on him as to cause him to desist from his prosecuting with so much eagerness his beloved studies for the sake of his health. For not long after the publication of his book against Velenus came forth another, written by him in opposition to Luther, which he A.D 524. entituled, *A Defence of the Sacred Priesthode against Luther.* In this tract his Lordship refers to this little book of his against Velenus, in which, he says, he has shewn, that the succession which began from Christ is not to be ended before that all things which are predicted by Christ shall be accomplished.

2. In a prologue prefixed to this book, the Bishop gives the following account of it. He had not, he says, without much grief of mind, read a great many books which Luther had some time since published: for that in them he found every where dispersed so much poison, wherewith the minds of the simpler sort, and that in no small number, were every day mortally infected. But he had never seen any book more pestilent, more unsound and impudent, than *that* to which Luther had given the title * *Of abrogating the Mass*, in which he attempts wholly to abolish the sacrifice of the body and blood of Christ, which has hitherto been reckoned by the Church principally salutiferous, and the great incentive of devotion in all the faithful servants of Christ. And that he may with greater probability effect this, he contends, says the

---

* *de abroganda Missa privata.*

Bishop, with abundance of prating, that there is no visible
priesthode; but that the priesthode which the ancient
fathers usurped for so many ages, was partly made up of
humane lies, and partly erected by satanical instincts.

3. It's much such another account that Maimbourg
gives of this book of Luther's, that in it he determined,
that the mass cannot be a sacrifice; that there is no purgatory, nor transubstantiation, but that the body and blood
of Jesus Christ are in the sacrament under the substance
of bread and wine: that both species of the sacrament are
to be given to the laity: that there is no difference betwixt
the clergy and laity, but that every one in the Church has
the same power of consecrating and administring the
sacraments, and also of teaching, altho', for order's and
decency's sake, this power be committed to elders, by
which he means presbyters and bishops, &c. But Seckendorf observed, that these things were represented more
invidiously than truly: that Luther inquiring more accurately into the distinction of clergy and laity, thought himself convinced by very plain texts of Scripture, that after
the taking away the priesthode of the Old Testament, and
Christ's being constituted the only priest of the New
Covenant, all true Christians, or all the faithful, were to
be accounted spiritual priests, and that there was no more
occasion for other priests, properly so called, than for a
sacrifice either bloody or ceremonial, and representative, unless it were to present themselves every day spiritual sacrifices unto God, and instead of a sacrifice, to offer prayers
and thanksgivings in spirit and in truth, and whatsoever
else of worship and observance which may please God
thro' Christ. But that Luther never denied, that particular
men ought to be appointed to preach the word of God,
and administer the sacraments; nor said, that, unless there
was the utmost necessity, any of the faithful might, of bro-
therly charity, do those things which ordinarily ought to
be done by the ministers of the Church. That if, therfore,
he had either wrote or said any things on this article more

Comm. de
Lutheran-
ismo, § cui

1 Pet. ii 9.
Apoc. v 10,
and xx.

freely, it was to depress the too great prerogatives of the clergy, which they thought their due by divine right, and very much abused.

4. The Bishop proceeds to tell us, that Luther endeavoured to shew, that there was no visible priesthode, by *three* arguments, and that therfore *he* should likewise attempt to brandish against Luther three other attacks, by which, as by a sponge, he would wipe out whatsoever Luther with his filthy and blasphemous mouth had objected to the priests. But that there may be no confusion, and the reader not left uncertain, as often as *attack s* are mentioned, whether he is to understand them of the Bishop or of Luther, he shall call, he says, his own *attacks, congresses*. The *first* of these, his Lordship says, shall be a prescription of the former truth, which has been infallibly conveyed down to us by the orthodox fathers, from the first founders of the Church themselves. The *second* will be a certain series of axioms digested from the Holy Scriptures, and placed in order, by which that priesthode, which Luther calls visible, will be plainly determined. The *third* will be a plain confutation of every one of Luther's arguments to the contrary.

I.   In laying down the ancient prescription, his Lordship begins with St. Augustine, and so goes backward, quoting the following writers of the Church, *viz.* Hierome, Ambrose, Hilary, Arnobius, Cyprian, Tertullian, Gennadius, Cyrillus, Chrysostome, Gregory Nazianzene, Basil, Eusebius, Origen, Egesippus, Ignatius, Polycarp, Dionysius, Philo, Clemens, without critically distinguishing betwixt those which are real, and such as are counterfeit. From the unanimous opinion of so many fathers, the Bishop observes, that it is most certainly to be collected, that the priesthode is by no means of yesterday or t'other day, but was instituted from the very infancy of the Church. To Luther's enquiry why the Apostles avoided this appellation of priesthode, the Bishop answers, because, as yet, the old priesthode was current, and sacrifices were daily offered in the temple; and therefore, that the legal and evangelical priesthode might not be confounded with one another, it pleased the Apostles in the mean while, instead of the name of priests, to use other new names. These, therfore, it's plain, they sometimes called presbyters, sometimes ministers, sometimes bishops and pastors, until the old priesthode, together with the temple, was utterly abolished. But when the temple was destroyed, and the old priests reduced to nothing, our presbyters were by all people every where called priests.

The *second* congress the Bishop introduces with shewing his design in it. He will not, he says, contend about words, i. e. by what name they are to be called whom at this day we stile priests; since he thinks it signifies nothing, as to this dispute, whether they are called priests or presbyters, or pastors, or any other name. He will shew, he says, that there ought to be some to act betwixt God and the people, who may for the people execute the same offices which we see at this day are born by priests. And this he will shew was not devised by men, or was no human invention, but was of divine institution. But before he does this, his Lordship thinks it proper to represent to the reader Luther's opinion in his own words, which he does as follows. Be assured, and don't suffer yourself to be deceived by any other persuasion, whosoever you are who have a mind to be sincerely a Christian, that there is in the New Testament no visible and external priesthode, unless that which is erected by Satan thro' the lies of men. But the one, and onely priesthode to us, is that of Christ, by which he offered himself for us, and all us with him; of whom Peter says, *Christ hath once died for our sins, the just for the unjust, that he might offer us unto God, being put to death in the flesh, but quickned by the Spirit;* and Heb. x. *By one suffering, he hath perfected for ever them that are sanctified.* This priesthode is a spiritual one, and common to all Chris-

CHAP. XVIII.

II

1 Epist iii.

tians; for all we who are Christians are priests by the
same priesthode by which Christ is a priest, i. e. we are
the sons of Christ, the High Priest. Nor have we need of
any other priest and mediator besides Christ. Luther, the
Bishop adds, thus expressed himself, because, as he said,
the dispensation of the mysteries of God was now dege-
nerated into so great a pomp of power, and a certain ter-
rifying tyranny, as that none of the powers of the world
are able to confer it, as if the laity were somewhat different from Christians. But then, says the Bishop, he owned,
that tho' it be true that we are all equally priests, we cannot, nor, if we could, we ought not all publickly to minister
and teach. He makes a great difference betwixt the
priests appointed by the Papal hierarchy, and the true
priests of Christ, or the faithful. But, in the mean time,
he does not deny, that there ought to be certain men appointed to preach the word of God, and administer the
sacraments; and that not without great necessity should
any of the faithful do what ought to be done ordinarily by
the ecclesiastical ministry. But to prove how full of error
these assertions of Luther's are, the Bishop lays down the
ten following conclusions, which he calls axioms.

I. It is agreeable to reason, that for the affairs which
concern the salvation of souls, some should be deputed
who should undertake the care of the whole multitude.

II. Christ himself, whilst he was here on earth, instituted some pastors who might take care of his sheep, and
feed, rule, and teach them.

III. It is fit, that they who in this manner are instituted
pastors to the Christian flock, should be endowed with a
more plentiful gift of grace above others.

IV. It is not only fit that it should be so done, but
Christ has in fact bestowed on these pastors of his Church
grace and power, wherby they might more commodiously
execute their office.

V. It was not only necessary that such pastors should

be instituted at the beginning of the Church, but this institution ought to be perpetual, till the building of the
Church be fully finished.

VI. No one does lawfully exercise the pastoral office
but he who is called, and rightly ordained and sent by the
prelates of the Church.

VII. As many as are thus lawfully instituted to the
pastoral office by the pastors of the Church, there is no
doubt but that they are likewise chosen by the Holy
Ghost.

VIII. They moreover receive at their ordination from
the same Spirit the gift of grace, wherby they are rendred
fitter for the performance of their ministry with greater
sanctity.

IX. Notwithstanding, this grace of the Spirit God
will have to be granted at the exhibiting some sensible
sign; which sign being duly performed, we believe, that
grace is forthwith given.

X. They who are thus lawfully ordained pastors of the
churches and presbyters, are to be accounted, and undoubtedly are, truly the priests of God.

In proof of this last axiom, that Christian pastors are
true and proper priests, the Bishop says, that it is plain,
that what is written, Esai. lxi. 6, *Ye shall be named the
priests of the Lord: men shall call you the ministers of
our God: ye shall eat the riches of the Gentiles, and in
their glory shall ye boast yourselves*, was said to the
Apostles and their successors: that Esaias here foretells,
that hereafter the princes of the Church should be called
the priests of the Lord, &c. But this, the Bishop says, he
shall likewise demonstrate out of the New Testament.
Luther, says he, cannot deny but that Christ himself was
a priest after the order of Melchisedech: which, if he
was, it is necessary that he should sacrifice with the same
things with which, it's plain, Melchisedech heretofore
sacrificed. Now of the sacrifice of Melchisedech, it's
plain by Gen. xiv. 18, that he sacrificed with bread and

wine: wherfore Christ ought to sacrifice with the same, which he is never read to have done but at the supper. But, says the Bishop, Luther will perhaps deny, that Melchisedech's sacrifice did consist of bread and wine. But this is a thing too well evidenced to be denied; for, as soon as the Scripture has told us, that Melchisedech brought forth bread and wine, it immediately adds, *for he was the priest of the most high God.* To what purpose has the Scripture subjoined *that* as a cause of this saying, *He brought forth bread and wine,* if it had not a mind by all means to be understood, that Melchisedec used those things in his priesthode? But here Luther, the Bishop supposes, will exclaim, that this place is not faithfully translated from the Hebrew, which has it thus, *And he was the priest,* &c. But be it so, that it may be thus translated: this makes nothing against his sacrificing bread and wine, but rather for it, since forthwith, as soon as bread and wine are mentioned, it is subjoined, that he was a priest of the most high God. I would therfore, says the Bishop, have Luther to answer me: what other sacrifices did Melchisedec ever use? If he was a priest, and of some peculiar order, it is necessary he should also offer a peculiar sacrifice. Wherfore, since there is plain mention made of bread and wine, in which Christ also instituted the sacrament of his body, and its no where read in the Scriptures, that Melchisedec, offered any other sacrifice, who will be so impudent as to cavil, that he did not sacrifice with *them?* Certainly its requisite, since it's not once only asserted in the Scriptures, that Christ is a priest after the order of Melchisedec, that the sacrifice common to both should somewhere be described. Wherfore, since there is no where any notice taken of any other sacrifice than this that is common to both, it follows, that this of bread and wine was the sacrifice which both offered. His Lordship then quotes the testimonies of the Latin fathers, Jerome, Augustine, Cyprian, Ambrose, and Arnobius, and of Chrysostome, Damascene, and Vulga-

rius, of the Greek Church.   He next cites the rabbis,   CHAP.
Semuel, Pinhas, Johai, Kimhi, and Selemon, as affirming,   XVIII
that the sacrifice of the Messias should be bread and
wine, or a wheaten loaf.   In rehearsing all these, his
Lordship says, he has been so prolix, that there might
remain no scruple but, that as Melchisedec sacrificed with
bread and wine together, so it should also be believed,
that Christ, who was constituted a priest after *his* order,
did likewise use the same things for his sacrifice, i. e. did
sacrifice with bread and wine.

In the *third* and last congress, the Bishop proposes to   III.
make it plain, that Luther has nothing to produce from
either the Scriptures, or the testimonies of the orthodox
to confirm his heresy.

CHAP. XIX.

1. The Bishop publishes a Defence of the King's book.
2. Some account of the contents of it.

1. THIS same year, in an answer to the book of Luther's against the King, our Bishop wrote a [a] *Defence of His Majestie*, which he published the next year. This he dedicated to Dr. Nich. West, at that time Bishop of Ely, and told him, that his Lordship had read a good part of this book *two* years ago, and had so read it, as very earnestly to desire to see the rest of it, and therefore had sent frequent messages to him to request, that he might have it as soon as it came out of the press: that he had hitherto deferred to publish it, partly on account of other business in which he was engaged; partly, for that some had entertained hopes, that Luther would return to a better mind, there being a report, that he with some of his followers thought of recanting, and were willing to retract some part of the things which they had formerly ill taught. Wherfore, that they might have some time to breath, he thought fit either altogether to suppress this little book in case they repented, or to put off the printing it to another time, if they did not in the mean while desist from their errors. But that so far were they from doing so, that they went forward in their pristine madness, and were become more distracted than they were. For that now, having by mutual agreement among themselves, divided and distributed the volumes of the Holy Bible, they were not ashamed filthily to corrupt them with impious commentaries, and every where to wrest them to the sense of their perverse heresies. For, as has been intimated before,

---

[a] The title of this book runs thus: J. Fisheri Defensio Assertionis Hen. viii. Regis Angliæ de vii Sacramentis contra Captivitatem Babilonicam Lutheri. Seckendorf says it was written 1525. *Postea an.* 1525 *contra eundem, Lutherum, pro Rege suo calamum strinxit.*

at this time, Luther, with Melancton, and others, under- CHAP. XIX.
took the translation of the Scriptures into German. They
first published the Gospel of St. Matthew, then of St. Secken-dorf, Com. de Luther. § 125.
Mark, and the Epistle to the Romans, and in the same
manner the other books of the New Testament, that so
they being printed separately, and in a small volume, they
might be bought for less money. The whole came forth
first of all in September, 1522.

2. In his prologue to this work, our Bishop quotes
those words in the canticles, *Take us the foxes, the little
foxes that spoil the vines.* These he applys to Luther,
who, he says, if he had been taken when he was a cub, or
a little fox, there had not been then so great a tempest in
the Church, and such a confusion of every thing; but that
now he is grown a great, old, and crafty fox, and has
learned so many arts, such wile and cunning, there's no
taking of him. Having said this, the Bishop recollects
himself, as if these were too good words to give so bad a
man in his opinion. It is, says he, little to call him fox. I
should have called him a mad dog, nay, a most rapacious
wolf, or a cruel she-bear, which having her whelps taken
from her, is transported with fury, or rather all these
together: for that this monster Luther nourishes many
beasts within him. Sometime he acted the part of a fox
with frauds, lies, and subterfuges; then he became a mad
dog by his impudence, barking, and fierceness; afterwards
he shewed himself a wolf by his rapaciousness, wildness,
and tearing things in pieces: last of all, he shewed himself a lioness and she-bear, by his fury, outrageousness,
and cruelty. He is certainly a monstrous beast: he has
the eyes as it were of a man, and teeth of iron, such a
monster is Luther become of a little fox. The Bishop
next commends the King, in order yet further to expose
Luther, who, he says, instead of being thankful to His
Majesty, as a pious monitor, omitted no kind of slander or
reproach of him, and shewed no regard either to that
sacred erudition which he himself profest, or to the reve-

U

rence due to so great a prince.   The Bishop concluded
this prologue with setting down the order and manner of
his following dispute, which he digested, he said, into
XII. chapters, to answer the series which Luther had observed in his book.

1. That Luther's boasting arrogance is a lying one.

2. That his apology, wherby he labours to conceal some
notorious vices, is all in vain.

3. That the custom of the Church in communicating
the people with the bread only, ought to be observed.
Here, the Bishop says, he does not deny, that for some
time this sacrament was administred to all the faithful
under both species, and especially in the time of a raging
persecution, that so the faithful themselves, by the oft receiving of the blood of Christ, which he formerly shed,
and which they see before them under the species of wine,
might be the more animated to suffer martyrdome for
Christ's name sake.   But when persecution ceased, and
many [b] inconveniences did every day arise more and more,
with which the minds of the faithful began to be struck
with horror, insensibly, by a sort of tacit consent one species was taken away in all the churches, and so the people,
to avoid frequent perils, gave their assent that the sacrament should be exhibited to the laity under one species
only.   To justify this, he asserts, that [c] it is lawful for any
general council, for urgent causes, to make some alterations in the institutions of Christ, as it was for the first
governors of the Church, who changed the form of
baptism.

4. The substance of bread does not remain with the
holy body of Christ.

[b] The inconveniences mentioned by the Bishop are, dying persons being
troubled with vomiting, and infants, who do not always swallow what is put
into their mouths.

[c] Dicimus licere cuipiam generali concilio nonnihil e Christi institutis, ob
urgentes causas, immutare, quemadmodum et primis ipsis licuit Ecclesiæ
proceribus, qui baptismi formam immutârunt.

5. The mass is by no means a testament.

6. The mass is rightly stiled by the orthodox a sacrifice, and a work of merit.

7. Some tricks, and lies, and cavils of Luther's, are detected.

8. The mass is not a promise only.

9. Some things are answered which Luther objected to the King.

10. The interpretation of Scripture, which the fathers have unanimously given, ought to be believed.

11. It rather appertains to the fathers to judge of opinions, than to the common people.

12. Order and matrimony are sacraments, and do efficaciously confer grace.

The Bishop concluded this book with telling his readers, that he thinks there's nothing in Luther's foul-mouth'd book that is of any moment which has been omitted by him, or passed over without a satisfactory answer, except his slanders, which, since they exceed all measure and malice, he has let alone, most justly to recoil on the head of the author.

To these books of the Bishop's, Luther seems never to have made any reply. [d]Erasmus tells us as much, and intimates as if Luther's reason for it was, that if he vouchsafed *him* and his other opposers an answer, he should do them too great an honour, and cause *them* to be taken notice of, who would otherwise be condemned to utter

Purgatio
adv Epist.
Lutheri
ver. finem.

[d] Nec illud ingratum fuerit quod minitatur, se contemptum Erasmum cum cæteris quibus non est dignatus respondere——Cum quibus? Cum Eccio, cum Emsero, cum Joanne Gocleo, &c. qui forsitan, ut ait, inclaruissent si eos fuisset dignatus responso. Poterat addere cum Jodoco Clithoveo, cum Jacobo Latomo, cum Joanne Phiscero Episcopo Roffensi, &c. He seems here to refer to what Luther said, in his fore-mentioned book *of the Babylonish Captivity*, concerning a frier at Leipsic, who had wrote against him about administring the communion to the laity in both kinds. *Video itaque hominem hunc——et eos qui colludunt, hoc quærere, ut per me nomen aucupentur in mundo, quasi digni fuerint cum Luthero congredi, sed frustrabitur eos spes sua, et contempti non nominabuntur a me in perpetuum. Unâ hâc contentus ero responsione ad universos eorum libros.*

obscurity and perpetual oblivion. But this great man was now out of humour with Luther, and therfore thus rallied him on a point which he knew to be not exactly true. We have seen, that for want of leisure Luther answered only a part of the King's book, and yet, it's said, that, so far was he from being afraid of writing the King into reputation, that he valued himself upon it, that so great a prince had entred the lists with him. But however this be, Seckendorf speaks of the Bishop with a great deal of respect, and says, [e]he was beyond all question the most learned of all those who wrote against Luther. But what opinion our Bishop himself had afterwards of these

writings of his, appears by the following story. A gentleman, it's said, was commending to the Bishop the great pains he had taken in confuting Luther's books; to which the wise prelate heartily replied, that he *now wished he had spent all that time in prayer and meditation which he had thrown away upon such useless wranglings.* Such reflections we find made by even the wiser sort of the heathens. Thus Seneca observes to Lucilius: [f]*Our forefathers,* says he, *only taught their children what they should do, and what they should avoid, and then were there better men. But when men strove to be learned, they then did not take so much pains to become good; since that plain and open vertue which before was practised, was turn'd into obscure and cunning science, and men were taught to* [g]*dispute, and not to live.* Controversies, especially religious ones, it's certain, are apt to spoil a very good temper. Persons engaged in them flatter themselves, that they are doing

---

[e] —— inter quos doctissimus absque dubio habendus est Johannes ille Fischer, Roffensis in Anglia Episcopus, qui non solum Assertiones thesium Lutheri refutavit, sed et postea anno 1525 contra eundem pro Rege suo calamum strinxit.

[f] Antiqua Sapientia nihil aliud quam facienda et vitanda præcepit. Et tunc meliores erant viri. Postquam docti prodierunt, boni desunt. Simplex enim illa et aperta virtus in obscuram et solertem scientiam versa est: docemurque disputare, non vivere.

[g] Major devotio in laicis et vetulis, quam in clericis, &c. *Nicho. Gorrham.*

God service, and so they throw off all restraint, and suffer their ill nature, to which they give the name of zeal, to rage in its full fury. Of this every one of the persons now mentioned are unhappy instances. The King checks the intemperance of Luther's language with as great or greater of his own. Luther in return flies out into the last excesses of railing, and seems to have thought himself justified by his cause in neglecting all the rules of decency and civility, and using the coarsest and rudest terms. Even our Bishop, tho' so justly offended with Luther's behaviour, is himself so unhappy, as to make the same mistake, and instead of answering Luther's arguments, to make it his business to expose and abuse his person. Nay, he very zealously contended for the use of force and violence, of fire and sword, in matters of conscience, as if he never reflected, that making bonfires of men and women's bodies is a very improper means of enlightening their minds; or, that the ruining them in this world is not the way to convince them that we desire their salvation in the next. Thus has it been observed of Sir Thomas Moore, that his Latin answer to Luther is thro'out nothing but downright ribaldrie, without a grain of reasoning to support it, so that it gave the author no other reputation, but that of having the best knack of any man in Europe at calling *bad names* in *good Latin:* tho' his passion is sometimes so strong upon him, that he sacrifices even his beloved *purity* to it. His English writings on the same occasion deserve the same character. And yet was this fine gentleman naturally of so great mildness and candor, that his son-in-law, Rooper, tells us, that in above sixteen years which he lived with him in his family, he never once saw him in a fume or passion. A most sad proof of the tendency of disputes to debase the most raised humane mind!

Answer to Considerations on the Spirit of Martin Luther, p 41.

Life of Sir Thomas Moore, MS.

CHAP. XX.

1. *The Protestants are divided among themselves about the Sacrament.* 2. *Oecolampadius writes a book on this subject.* 3. *The Bishop answers it.* 4. *The Boors in Schwabenland rise: Luther's apprehensions concerning this rebellion.* 5. *The Bishop insults the Protestants on this occasion. An account of the Bishop's book against Oecolampadius.*

A.D. 1524. 1. ABOUT this time a very unhappy difference arose
Sleidan's among the Protestants themselves about the Eucharist,
Histo. of which was continued for above three years with a great
the Refor. deal too much passion and animosity. Luther understood
&c. Book those words of Christ, *This is my body,* literally, and pro-
v. perly, without admitting any figurative interpretation, and affirmed the body and blood of Christ to be *really* in or with the bread and wine, and to be verily and indeed received and eaten by believers. But Ulrich Zuinglius, minister of the church at Zurich in Swisserland, tho' in almost all other things he agreed with Luther, dissented from him in this; maintaining it was a *figure,* and expounding the words, *This is my body* to mean, *this* signifies *my*
Secken- *body.* Accordingly he affirmed, that in the sacrament the
dorf. bread was as pure bread as when it was in the market, without any real change into flesh. With him joined Leo Judæus and Oecolampadius, &c. But both they and Luther agreed in this, that the body and blood of Christ are received *spiritually,* not *bodily,* with the heart, not with the mouth.

2. The last of these, Oecolampadius, was upon this unhappy occasion drawn to write and publish a book in Latin, entituled, *Of the true meaning of the words of the Lord,* This is my body, *or an exposition of the words of the Lord,* &c. The unhappy dispute that had been raised about them, as it very much affected all those who had religion at heart,

so it put them upon using all proper methods to put an CHAP.
end to it. And therfore knowing Oecolampadius to be a XX.
man of great learning and temper, they never left him, till
at their request he wrote this book. But it being against
the corporal presence, it was not allowed to be printed at
Basil, and therfore he was forced to procure it to be done
at Argentine or Strasburg. For Oecolampadius in it
maintained, that in the words of Christ, *This is my body*,
&c. there was a *trope*, or that they are not to be understood strictly and literally, but [a]figuratively.

3. To this book of Oecolampadius, the Bishop, two A.D. 1527.
years after, published an answer, which he intituled, [b]*Of
the Truth of the Body and Blood of Christ in the Eucharist*, &c. This he dedicated to Richard Fox, then Bishop
of Winchester; to do which, he tells his Lordship, he was
induced on these two accounts: first, that his Lordship
had lately founded a college in Oxford, to which, out of
devotion to the sacrament, he had given the name of
Corpus Christi, and next, that he had been particularly
kind to him in encouraging and rewarding his studies.
These things, he said, moved him to offer this book to his
Lordship, which, unless his judgment deceived him, contained the most solid and inevertible demonstrations for
asserting the truth of the body and blood of Christ, which
Oecolampadius, tho' otherwise famous for learning, and
full of it even to surfeiting, had sharply and copiously opposed. This dedication is dated at Rochester, 1526.[c]

---

[a] Dissidium magis est de *modo præsentiæ* vel *absentiæ*, [Christi in Cæna]
quam de ipsa præsentia vel absentia. Nemo enim tam obtusus est qui as-
serat *omnibus modis* adesse vel abesse Christi Corpus. *Quid de Eucharistia
Veteres, &c senserint. Autore Joanne Oecolampadio*, 1530.

[b] De Veritate Corporis et Sanguinis Christi in Eucharistia, per reverendum in Christo patrem ac Dominum D. Johannem Roffensem Episcopum adversus Johannem Oecolampadium. Coloniæ, A.D. MD XXVII. Æditio prima

[c] Whether Oecolampadius made any reply to this answer of the Bishop's
I don't know. But by what he says of him in his book of the Eucharist,
published *three* years after, it seems to me as if he so far resented the   1530.
Bishop's manner of treating him, as to resolve to neglect him Thus Na-
thanael speaks in the dialogue. Rofenses, Clichtovæos, Fabros, *et multo
alios magis maledicos quam theologos, non est mirum si negligas.*

CHAP.
XX.
_____
Sleidan,
Hist. of the
Refor.
A.D. 1524.

4. A few years before, the boors of Schwabenland had began to rise against their lord, the Count of Lupsic, pretending to be overcharged by him in their rents: which was the beginning of an extraordinary and dangerous commotion, which in process of time embroiled a great part of Germany. With their civil grievances, as is usual, they mixed religious ones, and in the publick declaration which they made of their demands, appealed to Luther as to the justice of them. On this Luther wrote an answer to this declaration of their's, in which he advised all men to abstain from sedition, and very sharply reprimanded the appealers for pretending to follow the rule of God's word, and yet, in direct opposition to it, to take the sword and resist the magistrate whom God hath appointed. He likewise addressed a monitory to the princes and nobility, and another to the nobles and boors: but finding that all his endeavours to compose this tumult were fruitless, and to no purpose, and that the boors still continued to do a great deal of mischief, he published another book, wherin he exhorted and stirred up all men to hasten to the destruction of these villanous traytors, robbers, and parricides, as they would run to the quenching of a public fire: for which he was censured as too sharp and bloody-

Andrew
Bodenstein

minded. But Andrew Carolostadius, another leading man who favoured the Reformation, but of too warm and violent a temper, took, it seems, different measures. He, instead of pacifying them, stird up the people in a tumultuary manner to destroy the images of the saints set up in churches, and to cast them out. This Luther very much blamed, and argued, that removing the images out of the minds of the people was what ought first to have been done; and they taught, that by faith alone they please God, and that images in churches avail nothing, or no wise profit them: that if the minds of the people were thus rightly informed, images could do them no hurt; but if they were to be removed, it ought to be done by the authority of the magistrate, and not by the rabble, and a promiscuous multitude. This created a sort of coldness betwixt Luther and Carolostadius, insomuch that, in opposition to Luther, Carolostadius favoured the opinions of the new enthusiasts, and at length forsook his station at Wittenberg, or, as others say, was banished thence by the Elector, and went over to them. But after the suppression of this popular insurrection, when in all places many were dragged to execution, Carolostadius, being in great straits, wrote a book, wherin he took a great deal of pains to justifie himself against those who reckoned him among the fautors or encouragers of the rebellion, affirming it to be an injury done to him, and offering to come to a fair trial, and to submit to the judgment which should be passed upon him. However, this was no small ᵈaffliction to Luther, who was not insensible how much the common cause would suffer by it, and what advantage their enemies would make of it, by representing them, as had been done before in the case of Wiclif, as preaching an armed Gospel, and teaching doctrines very unserviceable to the crown, and sapping the foundations of civil government, and therby exposing them to the jealousie and hatred of all princes and magistrates.

5. In this Luther was not at all mistaken. Our Bishop, in particular, insulted them on it, and thus wrote in a preface, which he præfixed to the *first* of those *five* books, into which his answer to Oecolampadius is divided, in which he proposed, as he expressed himself, to establish the truth of the body and blood of Christ in the Eucharist from the dissentions of the heretics. " We could not," says his Lordship, " have wished for any thing for a " greater discomfiture of our adversaries than what has " now happened, and that no doubt by the deep provi- " dence of a most gracious God. But let not any one " think, that I say this on account of the immense slaugh-

---

ᵈ De Carolostadio doleo, cui et si facile resisti potest, tamen adversariis nostris gloriandi dabitur occasio de intestina nostra discordia, magno scandalo infirmorum. *Epist. ad Amsdorfium*

" ters of those who have embraced the most pestilent opi-
" nions of Luther, altho', in that matter, the most powerful
" God has given a specimen of his wrath, perspicuous
" enough to all, against that accursed sect, in which the
" blood of so many thousands has been spilt, not by the
" sword of any foreign enemy, but by intestine divisions,
" God taking vengeance on this so great a rebellion
" against the Church. For who is so blind as not to see
" the raging hand of an angry God in this so grievous a
" destruction, and to whom do the Germans owe this but
" to [e] Luther and his followers?" But besides this, the
Bishop observed another also, and a much more bitter
vengeance had overtaken the heads of this faction, in that
they were, to use the words of Paul, *delivered up to a reprobate mind, to do those things which are not convenient.*
For what, says he, is more absurd, yea, what is more accursed, than that they, who once vowed their chastity to
God, and stoutly kept their vow during the heat of their
youth, should now, when they are grown old men, indulge
obscene lusts, and not only do it themselves, but persuade
others to do it? Insomuch, that you now every where see
not only priests, who a little while ago seemed graver
than Cato himself, but even monks, married to nuns, and
that publickly without any shame. So that one may well
say of every one of them, *Thou hadst a whore's forehead,
thou refusedst to be ashamed.* This seems intended as a
personal reflection on Luther and Carolostadius, who both
of them married after they left the Roman Church, and
the former a nun; that as Maimbourg represents it, they
might destroy the cælibate of churchmen, not only by their
doctrine, but by their example. The Bishop adds, that
by these means they had not vessels fit for the reception
of D. wisdom: since, as is said in the Book of Wisdom,

---

[e] So Sir Thomas Moore calls the followers of Luther; a most ungracious
sect; bestys more hote and more busy than wolde the grete Turke, from
howre to howre embruynge their handes in bloode, &c. *Dialogues*, lib. iv.
fol. 106, ed. 1529.

She does not dwell in the body that is subject unto sin. CHAP.
Who therfore does not plainly see by these things the XX.
avengeful hand of God himself not only on those masters,
but also on their followers, who are so altogether blinded
by the just judgment of God, being so often admonished
of their pernicious errors? for they have a great many of
their own countrymen who apply themselves to this with
great earnestness. As, first of all, ᶠErasmus, who unan-
swerably has shewn, that every one ought to follow or
take the part of the Catholic Church. John Cocleus,
John Eckius, Jerome Emser, Gaspar Statzger, John
Dittenburg. Nor do they want the assistance of fo-
reigners, among whom the most illustrious K. Henry VIII.
of England merits the principal place. Thomas More,
Knight, *John Powel, William Melton, Chancellor of the
Church of York, and our Bishop's tutor in the University, *theologus non vulga-
ris.
who, the Bishop says, had written of some points of Luther's heresies, but his book was not yet printed, as were
not a great many of the others, and must therefore be
here remembred by the Bishop rather to honour the
writers of them, than to prove that they have been of any
use to the Lutherans to convince them of their errors. He
adds, that out of France the Lutherans have had, Judocus
Chlictoveus, and Stephen Longolus; and from Flanders
and Italy, James Latomus and Ambrose Catharinus.

ᶠ Vives names *him* and Longolus, with others, as having written against
Luther, in answer to the prejudice, which, it seems, was then taken up in
the Lutherans' favour, *viz.* that they were men of better learning than their
adversaries At docti sunt Græci ac Latini sermonis Lutherani, et Lutherus
ipse quos Pontifex Romanus et Academiarum consensus damnavit. Quid?
num non etiam Lutherus dialecticus, et sophista et Theologus Scholasticus,
et quidem magis quam Latinus? Nam Græcè nihil penitus noverat quum
ad scribendum accessit, Latinè parum admodum Lutherani sunt Pomera-
nus, et Lambertus· an non magis Latini Rex Angliæ, Roffensis, Ruseus,
Latomus, Chlictoveus: et in eadem Germania, Mosellanus, Joannes Faber,
Capito, Eccius? Contra Lutherum, Erasmus et Longolius scripserunt; an
non his Lutherani omnes in oratione concedunt? Tam abest ab omni hæresi
Budæus quam dulce ab amaro· vivitne quisquam hodiè utriusque linguæ
callentior? Quid huc adferam Alexandrum, Tonstallum, Morum, Sadole-
tum, Bembum, Lascarem, Brixium, tot philosophos, tot theologos lingua-
rum peritos. *De Disciplinis*, lib ii.

There is something yet, adds the Bishop, more clear, in which we very plainly perceive the vengeance of God upon them. For it's said in the Book of Genesis, of some who attempted to build a tower whose top should reach even unto heaven, that when they were one people and of one language, God so revenged their pride, and so confounded their language and speech, that they could not understand one another's meaning. The like vengeance has overtaken these factious followers of Luther; since *they* also had designed to erect a sort of new Church, in order to spread their fame thro'out the whole world, in which attempt it's wonderful how much they were united and confederated together, insomuch, that they seemed as it were all one man of one heart and of one mind. Nor did they ever cease from this work till God, looking from on high, had compassion on his Church, and restrained this madness of their's by confounding their language: for now he has caused, that they who were esteemed as peers and pillars among them, should not understand one another. For instance, the [g]Carolostadians have long since dissented from the Lutherans, as you may see by the [h]letters lately printed under Luther's name; nay, even Melancton does not well agree with Luther. And now another of their chiefs has started up, *viz.* John Oecolampadius, who violently dissents from Luther in a great many things, whom yet before he zealously followed. Lu-

[g] Odiosam—maxime fecerant doctrinæ Evangelicæ causam Carolostadij excessus. *Seckendorf*, Com. § 119.

[h] Ego Carolstadium offendi quod ordinationes suas cassavi, licet doctrinam non damnarim, nisi quod displicet quod in solis ceremonijs et externis faciebus laborasse eum, neglecta interim vera doctrina christiana, hoc est, fide et charitate. Nam sua inepta docendi ratione eo populum perduxerat, ut sese Christianum arbitraretur per has res nihili, si utraque specie communicaret, si tangeret, si non confiteretur, si imagines frangeret. En malitiam Satanæ ut per novam speciem molitus est erigere se ad ruinam Evangelij! *Lutheri litera apud Seckendorf*, Com. § 121.

Illa, controversia circa presentiam realem, hoc tempore nondum eruperat, neque Lutherus manifeste doctrinam Carolostadij, sed importunitatem taxavit. *Seckendorf*, ibid. § 122.

ther every where obstinately maintains, that the Sacrament
of the Eucharist is the New Testament. Oecolampadius
plainly teaches, that it is not a testament, but the sealing
of a testament. Luther boldly invites all, be they never
so wicked and scandalous, to receive the sacrament of the
body and blood of Christ. Oecolampadius thinks they
ought to be repelled who come not with a purpose of
amending their lives. Luther constantly teaches, that in
the Eucharist the very body of Christ is contained together with the substance of bread. Oecolampadius openly
denys, that the body of Christ is at all there present.
Who, says the Bishop, does not here plainly see the
avengeful hand of God, which by so great a dissent has
confounded their tongues? His Lordship therfore thus
insults the Lutherans. He applys to them the words of
St. Paul, Rom. i. 28, 29, 30, 31, 32, as if they deserved
the very same character as the Apostle gives to heathen
idolaters, who changed the glory of the incorruptible
God into an image made like to corruptible man. He
asks, where now is that which Luther so often boasts of,
that the Holy Scripture is of itself the surest, most easy,
and plainest interpreter of itself? how has Luther's boast
vanished, that he had all his opinions from heaven? whither now has the certainty of the people's judgment of opinions fled, which Luther, to make himself popular, has
attempted to establish? where is the faith, of the residence of which in *their* breasts, these pestilent heretics
so much glory? But this advantage, his Lordship observes, they have by their disputes with one another, that
they see, that the true faith, which thro' an uninterrupted
succession of the fathers from the first Apostles themselves is descended to us. is perpetuated in the Catholic
Church. The Bishop concludes this preface with an admonition to the reader of the tricks, arts, and deceits,
which, he says, 'Oecolampadius all along uses: such as
trusting in lies, mangling and calumniating of authors, de-

---

[1] Altingius tells us, that this Oecolampadius was tutor to Prince

nying their books to be written by them, wresting their sense and meaning, promising things which are not to be performed, boasting of victory, arrogating to himself the knowledge of tropes or figures, making obscure things more obscure, deceiving by æquivocation, and returning wrong answers. But these things, he says, he observes with no other intent than to admonish all Christians to be on their guard, and beware of the arts and deceits of this jugler. For that it's very plain to *him*, that out of mere malice, and a diabolical instinct, Oecolampadius endeavours by what cunning he can, to seduce all men from the truth of this most divine sacrament now believed for so many ages, to the utmost hazard of their souls.

In discussing the title of this book of Oecolampadius's, the Bishop observes, that this is his own exposition, and is so proper and peculiar to *him*, that it neither agrees with the orthodox from whom Luther has long since separated, nor with Luther himself; and, which is still more to be admired, differs from even Oecolampadius, as appears by a printed sermon of his: that his falling into this inconstancy is owing to his trusting too much to the strength of his own parts, and searching too curiously into so great a mystery: that a disposition more inclined to curiosity than is fit, and too great a confidence in his learning and ingenuity, had no doubt precipitated him into this profane darkness. In the book itself, his Lordship, among other things, censures Oecolampadius for impiously contending, that it is lawful for any one to search or pry into the sacraments of God, and profanely denying, that they are unsearchable: for promising to shew, that there's no miracle in the Eucharist: producing frivolous and empty conjectures against the miracles in it, and ascribing to Sathan the miracles done by God in its behalf: attempting to darken the miracle which Ambrose

Wolffgang, the Elector Palatine's brother, *a quo, cum alijs fratribus minoribus, bonis literis et pietate imbutus fuerat.* Apud Seckendorf, Com. Supple. ad § 13.

relates to have happened to his brother, [k]Satyrus, and
concluding, that because in the Scriptures there is no
mention of any miracle done in behalf of the Eucharist,
therfoie there is none: cavilling at the ceremonies which
are observed by devout people in honour of so great a
sacrament, and taxing the indulgences or pardons of the
popes as solemn pomps. Lastly, promising to himself
the attaining to the true sense of Sciipture by prayer,
which also the other heretics pretend to be sure of. On
the contrary, the Bishop observes, that no one is against
making enquiry about the sacraments, that it is lawful
so to do, provided it be done with faith, and a desire
of leaining: but in sermons to the ignorant people, to
make a doubt of, or call in question, what the whole
Church has hitheito approved, is wicked and accursed:
that Oecolampadius is condemned out of his own mouth
for denying these sacraments to be of the kind of incom-
prehensibles, since he owns he cannot comprehend the
presence of the body of Christ under this sacrament; and
what is this else but to confess the incomprehensibility of
it? Oecolampadius had observed, that the sacraments
are called mysteiies, not because they are hidden from
those who are of the houshold of faith, but from those
who are without. To this, the Bishop replys, what if the
sacraments themselves be otheiwise known to the faith's
domestics than to strangers, it does not therfore follow,
that the secret powers of the sacraments, and what the

---

[k] That which St. Ambrose informs us of his brother Satyrus was still more
bold, *who being shipwrecked at sea, and not yet having been baptized, lest he
should die without the mystery, he beg'd of those that were baptized to let him
have that Divine Sacrament of the faithful,* the custom then being to have it
reserved about them, *which they granting, he bound it in his * neckcloth, which* * *orarium, a*
he rolled about his neck, and so threw himself into the sea. Whatsoever con- strip of li-
ceits Satyrus might have when he borrowed it, yet those that let him have it nen worn
could never think fit, if they believed it the very flesh of Christ, to deliver it about the
into the hands of one not yet a perfect Christian, nor to be wrap'd about his neck; the
neck, to serve instead of a cork or bladder, to keep him from drowning. *A* Latins call
full View of the Doctrines, &c. of the ancient Church relating to the Eucha- it a *stole.*
rist, p. 158, 159

Spirit effects by them, are otherwise known to the initiated than by faith. But Oecolampadius says, adds the Bishop, that he shall shew by a very clear testimony of St. Augustine, that there is not any thing in this sacrament that is either a miracle, or that exceeds humane capacity: to which, his Lordship replys, that he promises mountains of gold, but that he knows he cannot perform any thing of what he says: since he is not able to shew, that Augustine never said, that the Spirit of God does not divinely operate on the bread that it may be made so great a sacrament; and it is most certain, that whatsoever the Spirit of God invisibly operates in this sacrament, is above all human capacity. Oecolampadius, to prove this assertion of his concerning Augustin, observes, that in his books of the Trinity, he mentions *nine* kinds of signs and miracles, the last of which he thus expresses.

But the Bishop answers, that the father is here to be understood as speaking of the shew-bread, and not of the bread of the Eucharist, which he agen and agen says is consecrated by a mystical prayer, and sanctified by the invisible operation of the Spirit of God, that it may become the great sacrament. But, adds Oecolampadius, that Sathan might feign an hidden miracle where there is none, how many May-games has he contrived? As in some places the bread is seen turned into flesh; elsewhere it has the shape of a finger; in another place the figure of a little boy is seen in it: sometimes it's reported to have bled, and that blood is kept in some places, and made to serve to a new idolatry by its having festivals appointed upon that account. To this, the Bishop answers, that he can never be brought to believe, that these miracles were done by devils: but if they were done by good angels, as no doubt they were, Oecolampadius should consider with

himself whether it's becoming them, who, as Paul says, are
deputed to minister to the faithful, to lead so many devout
persons into so great an error, if yet it be one, as to Oecolampadius the belief of Christ's corporal presence in the
sacrament seems to be. As to particulars, Oecolampadius
mentions, among others, the miracle aforementioned of
Satyrus's being saved in a shipwreck, and of a priest, who
carrying the Eucharist thro' a fire, escaped unhurt. To
which, the Bishop replys, that he is obliged to him for
producing so many miracles which do so plainly militate
for the faith: that what so great a man as Ambrose has
so faithfully related is not to be despised; and that no one
can doubt but that Satyrus believed, that Christ was truly
contained in the Eucharist. Oecolampadius thus sums
up this head, that the Scripture has no more *distin- *insignivit.
guished this sacrament by miracles, than it has [1]baptism;
that the body of Christ may be corporally latent in the
bread; to which the Bishop answers, that Christ has
established his whole doctrine by innumerable miracles,
but not so that he has wrought some miracles for every
particular doctrine: and that Christ has sufficiently made
it known, that his body lies hid in the Eucharist under the
species of bread, by calling it *life*, the bread of life, &c.
Oecolampadius next desires to be taught where that immoderate apparatus of ceremonies is prescribed, the ado-
ration and gazing? since every where it is intimated, that
religion is pure and simple. If we are obliged by a divine
law to keep that holy bread with so great devotion as it is
now kept, and to adore and celebrate it as we now do,
what excused the Apostles from it? Why did not Paul
beg of the Macedonians and Corinthians, that he might
have wherwith to adorn the reserved bread, and that Christ
being present, may be adored? He adds, that he does not
say this, as if he thought sacred things should be treated

---

[1] Quemadmodum Veteres Eucharistiam valdè extollunt, ita et aliquando
Baptismum, asserentes illum esse *omnium Dei donorum excellentissimum et
præclarissimum.* Albertinus de Eucharistia, lib 1. c. 29.

indecently, but to shew from the Apostles' times what the
worship was which they gave to Christ when his blood
newly shed distained those breasts which were all in a
flame with the love of him.   To this, the Bishop replys,
that there is no need, that in the Scriptures those things
which he mentions should be explained : that they who
truly believe, that Christ is really contained in this sacrament, don't at all doubt but that his presence requires
many more ceremonies, parades, and adorations, and that
those which are now used are much beneath so great a
dignity : that he does not at all doubt but that the Apostles worshipped and adored Christ in this sacrament, tho'
they had but little regard to pomp and ceremonie, which
seems designed by the Holy Spirit for those who are
weaker, that by such ceremonies, and so great solemnity,
they might have their devotion towards this sacrament
more raised and enflamed : that Paul himself will answer
his enquiry concerning *him*, who says, God did not send
him to baptize, but to preach the Gospel.   Lastly, that if
he would not have sacred things indecently treated, why
does he with so much eagerness and delight cavil at the
honour which the people bestow on this sacrament in
pomp and ceremonies?   Oecolampadius proceeds, if the
Eucharist be so holy and devout, what need is there of
the Pope's bulls for it? but this is an argument that the
more learned and wiser bishops did in the beginning refuse this pomp: it's plain, adds he, with how great pride,
immoderate luxury, and great solemnity, the feast of Corpus Christi is kept; that the superstitions in purifying the
houses and fields are enlarged beyond all measure; that
women, in the dress of harlots, priests, like lovers, made
spruce and fine with royal pomp, souldiers, dreadful in
armour, and whatever else was formerly had in contempt
by the Apostles, now the glory of the cross is made void,
are set forth as the chief of all; so that there is now to be
seen gold, silver, jewels, tables, images, sights, cymbals,
cushions of tapestry, purple, flours, guns, drinkings, and

so little of sobriety, that there is the less, nay, almost nothing of true religion.   To this, the Bishop says, that to
repent and begin a new life in Christ is a holy and pious
thing, and yet it's so remote from the hearts of many,
that unless they were invited therto by the pope's bulls, a
great many would never, or very late, at all think of this
business: that he has before shewn, that the bishops, the
most learned as well as the best, have asserted, that Christ
is contained in the Eucharist; and who is so profane as
not willingly to adore Christ with all his heart whersoever
he is? that there was nothing ever so good and holy as on
no occasion to be abused; but that whoso considers the
coldness and dulness of the common people, will not think
it unmeet, that they be drawn to the faith of this sacrament by honourable pomps of ceremonies, and solemnities
of this nature.   Oecolampadius farther insisted on Christ's
frequent speaking in parables, and doing all his life long
things, which designed something hid under them; for
this end, he said, Christ cursed the barren fig-tree, turned
water into wine, washed his disciples' feet, &c. to recommend more sublime mysteries, since he had other ways to
signifie his power and humility.   To which, the Bishop
answers, that no one can deny, that Christ spoke in parables, but that it's as plain that he did not always speak so.
Now, say his disciples to him, *speakest thou plainly, and* John, xvi.
speakest no parable.   Certainly, Christ spake plainly, and
without a parable, when he said, *This is my body*. Agen,
Oecolampadius had observed, that the meaning of Christ's
words was not so hidden and abstruse, but that without
much difficulty we might attain to the knowledge of it
with the help of devout prayer, and a faithful comparing
of the Scriptures, which are both to be joined together:
to which, the Bishop answers, that he will never be able
to enter into their meaning, unless he first lay aside the
swelling arrogance of his mind, since he is above measure
puff'd up with the sense of his own abilities, and attributes
much more to his own wit, than to the unanimous judg-

ment of the most holy and learned fathers which have
gone before us.

These are some of the particulars of the Bishop's *first*
book, and may serve as a specimen of Oecolampadius's
way of arguing, and of the Bishop's answer to it. However, the Bishop acknowledges him to be a great and
learned man : but he treats him very roughly, and especially in the conclusion of this book. He not only calls
him heretic, and a most trifling caviller, &c. but tells him
that he [m]plainly sees he is distracted, as if it was any wise
worth his Lordship's while to take so much pains to answer a madman, or that he could expect to get any credit
by it. He represents him as one whom Satan had filled
with the greatest malice, and who was agitated by some
malignant spirit; and therfore he asks him, [n]why *he* besought them by Christ? since *he* had nothing to do with
Christ, who endeavoured to infect his spouse with so great
a plague; who had no place in the Catholic Church, but
was very far separated from Christ, and at a vast distance
from the body of his spouse; being a wolf under the
covering of piety, every where devouring the sheep of
Christ.

In the proeme of his *third* book, the Bishop produces
fourteen of what he calls *corroborations;* by which, he
says, every Christian may undoubtedly solidly establish his
mind in the faith of this sacrament. The truth of Christ's
body in the Eucharist, the Bishop says, is proved : 1. By
Christ's express words; 2. By the immensity of the love of
Christ; 3. By the consent of the fathers; 4. By the promises of Christ; 5. It is established by a great many
councils; 6. It is demonstrated by numberless miracles;

[m] Planè video te mente captum esse.

[n] Quid tu nos per Christum oras? Nihil enim tibi cum Christo, qui tanta
peste sponsam ejus corrumpere studes. Nihil tibi cum Christo, qui nullum
in Ecclesia Catholica locum obtines, longissime divisus es a Christo, qui a
corpore sponsæ suæ tanto disjungeris intervallo, lupus es qui sub tegumento
pietatis, oves Christi passim devoras. *Lib.* i. c. 2.

7. It is defended by revelations very worthy of credit; CHAP. XX.
8. The patronage of Christ has never been wanting to defend it against heresies; 9. The devout frequenters of this sacrament have profited in all virtue; 10. It has succeeded unhappily to those who have thought ill of it; 11. The enemies of this sacrament have no plain Scriptures for them, 12. They do not bring the solid testimony of any one orthodox person; 13. They cannot produce any miracles or revelations in their behalf; 14. The dissenters from the common faith of the Church do mutually confute one another.

Under the head of *miracles* his Lordship mentions *eight*. His *first* story is taken from Eusebius, who reports Hist. lib. vi. c. 36 how a presbyter, who was sick, and could not go himself, sent by a little boy to Serapion, who lay a dying, *a little bit of the Eucharist*. But this, it's intimated, is very in- — βραχυ της ευχα- ριστιας. consistent with the doctrine of transubstantiation: since the Roman Church confesses the natural body of Christ to be impassible; wheras the Eucharist is here represented as divided and parted, or broken into little bits. His Lordship's next story is taken from St. Cyprian, of a little de lapsis Christian girl, that by her nurse's wickedness had received polluted bread in an idol's temple, and afterwards, according to the usage of the Church at that time, was brought by her mother, who knew nothing of what the nurse had done, into the Church to receive the holy communion. He relates how the child, when its turn came to receive the cup, turn'd away its face, shut its lips, and refused to drink the wine. But the deacon persisted; and tho' the girl strove against it, did pour into her mouth some of the sacrament of the cup, &c. How must a Romanist, full of the conceit of transubstantiation, or the corporal presence, start at the thoughts of pouring the wine as this deacon did into the mouth of this strugling child? One need but read the *twelfth* rubric before the Roman missal, wherby de defecti- bus in ipso so wise a provision is made in case any part of the blood, ministerio as the wine is called, be spilt, to be throly sensible of the occurrenti- bus.

fright and consternation he must be in at the seeing some
of the blood spilt, as it must have been, in this odd
struggle.

Under the head of *revelations*, the Bishop reports the
same number, *viz. eight*, for which he quotes ° Hildegardis,
Elisabeth, Brigitt, and Mechtildis, all holy virgins, the
Bishop says, tho' one of them, Brigitt, had seven children,
who themselves have written an account of their visions
and revelations, though this does not appear to be true of
any of them but Mechtildis. To which the Bishop adds
two stories out of a spurious book fathered on St. Chrysostome, and called his *Dialogues*, least, says his Lordship,
any one should cavil that I have produced only the testimonies of women.

Cave's
Histo.Lite-
raria,vol.i.
Hildegardis, the first of these, was born at Spanheim,
in Germany, A. D. 1098. At eight years old she took
upon her the habit of a nun, and became at length Abbess
of the monastery of S. Rupert, on the hill at Binge, near
the Rhine. She *flourished*, A. D. 1170, or rather one
would think *died*, being then seventy-two years old. She
began to be famous for heavenly visions and prophecies
when she was forty years old: with the report of which
Pope Eugene III. and the principal bishops and abbots of
France and Germany, and among them St. Benard, having their curiosity raised, they, in the year 1148, ordered
those prophetic visions to undergo a stricter scrutiny, and
having discovered those which were counterfeit, confirm'd
the real ones in the council of Treves. This sentence was
confirmed by the Popes Anastasius IV. and Hadrian IV.
who in their letters to Hildegardis recommended themselves and the Roman Church to her prayers. She died
Sept. 17, A. D. 1180, being eighty-two years old, and her
visions or revelations were printed in *three* books at Paris,
1513.

° *See* **Liber trium virorum et trium spiritualium Virginum, Parisiis 1513.**
Iis qui huic devoto pioque operi emittendo quomodocunque invigilarunt:
prosint apud deum piæ preces legentium.

Elizabeth was likewise a German, and Abbess of Scon-haug, in the diocese of Treves. She was famous for visions and revelations about the year 1154, and died June 18, 1165, when she was but thirty-six years old. Her visions were also printed at Paris in *three* books, A. D. 1513.

Brigitt was a Swede of the blood royal, who, as it's said, was not unacquainted with D. visions in the very cradle. Being married to Wulfo, Prince of Nericia, and having had seven children by him, she began to desire the monastic life, and accordingly persuaded her husband to go into a monastery, where he soon after ended his days. Brigitt being thus a widow instituted a new monkish order, which she named the order of St. Saviour, and about 1363 grew very famous for frequent visions. She died July 23, 1373, and Pope Boniface IX. canonized her for a saint. Her revelations, in eight books, were printed at Lubec, 1492, and at Norimberg, 1521.

Mechtildis was a German of a noble family, and became a Benedictine nun. She flourished, A. D. 1280, and died before 1290, having written in her mother tongue what she called a *Revelation,* or *five books of spiritual grace*, which were afterwards translated into Latin, and printed at Paris, 1513, together with other little tracts of the same stamp, and separately at Colon, 1536, and elsewhere more than once.

Of these visions, or *revelations*, I'll only transcribe the following one, as a sample of the rest. The Bishop quotes for it a book of the most holy virgin or nun, Elizabeth, entituled, *Of the ways of God.* " It happened once upon " a time, that there came a certain frier bearing in the " pyx the divine sacrament of God's body to a certain " sick nun; and whilst we stood round about it, and I and " some of the nuns were talking together concerning it, " lo, of a sudden my heart was melted, and almost in an " extasy. And behold a great brightness shone in the " pyx, and I look'd into it, when yet it was shut, and there

" appeared really the species of flesh in it. I tremble in-
" deed whilst I speak these things, as I also then trembled
" when I saw them: but God is my witness, that in all
" these things I have spoken nothing by way of fiction, or
" seeking mine own glory." And who now can help being
convinced by such idle tales, that the body of Christ is
verily and indeed in the Eucharist? But if the reader be
not satisfied with this sample, I refer him to the Bishop's
book, and to another written by father Toustain Bridoul,
of the Society of Jesus, entituled, *The School of the Eucharist, established upon the miraculous respects and ac-
knowledgments, which beasts, birds, and insects, upon
several occasions have rendred to the Holy Sacrament of
the Altar*, printed in French at Lille, 1672, and translated
into English, 1687. With the reader's leave, I'll transcribe
one of the stories here told, least he should not have the
book, and that he may judge of the rest, which are all of
the same marvailous nature.

" A certain woman, not being able to believe that God
" was in the sacrament, was tempted by the devil to take
" some proof from thence to satisfie her fancie. And altho'
" her confessor, and also Albert, Bishop of Perusia, had
" exhorted her to yield to the publick belief, approved by
" so many knowing and vertuous persons, without desiring
" to be instructed and confirmed herein by a miracle, not-
" withstanding after all, she was led away by her fancy to
" make the trial. She went therfore one day to the com-
" munion, and having taken the host out of her mouth,
" she went and threw it into the hogs' trough: upon the
" noise she made, the hogs all ran greedily to their trough,
" but instead of opening their mouths to swallow the host,
" they all kneeled down to adore it. The unhappy woman
" stopt not here, but put the host upon the spit to roast it
" at the fire; but as she turned the spit, she saw drops of
" blood that distilled from the host. Still she continued
" obstinate in her false opinion, and being afraid to be
" apprehended and put to death, if what she had done

" should be discovered, she digged a hole in the ground,
" and there buried the host, that it might be spoken of no
" more. But perceiving that the blood bubbled out of the
" earth, and ran in abundance like a stream, the hardness
" of her heart was softened, so that her understanding
" being inlightened in this truth, and repenting of her un-
" belief, she went to find out the aforesaid Bishop of
" Perouse, who having heard her confession, imposed a
" penance on her to perform during her whole life." But
one need not much to admire, that the common people,
who are strangely affected with any thing that is marvailous and wonderful, should be imposed upon by such ridiculous stories as these, when one of the Bishop's great
learning and good sense could be carried to so extravagant a degree of credulity, as seriously to quote and transcribe them, as a proof of the verity of Christ's body in the
sacrament of the Eucharist.

To this answer of the Bishop's, Oecolampadius made
no reply. He thought, that his [p] Lordship used him in a
manner unbecoming a divine and man of learning, and,
that such ought to be neglected who treated their adversaries with ill language. He therfore contented himself
with publishing, three years after, a learned account of
the opinions of the ancients, both Greeks and Latins, concerning the Eucharist, in order to demonstrate, that the
opinion *he* maintained, and for which he was so ill used by
the Bishop and others, was not a *new doctrine*, nor peculiar to *him :* and, that they who thus represented it, did
either not know what his opinion was, or were otherwise
unlearned. This tract was published 1530, but without
the name of either the place or printer.

---

[p] Rofenses, Clichtouæos, Fabros, et multos alios magis maledicos quam
theologos non est mirum si neglîgas. Maledicentiam etiam ipse abominor,
adeo ut virulenta ista sæpius a lectione ipsorum me absterruerint, utut alios
convitia inescent. Quo nomine et Lutherus a suis libris me nonnihil alien-
avit. *Quid de Eucharistia Veteres tum Græci tum Latini senserint Dialogus,*
&c. Autore Joanne Oecolampadio, 1530

I've only to add, that by the Bishop's register it appears, that one Paull Lomley, who is stiled a weddid man of Gravesend, now abjured his saying, that *these prestis makith us to beleve, that the synginge brede they holde ouer their hedes is god, and it is but a cake*. Cardinal Wolsey also issued a commission to admonish those who had Luther's books containing the translation of the New Testament into the vulgar tongue, to deliver them to the bishop of the diocese, on pain of being proceeded against as heretics. This commission was given under the cardinal's seal at his mannor of Moore, Septem. 30, 1526.

CHAP. XXI.

1—7. The Bishop one of the examiners of Bilney and Arthur. 8. Concerned in the prosecution of Thomas Hitton.

1. TOWARDS the latter end of the next year, we find the Bishop, together with the Archbishop of Canterbury, Tonstall, Bishop of London, West, Bishop of Ely, Voysey, Bishop of Exeter, Longland, Bishop of Lincoln, Clerk, Bishop of Bath and Wells, and Standish, Bishop of St. Asaph, &c. accompanying the Cardinal in the chapter-house of Westminster, in order to the examination and trial of Thomas Bilney and Thomas Arthur, who were accused of heresy. Bilney was of Trinity-Hall, in Cambridge, where he took the degree of Bachellour of Laws. Sir Thomas More tells us he had learning, and had been accustomed in moral vertues. By reading the Scriptures, he came to have some scruples about the public worship, as it was then celebrated : particularly praying to saints, and using them as mediators and intercessors with God : the vain and expensive decking and adorning of images then in fashion, and the offering to them candles, wax, and money, and going on pilgrimages. These things he had preached against at Ipswich and Willesden, in the diocese of Norwich, and, as was afterwards deposed, was no less than three times pulled out of the pulpit by the priests that heard him, for his thus instructing and admonishing the people. At length he was complained of to the Cardinal, who was Lord Chancellor, and who accordingly issued out his warrant for apprehending Bilney, and his companion, Arthur, who were both, as has been said already, brought before his Lordship. But the Cardinal being otherwise occupied about the affairs of the realme, committed the hearing of the matter to the Bishops of London, Rochester, Ely, &c. These *three* therfore met at the Bishop of Norwich's house, where having

Novem. 27.
A. D. 1527.
Fox's Acts,
&c. p 258,
&c.

sworn witnesses against Arthur, as they had done the day before against Bilney, they proceeded to the examination of Arthur upon certain interrogatories. On December 2, the bishops met again in the same place, and sware more witnesses against Bilney, and then called for Arthur, and exhibited against him *eight* articles, *three* of which he denied: the other *five*, which were his preaching "against " licenses to preach, as being against God's laws; the " multitude of crosses and ecclesiastical laws; that the " preaching of the Gospel ought not to be omitted for " fear of persecution; that every Christian man is a priest " offering up the sacrifice of prayer; and that a Bachellor " of Divinity admitted of the University, or any other " person having or knowing the Gospel of God, should " go forth and preach in every place, and let for no man, " of what estate or degree soever he was, and if any " bishop did accurse them for so doing, his curses should " turne to the harme of himself," he confessed, and afterwards revoked and condemned, and submitted himself to the judgment and punishment of the Church. This Arthur had, it seems, the lord Cardinal's and the Universitie's license to preach, and was an intimate friend and inseparable companion of Bilney's.

2. The *third* day of December, the aforesaid bishops met again in the same place, when, upon Bilney's refusal to submit himself, the Bishop of London exhibited several letters which Bilney had written to him. He and Arthur had been before examined by them on thirty-four interrogatories. By Bilney's answers to them, it appears, that he believed that the assertions of Luther which had been impugned by the Bishop of Rochester were justly and lawfully condemned, and that Luther was a wicked and a detestable heretic; and that the Catholic Church cannot err in faith. But then by the Catholic Church, he said he did not mean the Pope and his cardinals, but *the whole congregation of the elect known only unto God.* So he said, he believed, that many of the Pope's laws were pro-

fitable and necessarie, did prevaile unto godliness, and were not in any point repugnant unto the Scriptures, but St. Augustine, he said, much complained of the multitude of them, and Gerson marvailed, that he could by any meanes live in safety amongst so many snares of constitutions. He likewise owned, that the images of saints were christianly set in churches: but then he said, tho' they were the books of the laity, we ought not to adore the image, but the prototype. To the *sixth* interrogatorie, he answered, that he did not believe that the souls of Peter and Paul, and of our lady, were in heaven. To the *fourteenth, fifteenth,* and *sixteenth,* he answered, that the 14th chap. of St. Paul's first Epistle to the Corinthians moved him to believe, that it is best for the people to have the Lord's prayer and the Apostle's creed in English; that he could wish, that the Gospels and Epistles should be read in English, however, that those of the day should be so read, that the people might be the more apt to hear sermons. As touching the Pope's pardons or indulgences, he said, that as they were used, and had too long been, it were better that they should be restrained. Two days Decem 4. after, the Bishop of London, with the other bishops, his assistants, met in the chapter-house of Westminster, whither Bilney was brought before them, and admonished three times to abjure and recant, which, on the third admonition, he did with great reluctancy, and having openly read his abjuration, and subscribed it, and delivered it to the Bishop, he was absolved, and for his penance enjoined to continue in the prison appointed by the Cardinal, till by him he should be released, and the next day to go before the procession in the Cathedral Church of St. Paul bareheaded, with a faggot on his shoulder, and to stand so before the preacher at Paul's Crosse all the sermon time.

3. Sir Thomas More tells us, that this is the man, of whom, without naming him, he spake so much in his *dya-* English *logue,* who being convict by twenty witnesses and above, Works, p. dyd yet stick still in his denial, and said, they were all for- 346.

CHAP.
XXI.
_____

Dyaloge,
fol. 6. a. col.
1.

fol. 73, a.
col. 2.

sworne, and had utterly belyed him. It seems Bilney had so good a character for his excellent learning and great piety, that this prosecution of him gave very great offence. It was reported, Sir Thomas said, that the spiritualtie did him wrong, and, that their displeasure against him was occasioned by his preaching against their viciouse living. The articles, wherwith he was charged, Sir Thomas said, were, that we should do no worship to any images, nor pray to any saintes, or go on pilgrimages, which things, he supposed, every good Christian man would agree for heresies. Of these, he added, Bilney was convicted, not by the words of one or two, but by the oaths of one or two above twenty, honest men, and almost of all sorts, of religious folke, husband-men and gentil-men. But it was said, that Bilney offered to bring twice as many, and that of such as were present as well as they, and stood as near him as they, and understood as well as they, and slepte no more at his preaching than a person doth at his offering, who would depose plainly *for* him; but their evidence would not be admitted. Sir Thomas said, Bilney was himself well learned in the law, and never could say, that he was denied any favour that the law would grant: and that many a witnesse was there, to whom he laid no exception, nor could say the contrary, but that they were at his sermons and heard them. Among other things, it was articled against Bilney, that he preached so and so in certain churches at London. Now to invalidate this evidence, there were, it seems, two beneficed men of great character for their learning, who affirmed, and offered to depose, that they heard the sermons he preached in those churches, and that he preached not the things which he was accused of. But Sir Thomas said, that then was his detection and the proof made thereupon of those heresies preached at several places out of London. To shew yet further, that Bilney was not hard used by the bishops, Sir Thomas says, he had also before this been accused to the greatest prelate in this realme, who for his tender favour borne to the Universitie, did not proceed far in the matter against him. But accepting his denial with a corporal oath, that he should from that time forth be no setter forth of heresies, but in his preachings and readings should impugne them, dismissed him very benignely, and of his liberal bountie gave him also money for his coste. And yet was none of all these matters laid unto his charge, which, if they had been, would peradventure have put him to peril. Sir Thomas added, that several days were his judges fain of their favour to give him, with sufferance of some of his best friends, and whom he most trusted to resorte unto him: and yet scarcely could all this make him submit himself to make his abjuration. And, finallie, were they faine for saving his life, to devise a forme of abjuration, wherof he, Sir Thomas, never saw the like, nor in so plain a case never would, was he the judge, suffer the like therafter. That was, that wheras they were wont to confesse in their own abjuration, that they had holden such heresies, and were guiltie therof, *that* would he do in no wise, tho' he was to die therfore, but alway stood still upon his oath, that all they that swore against him belyed him: *his* abjuration therfore was, that he therin only abjured and forsware all heresies, and acknowledged himself lawfully convict.

4. However this be, Bilney soon relented what he had done. What time he had borne his faggot, and was come again to Cambridge, he had such conflict within himself, was in such an anguish and agony, beholding this image of death, that his friends were afraid to let him be alone; nothing did him any good, neither eating nor drinking, nor any other communication of God's word. As for the comfortable places of Scripture, to bring them unto him, it was as though a man should run him through the heart with a sword; for he thought all the whole Scriptures were against him, and sounded to his condemnation, so that all things whatsoever any man could allege to his comfort, seemed to him to make against him. Yet for all

Bp. Latimer's Sermons. fol. 80, a. ed. 1596

CHAP.
XXI.
this, Bishop Latimer tells us, he was afterward revived, and came again to himself, and was indued with such strength and perfectness of faith, that he not only confessed his faith in the Gospel of our Saviour Jesus Christ, but also suffered his body to be burned for that same Gospel's sake, which is now preached in England, and took his death patiently, and died well against the tyrannical See of Rome. Fox tells us, that in the year 1531,

Acts, &c.
vol. ii. p.
272, col 1.
A D. 1531.
being resolved, and fully determined, to give over his life for the confession of that truth which before he had renounced, (tho' Sir Thomas More, as has been shewn, said, he only renounced all heresie, and would not own that he held any,) he took his leave of some of his friends in Trinity-Hall, at ten of the clocke at night, telling them he would go to Hierusalem, and went into Norfolke, where he first preached privately to some select families, and afterwards openly in the fields, confessing his fault in abjuring, and willing all to take warning by him, and never to trust to their fleshly friends in causes of religion. From thence he went to Norwich, to an anchoress whom he had converted, and to whom he now gave a New Testament, of Tyndal's translation, and his *Obedience of a Christian Man;* whereupon he was apprehended and carried to prison. Soon after he was examined, and condemned, as a relapse, before Dr. Pelles, LL. D. and Chancellor, and being degraded by the Bishop suffragan, Underwood, he was immediately delivered over to the secular arm. Thomas [a] Necton, one of the sheriffs of the city, was Bilney's special good friend, who therfore kept him in the Guildhall, and caused him to be more friendly looked unto, and to be more wholesomly kept as to his diet, than he was before in the Bishop's prison.

English
Works, p.
346.
5. Sir Thomas More tells us, that when Bilney came to examination, he waxed stiffe and stubborne in his opinions:

---

[a] Sir Thomas More mentions one Richard Necton, who was by Constantine's detection taken and committed to Newgate, as a relapse, where, he said, he stood in great peril to be burnt ere it was long

but yet God was so good and gracious lorde unto him,
that he was finallie so fullie converted unto Christe and his
true catholic faithe, that not only at the fire, as well in
wordes as in wiiting, but also many days before, he had
ievoked, abhorred, and detested such heresies as he had
before holden: that forthwith upon his judgment and de-
gradation, he kneeled down before the Bishop's Chancellor, in the piesence of all the people, and humbly besought
him of absolution fiom the sentence of excommunication,
and with his judgment held himself well content, and acknowledged, that he had well deserved to suffer the death
he then wist he should die; that upon this his humble ie-
quest and prayer, he was there in presence of all the
people absolved, before that he was carried out of the
court: that he laboured, and made great instance certain
days after his judgment, that he might be suffered to receive the B. body of Christ in forme of bread; wherin
the Chancelloi, making a while great sticking and diffi-
cultie, to the intent that he would the better and more
clearly perceive what devotion the man had therto, and
finally seeing him to be of a true perfect faith, and his
desire to pioceed of a fervent mind, it was agreed and
granted; and that thereupon was he howselled in so true
and perfect a faith, and so great devotion, that every good
Christian had great cause to rejoice therin: that when
his confessor in the end of the masse, which Bylney heard
full devoutly upon his knees, brought unto him the body
of Christ upon the patin of the chalice, with very good
and godly exhortation used unto him, that, except he
were in heart as he was in word and outward semblance,
he should else forbear to receive that blessed bodie, sith
he should then undoubtedlie receive it on his own condemnation, it would have gladded any good Christian
heart to have heard his faithful Christian answere, as they
reported and testified that were at that time by. Lastly,
that moreover, wheias in the presence of that holy sacrament holden yet upon the patin in the priest's hands,

Bilney, before he received it, said the collect *Domine Jesu Christe*, and when he came at these words, *Ecclesie Tue pacem et concordiam*, he divers times repeated these words with tunsions and knockings upon his breast, and thereunto God confessed and asked his mercy, that he had so grievously erred in that point, and so sore offended him in contemning his Church.

Fox, Acts,
&c. vol. ii.
p. 277.

6. The Friday following after his condemnation, &c. Bilney had several of his friends with him, some of whom put him in mind, that though the fire, which he should suffer the next day, should be of great heat to his body, yet the comfort of God's Spirit should coole it to his everlasting refreshing. Upon which Bilney, putting his hand toward the flame of the candle, and feeling the heat therof, *O*, said he, *I feele by experience, and have known it long by philosophie, that fire by God's ordinance is naturallic hot, but yet I am persuaded by God's holy word, and by the experience of some spoken of in it, that in the flame they felt no heat, and in the fire they felt no consumption*, &c. The next day being St. Magnus's day, August 19, when the officers of execution, with their gleves and halbers, were ready to receive him, Bilney, who was little and mean in person, came forth into the streets in a lay habit, accompanied by one —— Winter, D. D. and parson of Winterton, whom he chose, as his old acquaintance, to be with him, for his spiritual comfort, and giving much alms by the way, by the hands of one of his friends, and so he was conducted to the place of execution without Bishop's-gate, in a low valley, commonly called the Lollards' pit, under *St. Leonard's hill. Being obliged to wait for the getting ready the fire, he desired to speake a few words to the people, and spoke to them to this effect: that he was come thither to die, and that they might testifie that he died as a true Christian, he rehearsed unto them the articles of his creed, which he accordingly rehearsed, as they are in the common creed, often lifting up his eyes and hands to Almighty God : coming to the word

* so called from a chapel dedicated to that saint, anciently built on it.

crucified, he humbly bowed himself, and made great reverence: when he came to the words, *I believe the Holy Catholic Church*, there he paused and said, he must here confess he had offended the Church, in preaching once against the prohibition of the same, at a poor cure belonging to Trinity Hall, where he was Fellow, but that he was earnestly intreated therto by the curate, and other good people of the parish, who assured him, that they had had no sermon there of a long time before, and so being moved in his conscience, he did preach to them, and therby ran into the disobedience of certain authoritie in the Church, by whom he was prohibited; howbeit he trusted at the general day, charity, that moved him to this act, should bear him out at the judgment seat of God. Having said this, he put off his gowne, and went to the stake, where kneeling down upon a little ledge coming out of the stake, whereon he should after stand to be better seen, he made his private praier. After which, he turned himself to the officers, asking them if they were ready? who answering they were, he put off his jacket and doublet, and stood in his hose and shirt, and went unto the stake, standing upon the ledge, where before he kneeled, and the chaine was cast about him. When this was done, Dr. Warner came to him to take his leave of him, who said but little to him for weeping. But Bilney kindly smiling on him, bowed towards him to give him thanks, and the last words he said to him were, *O master Doctor, feed your flock, feed your flocke, that when the Lord cometh he may finde you so doing. Farewell, good master Doctor, and pray for me.* And so the Doctor left him with an heavy heart, and eyes full of tears, without making him any answer   While he thus stood ready for the fire's being put to him, certain friers, doctors, and priors of their houses being present, desired Mr. Bilney to declare his charitie toward them, and discharge them of being the causers of his death, since the people were persuaded, that *they* had procured it, and therupon, very probably, would withdraw from them their charitable alms. Wherupon Bilney, with a loud voice, prayed the people to be never the worse to those men for his sake, for they were not the authors of his death. Then the officers put reed and faggots about his body, and set fire to the reed, which, tho' it made a great flame, yet thro' the violence of the wind, which blew very high, it only scortch'd him, and was blown away from him three times, so that he stood for a little pause without fire, in the mean time holding up his hands, and knocking his breast, and crying sometimes *Jesus*, and sometimes *Credo*, till at length the wood took strength, to be the sharper to consume him, and then he gave up the ghost ; and his bodie being withered, bowed downward upon the chain. This account of Bilney's suffering, Fox tells us he had from Archbishop Parker, who was a Norwich man, and actually present to see Bilney burnt.

7. Sir Thomas More, as has been said, sometime after Bilney's death, told the world, that at the fire Bilney revoked, &c. the heresies which he before had holden, and that in *writing* as well as in words ; that he there read his revocation himself. The Archbishop therefore added, that after his pausing, and saying as above, on his repeating the article of his creed, *I believe the Holy Catholic Church*, he proceeded on to the end of it, without any manner of words of recantation, or charging any man with procuring his death. Nay, Fox assures us, that the Archbishop constantly affirmed, that Bilney not only did never recant, but also, that he never had any such bill, script, or roll, in his hand to read, either softly or apertly. But wheras in this account of the Archbishop's it's said, that the day of Bilney's burning was St. Magnus, August 19, we are told, that in the margin of Tonstal's register is this note : *Iste Thomas Bilney postea die Sabbati* 31 *Augusti* 1531, *combustus fuit Norvici propter Hæresim et relapsum in eandem.* But I believe upon examination it will be found, that the one-and-thirtieth of August, 1531,

does not fall on a Saturday, but on Thursday. Tho' if
the copy of the abjuration given us by Collier be a true
one, the Bishop of Rochester, it seems, was not present
when Bilney signed it; and, very probably, if he had, he
would have been of Sir Thomas More's mind, and not
have consented to the making any alteration in the usual
form of abjuration to bring Bilney to comply. However
this be, Bishop Latimer, who was cross-bearer at Cambridge at the same time that Bilney was there, and very
intimate with him, gave him the following character several
years after. Master Bilney, or rather Saint Bilney, that
suffered death for God's word sake, the same Bilney was
the instrument wherby God called me to knowledge, for I
may thanke him, next to God, for the knowledge that I
have in the worde of God. For I was as obstinate a
papist as any was in England, insomuch, that when I
should be made Bachellor of Divinitie, my whole oration
went against Philip Melancton, and against his opinions.
Bilney heard me at that time, and perceived, that I was
zealous without knowledge; and he came to me afterward
in my studie, and desired me for God's sake to hear his
confession: I did so: and to say the very truth, by his
confession I learned more than before in many yeares. So
from that time forward, I began to smel the word of God,
and forsooke the schoole doctors, and such fooleries. Now
after I had been acquainted with him, I went with him to
visit the prisoners in the Tower at Cambridge, for he was
ever visiting prisoners and sick folk: so we went together,
and exhorted them as well as we were able to do, moving
them to patience, and to acknowledge their faults.

8. About the same time was Bishop Fisher concerned
with the Archbishop in the prosecution of Thomas Hytton, a priest, who preached at Maidstone in Kent. Sir
Thomas More gives the following account of him. " He
" was," says he, " a priest, and, fallinge to Luther's sect,
" and after that to the sect of frere *Huskin and Zuing-
" lius, cast off matins and masse, and all divine service, and

CHAP
XXI

The domi-
nical letter
is A, which
is the 6th of
Aug. and
St. Magnus
the 19th,
Saturday.

First Ser-
mon upon
the Lord's
Prayer.

English
Works, p
344, 345,
346
* Tyndal.

" so became an Apostle sent to and fro betweene our
" English heretikes beyond the sea, and such as were
" here at home.   Now happened it so, that after he had
" visited there his holy congregations in divers corners and
" huskes lanes, and comforted them in the Lord to stand
" stiffe with the Devil in their errors and heresies, as he
" was going back again at Gravesend, God, consideringe
" the great labor he had taken already, and determyning to
" bring his business to his wel-deserved ende, gave him
" sodeinly such a favour and so great a grace in the visage,
" that every man that beheld him tooke him for a thiefe.
" For wheras there had been certaine lynnen clothes pil-
" fred awaye that were hanging on an hedge, and Sir
" Thomas Hytton was walking not far of, suspiciously in
" the meditacion of his heresies ; the people, doubting that
" the beggarly knave had stolen the cloutes, fell in ques-
" tion with him, and searched him, and so founde they
" certaine letters secretlie convaied in his coat, written
" from evangelical brethren here unto evangelical heretics
" beyond the sea.   And upon those letters founden, he
" was with his letters brought before the most reverende
" father in God the archbishop of Canterbury, and after-
" ward, as well by his Lordship, as by the reverend father
" the Bishop of Rochester, examined, and after, for his
" abominable heresies, delivered to the secular hands, to
" be burned.   In his examination, he refused to be sworne
" to say truth, affirming, that neither bishop nor pope had
" authoritie to compell him to sweare. His father and
" mother he would not be aknowen of what they were ;
" they were some so good folke, of likelihode, that he could
" not abide the glory. He would not be aknowen, that
" himself was prieste, but said, that he had by the space
" of *nine* years ben beyond the sea, and there lived by
" the joiners' craft." Of his teaching these things were
part :—

I. As for *baptism*, he agreed it for a sacrament necessary to salvation, howbeit every lay-person, he said, might

as well baptize as a priest, were the child in necessite or CHAP.
XXI. not: and that the forme of baptisyng used in the Church were much better if it were spoken in ᵃEnglishe.

2. Of *matrimonie*, whether it were a sacrament or not, he said, he wist nere. But he said yet, that it was a thing necessary, and of christen people to be observed and kept; howbeit, as for the solemnizatioun of marriage at church, he agreed it for good, but that it needed not.

3. The *extreme unction*, or anelyng and confirmation, he said, are no sacraments of the Church, nor nothing necessary to the soul.

4. The sacrament of *order*, he said, is no sacrament of the Church, nor was never ordained by God in the New Testament, but onely by man.

5. The *masse*, he said, should never be said; for that to say masse after the manner of the Churche, is rather sin than vertue.

6. *Confession* made to a priest, he said, nothing profiteth the soul: nor *penance* enjoined of the priest unto the penitent confessed, is nothing necessary.

7. *Purgatory* he denied, and said also, that neither praier nor fasting for the souls departed can do them any good.

8. To vow and entre into any religion approved by the lawe, he said, availeth not, but all that enter into religion, sin in so doing.

9. No man, he said, hath any free-will after that he hath once sinned. In like manner he affirmed, that

10. To say any divine service after the ordinance of the Church availeth nothing: and that all divine service may be left unsaid without any sin.

ᵃ Quilibet Sacerdos parochialis debet parochianis suis formam baptizandi in aqua pura naturali et recenti——frequenter in diebus dominicis exponere Ut si necessitas emergat sciant parvulos in forma Ecclesie baptizare, proferendo formam verborum baptismi in lingua materna——sic dicendo, *I* Lyndwood *cristene the N. in the name of the fadir and of the sone and of the holy gost,* Provinci. *amen.* Manuale Secundum usum Sarum.   p. 245.

11. All the images of Christ and his saints should be throwne out of the Church.

12. Whatsoever the Pope or the general counsaile make, beside that that is expressly commanded in Scripture, every man may lawfully breake it, without eny manner of sin at all, either mortal or venial.

13. It is not lawful neither for the King of England, nor for any other Christen prince, to make any law or statute, for the punishment of any thefte, or any other crime, by which law any man should suffer death: for that all such laws be contrary to the Gospel, which wills no man to die.

14. As touching the blessed sacrament of the altar, he said, it is a necessary sacrament; but that after the consecration, there was none other thing therin, but only the very substance of material bread and wine.

Such was the representation that Sir Thomas More was pleased to make of this man and his opinions: but any one may see, that it savours of very strong prejudice and partiality. For however scrupulous and tender that excellent person was in other matters, it's but too plain, that his zeal against heresy and hereticks, hurried him to make but little conscience of what he said or wrote of them, or how he acted towards them. As to Hitton's refusing to be sworn, it was no more than Sir Thomas himself did afterwards on a like occasion, telling the council, that verily he never purposed to swear any book oath more while he lived. Hitton's refusing to disclose his parents, or tell who they were, admitted of a better construction than that of his being ashamed of them. Rather he was afraid of bringing them into danger; and therfore would not discover them, for the same reason that the parents of him who was born blind, and restored to his sight by our Lord, would not own that they knew how he recovered his sight, because they feared the Jews. Such is the construction that Sir Thomas put on Hitton's opinion of matrimony, conceived in terms that must be offen-

English
Works, p.
1452.

John, ix.

sive to chaste and modest ears. "The man," says he,

CHAP XXI

"meant by likelihood, that it was good enough to wed "upon a cushion when the dogs be abed, as their priests "wedd, I wene, where their persons be known; for else "they let not to wedde openly at churche, and take the "whole parish for witnesses of their beastly bitchery." As to the *thirteenth* conclusion, relating to Christian princes making laws to punish any crime with death, the Anabaptists were charged with holding, that no such laws ought to be made; but it's well known that *they* were not followers of either Wiclif or Luther; and besides, Sir Thomas himself was once of opinion, that *servitutis incommodo* *punire et sceleratis non minus triste et Reipublicæ magis commodum quam si mactare noxios et protinus amoliri festinentur.*

de optimo Reipublicæ Statu.

But however this be, Sir Thomas tells us, that Hitton, after much favour shewed him, and much labour charitably taken for the saving him, was delivered in conclusion for his obstinacie to the secular hands, and burned up at Maidstone in Kent, in his false faith and heresies, wherof he learned the great part of Tyndal's holy booke· and that now the spirit of error and lying hath taken his wretched soul with him from the short fire to the fire everlasting. To all which he added, that in the kalendar before the primer published by George Joye, in English, this Thomas Hyton is set in the vigil of the B. Apostle St. Matthias, Feb. 23, by the name of St. Thomas the Martyr.

p. 346, col 1.

CHAP. XXII.

*1, 2, &c. Reflections on the Bishop's writings. 7. His
partiality in charging Luther with consequences which
he disowns. 8. Dr. Barn's reflections on some of the
Bishop's notions. An account of John Frith's answer to
the Bishop.*

1. THO' it does not appear that ever Luther, whose
time, as has been said, was taken up about things more
necessary and important, answered these books of the
Bishop's: yet by others have there several reflections been
made on them. The concessions which his Lordship
makes in the course of his dispute have been remarked as
very favourable to the cause which he with so much zeal
opposed; as that " the Scriptures are now better under-
" stood than they were in times past, and that those parts
" of them which are yet dark and obscure, he did not
" doubt but that to their posteritie they would be more
" plain and clear: that for this end was the Scripture left
" with us, that it might be understood by us exactly, and
" in every particular: that his Lordship agreed with the
" Protestants in their notion of *venial* and *mortal* sin: that
" at the beginning of Christianity there was no use of in-
" dulgences; that in the commentaries of the Greek
" fathers there is seldom or never any mention made of
" purgatory; and that neither did the Latines altogether
" conceive the truth of it; that the belief of it was not so
" necessary to the primitive Church as it is now, since on
" *that* depends all the reputation of indulgences, which we
" should no way need if there was no purgatory; and that
" therfore we are to consider purgatory as what was some-
" time unknown, and then by degrees lately discovered to
" some partly by revelations, partly by Scripture: that in
" the primitive Church they communicated with both
" forms, or the species of bread and wine: that transub-

Gerhard,
Loci Com.
vol. i. p.
196, col. 2.

" stantiation cannot be proved from Scripture, since with-
" out the interpretation of the fathers, and the usage by
" them delivered down to us, no body can prove from the
" bare words of the Gospel, that any priest in these times
" consecrates the true flesh and blood of Christ; and that
" the name, however, was not above four hundred years
" old: that the fathers sometimes erred, since they were
" men as we are: that Christ promised, that his disciples
" should cast out devils, which promise we plainly see has
" no effect at this time, since there is nobody now who
" corporally casts out devils or heals diseases; and yet we,
" no wise doubt but that there are a great many at this
" time who have the same faith which the antient believers
" had ; and that notwithstanding the promise is not void,
" since Christ would not that it should have a *perpe-*
" *tuall* efficacy, but only an occasional one during the
" time of the Church's birth and nonage." Which con- Gerhard,
cession, it is observed, evidently proves, that miracles are Loci Com.
to.v p 483.
not requisite in all ages of the Church, and that therfore col. 1.
they cannot be, as the present Roman Church pretends, a
genuine and proper note of the Church, as not being perpetuated to it.

2. The Bishop owns, that both the Marcionites and
Valentinians would be called catholics and orthodox themselves, whilst they stiled others heretics: and that the
Novatians called themselves pure, and all others impure ;
which shews how uncertain the sense is which is fixed to
the terms orthodox and heretic.

3. As warmly as the Bishop opposed Luther for saying, that we are justified by faith only, as if by saying so
he denied the necessity of good works; his Lordship
himself declared that he did not deny, but that faith without the production of good works, that is, when it has not
yet brought forth works, does justifie, but that then it is
actually big with them, and ready to bring them forth
whenever there is occasion.

4. The barbarous custom of tormenting and burning

those they called heretics, a name which the unbelieving Jews gave even to the Apostles and their followers, however the Bishop pleaded for it, and endeavoured to defend it, he yet ingenuously owned was not from the beginning: for which he gives this very good reason, that then there were no Christian princes or magistrates to be the hangmen or executioners of the zealous churchmen, to put in execution their cruel and bloody laws. His Lordship further owned, that this cruelty of punishing what they called heresy with death, Christians did not arrive at all at once: that this was the unhappy effect of their drawing blood in controversy, by which their passions were raised, and they became exceeding mad against one another. St. Austin was one unhappy instance of this; he owned, that he was first of opinion, that no one was to be ªcompelled to the unity of Christ; that he was to be treated by persuasion, fought with by disputation, and overcome by reason, that so we might not have those dissembled Catholics whom we had known to be open heretics. But he altered his opinion, because the Donatists with whom he disputed, were not convinced by his arguments, and had not the same opinion of their weight and solidity that the good father himself had. This he imputed to their dulness and security, and therfore was for having them compelled by fire and sword to raise and quicken their attention, and improve their understanding.

5. To any one who has ever read the Scriptures, what the Bishop says to prove, that Christ administred the sacrament of his Supper in bread only without wine, must appear exceeding mean and trifling. It's no less than a falsification of history, to represent St. Luke's account of

---

ª Illi in vos sæviant qui nesciant cum quo labore verum inveniatur, et quam difficile caveantur errores: illi in vos sæviant qui nesciant quantâ cum difficultate sanetur oculus interioris hominis, qui nesciant quantis suspiriis et gemitibus fiat ut ex quantulacunque parte possit cognosci Deus: postremò illi in vos sæviant qui nullo tali errore decepti sunt quali vos deceptos vident. *Augustin.* c. epist. Mani. cap. 2.

Christ sitting at meat with the two disciples, whom he CHAP.
overtook in the road to Emmaus, as he does. The history XXII
itself says not a word of Christ's blessing the bread with
his hands, and tasting it before he gave it to *them*. The
very same may be said of his representation of the history
of St. Paul, Acts xxvii. where there is not a word of the
Apostle's blessing bread, and with his own hand giving it
to Luke and the rest of his disciples. On the contrary,
the history informs us, that this eating was in complyance
with Paul's advice to *all* the ship's company, who had not
had time for fourteen days together to take much refreshment. Wherfore Paul prayed them to take meat: and
on their consenting so to do, he took bread, by which is
meant food in general, and gave thanks to God; and
when he had broken, he began to eat, and they also took
meat, *viz.* all the ship's company, who were two hundred
and seventy-six in all.

6. Nor is what the Bishop says in behalf of Peter's primacy, or his being the prince and soveraign of the Apostles more important. His distinction betwixt *heavens* in
the plural, and *heaven* in the singular number, is very low
trifling. His observation of Christ's joining Peter with
himself in the payment of the tribute money, to shew
Peter was his equal, and as a token of a certain pre-eminence which Peter was to have, exclusive of, and superior
to the other Apostles, is not much better, and proves only
the Bishop's ignorance of the Jewish history and customs.
But thus does zeal for a cause often blind men's eyes and
pervert their judgments. But as it is not my business
here to dispute, I wave taking any further notice of his
Lordship's escapes in his writings, and only observe,

7. His Lordship's partiality in fixing on Luther such
consequences of his opinions as he himself declared he
abhorred. Thus the Bishop accused him of holding good
works, or a holy life, to be unnecessary; and of his making God the author of sin, since he asserted the absolute
necessity of future events. This last opinion, the Bishop

CHAP. XXII. says, Luther had from Wiclif, tho' it seems as if he had no other authority for Wiclif's being of this mind than the Council of Constance. That learned confessor thus

Trialogus, lib. 1. cap. 10. expressed his own sense of this matter. God, says he, has ordained eternally that which he will blame, but he has not ordained, that man shall sin; that all the prohibitions of God which are expressed in Scripture are understood with a tacit condition, that if you do so, you shall necessarily be punished; that as to the liberty of the divine power, it is plain that it is highly free; and yet whatsoever it does, it shall necessarily come to pass: as God the Father very freely produces a son, and yet abso-

cap. 8. lutely necessarily. In his *third* book he continues the same argument, that all things come to pass by an absolute necessity, according to which God cannot, he says, produce or understand any thing but what in fact he understands and produces. But then, he says, he supposes this as possible, if God will: and when he comes to answer the objection, that wicked men may take occasion from that opinion to commit many wickednesses, and that if they may, they will actually do them; he answers, that who they are is to him unknown, as it is unknown to him whether any one shall necessarily break his head, and shall say, by way of excuse, that since it was necessary for him so to do, he could not help it: but, says he, I would say to him, that for so unreasonable an act he was necessarily to be blamed. To the same purpose in the next chapter. It

cap. 9. remains, says he, that the purpose of God be necessarily fulfilled, and so every thing future do necessarily come to pass.

Works, p. 237 8. Dr. [b]Barnes reflected on the Bishop for saying, that faith doth begin justification in us, but works do perform

Assert Luther. Confuta. Art. I. it, and make it perfect. *Per fidem initiari dicitur Justitia solum, non autem consummari, nam consummata Justitia non aliter quam ex operibus natis et in lucem editis acquiri potest. Opera consummatè justificant, fides primum*

[b] He had been Prior of the House of Anstin friers in Cambridge.

inchoat. For this saying of the Bishop's, Barnes thus expostulates. What christened man would think, that a Bishop would thus trifle and play with God's holy word? Doth not Paul say, that our justification is alonely of faith, and not of works? How can you avoid this same *non ex operibus,* not of works? If that workes do make justification perfect, then are not St. Paul's words true. He adds, that many there be that say works do not justifie, as St. Paul and all his scholars, but no man denieth good works, or ever did say or teach, that men should do no good works.

Next, Barnes finds fault with the Bishop for saying, where that the Pope and the Council doth not agree all in one, there will he suspect the Council not to be right. Who, says Barnes, did ever hear such a rule of a Christian man, yea, and of a Bishop, and of a Doctor of Divinitie? to reckon a Council to be true, because that the Pope, and so many men doe agree in one, yea, and that such men as so often have erred in their councils, as he does own himself.

Lastly, Barnes objects to the Bishop his saying, to maintain this error of communicating the people in one kind only, that Christ spake these words, *Drink ye all of it* only to his Apostles (for there were no other men there but the Apostles) and therefore *they* must alonely drink thereof. I answere, says Barnes, my Lord, if this thing were alonely lawfull unto the Apostles, how will you discharge the primitive Church, in the which were those men that Christ ministred this sacrament unto? Yea, and the selfe same men did minister it under both kindes to the whole congregation, according to this commandment, *Drink of it all.* Doubt not but they understood Christ's will as well as you in this commandment.

John Frith observed of the Bishop, that he is the first patron and defender of this fancy of *purgatorie:* and that to confirm his opinion he reckoneth up the doctors by heape; and that he writeth himself upon the 18th Article

An Aunswere to my Lord of Rochester

in this manner.ᶜ There is no orthodox man now adaies that doubteth of purgatorie, and yet among the old ancient fathers was there either none, or else very seldome mention made of it. And also among the Greeks even unto this day is not purgatorie believed. As long as no man minded purgatory, no body sought after indulgences, for all the estimation of indulgences dependeth on *that*. If you take away purgatory, what occasion is there for indulgences? To which Frith answers, that he cares not tho' he grant the Bishop this; that he thinks that money was the parent of both purgatory and indulgences, and, that out of the Scripture he will not be able to prove either. But mammon is a great god, even of power enough to invent such knacks, yea, and to make them articles of faith, and to burne those that cannot believe them.

Next, Frith observes, that the Bishop writeth on this manner, *Article* 37. " The Pope hath not so allowed the " whole doctrine of S. Thomas, that men should believe " every point he wrote was true. Neither hath the Church " so approved either S. Austin or S. Hierome, nor any " other author's doctrine, but that in some places we may " dissent from them; for they in many places have openly " declared themselves to be men, and many times to have " erred." Now, says Frith, sith the doctors sometime erre, and in certain places are not to be admitted, how should we know when to approve them, and when to deny them. Therfore we must have a judge to discern between truth and falshood: and who should that be? Verily the Scripture and Word of God, which was given by his Son, confirmed and sealed by the Holy Ghost, and testified by miracles and the blood of martirs.

Frith remarks further, that the Bishop thus reasons in behalf of purgatory. Of the souls that are departed, some are already damned in hell, and some are already in

---

ᶜ Polydore Vergil quotes these words of the Bishop to shew, that indulgences began after people had for some time stood in fear of the pains or torments of purgatory. *De inventoribus rerum*, lib. viii. c. 1.

heaven : and that to prove this true he alledgeth the parable of the rich man, Luke xv.   But Frith, says he, is sure
my Lord is not so ignorant as to say, that a parable proveth
any thing.   But the Bishop adds, " Neither is it credible,
" that all which are cast into hell should straitway goe to
" heaven, therfore must we put a purgatorie where they
" may be purged."   To this Frith answers, that all that
live are faithful or unfaithful.   If he be unfaithful, then is
he damned.   If he believe, then is he not condemned, but John, iii
is gone from death to life.   The righteous man when he 3 John, v
dieth, shall rest in peace.   If the faithful ᵈrest in peace,
let the Bishop call that what he will, whether to rest in
heaven, or to rest in their faith till the last day, Frith is
sure, he says, there is no man so mad as to say, that to rest
in peace signifies to lie in the pains of purgatory.

Next, Frith shews how the Bishop and Sir Thomas
Moore disagree in their defences of *purgatory*.   The
Bishop, he says, is compelled to grant that the souls in
purgatory obtain there neither more faith, nor grace, nor
charitie, than they brought in with them.   Wheras Sir
Thomas saith, that both their grace and charitie is encreased.   The Bishop confirmes purgatory out of the
66th Psalm, which saith, *We have gone thro' fire and
water, and thou hast brought us out into coolness.*   Wheras
Sir Thomas alledgeth, Zacha. ix. *I have sent forth thy
prisoners out of the pit wherein is no water ;* and affirmeth
there is no water in purgatory.   Sir Thomas says, that
they are not men, but devils which torment the soules in
purgatory.   Notwithstanding, says Frith, my Lord of
Rochester, good man, affirmeth, that they are angels
which torment the souls there.

Frith proceeds to remark, that the Bishop flieth unto
the Church, and saith, because the Church hath affirmed

ᵈ As touching this point *where they rest*, I dare be bold to say that they
are in the hand of God, and, that God would that we should be ignorant
where they be, and not to take upon us to determine the matter.   *Frith's
Answer, &c*

CHAP.
XXII.

that there is a purgatory, we must needs believe it, for the Church cannot erre. But, says Frith, Christ's Church never determined any thing; it is the synagogue of Sathan that maketh articles of faith, and bindeth mens consciences further than the Scripture will. Then, saith Frith, his Lordship waxeth somewhat hot against Martin Luther, because he would that no man should be compelled to believe purgatory. For, my Lord saith, it is profitable and well done, to *compel* men to believe such things whether they will or will not. And to stablish his

Luke, xiv.

opinion, he plucketh out a word of the parable, that a certain man made a great supper, and sayd unto his servants, *Go forth quickly into the ways and compell them to enter in.* To this Frith answers; verily there Christ meant no other thing, but that his Apostles should go forth into all the world, and preach his word unto all nations, opening unto them the miserable state and condition that they are in, and againe what mercy God hath shewed them in his son Christ. This would Christ, that his Apostles should expound and lay out so evidently, by reasons, scriptures and miracles unto the Gentiles, that they should even by their manifest persuasions be compelled to grant unto them, that he was Christ, and to take upon them the faith that is in Christ. But to say, that Christ would have his disciples to compel men with prisonment, fetters, scourging, sword and fire, is very false, and far from the mildnesse of a Christian spirit, although the Bishop approve it never so much. For Christ did forbid

Luke, ix.

his disciples such tyranny, yea, and rebuked them because they would have desired that fire should descend from heaven to consume the Samaritanes, who would not receive Christ. But he commanded them, that if men would not receive their doctrine, they should depart from thence, and sprinkle of the dust of their feet, to be a testimonie against the unfaithful, that they had been there, and preached unto them the word of life: but with violence

2 Corin. i.

will God have no man compelled unto his law. Paul also

testifieth, that he had not rule over the Corinthians as
touching their faith. By our faith we stand in the Lord,
and by our infidelitie we fall from him. As no man can
search the heart but only God, so can no man judge or
order our faith but only God through his Holy Spirit.
Furthermore, faith is a gift of God, which he distributeth
at his own pleasure : if he give it not this day, he may
give it to morrow. And if thou perceive by any exteriour
work, that thy neighbour have it not, instruct him with
God's word, and pray to God to give him grace to believe :
that is rather a point of a Christian man than to compell a
man by death or exterior violence. Finally, what doth thy
compulsion and violence? verily nothing, but make a
starke hypocrite : for no man can compel the heart to believe a thing except it see evidence and sufficient proof. I
have heard tell of a boy who was present at his father's
burning for his belief, and as soon as the officers had
espied the boy, they said one to another, let us take him,
and examine him also, peradventure we shall finde him as
great an heretick as his father. When the boy saw that
his father was dead, and that the catchpoles began to
snatch at *him*, he was sore dismaied, and thought he
should die too. And when one of them apposed him,
asking him how he believed, he answered, *Master, I believe even as it pleaseth you.* Even so by torments and
crafty handling a man may be compelled to say, that he
believeth the thing which he neither thinketh, nor yet can
believe : for a man's faith is not in his own power. But
how doth God accept this thing, to say, that I believe
that which indeed I believe not? verily he utterly condemneth it, whether the opinion be true or false. For if
the opinion be true, as for example, that the faith in
Christ's blood justifieth me before God, and I confesse it
before all the Bishops in England with my mouth, and
believe it not with mine heart, then am I nothing the
better, but I am much the worse. For first God condemneth me, who judgeth me after mine heart, and also

CHAP.
XXII.

2 Cor xii.

CHAP.
XXII.

mine own heart condemneth me, because I have openly
granted that which my heart denieth. And contrariwise, if
I should believe this fully in my heart, and yet for fear of
persecution should deny it when I was examined openly
of my faith, then shall I be condemned of God, except I
repent, and also mine own heart shall be a witness to condemn me.

Frith further observed of the Bishop, that he confirms
both pardons and purgatory by the text that Christ spake
unto Peter, *To thee will I give the keyes of the kingdom*
of heaven, &c. But these words, saith my Lord, had been
spoken in vain, if he, Peter, could not give pardons, and
lose men out of purgatory, &c. To this Frith replys: as
touching the keyes, there is but one key of heaven, which
Christ calleth the key of knowledge; and this key is the
word of God. This key or keyes, Christ delivered unto
Peter, and unto his other Apostles alike, which you shall
easily perceive if you mark when and where they were
given. For Matt. xvi. they were only promised, and not
yet given: for Christ sayd, *I will give thee the keyes,* and
not *I give thee.* But after that he was risen from death,
then performed he his promise, and gave the keys to all
indifferently, as thou mayst see, John, xx. and expoundeth
it, that he opened their wits to understand the Scripture,
that repentance and forgivenesse might be preached, &c.
Therfore it is the word that bindeth and loseth, through
the preaching of it. Frith adds, that he thinks the Bishop
wadeth too deep to descend to purgatory by this text.
For the text saith, that *whatsoever he bindeth on earth,*
shall be bound in heaven, and whatsoever he loseth on
earth, &c. But now they grant themselves, that *purga-*
tory is not *on earth,* but the third place in hell, and therfore it passeth the Bishop's bounds to stretch his hand to
purgatory, and so this text cannot serve him.

Last of all, Frith remarks, that notwithstanding the
Bishop is not content to give the Pope this power only,
but he has granted him full authoritie to deliver all men

Matt. xvi.

Luke, xi.

Luke, xxiv.

from hell, if they be not damned already. *For*, saith he, *whosoever hath committed a capital crime, hath thereby deserved damnation: and yet may the Pope deliver him both from the crime, and also from the paine due unto it.* Upon this point, says Fiith, will I reason a little with my Lord, and so will I make an end   If the Pope may deliver any man from the crime that he hath committed, and also from the pain due unto it, then may he, by the same authoritie, deliver twenty, an hundred, a thousand, yea, and all the world : for I am sure there can be no reason why he may deliver some, and not all.   If he *can* do it, then let him deliver every man that is at the point of death, both from the crime and from the pain, and so shall never man more neither enter into hell, nor yet into purgatory : which were the best deed and most charitable that ever he did.   Now if he *can* do it, and *will* not, then is he the most wretched and cruell tirant that ever lived. If any man say that he may do it, but that it is not meet for him to do it, because that by their pains God's justice may be satisfied ; I say that this their evasion is nothing worth.   For my Lord saith himself, that the Pope must pacifie God's justice for every soul that he delivereth from purgatory, and therefore hath he imagined, that the Pope hath in his hand the merits of Christ's passion, which he may apply at his pleasure where he will.   And also he saith, that the merits of Christ's passion are sufficient to redeem all the sins in the world.   Now, since these merits on their part are sufficient to satisfie the justice of God, and redeem the whole world, and also that the Pope hath them in his hand to distribute at his pleasure, then lacketh there no more but even the Pope's distribution unto the salvation of the world.   *"For he may pacifie God's wrath,* " *and satisfie his justice,* sayth my Lord, *by applying these* " *merits to them that lacke good workes.*   And so, if the " Pope will, God's justice may be fully satisfied, and the " whole world saved.   Now if he may so justly and easily " save the whole world, charity also moving him unto it,

" and yet will not apply these merits so fruitfully, then is
" the fault only his, and he the son of perdition, and
" worthy more pain than can be imagined."

Such were the remarks made on the writings published
by the Bishop against Luther. Some of them, very probably, his Lordship saw and read, but it does not appear
that *he* took any more notice of them, than Luther did of
what was written by the Bishop in opposition to *him*.
The reason of this, perhaps, may be, that now the Bishop
was otherwise emploied in studies and disputes of another
nature.

END OF VOL. I.

Lightning Source UK Ltd.
Milton Keynes UK
UKOW010222160612

194506UK00006B/47/P